SMYTHE GAMBRELL LIBRARY
WESTMINSTER SCHOOLS
1424 WEST PACES FERRY RD NW
ATLANTA GEORGIA 30327

The Professional Collection for Elementary Educators

The Professional Collection for Elementary Educators

PATRICIA POTTER WILSON

H. W. Wilson Company / 1996

Copyright © 1996 by Patricia Potter Wilson. All rights reserved. No part of this work may be reproduced or copied in any form or by any means, including, but not restricted to graphic, electronic, or mechanical—for example, photocopying, recording, taping, or information and retrieval systems—without the express written permission of the publisher, except that a reviewer may quote and a magazine or newspaper may print brief passages as part of a review written specifically for inclusion in the magazine or newspaper.

Printed in the United States of America

Library of Congress Cataloging-in-Publication Data
Wilson, Patricia Potter.
   The professional collection for elementary educators / Patricia Potter Wilson.
     p. cm.
   Includes bibliographical references and index.
   ISBN 0-8242-0874-9
   1. Education libraries—United States. 2. Media programs (Education)—United States.
I. Title.
Z675.P3W55   1996
027.8—dc20   96-8594
                                                                                                    CIP

Contents

List of Consultants	vii
Acknowledgments	xi
Introduction	xv
1 / The Status of Elementary Professional Collections	1
2 / School Library Media Programs *Consultant: Dr. Ken Haycock*	12
3 / General Education *Consultant: Dr. Allen R. Warner*	31
4 / Reading *Consultant: Dr. Timothy Shanahan*	40
5 / Language Arts *Consultant: Dr. Julie M. Jensen*	56
6 / Children's Literature *Consultant: Dr. Richard F. Abrahamson*	72
7 / Science *Consultant: Dr. James P. Barufaldi*	81
8 / Math *Consultant: Dr. Paul Trafton*	101
9 / Social Studies *Consultant: Dr. Dorothy Skeel*	112
10 / Music *Consultant: Dr. Cornelia Yarbrough*	121
11 / Visual Arts *Consultant: Dr. Eldon Katter*	129
12 / Theatre *Consultant: Kim A. Wheetley*	139

13 / Health and Physical Education 153
    Consultant: Dr. George M. Graham

14 / Early Childhood Education 163
    Consultants: Dr. Shirley C. Raines, Dr. Pamela O. Fleege,
        Dr. Susan Gomez

15 / Special Education 183
    Consultants: Dr. William L. Heward, Dr. Teresa A. Grossi

16 / Gifted and Talented Education 202
    Consultant: Dr. Karen L. Westberg

17 / Multicultural Education 216
    Consultant: Dr. Andrea B. Bermúdez

18 / Instructional Technology 227
    Consultants: Dr. Kent L. Gustafson, Dr. Melvin M. Bowie

19 / Promoting the Professional Collection 242

Appendix / The Status of Professional Collections in Elementary
    Schools: A National Survey of Library Media Specialists 261

Author and Title Index 269

Subject Index 291

Committee of Consultants

Dr. Richard F. Abrahamson
Professor of Literature for Children and Young Adults
University of Houston
Houston, Texas
(Children's Literature)

Dr. James P. Barufaldi
Professor of Science Education and
    Director of Science Education Center
University of Texas
Austin, Texas
(Science)

Dr. Andrea B. Bermúdez
Professor of Multicultural Education
   and Director of the Center for
     Multicultural and Bilingual Education
University of Houston-Clear Lake
Houston, Texas
(Multicultural Education)

Dr. Melvin M. Bowie
Associate Professor
Department of Instructional Technology
The University of Georgia
Athens, Georgia
(Instructional Technology)

Dr. Pamela O. Fleege
Assistant Professor of Early Childhood Education
University of South Florida
Tampa, Florida
(Early Childhood Education)

Dr. Susan Gomez
Assistant Professor of Child Development
California State University
Sacramento, California
(Early Childhood Education)

Dr. George M. Graham
Professor of Health and Physical Education
Virginia Tech
Blacksburg, Virginia
(Health and Physical Education)

Dr. Teresa A. Grossi
Assistant Professor of Special Education
University of Toledo
Toledo, Ohio
(Special Education)

Dr. Kent L. Gustafson
Professor and Chair of Department of Instructional Technology
University of Georgia
Athens, Georgia
(Instructional Technology)

Dr. Ken Haycock
Professor and Director of
    School of Library, Archival, and Informational Studies
University of British Columbia
Vancouver, British Columbia
(School Library Media Programs)

Dr. William L. Heward
Professor of Special Education
Ohio State University
Columbus, Ohio
(Special Education)

Dr. Julie M. Jensen
Professor of Curriculum and Instruction
University of Texas
Austin, Texas
(Language Arts)

Committee of Consultants

Dr. Eldon Katter
Professor of Art Education
Kutztown University
Kutztown, Pennsylvania
(Visual Arts)

Dr. Shirley C. Raines
Dean
College of Education
University of Kentucky
Lexington, Kentucky
(Early Childhood Education)

Dr. Timothy Shanahan
Professor of Urban Education
Director of UIC Center for Literacy and
 Coordinator of Graduate Programs
 in Reading, Writing, and Literacy
University of Illinois at Chicago
Chicago, Illinois
(Reading)

Dr. Dorothy Skeel
Professor Emerita
Vanderbilt University
Nashville, Tennessee
(Social Studies)

Dr. Paul Trafton
Professor of Mathematics Education
University of Northern Iowa
Cedar Falls, Iowa
(Math)

Dr. Allen R. Warner
Dean
College of Education
University of Houston
Houston, Texas
(General Education)

Dr. Karen L. Westberg
Assistant Professor
National Research Center on the Gifted and Talented
University of Connecticut
Storrs, Connecticut
(Gifted Education)

Kim A. Wheetley
Director of Dramatics
Southeast Institute for Education and Theater
University of Tennessee
Chattanooga, Tennessee
(Theatre)

Dr. Cornelia Yarbrough
Professor and Chair of Music Education
School of Music
Louisiana State University
Baton Rouge, Louisiana
(Music)

Acknowledgments

Throughout this project the consultants in the various content areas called upon other professionals in their fields for input and assistance. Several consultants wish to express gratitude to the following individuals for providing the support they needed.

Chapter 2: School Library Media Programs
Dr. Haycock wishes to acknowledge Linda Dunbar of the Vancouver (British Columbia) School Board Teachers' Professional Library for her assistance in selecting, documenting, and annotating the titles, as the project would not have been possible without her expertise, experience, and cooperation.

Chapter 4: Reading
Dr. Shanahan wishes to acknowledge Laura Blackwell of the University of Illinois at Chicago for the valuable support she offered the project.

Chapter 16: Gifted and Talented Education
Dr. Westberg wishes to acknowledge Mr. Bruce Berube, a graduate student at the University of Connecticut, for the assistance he provided during the project.

There are many library media specialists, university professors, and friends who supported me throughout this project. First, I want to express my gratitude to the twenty-one consultants listed in the preceding section who shared their expertise, valuable time, and resource selection skills to make this project possible. Their recommended collections in the various subject areas serve as the heart of the book and reflect the enormous amount of time and skill that went into selecting and annotating titles. It has been truly an honor and a pleasure to work with these talented experts, and I'm very grateful that they agreed to participate in the project. Although I'm pleased to see the project come to a successful conclusion, I feel a little saddened that I will be losing touch with many of these dedicated professionals.

I also wish to thank the school library media specialists across the nation who took the time to complete the national survey which served as the springboard for this project. With their help I was able to better delineate the professional collection at schools and in the district teacher centers. The library media specialists and teacher center directors who spent hours discussing professional libraries during telephone interviews played an important role in the development of this book. Particular recognition should be given to the library media specialists in Texas who so eagerly gave of their time and ideas.

My colleagues in the School of Education at the University of Houston-Clear Lake shared generously their time and knowledge. Their patience with my constant questions, their sharing of ideas, and their enthusiasm for the project were much appreciated.

Special thanks go to my sounding boards—Dr. Josette Lyders and Ms. Patricia Powell—with whom I spent many productive hours discussing the book. When I felt mentally drained I'd turn to Josette or Pat for suggestions, and they would breathe new life into the project.

Dr. Ken Black, Dr. Maureen White, Ms. Ann Kimzey, and Dr. Karen Kutiper were always there to advise me and provide the moral support I needed. Their encouragement and confidence in me are sincerely appreciated. The book could have never been completed without the computing skills of Ms. Barbara Dressler and Mr. Isidro Grau—my sincere thanks to both for their support.

A deep appreciation goes to my husband, Wendell Wilson, and my sister, Debbie Potter Parker for their love, continuing support, and never failing confidence.

While many librarians were involved in this project, I want to extend a special thank you to five outstanding library media specialists who took much time out of their busy schedules to visit with me, take me on tours of their facilities, answer numerous questions, and mail me helpful materials. They were always cheerful and available for my constant questions, and because of their experiences of working with professional collections I was able to more fully visualize the direction in which we hope professional libraries will move. My special thanks to the following library media specialists and teacher center directors:

Karen Dowling
Director of Professional Library
Montgomery County Schools
Rockville, Maryland

Acknowledgments

Elizabeth Polk
Administrative Supervisor
Library Media Center
Austin Independent School District
Austin, Texas

Patricia Powell
Coordinator of Teacher Center
Clear Creek Independent School District
League City, Texas

Doreen Velnich
Head Librarian
Pedagogical Library of Philadelphia
Philadelphia, Pennsylvania

Julie Walker
Director of Library and Media Services
Round Rock Independent School District
Round Rock, Texas

Finally, I want to extend my sincere gratitude to my outstanding editor, Judith O'Malley of the H. W. Wilson Company, whose commitment to the project made the whole thing work! Never too busy to discuss the project or answer questions, Judy spent many hours on the telephone discussing the book with me and refining chapters.

Introduction

A language arts teacher is in search of costume ideas for the Thanksgiving play. The social studies teacher needs a list of elementary-level trade books on the Civil War. The science teacher is preparing a learning center on earthworms. A third grade teacher wants information on portfolio assessment. Where can all of these educators find the sources and materials they need? In a well-conceived and -maintained professional collection. A professional collection offers teachers convenient access to print and nonprint materials which provide information and ideas for carrying out classroom lessons and activities. At the same time, the professional collection can also support and enrich the intellectual growth of educators as they update their knowledge.

The Importance and Identity of Professional Collections

Today, more than ever before, strong emphasis is being placed on professional development for teachers. The move toward site-based management in schools in many states is finding more and more principals highlighting professional growth through workshops and special activities. Specialized training and continuing education at individual schools and across districts require resources that leaders preparing the workshops as well as participants in the professional development experience can use. Professional collections within school libraries or full professional libraries in district centers can provide resources that support such training as well as the ongoing professional growth of teachers. For example, a school library media specialist is conducting a workshop for teachers on the Internet. He turns to the professional collection to help in the preparation and, in the process, he develops a bibliography of resources related to the Internet that are found in the professional library. This bibliography will be shared during the workshop and should encourage teachers to use the professional collection.

Teachers can use the works found in the professional collection of the school or district library for a variety of reasons: (1) to prepare lessons and special units for the classroom; (2) to glean background information on specific topics; (3) to gather creative ideas for activities to use in the classroom; (4) to obtain information about teaching styles and methods; (5) to keep up-to-date with current methodologies, philosophies, materials, and technology; (6) to prepare assignments for graduate courses in which they are enrolled; (7) to prepare presentations to use at conferences and workshops; and (8) to do the research necessary to prepare for an upcoming in-service event.

Ideally, a sizable professional library is centrally located within the school district and smaller collections are housed at individual schools. The combination of these two professional facilities offers educators breadth and depth in resource materials as well as personalized service in their use. Funding, however, is almost always a primary problem, and the ideal may not be possible. This book offers information and suggestions that can work for any district or individual school.

Where the optimal situation exists, resource sharing through a strong, centralized professional collection available to all teachers is actually an economical approach. Proponents of district collections see them as a way of saving money through sharing the use of all materials. The control of resource acquisition and the ability of the district professional library to provide a larger and more varied collection of materials for all educators are a few advantages of the centralized collection. Additionally, specialized services such as an instructional materials production center can be provided for all teachers at these centralized libraries.

Professional collections housed at individual schools offer a customized approach to meet the needs of individual teachers through the help of the school library media specialist. By zeroing in on the journals and professional materials that will be frequently used at the school site, the librarian can provide for immediate needs and see that hands-on information is ready to be put to use in the classroom.

Contents of a Professional Collection

Just as the selection process for the children's collection in an elementary school library is based on need and interest, the same holds true for a professional collection. The establishment of a professional library or collection requires an important investment of funds and time. It should include a variety of print and nonprint materials related to professional needs of ed-

Introduction

ucators. Books, documents, nonprint materials, and journals are the resources typically found in a professional collection. Professional books that focus on the various content and specialized areas such as reading, math, music, gifted education, and physical education form a necessary part of any professional library, and they should also contain the national and state documents, guidelines, standards, and information on professional organizations specific to the various content areas. Additionally, a wide range of journals should be included. Those published by professional organizations such as *Reading Teacher* and *Science and Children* keep the educator up-to-date on latest materials and philosophies in particular content areas. At the same time, the idea-type journals such as *Mailbox* and *Good Apple* are frequently used by teachers who are in search of specific activities and ideas that meet classroom needs. Nonprint materials (including videos, cassettes, and CD-ROM) should also be considered when establishing and maintaining the collection.

For the investment to be worthwhile, the collection must actually be used by teachers, and careful selection of the materials plays an important role in this usage. Selection aids are readily available to help librarians choose books and nonprint materials to include in the children's collection, but there are few aids available to help them choose materials for the professional collection. Librarians often rely on recommendations from the teachers themselves. They also rely on their own knowledge of educational resources and on reviews found in professional journals for the various curriculum areas.

This book is a compendium of recommendations from experts in the various content areas to help library media specialists establish or develop the contents of professional collections in all the elementary school curriculum areas and in other areas of professional growth. The book can also provide elementary educators with highly recommended titles which may meet their specific professional needs. *The Professional Collection for Elementary Educators* encompasses documents and standards, books, nonprint materials, and journals.

Preliminary Research on Professional Collections

As preliminary research for this book, the author conducted a national survey which investigated the status of professional collections at the elementary level. Surveys were mailed to one thousand school library media specialists, and an astounding 51.6 percent responded. Additionally, the author interviewed numerous library media specialists within elementary schools and five directors of district professional libraries to gather more information concerning the status of professional collections as well as ways to promote the professional collections.

Chapter 1 provides an overview of the research results and a look at what professional books library media specialists and teachers are using. The survey results, presented under topic headings relevant to this book, are shown in the Appendix.

About the Contributors to this Book

The author asked nationally recognized experts in the various curriculum areas to select and annotate a list of recommended titles in his or her field for this guide.

The consultants who put together this model professional collection were selected on the basis of national reputation and knowledge of their curriculum area for the elementary level. Confidence in any selection aid is enhanced by the credentials of the selectors, and such credentials are provided within the content-area chapters. All consultants are university professors and currently hold teaching positions at universities across the nation. Additionally, some of the consultants hold administrative positions or serve as directors of university centers related to their particular curriculum area. Each consultant works continuously with the professional materials in his or her curriculum area, using the materials daily with teachers and students. Many of the consultants review materials on a routine basis for journals, and all keep up to date with the latest print and nonprint materials.

While all have published professional articles related to their areas of expertise, many have also published recognized books in their fields, and some are editors or have served as editors of journals in their content areas. All are frequent speakers at national and state conferences and are actively involved in their professional organizations, with many currently or previously serving on the board or holding top offices in their national and state organizations. With such strong backgrounds and knowledge concerning professionalism, each consultant is committed to providing teachers with the richest collection of professional materials.

Criteria Used for Selection of Materials

As there is an abundance of materials available in each of the curriculum areas, the goals of the consultants for this project were to select the very

Introduction xix

best available materials for elementary teachers and to prepare an annotated list that represents a balanced collection of resources reflecting various philosophies. They were asked to create a varied collection of professional resources that teachers would really use for daily planning and decision making, and that they would consult when preparing for university course work. Each consultant's suggested collection focuses on current curricula, philosophies, and teaching methods that contribute to the teaching/learning process.

Consultants were asked to examine materials in light of basic selection criteria, and they were also urged to keep one major question in mind: "Will this book or nonprint material be truly useful to elementary teachers?" While materials selected should have a solid theoretical basis, consultants were asked to strive to establish a substantive, interesting, and exciting collection that teachers can rely on and look forward to using. This book is not an attempt to provide a listing of the classic texts from all curriculum areas.

Consultants used a common body of selection criteria in this process:

- Authority
- Scope
- Appropriateness of content for users
- Accuracy of information
- Treatment
- Arrangement/Organization
- Literary merit
- Special features
- Physical format
- Ease of use (indexes, tables of contents, etc.)

Further explanation of the selection criteria can be found in works such as Phyllis Van Orden's *The Collection Program in Schools: Concepts, Practices, and Information Sources*.

Additionally, consultants were asked to consider the following overarching concerns as they examined each professional work:

Provision of a Balanced Collection. Each selection should be based on the value it adds to the collection. The list should include works that focus on differing philosophies. Biases and personal preferences should not affect selections. Objectivity should govern the search for the best professional materials.

Format. The materials should include books, nonprint materials, documents/guidelines/standards, and journals.

Audience. The annotations should be written for educators at the elementary level. Library media specialists will be using the recommended titles to build the professional collection. Additionally, teachers, principals, graduate students, and other educators may use the tool to locate materials to meet their professional needs.

Content. The impact of the work's intellectual content should be considered. Resources that provide activities and strategies based on current theories and philosophies are to be included. Teacher supply stores abound with "activity books," and with so many available, only the best of such works that are supported by sound educational research and that will enrich instruction should be recommended.

Publication Date of Materials. Books or nonprint materials included in the collection must be up to date, but not necessarily limited by a specific time period. Certain older works are timeless and should be part of any professional collection; more recent works that have an impact on teachers should also be included. Since this will be a selection aid for library media specialists to use in ordering books, out-of-print items are not appropriate.

Classic Texts or "Keystone Books" Necessary to Any Definitive Collection. There are a few valuable works in each of the fields which are quite expensive and are likely to be used infrequently by teachers even though they are considered classics of the field. Such key works are placed under a brief subheading at the beginning of each section labeled "Keystone Books." (This subheading will provide a purchasing distinction. If a district collection is available, these highly recognized works would best be placed in the district collection. School library media specialists building professional collections at the school level may want to check on the availability of these key books in the district, then focus first on ordering the recommended works they know teachers will use regularly.)

Inclusion of Consultants' Own Works. Consultants' own works are included where they are relevant. It is recognized that since the consultants were selected because of their reputations in specific curriculum areas, they would certainly need to examine their own works objectively during the selection process.

Resources to Help Consultants With Selection

While the consultants reported a variety of methods they used in their searches for the best materials in the various content areas, many noted that they began by examining the reviews and articles in their professional journals. To consider the recently published materials, the selectors also re-

Introduction

viewed catalogs of publications compiled by professional publishers and organizations and requested review copies. Additionally, they were urged to examine the major library review journals such as *Booklist* and *School Library Journal* as well as review journals in their own specialized fields such as *School Arts* and *Young Children*.

While all consultants called upon their vast backgrounds and working knowledge of professional materials, the majority also conferred with colleagues in their specific fields—fellow professors, practicing teachers, and graduate students—for suggestions. Some turned to technology and the Internet to ask teachers and experts in their user groups to recommend titles of materials to include in the collection. Others visited exhibits and talked to colleagues at conferences and professional meetings in their search for the best resources.

Following careful reflection and examination of numerous materials over a six to eight month period, as well as informal surveys of colleagues and practitioners, the consultants finally selected a list of "no more than fifty" print and/or nonprint materials that elementary teachers could call upon to meet their professional development needs. Regardless of the variety of methods consultants used for selection, in the end they were asked to have hands-on experience with the resource. Out of the hundreds and perhaps thousands of works available in their fields, they chose cohesive groups that appear under their chosen headings.

The consultants did not tackle the selection process with an intent of selecting the "only" professional collection for teachers. Any selection process, regardless of how unbiased, relies on the personal experiences and backgrounds of the selectors. The consultants for each content area, using their professional background and wide experiences with the professional literature, grappled with the difficult task of selecting a useful and practical collection of no more than fifty print and/or nonprint resources. With this carefully compiled list of resources in hand, elementary librarians and teachers can select works relevant to their specific needs.

Summary Purposes of Book

There are at least seven potential purposes or uses for this volume:

1. A resource for library media specialists to use when selecting professional trade books and journals for a professional collection for elementary teachers at the school level.

2. A source of recommended works to include when establishing a new professional collection or maintaining an existing one at the district level.
3. A recommended list of professional materials for faculty in private schools.
4. A recommended collection of professional readings for elementary teachers in their specific content areas. The lists, arranged by content area, can guide teachers to materials that may meet their specific needs.
5. A recommended list of professional materials for principals who wish to encourage faculty to participate in professional growth through reading.
6. Recommended titles of professional materials for universities which have education training programs for elementary teachers.
7. Suggestions based on research for library media specialists at school and district levels concerning the development and promotion of professional collections.

Organization and Use of The Professional Collection for Elementary Educators

1. Chapter 1 forms the framework around which the book is developed. Based on the author's research, it provides educators with data concerning the status of professional collections within schools across the United States. Chapter 19 highlights ways to facilitate educators' access to the professional materials.
2. In Chapter 2, Dr. Ken Haycock, President-Elect of The American Association of School Librarians for 1997–98, recommends more than one hundred useful professional resources for library media specialists. Other educators will also find these titles valuable, as they include materials related to timely topics such as copyright, intellectual freedom, and the Internet.
3. The recommended professional materials in Chapters 3–18 are organized according to elementary curriculum areas and specialized fields. The approximately fifty professional resources in each chapter were selected by experts in the field. To better match educators to materials related to their specific needs and interests, most chapters are organized according to subcategories. The Table of Contents may first be used to determine the page numbers related to your specific area of interest. Overlaps in curriculum areas should be considered when

Introduction xxiii

searching for professional materials to meet your needs. For example, language arts teachers will certainly find the theatre chapter useful. Math and social studies teachers will find the children's literature chapter of interest. The indexes also provide excellent access points.
4. Each chapter provides a short biographical sketch of the consultant who selected, recommended, and annotated the various materials.
5. The recommended materials in Chapters 3–18 are organized within each chapter in the following manner:

> Documents/Guidelines/Standards (if any)
> Keystone Works (if any)
> > This category includes those works in each of the fields which are quite expensive and are likely to be used infrequently by teachers even though they may be considered classics of the field.
>
> Subcategories of Books Related to the Subject Area (if any)
> > These are arranged in alphabetical order.
>
> Nonprint Materials (if any)
> Professional Journals
> Membership Information Concerning Professional Organizations

6. In Chapters 2–18, a special symbol (•) is inserted before each of the materials which were recommended by more than one consultant.

Works Cited

Booklist. Chicago, IL: American Library Association.
Good Apple. Carthage, IL: Good Apple Publishing Company.
Mailbox. Greensboro, NC: Education Center.
Reading Teacher. Newark, DE: International Reading Association.
School Arts. Durham, KS: Davis Publishers.
School Library Journal. New York, NY: Cahners Publishing Company.
Science and Children. Washington, DC: National Science Teachers Association.
Van Orden, Phyllis. *The Collection Program in Schools: Concepts, Practices, and Information Sources.* 2nd ed. Englewood, CO: Libraries Unlimited, 1995.
Young Children. Washington, DC: National Association for the Education of Young Children.

1

The Status of Elementary Professional Collections: A National Survey

With the multitude of professional materials available for elementary educators, how do library media specialists choose the exciting, fresh resources that can breathe life into a professional library collection? One approach is to determine the resources that teachers actually use. Another approach is to ask experts in the various curriculum areas to identify the resources they consider the most useful for elementary teachers. To help ensure that the materials librarians select for professional collections will be used by teachers, this book focuses on recommendations of both sets of professionals—the teacher-users as well as the experts in the various fields. This chapter will provide the titles of the most frequently circulated professional resources in elementary libraries, and in the chapters that follow experts in the various content areas will recommend professional materials to include in the school library professional collections.

However, before examining these popular and recommended resources, it is important to gain information concerning the current status of professional collections at the elementary level. Answers to the following questions will provide a background of knowledge that may prove useful when tackling the development of a professional collection: How many elementary libraries actually enjoy a professional collection? What is the size of these professional collections? What types of resources are found in professional collections? How often are the professional resources used by teachers and library media specialists? Which resources are the most frequently used by educators? After a detailed search for information about professional collections in elementary schools revealed very little, I conducted a national survey which focused on questions about the topic.

The 1993–1994 survey of one thousand school library media specialists provides insight into the professional collections at the elementary school level across the nation. Surveys were sent to elementary library media specialists across the country. The librarians in the sample were randomly selected by computer from the membership list of the American Association of School Librarians. The survey contained a total of forty items. Thirty-four of these items were multiple choice and examined the status of professional collections at the school and district levels. Six open-ended questions appearing at the end of the survey focused on popular titles for the professional collection. A letter and survey were mailed out along with a self-addressed stamped envelope for return of the survey. Completion of the survey was strictly voluntary, and confidentiality was assured as the surveys and envelopes contained no coding. Three weeks later the survey was again mailed out to the one thousand elementary library media specialists, requesting that those who had not yet participated in the survey take part.

Each answer was given a numerical value and entered onto a spreadsheet, Quattro Pro. Then the spreadsheet file was imported into SPSS/PC+, a statistical software package, and an analysis was run to determine the frequencies and valid percentages.

An overwhelming total of 516 library media specialists (51.6 percent) responded to the survey. Almost 56 percent of the library media specialists responding indicated more than ten years experience as school librarians. Approximately 52 percent of the respondents were from suburban school districts, with almost 28 percent from urban and almost 21 percent from rural districts. Almost 53 percent of the librarians were from small districts with ten or fewer elementary schools, and almost 65 percent of the library media specialists responded that there were thirty or fewer teachers in their schools.

The survey provides interesting insight concerning the status of professional collections at school and district levels: their importance, location, size, usage, currency, and problems. (The survey results can be found in the Appendix.) Additionally, the responses to the open-ended questions found at the end of this chapter provide educators with the titles of frequently circulated professional materials.

Status of Professional Libraries Within the Elementary Schools

Surprisingly, 96.1 percent of the 516 library media specialists responding to the survey stated that they included a professional collection for teachers in their elementary libraries. Caution must be used when considering this reported large percentage of elementary schools with professional collections. Several factors could have influenced this percentage: (1) The sample of library media specialists used in this study were members of the American Association of School Librarians, and due to their affiliation with a professional organization may be more likely to recognize the importance of a professional collection; (2) The library media specialists in the sample who responded to the survey may have chosen to take part because of their existing interest in professional collections; (3) Although the cover letter attached to the survey defined the meaning of "professional collection," the respondents' use of the term may vary according to depth and type of materials. For example, a library media specialist who orders several professional journals for teachers may consider this a professional collection.

It is encouraging that approximately 84 percent of the library media specialists who indicated that a professional collection was available to teachers look on the professional collection as a necessary service. A total of 51.9 percent of the library media specialists responded that it was "very important" for teachers to enjoy access to a well-organized professional collection, with 32 percent saying it was "important."

When asked to select a statement that best describes their professional collection within the school, almost 63 percent of the librarians said that "it adequately meets teacher needs." Yet only 3.7 percent thought that "it is an excellent collection and surpasses most of the teachers' needs." Another 31 percent stated that teachers "rarely find what they need" due to size and currency. Furthermore, it appears that most collections are made up of materials selected and ordered by the school library media specialist (59.4 percent), with very few depending on donated materials (3.6 percent).

Librarians were also asked to identify the location of their professional collections. Approximately 72 percent of the librarians reported that their professional collections are located within the school library. Another 14 percent stated that while the major part of the collection was housed in the library, journals were available in the teachers' lounge. Approximately 7 percent house their professional collections in the teachers' lounge area and 4 percent in the work room.

The size of the professional collections was also examined: "Excluding journals, approximately how many materials are included in the professional collection at your school?" A total of 17 percent reported that their collections consist of 250–400 books. Another 31.1 percent mentioned 100–249 books, 24.8 percent told of 50–99, and 18.7 percent noted less than fifty. A few elementary schools enjoy large professional collections, with 8.4 percent of the library media specialists pointing to collections of over four hundred books. The small size of many collections makes it more important than ever that librarians carefully select materials teachers will use.

The size of the journal collections was also a focus of the study. Approximately 10 percent of the professional collections include twenty or more journals, with 38.1 percent reporting eleven to nineteen and 51.6 percent less than ten. Although librarians recognize the importance of providing teachers with professional journals, their comments indicate that journals are often the first materials to go during budget cuts. Even though many teachers and librarians subscribe to journals on a personal basis, journals should be readily available at the school or district level if teachers are expected to keep current in their content areas.

The survey also asked librarians: "Approximately how many total checkouts (including journals) do you have per week by faculty members using professional materials from the collection?" A total of 10.4 percent reported more than fifteen, with 12.3 percent pointing to eleven to fifteen checkouts each week. Another 27.5 percent noted six to ten checkouts. A total of 46.5 percent counted one to five. Various factors could influence this seemingly low number of checkouts—the lack of interesting and useful materials within the collection, too few materials, lack of interest in professional growth, or lack of promotion of the collection. Librarians and teachers might also add "lack of time." Tips for encouraging teachers to use the professional collection will be the focus of Chapter 19.

When examining the library media specialists' use of the professional collection, the survey indicated that almost 78 percent of the library media specialists used the professional collection frequently or very frequently as an aid in selecting books, with less than 8 percent reporting that they seldom or never use it. Almost 54 percent went on to say that, in addition to selection purposes, they most often use the collection for class preparation; over 35 percent stated that they used it to gain knowledge on topics for their own satisfaction. When asked specifically: "Aside from book selection, how often do you use the professional collection to meet your own needs?" over 55 percent of the librarians affirmed they use it frequently or very frequently, and 32 percent said that they sometimes use the professional collection.

Over 75 percent of the school librarians consider their professional collections to be current. While only 8.7 percent of the library media specialists responded that their collections were outstanding in regard to currency, a total of 30.6 percent stated that they were good, and 35.9 percent characterized theirs as average.

It comes as little surprise that 65 percent of the librarians say that their biggest problem in maintaining the professional collection is lack of funds. Another 12.4 percent reported that lack of time was the biggest problem. Throughout the surveys and interviews with school library media specialists,

The Status of Elementary Professional Collections

the issue of too little funding to support a professional library was a chief concern. This issue will be discussed in detail in Chapter 19.

Status of the District-Level Professional Collection

Examination of the district-level collection was also included in the survey. Over half (56 percent) of the library media specialists responding reported that a professional collection was available at the district level. Their satisfaction with district collections is reflected in 61 percent of librarians describing their collection at the district level as good or better. Over 40 percent of the librarians responded that their district collections contained over five hundred works, and 33.7 percent noted that they did not know the number of materials in the district collection.

Library media specialists think that teachers most often use the professional collection at the district level for university course assignments (48.5 percent) or classroom preparation (31.6 percent). Only 6.9 percent reported that teachers most often use it to gain more knowledge for personal satisfaction, and 11.5 percent said that they most often use it to prepare for professional presentations. While 53.8 percent of the librarians reported that their "teachers rarely use the collection," approximately 22 percent noted that one to three teachers use the district collection each week. It is encouraging that almost 16 percent of the librarians said that four to ten teachers use the district collection each week, and over 8 percent reported more than ten. Again, as in the case of the school collection, inclusion of materials that teachers will use as well as promotion of the collection are critical features in increasing circulation.

Popular Titles in the Professional Collection

Included in the survey were four questions for library media specialists to answer concerning those titles that are frequently circulated. Librarians were also asked to recommend titles for the professional collection. The titles listed by library media specialists were compiled and analyzed according to frequency of response. In the following lists, an asterisk (*) is placed beside these titles when recommended by one or more consultants in the chapters. The consultants were not informed of the results of the survey until they had completed their own recommended collections, and it is interesting to note the high degree of match between the consultants' selections and the librarians' recommendations and the most frequently circulated resources. It is also interesting that all the titles listed by librarians as "the most often used by teachers" are related to language arts, reading, or children's literature.

Although the survey was completed in 1994, the following citations reflect the most recent editions of the frequently circulated works. These up-to-date citations should aid librarians who plan to order the resources.

Professional Books School Librarians Use to Meet Their Own Needs

SURVEY QUESTION: What was the title of the book you last used to meet your own needs from the professional collection in your school or at district level?

Approximately 220 different titles were named by school library media specialists across the country. Of these, the following twenty titles were listed by four or more school library media specialists. The titles are ranked according to frequency of occurrence on the surveys, and the frequency is displayed at the end of the citation.

TOP 20

*ptr*A to Zoo: Subject Access to Children's Picture Books.* Written by Carolyn Lima and John A. Lima. Bowker, 1993. ISBN 0-8352-3201-8 (hardcover). (26)

Children's Catalog. 17th ed. H. W. Wilson, 1996. ISBN 0-8242-0893-5 (hardcover). (19)

Books Kids Will Sit Still For: The Complete Read-Aloud Guide. 2nd ed. Written by Judy Freeman. Bowker, 1990. ISBN 0-8352-3010-4 (hardcover). (17)

Elementary School Library Collection: A Guide to Books and Other Media. 20th ed. Edited by Linda Homa. Brodart, 1996. ISBN 0-87272-105-1 (hardcover). (16)

Information Power: Guidelines for School Library Media Programs. American Library Association, 1988. ISBN 0-8389-3352-1 (paper). (11)

Invitations: Changing as Teacher and Learners K-12. Written by Regie Routman. Heinemann, 1991. ISBN 0-435-08593-X (hardcover); 0-435-08578-6 (paper). (8)

Best Books for Children: Preschool Through Grade 6. 5th ed. Edited by John T. Gillespie and Corinne J. Naden. Bowker, 1994. ISBN 0-8352-3455-X (hardcover). (7)

Celebrations: Read-Aloud Holiday and Theme Book Programs. Written by Caroline Feller Bauer. H. W. Wilson, 1985. ISBN 0-8242-0708-4 (hardcover). (6)

The Status of Elementary Professional Collections 7

*Abridged Dewey Decimal Classification, 12th ed. Forest Press, 1990. ISBN 0-910608-42-3 (hardcover). (6)

*Story Stretchers for the Primary Grades. Written by Shirley D. Raines. Gryphon House, 1992. ISBN 0-87659-157-8 (paper). (6)

The Read-Aloud Handbook, rev. ed. Written by Jim Trelease. Viking Penguin, 1985. ISBN 0-14-046727-0 (paper). (6)

*Children's Literature in the Elementary School. 5th ed. Written by Charlotte S. Huck, et al. Harcourt Brace College Publishers, 1993. ISBN 0-03-047528-7 (hardcover). (5)

*The Bookfinder, Vol. 4. Written by Sharon S. Dreyer. American Guidance Service, 1989. ISBN 0-913476-50-1 (hardcover); 0-913476-51-X (paper). (4)

Children's Books In Print. Bowker, 1995. ISBN 0-8352-3593-9 (hardcover). (4)

*Flexible Access to Library Media Programs. Written by Jan Buchanan. Libraries Unlimited, 1991. ISBN 0-87287-834-1 (hardcover). (4)

*The New Read-Aloud Handbook. 2nd ed. Written by Jim Trelease. Viking Penguin, 1989. ISBN 0-14-046881-1 (paper). (4)

Read for the Fun of It. Written by Caroline Feller Bauer. H. W. Wilson, 1991. ISBN 0-8242-0824-2 (hardcover). (4)

*Sears List of Subject Headings. 14th ed. H. W. Wilson, 1991. ISBN 0-8242-0803-X (hardcover). (4)

*Taxonomies of the School Library Media Program. Written by David V. Loertscher. Libraries Unlimited, 1988. ISBN 0-87287-662-4 (paper). (4)

*This Way to Books. Written by Caroline Feller Bauer. H. W. Wilson, 1983. ISBN 0-8242-0678-9 (hardcover). (4)

Professional Materials for School Library Media Specialists

SURVEY QUESTION: Suggest three to five titles of professional books that meet the professional needs of school library media specialists that you would include in a professional collection.

More than 200 different titles were mentioned by school library media specialists for this survey question. The following twenty titles were suggested by more than ten library media specialists.

TOP 20

*A to Zoo: Subject Access to Children's Picture Books. Written by Carolyn Lima and John A. Lima. Bowker, 1993. ISBN 0-8352-3201-8 (hardcover). (76)

*Information Power: Guidelines for School Media Programs. American Library Association, 1988. ISBN 0-8389-3352-1 (paper). (69)

Children's Catalog. 17th ed. H. W. Wilson, 1996. ISBN 0-8242-0893-5 (hardcover). (55)

Elementary School Library Collection: A Guide to Books and Other Media. 20th ed. Edited by Linda Homa. Brodart, 1996. ISBN 0-87272-105-1 (Hardcover). (52)

Books Kids Will Sit Still For: The Complete Read-Aloud Guide. 2nd ed. Written by Judy Freeman. Bowker, 1990. ISBN 0-8352-3010-4 (hardcover). (35)

This Way to Books. Written by Caroline Feller Bauer. H. W. Wilson, 1983. ISBN 0-8242-0678-9 (hardcover). (28)

The Read-Aloud Handbook, rev. ed. Written by Jim Trelease. Viking Penguin, 1985. ISBN 0-14-046727-0 (paper). (25)

The New Read-Aloud Handbook. 2nd ed. Written by Jim Trelease. Viking Penguin, 1989. ISBN 0-14-046881-1 (paper). (24)

Sears List of Subject Headings. 14th ed. H. W. Wilson, 1991. ISBN 0-8242-0803-X (hardcover). (24)

Abridged Dewey Decimal Classification, 12th ed. Forest Press, 1990. ISBN 0-910608-42-3 (hardcover). (24)

Taxonomies of the School Library Media Program. Written by David V. Loertscher. Libraries Unlimited, 1988. ISBN 0-87287-662-4 (paper). (24)

Flexible Access to Library Media Programs. Written by Jan Buchanan. Libraries Unlimited, 1991. ISBN 0-87287-834-1 (hardcover). (20)

Best Books for Children: Preschool Through Grade 6. 5th ed. Edited by John T. Gillespie and Corinne J. Naden. Bowker, 1994. ISBN 0-8352-3455-X (hardcover). (18)

The Bookfinder, Vol. 4. Written by Sharon S. Dreyer. American Guidance Service, 1989. ISBN 0-913476-50-1 (hardcover); 0-913476-51-X (paper). (17)

Celebrations: Read-Aloud Holiday and Theme Book Programs. Written by Caroline Feller Bauer. H. W. Wilson, 1985. ISBN 0-8242-0708-4 (hardcover). (15)

Children's Literature in the Elementary School. 5th ed. Written by Charlotte S. Huck, et al. Harcourt Brace College Publishers, 1993. ISBN 0-03-047528-7 (hardcover). (15)

Helping Teachers Teach: A School Library Media Specialist's Role. 2nd ed. Written by Philip M. Turner. Libraries Unlimited, 1993. ISBN 1-56308-125-3 (paper). (15)

Booktalk! 2: Booktalking for All Ages and Audiences. 2nd ed. Edited by Joni Richards Bodart. H. W. Wilson, 1985. ISBN 0-8242-0716-5 (hardcover). (14)

Story Stretchers for the Primary Grades. Written by Shirley C. Raines. Gryphon House, 1992. ISBN 0-87659-157-8 (paper). (13)

Read for the Fun of It. Written by Caroline Feller Bauer. H. W. Wilson, 1991. ISBN 0-8242-0824-2 (hardcover). (11)

Most Frequently Used Professional Books For Teachers

SURVEY QUESTION: Give the titles of three books from the professional collection in your school or district that are most often used by teachers.

The Status of Elementary Professional Collections

Over three hundred different titles were provided by the school library media specialists. The following twenty titles were listed by five or more school librarians. They are ranked according to the number of times librarians involved in the survey identified the title as the "most often used by teachers."

TOP 20

Invitations: Changing as Teacher and Learners K–12. Written by Regie Routman. Heinemann, 1991. ISBN 0-435-08593-X (hardcover); 0-435-08578-6 (paper). (33)

Transitions: From Literature to Literacy. Written by Regie Routman. Heinemann, 1988. ISBN 0-435-08467-4 (paper). (27)

**A to Zoo: Subject Access to Children's Picture Books*. Written by Carolyn Lima and John A. Lima. Bowker, 1993. ISBN 0-8352-3201-8 (hardcover). (23)

**The New Read-Aloud Handbook*. 2nd ed. Written by Jim Trelease. Viking Penguin, 1989. ISBN 0-14-046881-1 (paper). (21)

**Story Stretchers for the Primary Grades*. Written by Shirley C. Raines. Gryphon House, 1992. ISBN 0-87659-157-8 (paper). (16)

**In the Middle: Writing, Reading and Learning with Adolescents*. Written by Nancie Atwell. Boynton Cook, 1986. ISBN 0-86709-164-9 (hardcover); 0-86709-163-0 (paper, 1987). (13)

**Books Kids Will Sit Still For: The Complete Read-Aloud Guide*. 2nd ed. Written by Judy Freeman. Bowker, 1990. ISBN 0-8352-3010-4 (hardcover). (11)

The Whole Language Evaluation Book. Edited by Kenneth Goodman. Heinemann, 1988. ISBN 0-435-08484-4 (paper). (11)

The Art of Teaching Writing. 2nd ed. Written by Lucy M. Calkins. Heinemann, 1994. ISBN 0-435-08817-3 (hardcover); 0-435-08809-2 (paper). (9)

An Author a Month (for Pennies). Written by Sharron L. McElmeel. Libraries Unlimited, 1988. ISBN 0-87287-661-6 (paper). (9)

**Using Picture Storybooks to Teach Literary Devices*. Written by Susan Hall. Oryx Press, 1990. ISBN 0-89774-582-5 (paper). (8)

**The Bookfinder,* Vol. 4. Written by Sharon S. Dreyer. American Guidance Service, 1989. ISBN 0-913476-50-1 (hardcover); 0-913476-51-X (paper). (4)

**For Reading Out Loud! A Guide to Sharing Books with Children*. Written by Margaret M. Kimmel and Elizabeth Segal. Delacorte Press, 1982. ISBN 0-385-28304 (hardcover); 0-385-29660-0 (paper). (6)

**Writing: Teachers and Children at Work*. Written by Donald Graves. Heinemann, 1989. ISBN 0-435-08504-2 (hardcover); 0-435-08203-5 (paper). (6)

**Children's Literature in the Elementary School*. 5th ed. Written by Charlotte S. Huck, et al. Harcourt Brace College Publishers, 1993. ISBN 0-03-047528-7 (hardcover). (6)

Children's Literature in the Reading Program. Edited by Bernice Cullinan. Books on Demand. ISBN 0-7837-4585-0 (paper); 2044303 (facsimile edition). (5)

Portfolio Assessment in Reading-Writing Classrooms. Written by Robert J. Tierney, et al. Christopher-Gordon Publishers, 1991. ISBN 0-926842-08-0 (paper). (5)

The Read-Aloud Handbook, rev. ed. Written by Jim Trelease. Viking Penguin, 1985. ISBN 0-14-046727-0 (paper). (5)

Science Through Children's Literature. Written by Carol M. Butzow and John W. Butzow. Libraries Unlimited, 1989. ISBN 0-87287-667-5 (paper). (5)

When Writers Read. Written by Jane Hansen. Heinemann, 1987. ISBN 0-435-08438-0 (paper). (5)

Journals Most Frequently Used by Elementary Teachers

SURVEY QUESTION: Give the titles of three journals from the professional collection in your school or district that are the most often used by teachers.

Of 110 different titles listed by library media specialists, twenty titles were mentioned by seven or more respondents. They are ranked according to frequency of mention. It is particularly important that library media specialists consider frequently used journals when ordering. The consultants for this book focused only on journals within their own content areas; therefore, many of the general journals related to classroom activities and ideas, which are so useful to teachers, were not included in the consultants' collections. When selecting journals to order for teachers, attention should be given to the general magazines from this list as well as the professional journals from the recom-mended lists within the various curriculum areas.

TOP 20

Mailbox. Greensboro, NC: Education Center. ISSN 0199-6045. (181) Contains literature-based activities, critical thinking ideas, art and bulletin board activities, and classroom management ideas.

Instructor. New York, NY: Scholastic. ISSN 1049-5851. (175) Features articles on a variety of topics of interest to elementary school teachers. Computer applications for teaching techniques, educational software reviews and children's fiction book reviews are a few of the features.

Reading Teacher. Newark, DE: International Reading Association. ISSN 0034-0561. (98) Devoted to literacy in the elementary years.

Teaching Children Mathematics (formerly *Arithmetic Teacher*). Reston, VA: National Council of Teachers of Mathematics. ISSN 0004-136X. (58) Articles, teaching ideas, and features of interest to teachers of mathematics in kindergarten through middle grades.

The Status of Elementary Professional Collections 11

School Days. Torrance, CA: Frank Schaffer Publications. ISSN 0746-2018. (55) Contains resources for teachers K–3: teaching units in literature, thematic and resource categories, hands-on and open-ended activities, file folder games, and a pull-out activity calendar.

Learning. Springhouse, PA: Springhouse Corporation. ISSN 0090-3167. (53) Contains teaching tips and curriculum ideas for kindergarten through middle school.

Good Apple Newspaper. Carthage, IL: Good Apple Publishing. ISSN 0884-688X. (44) Focuses on educational ideas and activities for teachers of grades 2–8.

**Book Links.* Chicago, IL: Booklist Publications. ISSN 1055-4742. (42) Focuses on thematic units. Designed for teachers and school librarians interested in connecting children with books.

**Science and Children.* Washington, D.C.: National Science Teachers Association. ISSN 0036-8148. (39) Devoted to preschool through middle level science teaching. Issues contain posters, games, lesson plans, and ideas for the elementary school teacher.

Teacher's Helper. Greensboro, NC: Education Center. ISSN 1078-6570. (39) Reproducible thematic units for teachers. Covers four grade-specific levels: Kindergarten, Grade 1, Grades 2–3, Grades 4–5.

Copycat. Racine, WI: Copycat Press. ISSN 0886-5612. (37) Provides enrichment materials for K–3 teachers.

Teaching K–8. Norwalk, CT: Early Years. ISSN 0891-4508. (27) Covers innovation and techniques of individualized instruction.

Creative Classroom. New York, NY: Children's Television Workshop. ISSN 0887-042X. (25) Presents hands-on teaching techniques for teachers of grades pre-K through 6.

**Language Arts.* Urbana, IL: National Council of Teachers of English. ISSN 0360-9170. (24) Focuses on teaching methods for the language arts.

**School Library Journal.* New York, NY: Cahners Publishing Company. ISSN 0362-8930. (18) Includes book reviews and articles of interest to librarians serving children and young adults in schools and public libraries.

**Phi Delta Kappan.* Bloomington, IN: Phi Delta Kappa. ISSN 0031-7217. (16) Publishes articles concerned with educational research, service, and leadership; issues, trends, and policy are emphasized.

Educational Oasis (formerly *Oasis*). Carthage, IL: Good Apple Publishing. ISSN 0892-2853. (12) Includes reviews of materials for the classroom, special units, and articles of interest to elementary teachers.

AIMS Magazine. Fresno, CA: AIMS Education Foundation. (9) Focuses on integrating math and science through hands-on activities, reflecting the acronym in the publication's title: "Activities Integrating Math and Science."

**Challenge.* Carthage, IL: Good Apple Publishing. ISSN 0745-6298. (9) Contains articles and reproducible activity worksheets to be used by teachers and parents who work with gifted children.

**Technology and Learning.* Dayton, OH: Peter Li Education Group. ISSN 1053-6728. (7) Features, reviews, news and announcements of educational activities and opportunities in programming, software development, and hardware configurations.

2

School Library Media Programs

Consultant: Dr. Ken Haycock
The University of British Columbia
Vancouver, British Columbia

Dr. Haycock is Professor and Director of the School of Library, Archival and Information Studies at the University of British Columbia in Vancouver, British Columbia. He earned an Ed.D. from Brigham Young University in 1991 and holds an A.M.L.S. from the University of Michigan as well as a Master's in Education from the University of Ottawa.

Until 1992 he was director of program services with the Vancouver (British Columbia) School Board, where his responsibilities included K–12 program development and implementation, the management of curriculum resources and technologies, and district and school-based professional and staff development and training for more than 7,000 staff members in 110 schools. Dr. Haycock worked as a teacher and teacher-librarian, as a district library media consultant, and as a coordinator of library media services for a large urban school board. He was also an elementary school principal.

Dr. Haycock has been honored by Phi Delta Kappa as one of the leading young educators in North America and received the Queen Elizabeth II Silver Jubilee Medal for contributions to Canadian society. For his work in teacher-librarianship he has received distinguished service awards from several associations. He has served as president of the Canadian School Library Association as well as the Canadian Library Association and remains very active in professional library and educator organizations.

In 1993, Dr. Haycock was named a Fellow of the Canadian College of Teachers, one of only ten in Canada. In 1994, he was also elected director for North America for the International Association of School Librarianship and also as chair of the school board of the West Vancouver (British Columbia) School District. He was elected President of the American Association of School Librarians division of the American Library Association for 1997–98.

Dr. Haycock has authored fifteen books and book chapters and more than eighty articles and columns. His most recent works include *What Works: Research About Teaching and Learning Through the School's Library Resource Center, Program Advocacy,* and *The School Library Program in the Curriculum.* He has also been editor and publisher of *Emergency Librarian,* a professional journal for teacher-librarians, since 1979.

DOCUMENTS/GUIDELINES/STANDARDS

•American Association of School Librarians and Association for Educational Communications and Technology. *Information Power: Guidelines for School Library Media Programs.* American Library Association, 1988. 182 p. ISBN 0-8389-3352-1 (paper).

The national guidelines for the implementation of effective school library media programs represent the best thinking in the profession; the guiding principles outlined here for the mission of the program and roles of school partners are reflected in exemplary schools. Similar guidelines have been developed in other countries too; for example, *Learning for the Future: Developing Information Services in Australia's Schools* (Curriculum Corporation, 1992, 58 p. ISBN 1-86366-217-0) and at the state/provincial level; for example, *Developing Independent Learners: The Role of the School Library Resource Centre* (British Columbia Ministry of Education, 1991, 101 p. ISBN 0-77261-300-1).

KEYSTONE WORKS

Kuhlthau, Carol Collier, ed. *School Library Media Annual.* Libraries Unlimited, annually. ISSN 0739-7712 (hardcover).

Always useful, always provocative, always thoughtful, always significant. This annual guide to professional thinking, research, and resources should be in every school district and relevant university collection and available to every teacher-librarian. First published in 1984, the most recent edition includes timely and important material on current trends and issues such as student assessment, critical thinking, and the changing library landscape, as well as the annual guide to professional associations and literature. Occasionally, sections of the annual are expanded for special subjects such as *Assessment and the School Library Media Center* (Carol Kuhlthau, Elspeth Goodin, and Mary Jane McNally, Libraries Unlimited, 1994, 125 p. ISBN 1-56308-211-X) and *The Virtual School Library: Gateways to the Information Highway* (Carol Kuhlthau and Laverna Saunders, Libraries Unlimited, 1995, 225 p. ISBN 1-56308-336-1); *School Library Media Annual 1993* (vol. 11, ISBN 1-56308-099-0); *School Library Media Annual 1994* (vol. 12, ISBN 1-56308-317-5); *School Library Media Annual 1995* (vol. 13, ISBN 1-56308-388-4).

Lance, Keith Curry, Lynda Welborn, and Christine Hamilton-Pennell. *The Impact of School Library Media Centers on Academic Achievement.* Hi Willow, 1993, 125 p. ISBN 0-931510-48-1 (paper).

Using more than two hundred Colorado schools as units of study, this 1989 study answers three questions: (1) is there a relationship between expenditures on school libraries and test performance? (2) what characteristics of the library affect this relationship? (3) does the teacher-librarian's instructional role and the extent of collaboration with classroom teachers affect test scores? The researchers found that there is indeed a positive relationship and that it is further affected by the size of the staff and the size and variety of the collection, as well as the degree of collaboration between teachers and teacher-librarians. The research methods are carefully and clearly explained. A review of the research literature and an annotated bibliography are included.

COOPERATIVE PROGRAM PLANNING AND TEACHING

British Columbia Teacher-Librarians' Association. *Fuel for Change: Cooperative Program Planning and Teaching.* UBC Access (The University of British Columbia, 1170-2329 West Mall, Vancouver, BC V6T 1Z4), 1986. Video.

Almost a "classic" as a model for cooperative program planning and teaching, the program, formerly three separate videos, focuses on the reasons for change and how to plan and implement resource-based programs at the elementary and secondary levels. An accompanying document includes a collection of planning guides and sample units developed in 1986 by teams of teachers and teacher-librarians from the British Columbia Teacher-Librarians' Association (100-550 West 6th Avenue, Vancouver, BC V5Z 4P2). Other videos for staff development include *Cooperative Program Planning—Elementary,* and *Cooperative Program Planning—Secondary,* both available from UBC Access (1994) and *Partnerships for Effective Learning: Cooperative Program Planning and Teaching* (Avalon Consolidated School Board, P.O. Box 1980, St. John's, NF A1C 5R5, 1990). Each is 20–35 minutes long.

Buchanan, Jan. *Flexible Access to Library Media Programs.* Libraries Unlimited. 171 p. ISBN 0-87287-834-1 (hardcover).

Designed to assist in the development of new programs or to provide clarification for existing programs, chapters cover the definition, the rationale, and the design, implementation and evaluation of flexible access programs. The essential elements of cooperative planning are also discussed. Because flexible scheduling and cooperative program planning and teaching are the basic elements of the library media program, Buchanan proposes that the philosophy of flexible scheduling must be understood and appropriate strategies are necessary for successful implementation. She also identifies the level of commitment, skills, and attitudes that each member of a staff must acquire to develop a successful program.

Calgary Board of Education. *The School Library Program: Teacher-Librarian Resource Manual.* School Library Program Office (3610-9 Street SE, Calgary), 1991. ISBN 1-55063-019-9 (loose-leaf).

Although specific to one major school board, this is an excellent resource for library media specialists as well as a superb model for districts looking to establish their own handbook. Emphasis here is where it should be—on learning, on cooperative program planning and teaching, and on enabling and leadership—as well as on management and evaluation. Strategies to assist librarians and teachers in the development and implementation of a learner-centered program are developed.

California Media and Library Educators Association. *From Library Skills to Information Literacy: A Handbook for the 21st Century.* Libraries Unlimited, 1993. 167 p. ISBN 0-931510-49-X (paper).

This well-organized book provides a research perspective, including implementation techniques to teach students how to analyze, synthesize, and evaluate the information needed for successful completion of the research project. Chapters cover the model for information literacy, stages of the research process, and instructional planning and strategies. Readers will be able to adapt the sample integrated curricular units and the guidelines for fitting the school's program into a local or state framework.

Dame, Melvina Azar. *Serving Linguistically and Culturally Diverse Students: Strategies for the School Library Media Specialist.* Neal-Schuman, 1993. 175 p. ISBN 1-55570-116-7 (hardcover).

Diversity of approach, important for diverse populations, is covered in the context of a discussion of the need for specialized materials and services. Stressing collaboration and integration, models and samples are provided for promoting voluntary reading, developing information skills and integrating them into the curriculum. Dame points out bias in collection development and cataloging, and suggests ways of adapting alternatives. The directory of resources is extensive, including books, periodicals, government documents, software, organizations, and other sources. Programs and resources are also covered in Carla Hayden's *Venture into Cultures: A Resource Book of Multicultural Materials and Programs* (American Library Association,

1992, 165 p. ISBN 0-685-60858-1). Excellent sources of resources are •Lyn Miller-Lachmann's *Our Family, Our Friends, Our World: An Annotated Guide to Significant Multicultural Books for Children and Teenagers* (Bowker, 1991, 710 p. ISBN 0-8352-3025-2), Ron Jobe's *Cultural Connections: Using Literature to Explore World Cultures with Children* (Pembroke, 1993, 155 p. ISBN 1-55138-007-2), and Patricia Roberts and Nancy Cecil's *Developing Multicultural Awareness Through Children's Literature: A Guide for Teachers and Librarians, Grades K–8* (McFarland, 1993, 216 p. ISBN 0-89950-879-0).

Eisenberg, Michael, and Robert Berkowitz. *Curriculum Initiative: An Agenda and Strategy for Library Media Programs.* Ablex, 1988, 180 p. ISBN 0-89391-486-X (hardcover).

Building on Bloom's taxonomy of educational objectives, and avoiding emphasis on discrete skills, the authors propose a conceptual framework and practical approaches for implementing a "Big Six" skills curriculum based on the information problem-solving strategies of task definition, information seeking, location and access, information use, synthesis, and evaluation. These "Big Six" strategies have been used successfully with elementary students from kindergarten up. Also available is the *Resource Companion* (Ablex, 1988, 162 p. 0-89391-498-3), with worksheets, masters, and other tools for implementation.

Haycock, Ken. *Foundations for Effective School Library Programs.* Libraries Unlimited, 1997. 210 p. ISBN 1-56308-368-X (paper).

Emphasis is placed on the essential foundations for effective school library media programs: a clear role for the teacher-librarian; a school-based continuum of information problem-solving skills and strategies; a commitment to cooperative program planning and teaching; and the ability to develop and implement an integrated and flexible program over a two- to five-year time period; both the "why" and the "how" are included. Betty Cleaver and William Taylor expand on *The Instructional Consultant Role of the Library Media Specialist* (2nd edition, American Library Association, 1989, 96 p. ISBN 0-8939-3377-7), while Hilda Weisburg and Ruth Toor offer specific suggestions through units integrated in a variety of curriculum areas in their *Learning, Linking and Critical Thinking for the K–12 Library Media Curriculum* (Library Learning Resources, 1994, 209 p. ISBN 0-931315-08-5).

Loertscher, David. *Taxonomies of the School Library Media Program.* Libraries Unlimited, 1988. 336 p. ISBN 0-87287-662-4 (paper).

With its focus on the viewpoints of the teacher-librarian, principal, teacher, and student, this book provides a comprehensive overview of the role of the teacher-librarian, emphasizing resource-based teaching and the integration of the library in the school curriculum. Discusses warehousing (collection development and management), direct services (client assistance), and in detail, his vertical program with examples of library skills, research skills and technology skills, with case studies.

Also included are detailed planning guides, sample questionnaires, checklists, and models for evaluation of personnel and programs.

Turner, Philip. *Helping Teachers Teach: A School Library Media Specialist's Role.* 2nd ed. Libraries Unlimited, 1993. 288 p. ISBN 1-56308-125-3 (paper).

Focusing more on instructional design than the process of collaboration, Turner provides step-by-step guidance in identifying needs and following through at the initial, moderate, and in-depth levels of involvement. The standard steps—learner analysis, objectives, performance assessment, development of strategies and activities, selection of materials, implementation, and evaluation—are included. Models, surveys, assessment and evaluation instruments, charts, lists, and scenarios are provided. Organized as a text, this work provides an impressive, well-organized approach to learning more about designing and implementing programs and lessons.

Vandergrift, Kay. *Power Teaching: A Primary Role of the School Library Media Specialist.* American Library Association/American Association of School Librarians (School Library Media Programs: Focus on Trends and Issues, No. 14), 1993. 171 p. ISBN 0-8389-3435-8 (paper).

Vandergrift surveys the educational context, stressing the teacher-librarian and multiple technologies in school reform, presents a variety of teaching models, and explains how the teacher-librarian might work with teachers to provide different opportunities using library resources. Semantic webbing as well as issues- and materials-centered research are discussed, and webbing is elaborated on as a means of providing alternative paths to organizing information and ideas. The importance of critical thinking and the evaluation of information for all ages is underscored using Christopher Columbus as an example. Evaluation instruments for time allocation and priorities and cooperation with the public library and information staff development and workshop initiatives round out the work. Of all the roles that teacher-librarians play, it is the teaching role that makes them equal partners in the educational process, and this is stressed here.

Walling, Linda Lucas, and Marilyn H. Karrenbrock. *Disabilities, Children and Libraries: Mainstreaming Services in Public Libraries and School Library Media Centers.* Libraries Unlimited, 1993. 418 p. ISBN 0-87287-897-X (hardcover).

A revised and updated version of *The Disabled Child and the Library* (1983), this work discusses attitudes toward children with disabilities, various disabilities and their effects on lives and lifestyles, planning services, materials selection, technologies and equipment which can be adapted for, or provide assistance to, those with disabilities, and the creation of appropriate physical environments. While these are designed to foster awareness and promote confidence in serving children with disabilities, they are topics which are of value for all library programs and clients. For selection of, or access to, children's resources on disabilities, refer to Margaret

Carlin, Jeannine Laughlin, and Richard Saniga's *Understanding Abilities, Disabilities and Capabilities: A Guide to Children's Literature* (Libraries Unlimited, 1991, 113 p. ISBN 0-87287-717-5); Joan Brest Friedberg, June Mullins, and Adelaide Weir Sukienniik's *Portraying Persons with Disabilities: An Annotated Bibliography of Nonfiction for Children and Teenagers* (Bowker, 1992, 385 p. ISBN 0-8352-3022-8); and Debra Robertson's *Portraying Persons with Disabilities: An Annotated Bibliography of Fiction for Children and Teenagers* (Bowker, 1992, 482 p. ISBN 0-8352-3023-6). Less well-known but of equal value is Sharon Spredemann Dreyer's *The Bookfinder,* volume 5 and *The Best of Bookfinder: Selected Titles from Volumes 1–3* (American Guidance Service); all five volumes were released on CD-ROM in 1995.

Young, Wendy. *Partnerships: Developing an Integrated School Library.* Wellington County Board of Education (500 Victoria Road N., Guelph, ON N1E6K2), 1992. 97 p. (paper).

An exceptional resource developed by a teacher-librarian for colleagues. Includes the principles of resource-based learning, the why and how of flexible scheduling, cooperative program planning guides, advice on principal support, and networking, all without being cute or idiosyncratic. Useful in and of itself but also helpful as a model for others to follow in developing their own district resource guide.

COOPERATIVE PROGRAM PLANNING AND TEACHING: INFORMATION PROBLEM SOLVING

Anderson, Duncan, and Elaine Blakey. *Focus on Research: A Guide to Developing Students' Research Skills.* Alberta Education Curriculum Support Branch (11160 Jasper Avenue, Edmonton, AB T5K 0L2), 1990. 86 p. ISBN 1-55-006-246-8 (paper).

Provides an overview of cooperative program planning and teaching and how educators can work together to teach students information problem-solving skills. Chapters cover the purposeful use of research activities, the roles of the players and of resources in research activities, the components of research, curriculum links, teacher preparation, and putting the theory into practice. Easy to read, practical information.

Eisenberg, Michael, and Robert Berkowitz. *Information Problem-Solving: The Big Six Skills Approach to Library and Information Skills Instruction.* Ablex Publishing, 1990. 156 p. ISBN 0-89391-757-5 (paper).

The "Big Six" steps of problem solving—task definition; information seeking strategies; location and access; use of information; synthesis; and evaluation—should be taught through the school library. Eisenberg and Berkowitz define the "Big Six" skills, explain the three levels involved and how they provide the framework for the information skills curriculum, and provide a variety of implementation strategies, exemplary units and lessons. Similar previous work developed in the U.K. has been reported by Ann Irving in *Study and Information Skills Across the Curriculum* (Heinemann, 1985, 228 p. ISBN 0-435-80520-7).

Stripling, Barbara, and Judy Pitts. *Brainstorms and Blueprints: Teaching Library Research as a Thinking Process*. Libraries Unlimited, 1988. 181 p. ISBN 0-87287-638-1 (paper).

Two essential elements are brought together: brainstorms—conceptual right-brain activities that encourage creative research projects—and blueprints—carefully delineated, left brain processes that bring order to the new ideas. A ten-step research process includes specific skills, explanations and teaching strategies with activities, examples and reproducible exercises. A research taxonomy may be used to elevate the amount of critical thinking required during the research project. Although aimed at Grades 7–12, the ideas and resources are easily adaptable for lower grades.

COOPERATIVE PROGRAM PLANNING AND TEACHING: LITERATURE-BASED PROGRAMS

Doerksen, Donna, and Patricia Finlay, comps. and eds. *Links to Literature: Literature-based Units and Ideas for Teacher-Librarians and Teachers*. British Columbia Teacher-Librarians' Association (Dianne Rabel, 1501-2nd Avenue, Prince Rupert, BC V8J 1J5), 1989. 208 p. (paper).

This volume is representative of the excellent resources published in the British Columbia Teacher-Librarians' Association's award-winning journal *The Bookmark*. Following an introduction to literature-based reading programs in the elementary school, the majority of the book is devoted to units, articles, and bibliographies related to the use of literature in the library resource center and K–12 classrooms. Creative and practical.

Kimmel, Margaret Mary, and Elizabeth Segal. *For Reading Out Loud! A Guide to Sharing Books with Children*. rev. ed. Delacort, 1988, 240 p. ISBN 0-385-29660-6 (paper).

The authors, librarians, and children's literature specialists, discuss the benefits of reading aloud to children, then cover technique and provide practical suggestions (some of which are clearly aimed at parents rather than librarians). The thorough, often one-page reviews of author-tested titles for elementary and middle level children include time required and ways to introduce the story at intervals at which the reader may end the session. For more recent titles, consider •Judy Freeman's *Books Kids Will Sit Still For: The Complete Read-Aloud Guide* (2nd ed., Bowker, 1990, 660 p. ISBN 0-8352-3010-4) and •Jim Trelease's *The New Read-Aloud Handbook* (Penguin, 1989, 220 p. ISBN 0-14-046881-1).

Krashen, Stephen. *The Power of Reading: Insights From the Research.* Libraries Unlimited, 1993. 119 p. ISBN 1-56308-006-0 (paper).

Citing study after study, Krashen makes a compelling case for the importance of fifteen minutes of free voluntary reading and of teacher-librarians and school libraries in this thoughtful and easy-to-read book. It becomes obvious that when children and less literate adults read for pleasure, their reading comprehension, writing style, vocabulary, spelling, and control of grammar improve. Free voluntary reading (FVR) is a far more powerful means of developing readers than direct instruction with drills and exercises; FVR is reading like you and I do—no book reports, no questions, no looking up words, no having to finish a book you don't like. With a simple but research-based solution to a compelling social issue, why doesn't every school have FVR every day?

Kullesied, Eleanor, and Dorothy Strickland. *Literature, Literacy, and Learning: Classroom Teachers, Library Media Specialists and the Literature-based Curriculum.* American Library Association, 1989, 44 p. ISBN 0-83893-376-9 (paper).

This is a concise, practical, usable, and readable presentation of theoretical concepts, research findings, innovative instructional practices, and evaluative processes that support and demonstrate successful literature-based literacy programs. It stresses the importance of using children's literature to assist in the development of good reading and writing skills. The book includes specific strategies for implementing a theme-centered program and examples of lesson activities. Both the role of the teacher-librarian in literature-based instruction and the partnerships among students, teachers, principals, teacher-librarians, and parents are discussed as essential in making the program work. To present the link between the library and the classroom to others, consider the 20-minute video with the same title (Frank Frost Productions for Encyclopedia Britannica Educational Corporation in association with the American Library Association, Britannica Learning Materials, 1990; also distributed by the International Reading Association).

Laughlin, Mildred Knight, and Claudia Lisman Swisher. *Literature-Based Reading: Children's Books and Activities to Enrich the K–5 Curriculum.* Oryx, 1990, 149 p. ISBN 0-89774-562-0 (paper).

In the context of encouraging reading and the teacher as reader, the authors focus on visual literacy, predicting, sequencing, characterization, plot line, theme, and vocabulary; for older children, an analysis of realistic fiction, biography, fantasy, and information books is also included. Each section includes student objectives, an annotated reading list, group introductory activities with one of the titles, and follow-up activities. Similar titles by the same principal author, and with the same subtitle and publisher, include *Literature-Based Social Studies* (1900, ISBN 0-89774-605-8), *Literature-Based Art and Music* (1992, ISBN 0-89774-661-9) and *Literature-Based Science and Math* (1993, ISBN 0-89774-741-0).

MANAGEMENT

Book Report and *Library Talk* editors; with Catherine Andronik. *School Library Management Notebook*. 3rd ed. Linworth (Professional Growth series), 1994. 300 p. ISBN 0-938865-29-3 (hardcover).

With short selections from the publisher's magazines, this binder provides innumerable tips and suggestions, organized through eight sections: goal setting and evaluation; getting organized; selection, weeding and inventory; circulation, processing, and overdues management; supervising aides and paraprofessionals; computers and new technology; and bibliography. Similar but more elementary school focused is Alice Yucht's *The Elementary School Librarian's Desk Reference: Library Skills and Management* (Linworth, 1992, 371 p. ISBN 0-938865-05-6).

•Carson, Ben, and Jane Bandy Smith. *Renewal at the Schoolhouse: Management Ideas for Library Media Specialists and Administrators*. Libraries Unlimited, 1993. 158 p. ISBN 0-87287-914-3 (paper).

Articles written by authorities cover school renewal/restructuring through program improvement, planning, leadership, personnel development and motivation and management of change and technology. Particularly valuable during periods of fiscal restraint are the discussions of time and budget management. The teacher-librarian's role is presented as collaborative and supportive.

Craver, Kathleen. *School Library Media Center in the 21st Century: Changes and Challenges*. Greenwood (Greenwood Professional Guides in School Librarianship), 1994. 216 p. ISBN 0-313-29100-4 (hardcover).

Placing school libraries squarely in their societal context, Craver documents trends that will affect every North American. Chapters explore technology, the economy, education, employment, and organization and management with background information, historical development, statistics, and quotations, together with challenges for the library and teacher-librarian. When you become tired of responding to technological change, anticipate new developments by reading Craver's work and discussing the implications for your school and library with colleagues and school administrators.

Klasing, Jane. *Designing and Renovating School Library Media Centers.* American Library Association (School Library Media Programs: Trends and Issues, no. 11), 1991. 260 p. ISBN 0-8389-0560-9 (paper).

Klasing, a director of learning resources who experienced many construction projects, an architect, and the directors of a library that underwent renovation provide three perspectives. In her model document chapter, Klasing emphasizes the most important part of the planning process—the educational specifications. Case studies for renovation and new construction include illustrated floor plans. Glossaries, a basic equipment checklist, and suggestions for selection of furniture and shelving make this a very practical guide. Pauline Anderson's *Planning School Library Media Facilities* (Shoe String, 1960, 260 p. ISBN 0-208002254-6) is useful for first-timers as she explains the people and issue problems related to these projects.

LM_NET.

The current and most useful "online network" of teacher-librarians available. Access through e-mail by sending a message to listserv@suvm.syr.edu "Subscribe LM_NET (your first name and last name)." Although this resource is listed under "management," the range of questions asked by teacher-librarians of teacher-librarians reflects the range and complexity of the job itself: new print and electronic resources; available jobs; current censorship issues; professional development opportunities—much chatter and much debate. This is an exciting and ground-breaking communication link, with access to the LM_NET archives through telnet or gopher to erecir.syr.edu, that links teacher-librarians around the world.

Morris, Betty; with John Gillespie and Diana Spirit. *Administering the School Library Media Center.* 3rd ed. Bowker, 1992. 567 p. ISBN 0-8352-3092-9 (hardcover).

A basic text for teacher-librarians, covering functions, facilities, budgets and personnel, as well as policies and procedures. This edition includes references to the latest guidelines and standards and substantially updates previous information. Practical tools include lesson plans, budget worksheets, and forms for evaluation. The fourth edition of the classic *School Library Media Center* has also been revised by Blanche Woolls as *The School Library Media Manager* (Libraries Unlimited, 1994, 336 p. ISBN 1-56308-304-3, hardcover, or 1-56308-318-3 paper) or as a course text, thus including exercises, discussion questions, and ten useful appendices.

Wright, Kieth. *The Challenge of Technology: Action Strategies for the School Library Media Specialist.* American Library Association, 1993. 122 p. ISBN 0-8389-0604-4 (paper).

Placing the school in the context of the information society by reviewing the research on the use of computers in instruction and presenting four models of education which influence the ways computers will or will not be used, Wright focuses on the roles of teacher-librarians, administrators, teachers, and computer specialists in implementing computer-based technologies. Strategies are suggested for eliminating barriers to the use of technology. For a practical planning guide, also review Gregory Zuct, Theresa Day, and Bruce Flanders' *Automation for School Libraries: How to Do It From Those Who Have Done It* (American Library Association, 1994, 138 p. ISBN 0-8389-0637-0) and Annette Lamb and Larry Johnson's *Strap on Your Spurs: Technology and Change Cowboy Style* (Vision to Action, 1994, 173 p. ISBN 0-9641581-0-8).

MARKETING AND ADVOCACY

Haycock, Ken. *Program Advocacy: Power, Publicity and the Teacher-Librarian*. Libraries Unlimited, 1990. 105 p. ISBN 0-87287-781-7 (hardcover).

This collection of articles focuses on the three key ingredients of any campaign to promote school libraries: the product, including the research base and sample presentation; the commitment, examining the importance of individual and group effort; and the strategies, those abilities and techniques for implementing change and building consensus and power. Several target groups are identified at the school and district levels, and teacher-librarians from a variety of backgrounds provide insights regarding marketing services and lobbying. Although aimed at secondary schools, Gary Hartzell's *Building Influence for the School Librarian* (Linworth, 1994, 196 p. ISBN 0-938865-32-3) is also useful for all teacher-librarians committed to improving understanding and support.

Kaleidoscope: New Visions for School Library Media Programs. Video. Follett Software Company/Follett Library Book Company, 1993. Part 1: 6 min.; Part 2: 23 min.

Featuring vignettes of actual activities from schools in Arizona, Kansas, and Massachusetts, Part 1, excerpted from Part 2, is designed for use with school and community groups, while Part 2 is designed for professional and staff development programs. Two themes are common to each of the vignettes: cooperative program planning and teaching between the teacher and teacher-librarian and the support of the principal. Ranging from a first grade unit to senior high research, the video is useful for awareness level orientation sessions. Helpful suggestions are included in *Using Kaleidoscope: New Visions for School Library Media Programs,* edited by Judy Pitts (American Library Association/ Follett Software, 1994, 55 p. ISBN 0-695-62014-2).

Laughlin, Mildred Knight, and Kathy Howard Latrobe. *Public Relations for School Library Media Centers.* Libraries Unlimited, 1990. 134 p. ISBN 0-87287-819-8 (hardcover).

The articles collected here underline the requirement for continuous positive public relations as a management component. Teacher-librarians and other educators provide brief introductory coverage on theoretical and practical issues. The book offers guidelines, techniques, and strategies and discusses cooperation among staff and between school and parents, community, and the media. Other titles to consider are Marian Edsall's *Practical PR for School Library Media Centers* (Neal-Schuman, 1984, 165 p. ISBN 0-918212-77-4), Rita Kohn and Krysta Tepper's *Have You Got What They Want? Public Relations Strategies for the School Librarian/Media Specialist: A Workbook* (Scarecrow, 1982, 222 p. ISBN 0-8108-1481-1), and Valerie Childress' *Winning Friends for the School Library: A PR Handbook* (Linworth, 1993, 217 p. ISBN 0-938865-24-2).

ORGANIZATION OF LEARNING RESOURCES

Intner, Sheila S., and Jean Weihs. *Standard Cataloging for School and Public Libraries.* Libraries Unlimited, 1990, 208 p. ISBN 0-87287-737-X (hardcover).

Covering the entire spectrum of tasks, from theory and principles to practical applications, the authors also examine automated networks, including local systems, and the MARC format along with such tools as AACR2, LCSH, Library of Congress and Dewey classification systems, and the Sears list of subject headings. The second edition of Sharon Zuiderveld's *Cataloging Correctly for Kids: An Introduction to the Tools* (American Library Association, 1991, 78 p. ISBN 0-8389-3395-5) includes articles explaining current standards and practices. For teacher-librarians facing conversion or needing an authority file, Joanna Fountain's *Headings for Children's Materials: An LCSH/Sears Companion* (Libraries Unlimited, 1993, 127 p. ISBN 1-56308-146-6) provides models for practical applications and makes it possible for the nonexpert to use subdivisions with little training.

Kogon, Marilyn, and Lynne Lighthall. *The Canadian Library Handbook: Organizing School, Public and Professional Libraries.* McGraw-Hill, 1993. 259 p. ISBN 0-07551552-0 (hardcover).

An unfortunate title for a comprehensive and comprehensible guide to organizing the school's collection; the "Canadian" signifies country of origin rather than content. Topics include acquisitions, descriptive and subject cataloging, classification, collection maintenance, and circulation. Also useful are the *Anglo-American Cataloging Rules* (2nd edition, American Library Association, 1988, 677 p. ISBN 0-8389-3346-7) or Michael Gorman's *The Concise AACR2* (1988 revision, American Library Association, 1989, 161 p. ISBN 0-8389-3362-9) for the beginner; the *Abridged Dewey Decimal Classification* (12th edition, edited by John Comaromi, Forest Press, 1990, 857 p. ISBN 0-910608-42-3); *Sears List of Subject Headings* (15th edition, edited by

Joseph Miller, H. W. Wilson, 1994, 758 p. ISBN 0-8242-0857-7); and *Sears List of Subject Headings: Canadian Companion* (4th edition, edited by Lynne Lighthall, H. W. Wilson, 1992, 88 p. ISBN 0-8242-0832-3).

•Lima, Carolyn, and John Lima. *A to Zoo: Subject Access to Children's Picture Books.* 4th ed. Bowker, 1993. 1158 p. ISBN 0-8352-3201-8 (hardcover).

Revised and expanded to (thirty-five hundred new entries), the new edition provides bibliographic information on fifteen thousand titles suitable for ages three to seven. The thorough subject coverage assists in locating materials in a collection as well as acting as a source of subject headings for cataloging or information files. There are five indexes: subject headings; subject guide; full bibliographic guide by author; title; illustrator. There are no annotations.

PROFESSIONALISM AND LEADERSHIP

Austrom, Liz, Roberta Kennard, Joanne Naslund, and Patricia Field. *Implementing Change: A Cooperative Approach.* Edited by Dianne Driscoll. British Columbia Teacher-Librarians' Association (100-550 West 6th Avenue, Vancouver, BC V5Z 4P2), 1989. 169 p. (paper).

Designed as a "self-help" guide for teacher-librarians wanting to become change agents (or who at least recognize that they have no choice), this work provides numerous frameworks for personal and staff assessment and evaluation and the design of action plans for effecting change. Change causes anxiety, and teacher-librarians need the skills and aptitude to lead others through phases of implementation of cooperative program planning and teaching and flexible scheduling. Information and strategies, based on the Concerns-based Adoption Model (CBAM), involve reflecting on current practice, assessing the present situation, articulating a vision for the program, developing effective communication skills, defining short- and long-term goals, identifying the steps to be taken, and evaluating the success of the process.

Educational Resources Information Center. Clearinghouse on Information and Technology (Syracuse University, 4-194 Center for Science and Technology, Syracuse, NY 13244-4100).

The Clearinghouse and its newsletter *ERIC/IT Update,* a semi-annual bulletin, cover the management, operation, and use of libraries, the technology to improve their operations, and the education, training, and professional activities of librarians and other information specialists. The newsletter highlights relevant new books and ERIC publications and provides ordering information for ERIC/IR monographs and software such as *Information Literacy for an Information Society: A Concept for the Information Age,* by Christine Doyle (1994, 80 p. IR-97) and *Libraries for the National Education Goals,* by Barbara Stripling (3rd edition, 1992, 119 p. IR-94).

Haycock, Ken. *What Works: Research about Teaching and Learning Through the School's Library Resource Center.* Rockland, 1992. 244 p. ISBN 0-920175-06-6 (hardcover).

What Works is organized into three sections to make school library research easy to read and easy to share: the intent is to provide evidence of the effect of school libraries and teacher-librarians on student achievement when programs are based on these research findings. The presentation of conclusions is organized to be used easily and effectively with principals, senior education officials, and school board members. Over six hundred research studies are identified and described, with twenty-eight general and specific findings provided to guide effective practice. The implications of research in a variety of areas are also provided in Blanche Woolls' *The Research of School Library Media Centers: Papers of the Treasure Mountain Research Retreat,* 1989 October 17, Park City, Utah (Hi Willow, 1990, 267 p. ISBN 0-93151-030-9).

Miller, Elizabeth. *The Internet Resource Directory for K–12 Teachers and Librarians (94/95 edition).* Libraries Unlimited, 1994. 199 p. ISBN 1-56308-337-X (paper).

The edition statement in the title suggests that this will be an annual publication: excellent! This is an essential title for each school and library providing support for information access through technology. Introductory material on getting started with the Internet is followed by chapters organized by subject, with further breakdown within the chapter. Access information, electronic address, and a description and instructions are included for each of the more than four hundred entries. For beginners, consider *The Easy Internet Handbook* by Javed Mostafa, Thomas Newall, and Richard Trenthem (Hi Willow, 1994, 140 p. ISBN 0-931510-50-3); the beginning or frustrated user will also find helpful Nancy Regina John and Edward Valauskas' *The Internet Troubleshooter: Help for the Logged-on and Lost* (American Library Association, 1994, 100 p. ISBN 0-8389-0633-8).

SELECTION OF LEARNING RESOURCES

Helmer, Dona. *Selecting Materials for School Library Media Centers.* 2nd ed. American Association of School Librarians, 1993. 111 p. ISBN 0-8389-7693-X (paper).

This annotated bibliography of selection tools for the teacher-librarian has been revised and updated. Indexes include author, source of materials at elementary and secondary levels, as well as journals with current reviews. This book is useful as a guide to specific selection tools for your situation and needs.

Lee, Lauren K., ed. *The Elementary School Library Collection: A Guide to Books and Other Media; Phases 1-2-3*. Brodart, 1994. 19th ed. approx. 1200 p. ISBN 0-87272-096-9 (hardcover).

This guide is aimed at pre-school to sixth grade, with about fourteen thousand recommended titles, including books, periodicals, big books, CD-ROMs, and a-v and computer software, in each volume. It is organized by Dewey classification, with full ordering information and annotation; reading levels, interest levels, and priority for purchase are included. Author, title, and subject indexes are complemented by listings of media for pre-school, books for beginning independent reading, and series books. The nineteenth edition (1994) versions have been made available with CD-ROM, priced as a supplement to the book, as a stand-alone and networkable. Also worthy of consideration is the *Children's Catalog* (17th ed., 1996, H. W. Wilson, ISBN 0-8242-0893-5); the main volume is published every five years, with four annual supplements. Compiled by specialists, this tool provides complete information for over six thousand books, plus five hundred per annual supplement. John Gillespie and Corinne Naden's *Best Books for Children: Preschool Through Grade 6* (Bowker, 1994, 1002 p. ISBN 0-8352-3455-X) is especially useful for undertaking thematic searches for materials, with thousands of subject categories indexing over eleven thousand titles; a comparable alternative is •*Adventuring with Books: A Booklist for Pre-K–Grade 6,* edited by Julie Jensen and Nancy Roser for the National Council of Teachers of English (10th edition, 1993, 603 p. ISBN 0-8141-0079-1).

Peterson, Carolyn Sue, and Ann D. Fenton. *Reference Books for Children*. 4th ed. Scarecrow, 1992, 399 p. ISBN 0-8108-2543-0 (hardcover).

This book includes more than a thousand recommended titles, published to mid-1990, with complete bibliographic citations and annotations. Titles include general reference books and subject-specific resources under more than fifty topics recommended for K–12. Useful as a selection checklist and as a resource for explanations of the reference process and of evaluation criteria. The improved access by specific entry number enhances the author/title and subject indexes. Reviews of reference books are also included in the *Children's Catalog* and the *Elementary School Library Collection*. The district resource center should also provide Margaret Irby Nichols' *Guide to Reference Books for School Media Centers* (4th edition, Libraries Unlimited, 1992, 463 p. ISBN 0-87287-833-3).

Reichman, Henry F. *Censorship and Selection: Issues and Answers for Schools*, rev. ed. American Library Association/American Association of School Administrators, 1993. 160 p. ISBN 0-8389-0620-6 (paper).

Authoritative, well-written, and well-organized to provide support for schools dealing with censorship issues, most recently adding violence, witchcraft, and alternate lifestyles to sexism, racism, sex education and profanity, real or imagined. Chapters dealing with the preparation of a selection policy and "What do we do if . . . ?" are applicable to real situations. Sample policies and procedures, and guidelines for student publications are included. Also recommended are *Censored Books: Critical Viewpoints,* edited by Nicholas Karolides, Lee Burress, and John Kean (Scarecrow, 1993, 524 p. ISBN 0-8108-2667-4) and *Censorship: The Problem That Won't Go Away,* by Edna Boardman (Linworth, 1993, 80 p. ISBN 0-938865-18-8).

Simpson, Carol Mann. *Copyright for School Libraries: A Practical Guide.* Linworth (Professional Growth Series), 1994. 104 p. ISBN 0-938865-31-5 (paper).

Following a brief history of copyright liability and fair use provisions, Simpson examines their application to print and audiovisual materials and computer software. Practical and specific suggestions include guidelines for librarians with realistic examples of copyright infringement and samples of school district compliance agreements, warning notices, and reprint permission requests. Janis Bruwelheid's *The Copyright Primer for Librarians and Educators* (2nd edition, American Library Association, 1994, 100 p. ISBN 0-8389-0642-7) also explains the complexities of copyright law, in question and answer format.

Sorrow, Barbara Head, and Betty S. Lumpkin. *CD-ROM for Librarians and Educators: A Resource Guide to Over 300 Instructional Programs.* McFarland, 1993. 155 p. ISBN 0-89950-800-6 (hardcover).

Includes bibliographic information, format, price, grade level, hardware and software requirements, distributor, and a review, organized by subject; criteria for inclusion include objectivity, timeliness, format, appeal, and credibility. The information on CD-ROM basics will be useful to those new to this medium. Warren Buekleitner's *High/Scope Buyer's Guide to Children's Software* (High/Scope, 1993, 288 p. ISBN 0-929816-53-6) reviews over five hundred programs each year for schools, libraries, and home, while Tiniki Roxton and Beth Blenz-Clucas' *Recommended Videos for Schools* (ABC-CLIO, 1992, 184 p. ISBN 0-87436-644-5) is a definitive guide to the best four hundred videos for school use. Current reviews are included in the *Elementary School Library Collection, Emergency Librarian,* and *School Library Journal* as well.

Stoll, Donald. *Magazines for Kids and Teens.* Educational Press Association and International Reading Association, 1994. 101 p. ISBN 0-87207-397-1 (paper).

An affordable guide which includes more than two hundred titles from around the world. Each description includes ordering information and age level. The most useful section is the list of magazines that publish readers' work. The district center should also make available *Magazines for Young People: A Children's Magazine Companion Volume,* by Bill Katz and Linda Sternberg Katz (2nd edition, Bowker, 1991, 361 p. ISBN 0-8352-3009-0) and *Magazines for Children: A Guide for Parents, Teachers and Librarians,* by Selma Richardson (2nd edition, American Library Association, 1991, 139 p. ISBN 0-8389-0552-8). Each school will also want to select based on titles included in the essential *Children's Magazine Guide* (Bowker, 9/year. ISSN 0743-89873).

Van Orden, Phyllis. *The Collection Program in Schools: Concepts, Practices, and Information Sources.* 2nd ed. Libraries Unlimited, 1995. ISBN 1-56308-120-2 (hardcover); 1-56308-334-5 (paper).

Well-written and comprehensive, this text provides excellent basic information on the processes and procedures associated with developing, maintaining, and evaluating a collection at the building level, with information on collection development and management, programs, policies and procedures, criteria for evaluation by format and administrative concerns. Sources of assistance and suggested approaches to handling a wide range of situations and demands on the collection are included. New features deal with copyright, intellectual freedom, multicultural materials, and resources to meet the needs of children with disabilities.

JOURNALS

Emergency Librarian. Rockland Press, ISSN 0315-8888.

Promotes excellence in library services for children and young adults through thought-provoking and challenging articles, regular review columns, and critical analysis of management and programming issues. Feature articles stress the relationship between the classroom teacher and the teacher-librarian in planning and teaching. Reviews professional books, outstanding new titles, paperbacks, videos, and software. Regular departments include Issues, One Minute Management, InfoTech, Portraits, Bestsellers, What Works, and the ERIC Digest. Each issue includes a buying guide on a theme and a poster.

Library Talk. Linworth. ISSN 1043-237X.

The strength of *Library Talk* (and other titles by Linworth, the publisher) is the "library media specialist to library media specialist" focus, meaning that you cannot beat the currency and relevance of the ideas even if the appropriateness is sometimes questionable. Sometimes, "how to do it better" applies to something that should not be done at all—for example, there are suggestions for dealing with rigidly scheduled library skills and literature classes rather than how to grow out of them. That having been said, however, this is an exceptional source for learning from your colleagues. Includes feature articles, regular columns, and profiles and reviews by teacher-librarians. The publisher has also started *Technology Connection: The Newsletter for School Library Media Specialists* (10/year).

• *School Library Journal.* Cahners. ISSN 0362-8930.

The highest circulation journal for teacher-librarians, with the most comprehensive reviews. Articles are current and well-written, covering the broad spectrum of service for students in school and public libraries. Besides the feature articles and book reviews, *SLJ* includes a checklist of free and inexpensive pamphlets and booklets and regular review of reference books, audio-visual material, and computer software. Reviews are concise, evaluative, and written by practicing professionals.

MEMBERSHIPS

American Association of School Librarians
American Library Association
50 East Huron Street
Chicago, Illinois 69611

Phone: (800) 545-2433
(312) 944-6780

Teacher-librarians will want to belong to both their state/provincial association and their national association, the American Association of School Librarians (AASL), a division of the American Library Association. AASL provides leadership in advocacy and lobbying for federal support, such as the re-authorization of the ESEA; in developing national guidelines such as *Information Power;* in producing resource materials such as *Kaleidoscope;* in seeking funding such as Library Power, a $43 million project to revitalize school libraries; and in supporting research to inform practice, such as through its grants and awards. Members also receive *School Library Media Quarterly* (ISSN 0278-4823), with three to four research-based articles per issue and listings of recommended resources, and Connections, sources of ideas from conferences. Canadian teacher-librarians will want to consider too the Association for Teacher-Librarianship in Canada (2651 Western Avenue, North Vancouver, British Columbia V7N 3L2), which publishes *Impact,* and the Canadian School Library Association (100 Elgin Street, Suite 602, Ottawa, Ontario K2P 1L5), which publishes *School Libraries in Canada.*

3

General Education

Consultant: Dr. Allen R. Warner
University of Houston
Houston, Texas

Dr. Allen Warner is Dean of the University of Houston's College of Education and Professor of Curriculum and Instruction. He received an Ed.D. in secondary education and educational administration as well as his master's in education from Northern Illinois University-DeKalb.

At the national level Dr. Warner represents the Association of Teacher Educators on the National Council for Accreditation of Teacher Education, a post he has held since 1981. He chaired the NCATE Specialty Area Studies Board and currently serves on NCATE's Executive Board and on the Unit Accreditation Board. Following a three-year term as chair of the Professional Ethics Committee of the National Council for the Social Studies, he completed a term on the NCSS Research Committee and is past chair of the editorial board of NCSS's journal *Social Education*. He served on the ATE Board of Directors, is past president of the Texas Association of Teacher Educators, served as a member of the Action Group on Teacher Competence Committee on Accreditation, and chairs the ATE Leadership Foundation for Teacher Education, among many other professional activities.

Among the recognition he has received are election as a Distinguished Member of the Association of Teacher Educators, the 1993 ATE Distinguished Educator Award, ATE President's Awards in 1984, 1985, 1986, and 1992 from four different presidents, the Ben Coody Distinguished Service Award from the Texas Association of Teacher Educators, the Finalist Award from ATE's Distinguished Program in Teacher Education, a Distinguished Achievement Certificate of Recognition from the American Association of Colleges for Teacher Education, and the first Distinguished Service Award from the University of Houston College of Education Foundation. In February 1990 he was recognized by the Association of Teacher Educators as one of the nation's 70 Leaders in Teacher Education and presented the Distinguished Educator Lecture at the 1993 ATE Annual Meeting. In March

1995 he was invited to keynote the Dutch Conference on Teacher Education in Amsterdam.

He is co-author of two books and has published numerous monographs as well as articles in various journals.

CHANGING SCHOOLS

Fiske, Edward B. *Smart Schools, Smart Kids: Why Do Some Schools Work?* Simon & Schuster, 1992. 304 p. ISBN 0-671-79212-1 (paper).

Ted Fiske is former Education Editor for the *New York Times*. In this work he seeks to describe schools across the country in which educational reform is working, and it is usually working because decision-making power over instruction has been delegated to principals, to teachers, and to those who are closest to learners. He sees the major obstacle to school reform to be the isolation in which many of these people work—most of them usually not knowing that someone else is trying something similar, elsewhere, and it's working.

Glasser, William. *The Control Theory Manager: Combining the Control Theory of William Glasser with the Wisdom of W. Edwards Deming to Explain Both What Quality Is and What Lead-Managers Do to Achieve It.* HarperBusiness, 1994. 123 p. ISBN 0-88730-673-X (hardcover).

As the rather laborious title indicates, this work is an extension of Glasser's reality therapy concepts for classroom management combined with Deming's work on Total Quality Improvement. The major issue in reading this work is the increasing realization that the professional teacher of the future will be more of a manager, orchestrating the design of learning environments and to some degree coordinating the activity of a variety of adults (including parents, teacher aides, counselors, and others who affect the environment of the child) to assist with the child's development.

———. *The Quality School.* Harper & Row, 1990. 171 p. ISBN 0-06-096513-4 (hardcover).

While "quality" is a term which tends to be so overused in education that it may turn some people off, this work is an important effort by one of our more prolific educational writers to examine elements of schools which can lead to quality. Glasser writes simply and eloquently. The ideas take time to ingest and apply. It's worth it.

Goodlad, John I. *A Place Called School: Prospects for the Future.* McGraw-Hill, 1984. 396 p. ISBN 0-07-023627-5 (paper).

John Goodlad's timing was impeccable in the publication of this work. It was published on the heels of *A Nation at Risk* (1983), the United States Department of Education report which brought schools and schooling to the forefront of the national agenda of the United States. There is much here to think about, from the conditions of schools and the teaching profession to what schools can and should become.

Kozol, Jonathan. *Savage Inequalities: Children in America's Schools.* Crown Publishing Group, 1991. ISBN 0-517-58221-X (hardcover); 0-06-097499-0 (paper).

Decades ago John Gardner said that American education was increasingly being caught in a crossfire between unloving critics and uncritical lovers. There are few more vehement critics of schools than Jonathan Kozol, but if one were to attempt to typify him by Gardner's dichotomy the conclusion comes quickly that his work reflects one who cares deeply but is outraged by the conditions of schooling which further disadvantage those children in the greatest need of help. This work should be read by everyone who cares deeply about children and the future.

DOING CURRICULUM AND INSTRUCTION

Eisner, Elliot W. *The Educational Imagination: On the Design and Education of School Programs.* 2nd ed. Macmillan, 1985. 386 p. ISBN 0-02-332110-5 (hardcover).

Eisner calls his unique approach to curriculum development and evaluation "educational connoisseurship," a concept he borrows from the arts. He's not easy to understand but he's challenging, and most important he shifts our attention from the contemporary fetish with accountability based on paper-and-pencil test scores to a more open, human, and humane approach to looking at what goes on in school settings. Whether one agrees or disagrees with his approach, it should be confronted as an alternative way of designing and evaluating school programs.

English, Fenwick W. *Deciding What to Teach and Test: Developing, Aligning and Auditing the Curriculum.* Corwin Press, 1992. 128 p. ISBN 0-8039-6126-X (hardcover); 0-8039-6019-0 (paper).

Fenwick English is one of the more prolific writers in the area of curriculum alignment—a concept of ensuring that the intent, goals, objectives, instruction, and evaluation all have a sound relationship to one another. This book is a very useful approach to that end. If we do nothing else in school settings, we need to seek congruence between the curriculum as it is intended, the curriculum as it is taught, the curriculum as it is apprehended by learners, and the curriculum as it is assessed by whatever means chosen. Too often each of those elements tends to be disconnected from the others.

Gardner, John W. *Excellence.* Rev. ed. W. W. Norton, 1984. 175 p. ISBN 0-393-30377-2 (paper).

John Gardner, Secretary of Health, Education and Welfare from 1965 to 1968 and the founder of Common Cause, analyzes our nation's conflicting values between equality and excellence. This is an important work for any teacher who struggles with trying to treat children with equity while at the same time recognizing and rewarding excellence. A wonderful quote from this book:

> "The society that scorns excellence in plumbing because plumbing is a humble activity and tolerates shoddiness in philosophy because it is an exalted activity will have neither good plumbing nor good philosophy. Neither its pipes nor its theories will hold water." (p. 102)

Glasser, William. *Control Theory in the Classroom.* Harper & Row, 1986. 144 p. ISBN 0-06-096085-X (paper).

Glasser's concept of control theory is not one of how to control others, but rather one which rests on the notion that the behavior of each of us rests in large measure on our need to have some control of the environment about us and that the teacher who knows how to use that powerful motivating force toward success in school is more likely to help children succeed. This is important stuff. It should be required reading for every school professional, whether one finally agrees or disagrees with the approach.

•Gollnick, Donna M., and Philip C. Chinn. *Multicultural Education in a Pluralistic Society.* 4th ed. Merrill, 1994. 352 p. ISBN 0-02-344491-6 (hardcover).

We are a nation of immigrants. Unless one has a substantial amount of Native American blood flowing through the veins, the issue is not whether we are natives, but when our ancestors arrived. The future of American society will depend in large measure on our corporate ability to create a pluralistic society in which one's talent, rather than conditions of birth, forms the basis for achievement. Schools must be the cornerstone of the foundation for social mobility. This is one of the better and more contemporary commentaries on the whole issue.

Good, Thomas L., and Jere E. Brophy. *Looking in Classrooms.* 6th ed. HarperCollins College Publishers, 1994. 525 p. ISBN 0-06-501918-0 (hardcover).

This is an excellent reference for understanding the dynamics of what goes on in classrooms. Chapters include topics such as classroom life, increasing teacher awareness, the role of teacher expectations, preventing problems, coping with problems, motivation, differentiating instruction, active teaching, and a host of more specific topics under those titles. Numerous current and important issues like cooperative learning, inclusion, and metacognitive awareness are addressed. The work is initially designed as a text. It can also be a substantial reference for teachers interested in improving their performance.

Mager, Robert F. Various works.

Robert Mager is the contemporary guru of instructional design in education and especially in training in business and industry. His works tend to be easily readable, instructive, and thought-provoking. The problem with any one citation is that he often issues multiple editions and frequently changes publishers with later editions. Among the titles which should be included in any Mager professional development collection are *Preparing Instructional Objectives* (Lake Publishing, 1984. ISBN 1-56103-341-3, paper), *Developing Attitude Toward Learning* (Lake Publishing, 1984. ISBN 1-56103-337-5, paper), *Analyzing Performance Problems* (Mager and Peter Pipe. Lake Publishing, 1984. ISBN 1-56103-336-7, paper), and *Measuring Instructional Intent* (2nd ed. Lake Publishing, 1984. ISBN 56103-340-6, paper).

Slavin, Robert E. *Effective Programs for Students at Risk*. Allyn & Bacon, 1989. 376 p. ISBN 0-205-11953-0 (hardcover).

There is no more "hot" contemporary topic in schools than at risk students—those who by conditions of birth and/or environment are disadvantaged in their likelihood of succeeding in school in a nation and in a world where the contributions of each individual will become more and more important. This work surveys programs in which those children increase their likelihood of school success and, by extension, their potential for success and societal contribution after schooling. Every school professional should find something of use here.

―――, Nancy L. Karweit, and Barbara A. Wasik. *Preventing Early School Failure: Research, Policy, and Practice*. Allyn & Bacon, 1994. 237 p. ISBN 0-205-13991-4 (hardcover).

Slavin's work is best known for his efforts in cooperative group learning. In this edited collection of readings he and his colleagues address issues of early childhood education and share the most current information available on topics such as the effects of birth-to-age-three interventions on school success, the impact of preschool, extra-year kindergartens and transitional first grades, school and classroom organization in beginning reading (including class size, teacher aides, and instructional grouping), and a host of other topics.

OLDIES BUT GOODIES

Benjamin, Harold. *The Saber-Tooth Curriculum.* McGraw-Hill, 1939. 139 p. ISBN 0-07-049151-8 (paper).

This little paperback book is a timeless classic. Originally written in 1939 as a series of interviews with professor of paleolithic education J. Abner Pediwell over tequila daisies in a bar in Tijuana, this satire continues to be thought-provoking. It causes any reader to question the functionality of what (s)he is teaching, the degree to which the things that are taught are the things children need—now and into the future. More than half a century after it was penned, *The Saber-Tooth Curriculum* is an easy, but stimulating, read.

Bloom, Benjamin S. *Human Characteristics and School Learning.* McGraw-Hill, 1982. 284 p. ISBN 0-07-006122-X (paper).

In this work Bloom, the patriarch of mastery learning, argues from an analysis of hundreds of studies on school achievement that there are three important variables to attend to in helping students achieve on any given learning task. Those variables are cognitive entry skills, affective entry characteristics [especially whether the learner believes (s)he can succeed, at least enough to try], and timely and effective feedback from the teacher and/or the learning materials. It's not necessarily easy reading but these are important concepts.

Illich, Ivan. *Deschooling Society.* Harper & Row, 1971. ISBN 06-091046-1 (hardcover); 0-06-132086-2 (paper).

Illich argues forcibly that perhaps one of the greatest contributions we could make to societal advancement is to "deschool" society, taking the massive funds spent on public education institutions (which invariably become institutions of social control) and devoting those funds to improving the lot of the poor. He suggests that creating learning networks may well be more valuable, linking someone who wishes to learn to be a welder with an experienced welder. Whether one agrees or disagrees, the argument should be engaged.

Postman, Neil, and Charles Weingartner. *Teaching as a Subversive Activity.* Dell Publishing, 1987. ISBN 0-440-38485-0 (paper).

In this reprint of a work first published close to twenty years ago, Postman and Weingartner argue that the greatest tools we can impart to each student are those needed to sort out among the various attempts to influence our thinking each day. They posit that because much of schooling is indoctrination into a specific culture and set of values, if we as teachers do our jobs we are in essence subversive because we prepare the young to critically examine their society rather than to simply accept it. Read it; debate it; don't ignore it.

General Education 37

Tyler, Ralph W. *Basic Principles of Curriculum and Instruction.* University of Chicago Press, 1969. ISBN 0-226-82031-9 (paper).

Ralph Tyler recently passed away after a career which included advising every president since Franklin Delano Roosevelt on educational issues. This little work is seminal, the first statement of Tyler's classic theory of systematic curriculum design. Everyone should read it. It was originally a syllabus for Education 305 at the University of Chicago and has influenced much of educational thought for the latter half of the 20th century.

THINKING AHEAD AND STAYING ALIVE

Covey, Stephen R. *The 7 Habits of Highly Effective People.* Simon & Schuster, 1989. 358 p. ISBN 0-671-66398-4 (hardcover); 0-671-70863-5 (paper).

Stephen Covey has become something of a contemporary guru in the arena of self-improvement. This work has several important potential applications in schools. The first is to be available to school personnel who often feel over-afflicted with conflicting demands and need personal, as well as professional, development and inspiration from time to time. The second is that many of these ideas can, and probably should, be applied in a holistic way when helping children make sense of their world and their potential place in it.

Naisbitt, John. *Global Paradox: The Bigger the World Economy, the More Powerful its Smallest Players.* William Morrow, 1994. 304 p. ISBN 0-688-12791-6 (hardcover).

The most recent in the Naisbitt series which includes *Megatrends, Megatrends 2000,* and a host of other popular publications, this pop-futures work attempts to help the reader grasp the impact of increasing interdependence among nations—especially the smaller ones. Only one military superpower remains—the United States—while nations with comparatively small populations (e.g., Yemen, Saudi Arabia, Jordan) have disproportionate impact on the world scene because the emphasis has shifted from military confrontation to economic development. The economic superpowers of Japan, Germany (with the European Community), and the United States now move into a whole new environment in which, in truth, no nation can be an island unto itself.

―――. *Megatrends: Ten New Directions Transforming Our Lives.* Warner Books, 1988. 290 p. ISBN 0-446-35681-6 (paper).

This is the original work which brought John Naisbitt and the Naisbitt Group of futures-studies specialists to the attention of the public. In the early 1980s Naisbitt argued that the trends were toward an information society, high tech/high touch, a world economy, long term thinking, decentralization, self-help, participatory democracy, networking instead of hierarchies, movement from the northern states to the southern states, and multiple options. To comprehend the present state of affairs it's useful to realize that the directions were apparent more than a decade ago. It's worth reading.

————, and Patricia Aburdenne. *Megatrends 2000: Ten New Directions for the 1990's*. Avon, 1990. 448 p. ISBN 0-380-70437-4 (paper).

The Naisbitt Group of futures-studies specialists has an interesting methodology for their work. Essentially, they comb newspapers and periodicals for themes of what is reported and coalesce their findings into trend-identification for the edification of the rest of us. This update to the original *Megatrends* includes trends which are often self-contradictory (the emergence of free-market socialism, privitization of the welfare state) as well as illuminating (the rise of women in leadership, the impact of biological advances, the religious revival of the third millennium). Whether one agrees or disagrees with their identified trends, this is thought-provoking reading.

Peters, Tom, and Nancy Austin. *A Passion for Excellence*. Warner Books, 1985. 575 p. ISBN 0-446-38639-1 (paper).

This follow-up piece to the original *In Search of Excellence* is primarily phrased in terms of business leadership. The fact of the matter, though, is that teachers are leaders and are in need of continuing leadership training. There is much here to chew on if the reader will take the additional time needed to think through and translate business leadership concepts into leadership attributes for children in school settings. It's a stretch but the effort can be worthwhile.

JOURNALS

Educational Leadership. Association for Supervision and Curriculum Development. ISSN 0013-1784.

The audience includes educational leaders at all levels who are interested in school curriculum, supervision, and leadership. Each issue focuses on special topics and contemporary issues of interest to school leaders as well as relevant research. Each issue also includes reviews of resources for educational leaders.

Phi Delta Kappan. Phi Delta Kappa. ISSN 0031-7217.

This quality journal is published by Phi Delta Kappa, the professional fraternity in education. Its articles focus on educational research, service, and leadership. Emphasis is placed on contemporary trends, issues, and policies in education.

Principal. National Association of Elementary School Principals. ISSN 0271-6062.

General Education

Available only through membership in NAESP, this journal is for principals at the elementary and middle school levels. It highlights current educational topics and research which are of interest to principals. The "Principal's Bookshelf" section reviews current resources that would be of interest to school principals.

MEMBERSHIPS

Association for Supervision and Curriculum Development
1250 North Pitt Street
Alexandria, Virginia 22314-1453

Phone: (703) 549-9110

The mission of ASCD states: "ASCD, a diverse international community of educators, forging covenants in teaching and learning for the success of all learners." Membership in this organization includes a subscription to *Educational Leadership*.

National Association of Elementary School Principals
1615 Duke Street
Alexandria, Virginia 22314-3483

Phone: (703) 684-3345

This organization serves twenty-seven thousand elementary and middle school principals through a wide variety of services aimed at helping principals do the best job possible. NAESP provides principals with the latest in professional development through its national conference and exhibits, *Principal* magazine, and a broad range of other periodicals.

Phi Delta Kappa
408 North Union
P.O. Box 789
Bloomington, Indiana 47402-0789

Phone: (800) 766-1156 or (812) 339-1156
Fax: (812) 339-0018

The purpose of the organization is to promote quality education, with particular emphasis on publicly supported education as essential to the development and maintenance of a democratic way of life. Membership includes a subscription to *Phi Delta Kappan*. Of particular interest to librarians is the *Kappan Fast Back* series (Phi Delta Kappa Educational Foundation), which includes quality professional literature on a variety of educational topics. Contact the organization and request the complete list of *Kappan Fast Back Books* that are in print.

4

Reading

Consultant: Dr. Timothy Shanahan
University of Illinois at Chicago
Chicago, Illinois

Dr. Timothy Shanahan is Professor of Urban Education at the University of Illinois at Chicago, where he is the coordinator of graduate programs in Reading, Writing, and Literacy and also serves as Director of the UIC Center for Literacy.

He was recipient of the Milton D. Jacobson Readability Research Award from the International Reading Association, and the Amoco Award for Outstanding Teaching. He served on the task force that wrote national standards for English Language Arts education, a joint project of the International Reading Association and the National Council of Teachers of English. For six years, he has been co-director of Project FLAME, a family literacy program in Chicago's Latino community.

Dr. Shanahan has published more than ninety research articles, chapters, and other publications, including the books *Teachers Thinking—Teachers Knowing* and *Multidisciplinary Perspective on Literacy* (both published by NCRE and NCTE). He is one of the authors of the *Treasury of Literature* (Harcourt Brace), a K–8 reading program. He edited the "Integrating Curriculum" column for *The Reading Teacher* and served as associate editor of *The Journal of Reading Behavior* and as the Director of Cooperative Research for the National Conference of Research on English.

DOCUMENTS/GUIDELINES/STANDARDS

Anderson, Richard C., Elfrieda H. Scott, Judith A. Scott, and Ian A. G. Wilkinson. *Becoming a Nation of Readers: Report of the Commission on Reading.* National Institute of Education (available from the International Reading Association), 1985. 147 p. (paper).

This document was sponsored by the National Academy of Education to analyze and make accessible recommendations based upon research from a variety of disciplines. The report was written for both lay readers and practitioners, and remains one of the clearest descriptions of school reading programs available. It masterfully describes reading, emergent literacy, literacy for the older student, teacher education, classroom organization, and testing. Specific recommendations are included in each chapter. This book provides useful background information for designing effective instruction, and can be used with the community to help parents and others to better understand school reading instruction.

KEYSTONE WORKS

Adams, Marilyn Jager. *Beginning to Read: Thinking and Learning About Print.* MIT Press, 1990. 494 p. ISBN 0-262-01112-3 (hardcover).

Debates about the role of phonics instruction have plagued American education for more than a century. This is an exceptionally cogent review of the research on how children perceive and think about print and the role of phonics instruction in reading development. Although this book is theoretical in nature, it is a valuable resource for teachers who must decide on instructional approaches and who must explain these decisions to the public. It makes a compelling case for the inclusion of explicit study of sound-symbol relationships, and explains how phonics can be part of a whole language program.

Barr, Rebecca, Michael L. Kamil, Peter Mosenthal, and P. David Pearson, eds. *Handbook of Reading Research (vol. II).* Longman, 1991. 1086 p. ISBN 0-8013-0292-7 (hardcover).

This second volume of research summaries treats thirty-four topics. All of the summaries are new; none has been carried over from the first collection. In some cases, such as beginning reading and comprehension instruction, the summary in the second volume is an entirely new analysis of a topic treated earlier. Several new topics are covered as well, including remediation, grouping, vocabulary, strategic reading, computers in reading and writing, and reading–writing relationships. Again, the reviews are comprehensive and authoritative, and both volumes are considered to be "classics" in the field. An essential reference guide to empirical work on reading.

Harris, Albert J., and Edward R. Sipay. *How to Increase Reading Ability: A Guide to Developmental and Remedial Methods.* 9th ed. Longman, 1990. 926 p. ISBN 0-8013-0246-3 (hardcover).

This book has been one of the leading textbooks and desk references in reading education for more than fifty years. It remains the most comprehensive treatment of reading instruction for teachers, with more than three thousand references. Clearly written, carefully indexed, practical, informative, and balanced, it provides useful advice for teachers on hundreds of topics, including assessment, vision and reading, reading rate, parent involvement, content area reading, and reading preferences. An especially thorough coverage of issues of reading disabilities, and a useful summary of published reading tests.

Harris, Theodore L., and Richard E. Hodges, eds. *A Dictionary of Reading and Related Terms.* International Reading Association, 1981. 382 p. ISBN 087207-944-9 (paper).

This useful reference tool provides definitions of more than five thousand terms concerning reading, language, and reading instruction. Both historical and modern entries are included. Although probably most useful for academic purposes, it can have practical value to facilitate communication between school and community. Definitions, many supported with illustrative sentences, are clear enough that they can be understood by laymen as well as educators, and the many related medical terms that are included are useful in dealing with information that sometimes appears in students' cumulative folders.

Pearson, P. David, ed. *Handbook of Reading Research.* Longman, 1994. 899 p. ISBN 0-582-28119-9 (hardcover).

This is a collection of twenty-five articles that summarize research on various topics concerning reading and reading instruction. The reviews are comprehensive and authoritative. Included are treatments of topics such as oral reading, classroom reading instruction, studying, reading comprehension, word identification, beginning reading instruction, individual differences, listening and reading, and assessment. This compendium is a valuable reference work that will provide teachers with empirical support for instructional decision-making, and will be a useful resource for those enrolled in graduate programs in reading.

Ruddell, Robert B., Martha Rapp Ruddell, and Harry Singer, eds. *Theoretical Models and Processes of Reading.* 4th ed. International Reading Association, 1994. 1275 p. ISBN 0-87207-438-2 (hardcover); 0-87207-437-4 (paper).

This theoretical collection analyzes research on the role of language, social context, and culture in the various aspects of reading development, including word recognition, motivation, comprehension, literary response, and metacognition. It explores various theoretical models that have been proposed to explain how readers read and learn to read, including those from cognition, sociolinguistics, and other disciplines. Surprisingly readable given the nature of the material and depth of analysis. Useful for graduate studies, to inform instruction, and as a reference.

Smith, Frank. *Understanding Reading: A Psycholinguistic Analysis of Reading and Learning to Read.* 5th ed. Lawrence Erlbaum Associates, 1994. 365 p. ISBN 0-89859-879-6 (paper).

This is a classic summary of cognitive theoretical work on reading. The author considers information drawn from psychology and linguistics to make sense of the reading process. It is especially thorough in its treatment of memory issues in work identification. On the basis of theory and research, the work derives principles of instruction that should be considered by teachers in designing classroom reading instruction. A good introduction to cognitive reading processes; a must for those engaged in graduate studies in reading.

ASSESSMENT

Farr, Roger, and Bruce Tone. *Portfolio and Performance Assessment.* Harcourt Brace, 1994. 383 p. ISBN 0-15-500485-9 (hardcover).

A very practical guide to developing student portfolios and performance assessments for evaluating student work. Demonstrates how to construct and store portfolios, and gives advice on how students might work with them. Specific guidance for helping students to engage in self-evaluation is provided, and criteria for teacher evaluation are recommended. The manual includes step by step instructions on how to develop performance assessments for rating students' abilities to read and write. An appendix includes several blackline masters of various checklists, rating forms, and other useful assessment materials.

Rhodes, Lynn K., and Nancy Shanklin. *Windows Into Literacy: Assessing Learners K–8.* Heinemann, 1992. 491 p. ISBN 0-435-08757-6 (paper).

Presentation of principles and practices of classroom literacy assessment. Emphasis is on teacher observation and judgment, rather than standardized tests. Shows how to collect and record assessment data within classroom instruction using observations, think alouds, retellings, interviews, portfolios, and performance samples. Practical information is provided, including observation checklists and performance criteria, for comprehension, metacognition, word recognition, emergent literacy, and writing. The authors provide guided reflection, activities, and practical advice to help teachers rethink their classroom reading and writing assessment.

Shearer, Arleen P., and Susan P. Homan. *Linking Reading Assessment to Instruction: An Application Worktext for Elementary Classroom Teachers.* St. Martin's Press, 1994. 259 p. ISBN 0-312-04765-7 (paper).

This worktext starts from the premise that instructional decision making is central to literacy teaching. It guides teachers towards a deeper understanding of both formal and informal assessment techniques that can be used to guide such decisions. It demonstrates how teachers can collect and interpret information appropriately in the classroom. Information is provided on conducting structured observations, interpreting standardized test scores, identifying problem readers, using informal reading inventories, and evaluating comprehension strategies, word recognition, and spelling ability. Each chapter includes work samples that teachers can use to improve their interpretive skills.

Valencia, Sheila W., Hiebert Elfrieda, and Peter P. Afflerbach, eds. *Authentic Reading Assessment: Practices and Possibilities.* International Reading Association, 1994. 317 p. ISBN 0-87207-765 (paper).

This collection emphasizes the use of non-traditional assessments in American education. It includes information on both classroom assessments as well as the newer large-scale assessments of reading that are being used in many states. The classroom assessment chapters are case studies that describe the author's experiences in developing and using specific innovative assessments. These emphasize the use of portfolios. Even the large-scale assessment chapters are written in a way that could be useful to classroom teachers who are trying to get beyond traditional assessment practices.

BEGINNING READING AND EMERGENT LITERACY

Clay, Marie M. *Becoming Literate: The Construction of Inner Control.* Heinemann, 1991. 366 p. ISBN 0-86863-279-1 (paper).

This important theoretical work describes how children come to take gradual control over print, and how teachers and parents can more effectively support this learning. The author demonstrates the logic of children's beginning construction of literacy through analyses of their beginning writing and spelling, their responses to print features such as directionality and orientation, and their attempts to match printed and oral words. She recommends instructional approaches that encourage and support children's efforts to read and write in their own ways with teacher observations and responses. and explains how teachers can recognize when students have gained control over print.

Harste, Jerome C., Virginia A. Woodward, and Carolyn Burke. *Language Stories and Literacy Lessons.* Heinemann, 1984. 252 p. ISBN 0-435-08211-6 (paper).

This book provides valuable theoretical analysis of beginning reading development. It describes an influential study of preschool literacy learning with important implications for beginning reading instruction. The study is so useful because it describes the early literacy and literacy learning strategies used by young children prior to receiving instruction. By revealing children's understanding of and approach to literacy before they enter the primary classroom, the authors show teachers how to take account of this knowledge in instructional planning.

McGee, Lea M., and Donald J. Richgels. *Literacy's Beginnings: Supporting Young Readers and Writers.* 2nd ed. Allyn & Bacon, 1995. 467 p. ISBN 0-205-16732-2 (paper).

This textbook focuses on reading and writing instruction through grade three. Useful resource on how children learn to read, how to develop a literacy-rich classroom, preschool literacy development, how to take account of the knowledge that children bring to school, and the needs of special learners. This includes information on big books, language experience approach, basal readers, predictable books, and other beginning reading instruction strategies and many examples of students' work samples and descriptions of classrooms.

•Strickland, Dorothy S., and Lesley Mandel Morrow, eds. *Emerging Literacy: Young Children Learn to Read and Write.* International Reading Association, 1989. 161 p. ISBN 0-87207-351-3 (paper).

This is a very practical collection of articles on various aspects of emergent literacy. Included are treatments of oral language, family storybook reading, use of literature with young children, reading to kindergarten children, home and school connections, a photo essay that illustrates the types of activities that will support emergent literacy development in the classroom, and the teaching of specific skills. Written for the practitioner, this book includes many examples of children's work and lots of practical suggestions for books and activities that will be of use in the classroom.

COMPREHENSION

Irwin, Judith Westphal. *Teaching Reading Comprehension Processes.* 2nd ed. Prentice-Hall, 1990. 209 p. ISBN 0-13-892738-3 (paper).

This book takes a unique approach to reading comprehension instruction. On the basis of research, it proposes that reading comprehension is made up of a number of underlying processes, including microprocesses (sentence level composition), integrative processes (connecting sentences together), macroprocesses (summarization and overall passage organization), elaborative processes (thinking about the overall sense of a text), and metacognitive processes (thinking about your own sense making). The book not only synthesizes research on each of these topics, but suggests many effective instructional techniques for helping students to comprehend better.

McNeil, John D. *Reading Comprehension: New Directions for Classroom Practice.* 3rd ed. HarperCollins, 1992. 221 p. ISBN 0-673-46425-3 (hardcover).

This useful handbook brings together a set of strategies and materials for developing students' reading comprehension. Based largely on constructivist theory that emphasizes the importance of the knowledge that students bring to reading, the book recommends a large number of practical instructional activities that can be used across the grades. Included is information on vocabulary development, comprehension of different types of texts, ways to elaborate on text, use of writing in comprehension, and other approaches for enhancing student understanding and interpretation of what they read.

CONTENT AREA AND UPPER GRADE READING

•Atwell, Nancie. *In the Middle: Writing, Reading, and Learning with Adolescents.* Boynton/Cook, 1987. 295 p. ISBN 0-86709-164-9 (hardcover); 0-86709-163-0 (paper).

One of the few books that emphasizes the teaching of reading in the upper grades, this is a delightful account of the author's own teaching in middle school. Proposing the use of reading workshops and mini-lessons as the center of a classroom reading program, it shows how the author helps students to develop ownership over reading through making their own guided choices. It is particularly useful in its approach to talking about books; many practical and insightful suggestions are included, as the author shows how reading skills are handled in a workshop context. Similar treatment of writing instruction is provided.

Cochran, Judith A. *Reading in the Content Area for Junior High and High School.* Allyn & Bacon, 1993. 326 p. ISBN 0-205-13404-1 (paper).

This practical book focuses on helping students to become independent readers in social studies, history, art, music, English, mathematics, science, and physical education. Although its focus is on high school and junior high, most of the information included should be helpful to anyone teaching reading in these subjects beyond the third grade. Helpful advice is provided on textbook use, vocabulary development, reading comprehension, writing, study skills, and technology. The book overflows with application exercises and teaching activities that can be applied in the classroom, including television reading activities, vocabulary games, textbook analysis forms, and scales for evaluation. Very readable.

Vacca, Richard T., and Joanne L. Vacca. *Content Area Reading*. 4th ed. HarperCollins, 1993. 416 p. ISBN 0-673-52215-6 (hardcover).

A widely used textbook about how to teach students to use reading to learn, this shows how to assess students, evaluate textbooks, plan instruction, guide text discussions, help students to activate their background knowledge, improve reading comprehension, teach text organization, develop strategies for studying, use writing to learn, and teach vocabulary. Clearly written and rich with examples of useful instructional activities and guides, it emphasizes general learning strategies over specialized approaches to different content areas, such as math, science, and history.

INSTRUCTIONAL METHODS

Cooper, J. David. *Literacy: Helping Children Construct Meaning*. Houghton Mifflin, 1993. 620 p. ISBN 0-395-64782-7 (paper).

This is a popular classroom reading textbook. Engagingly written, it provides a great deal of practical advice on teaching reading and writing in the elementary grades. Included are chapters on prior knowledge, vocabulary development, word identification, literary response and meaning construction, writing, modeling, content area instruction, and assessment. Illustrations abound, including guides for developing a thematic unit, study guides, minilessons, conference logs, graphic displays of information for classroom use, and story maps. A practical resource.

Crafton, Linda K. *Whole Language: Getting Started . . . Moving Forward*. Richard C. Owen Publishers, 1991. 322 p. ISBN 0-913461-19-9 (paper).

This practical book deals with the nuts and bolts of developing a "whole language" program. Each chapter emphasizes practical decisions that teachers must make to create a whole language classroom. The author shows how to get started, recommends twenty-five practical instructional strategies for supporting language learning, and includes descriptions of several thematic units. This volume could be used by teachers trying to develop complete whole language programs, or those who want to innovate within a more traditional framework. It includes information on classroom management, portfolio evaluation, working with parents and administrators, and the role of basals.

Daniels, Harvey. *Literature Circles: Voice and Choice in the Student-Centered Classroom.* Stenhouse Publishers, 1994. 200 p. ISBN 1-571-100-00-8 (hardcover).

This useful book shows how independent reading and cooperative learning can be combined to support children's reading development. The book provides specific techniques for starting Literature Circles (student reading groups), instructional variations for different types of students, photocopiable materials for use in English and Spanish, and practical suggestions for using Literature Circles across the curriculum. Lots of practical examples from classrooms.

Johns, Jerry L., Peggy VanLiersburg, and Susan J. Davis. *Improving Reading: A Handbook of Strategies.* Kendall/Hunt Publishing Company, 1994. 394 p. ISBN 0-8403-8984-1 (paper).

This resource book provides specific strategies and activities for use in the classroom reading program. Each section describes a difficulty with reading that students might be having, provides brief background information, and examines several ways to teach that aspect of reading more effectively, including ideas for practice and reinforcement. Emphasizing attitude, emergent literacy, oral reading, word recognition, comprehension, strategic reading, studying and test taking, and parent involvement, this book contains easily reproduced material (pages are perforated) that can be used to help assess or teach reading.

Nessel, Denise D., and Margaret B. Jones. *The Language-Experience Approach to Reading: A Handbook for Teachers of Reading.* Teachers College Press, 1981. 176 p. ISBN 0-8077-2596-X (paper).

The language-experience approach (LEA) is a widely used method for beginning and remedial reading instruction. It emphasizes the connection of reading with students' oral language development by using stories dictated by the students as the basic material of instruction. This book emphasizes its use in first grade classrooms, though much of it could be practical for work with older low readers, ESL, and special education students. This manual shows how to use LEA with groups, as well as how to support children's transfer into independent writing, and the reading of texts not composed through dictation.

•Routman, Regie. *Invitations: Changing as Teachers and Learners K–12.* 2nd ed. Heinemann, 1994. 502 p. ISBN 0-435-08837-8 (hardcover); 0-435-00836-X (paper).

Reading

This engaging book describes whole language instruction and theory, and provides support and encouragement for teachers trying to make the transition to this instructional philosophy. It provides specific strategies and demonstration lessons for reading and writing, literature, and phonics and spelling, as well as holistic advice about classroom organization and approaches to learning disabled children. The approach is never doctrinaire and always practical because of its basis in the author's own teaching experiences. Especially useful are the "blue pages," a 256-page supplement in the back of the book with resources for teachers, literature recommendations for each grade level, and exemplary themed units.

Slaughter, Judith Pollard. *Beyond Storybooks: Young Children and the Shared Book Experience.* International Reading Association, 1993. 167 p. ISBN 0-87207-377-7 (paper).

Increasingly, primary grade reading teachers are using big books and predictable books to teach reading. This practical guide shows how to use the "shared book experience" effectively. The shared book experience is one in which teachers read to children, and over time children join in and eventually take over the reading. It is a group or classroom emulation of the parent sharing a book with a single child. This book shows how to make big books of various kinds for and with children, and how to handle discussions, vocabulary, comprehension, and choral reading.

Tierney, Robert J., John E. Readence, and Ernest K. Dishner. *Reading Strategies and Practices: A Compendium.* Allyn & Bacon, 1995. 532 p. ISBN 0-205-16285-1 (hardcover).

This compendium includes descriptions of more than ninety different strategies for teaching reading. Strategies are organized by purpose or nature of activity, including such areas as reading comprehension, reading with writing, discussion and cooperative learning, vocabulary, literature and drama, content area reading, studying, listening, programs for "at risk" learners, and word identification. Several strategies from the professional literature are presented for each category. Each strategy includes a description of its specific purpose and rationale, intended audience, step-by-step description of the procedures, cautions and comments, and additional references.

INTEGRATED INSTRUCTION

Danielson, Kathy Everts, and Jan LaBonty. *Integrating Reading and Writing Through Children's Literature.* Allyn & Bacon, 1994. 234 p. ISBN 0-205-15314-3 (hardcover).

This practical book shows teachers how reading and writing instruction can be integrated effectively through an emphasis on children's literature. The authors describe how to organize a classroom around literature instruction, including alternative grouping approaches, as well as outlining ways to teach beginning reading and writing and to support reading comprehension through children's books. Skills—including word meaning, sight vocabulary, contextual analysis, phonics, literary skills, and study skills—are taught in the context of specific children's books. Each activity provides recommendations of several appropriate selections from children's literature.

Heller, Mary F. *Reading–Writing Connections: From Theory to Practice.* Longman, 1991. 322 p. ISBN 0-8013-0139-4 (paper).

This is a very practical textbook devoted to issues of how reading and writing can be taught together effectively. It takes a developmental approach to issues of integration in that it includes chapters on emergent literacy and primary, intermediate, and middle school instruction. It provides step-by-step descriptions of many useful instructional techniques, including invented spelling, the writing process conference approach, journals, directed reading lessons, and so on. Includes suggestions for creative variations on many useful instructional approaches and very useful chapters on vocabulary and classroom organization.

Shanahan, Timothy, ed. *Reading and Writing Together: New Perspectives for the Classroom.* Christopher Gordon, 1990. 277 p. ISBN 0-926842-04-8 (hardcover).

This book focuses on how reading and writing can be taught together most effectively. It emphasizes theory, research, and teaching practices for three different types of reading–writing relationships. Specifically, it considers the knowledge sharing that takes place across these language processes, the ways that readers think about authors and that authors think about readers, and how using reading and writing together can help students to accomplish goals more effectively. Additionally, there are chapters on classroom environment, the use of literature in fostering language connections, and assessment.

MOTIVATION

Cramer, Eugene H., and Marrietta Castle, eds. *Fostering the Love of Reading: The Affective Domain in Reading Education.* International Reading Association, 1994. 277 p. ISBN 0-87207-125-1 (paper).

This book is entirely devoted to issues of interest, attitude, motivation, and values for reading. The central premise of this collection of articles is that teachers should help children to learn the love of reading. Students who find reading to be satisfying and rewarding are more likely to be effective readers. This book includes both the theoretical foundations of this topic, as well as more directly applicable chapters on how to help children to choose books, developing motivational responses to literature, and using read-alouds and the visual arts effectively.

READING PROBLEMS

Gillet, Jean Wallace, and Charles Temple. *Understanding Reading Problems: Assessment and Instruction.* 4th ed. HarperCollins, 1994. 420 p. ISBN 0-673-52327-6 (hardcover).

This basic textbook describes various approaches to the diagnosis and instruction of reading disabilities. Unlike many other guides, its emphasis is on the use of informal assessment procedures, especially the informal reading inventory. It devotes one chapter to the description and interpretation of more formalized, norm-referenced measures. The book describes instructional techniques both for classroom and clinic, including activities that support learning of word recognition, comprehension, and spelling. It also contains useful discussions of learning disabilities, inclusion, and the assessment of the classroom reading environment.

Hiebert, Elfrieda H., and Barbara M. Taylor, eds. *Getting Reading Right From the Start: Effective Early Literacy Interventions.* Allyn & Bacon, 1994. 222 p. ISBN 0-205-15407-7 (paper).

At one time, schools waited until fourth grade before providing special assistance to children who were having difficulty learning to read. Increasingly, schools intervene earlier, as early as grade one, to prevent or alleviate reading problems. This useful book describes a number of early intervention programs that have successfully helped these types of children to succeed in learning to read. Included are descriptions of several models of early compensatory education, including Reading Recovery, Success for All, and various models of enhanced Chapter 1 and classroom instructional approaches.

Stires, Susan, ed. *With Promise: Redefining Reading and Writing for "Special Students."* Heinemann, 1991. 180 p. ISBN 0-435-08573-5 (paper).

This unique book approaches the reading needs of "special education" students in terms of whole language philosophy and practice. Rather than relegating such children to direct instruction in decontextualized language, the authors of this collection of articles show how integrated instruction in more authentic forms of literacy can support the learning of such children. Several of the articles were written by teachers, and there are many examples of children's work. The author provides specific information on topics such as motivation, oral reading, skills instruction, and mainstreaming.

SPECIAL POPULATIONS

•Allen, JoBeth, and Jana M. Mason, eds. *Risk Makers, Risk Takers, Risk Breakers: Reducing the Risks for Young Literacy Learners.* Heinemann, 1989. 351 p. ISBN 0-435-08483-6 (paper).

The chapters in this collection recommend policy changes and specific home and school practices that can be used to reduce the amount of failure in beginning literacy learning. Special emphasis is given to barriers to learning that are posed by racial and linguistic differences. Many specific instructional approaches are recommended, including collaborative learning, shared reading, little books, Reading Recovery, and family literacy, as well as several less well known and harder to label changes that are possible in any primary grade classroom. This work is valuable both for the research literature that is interpreted and the specific innovative projects and programs that are described.

•Au, Kathryn H. *Literacy Instruction in Multicultural Settings.* Harcourt Brace, 1993. 208 p. ISBN 0-03-076847-0 (paper).

Perhaps no issue in reading education is as troublesome as how to provide effective instruction to those from a variety of cultural backgrounds. Racial, ethnic, and linguistic differences often serve as barriers to literacy learning. This book offers practical advice on how to develop effective reading and writing instruction for students from different cultural backgrounds. It demonstrates how diversity can be valued successfully in the classroom. Specific instructional approaches are provided, including the use of multi-ethnic literature, dialogue journals, and adjustments to classroom discussions. This book shows teachers how to turn classroom diversity into an advantage in reading instruction.

Taylor, Denny, and Catherine Dorsey-Gaines. *Growing Up Literate: Learning from Inner City Families.* Heinemann, 1988. 234 p. ISBN 0-435-08457-7 (paper).

This is an analysis of the family literacy practices of inner city, African American families. The emphasis is on Black children who are learning to read and write despite extraordinary economic hardships. Important both because it dramatically demonstrates that race, locale, and economic circumstances do not necessarily preclude success with literacy, and because it describes the different educative styles of families that shape the literacy experiences of children. Insightful and moving accounts of home literacy practices.

VOCABULARY

Johnson, Dale D., and P. David Pearson. *Teaching Reading Vocabulary*, 2nd ed. Harcourt Brace College Publishers, 1984. 216 p. ISBN 0-03-062778-8 (paper).

This is a practical teaching manual that emphasizes word identification and word meaning instruction. The word identification chapters include information on sight vocabulary, phonics, structural analysis, and context analysis. Several chapters are devoted to word meaning instruction, including semantic networks, mapping, analogies, and dictionary and thesaurus instruction. The book also directs much attention to synonyms, antonyms, homophones, multi-meaning words, etymology, and other traditional issues in vocabulary development. Very practice oriented in its approach, with many specific exercises, assignments, and teaching activities.

Nagy, William E. *Teaching Vocabulary to Improve Reading Comprehension*. National Council of Teachers of English and International Reading Association, 1988. 42 p. ISBN 0-8141-5238-4 (NCTE, paper); 0-87207-151-0 (IRA, paper).

This practical booklet describes the qualities of effective vocabulary instruction, particularly with regard to its impact on reading comprehension, in a clear and efficient manner. Although the author indicates that most vocabulary learning takes place incidentally (that is, without direct instruction), he explains the role of direct instruction and describes several approaches to teaching vocabulary that can influence reading comprehension if used effectively, including semantic mapping, semantic feature analysis, hierarchical arrays, linear arrays, meaningful use, and repetition. Nice introduction to vocabulary.

WORD RECOGNITION

Cunningham, Patricia M. *Phonics They Use: Words for Reading and Writing*, 2nd ed. HarperCollins, 1995. 170 p. ISBN 0-673-46433-4 (paper).

A collection of practical, classroom-tested activities that help teach sound-symbol relationships, this is full of common sense advice on appropriate instructional practices in phonics and includes information on the development of phonological awareness, use of predictable books, word sorting, writing and spelling, blending, word families, and various phonic elements (consonants, digraphs, vowels, etc.). Very thorough in its approach to instructional issues in phonics; it would be possible to develop a very sound program of instruction in this area of reading from this source alone.

Heilman, Arthur W. *Phonics in Proper Perspective.* 7th ed. Macmillan, 1993, 145 p. ISBN 0-02-353065-0 (paper).

This book provides a clear description of the purpose and limitations of phonics instruction and recommends an organized collection of practices that can be used to teach phonics analysis to children. A very practical guidebook that shows how to teach visual discrimination of letters and auditory discrimination of language sounds, this is a thorough analysis of the teaching of consonants, vowels, and irregular relationships, including lots of word lists, and recommendations of specific activities for use with children.

NONPRINT MATERIALS

Association for Supervision and Curriculum Development. *Making Meaning: Integrated Language Arts Series.* Association for Supervision and Curriculum Development (available from IRA), 1992. Videos. Stock #614228.

This series of five videotapes explores how teachers can integrate reading with the rest of the language arts. It shows effective combinations of reading, writing, speaking, and listening in actual K–5 classrooms, emphasizing issues of time, choice, response, structure, and community. One tape serves as an introduction (20 minutes), while others deal with specific areas of integration, including primary grades (23 minutes), upper elementary grades (23 minutes), across the curriculum (22 minutes), and assessment (22 minutes). Includes a facilitator's guide, the book
• *When Writers Read* by Jane Hansen.

Center for the Study of Reading. *Teaching Reading Strategies from Successful Classrooms.* Distributed by the International Reading Association, 1991. Videos.

This set of six videotapes allows teachers to see effective research based, instructional practices in emergent literacy (43 minutes), connecting reading with writing (55 minutes), teaching word identification (50 minutes), literacy in content area instruction (44 minutes), fostering a classroom literacy culture (50 minutes), and teaching reading comprehension (34 minutes). Each tape has a viewer's guide that includes background information, theoretical rationale, and follow-up activities. Only available as a set.

JOURNALS

• *Language Arts.* National Council of Teachers of English. ISSN 0360-9170.

Reading

This journal is published eight times during the school year. It usually includes about six articles on different aspects of elementary language arts instruction, including reading. Each issue focuses on a particular theme, so some issues may have little on reading while others are entirely devoted to reading. Additionally, each issue contains departments that deal with children's books, children's authors, research on the language arts, and other relevant topics. One of the best sources of books for children.

The Reading Teacher. International Reading Association. ISSN 0034-0561.

This journal is published eight times during the school year. It usually includes four to six articles on different aspects of elementary reading instruction, and each year publishes "Children's Choices," an annotated list of the most popular children's books in various categories. Each issue has a number of departments that deal with children's books, work from the National Reading Research Center, professional development, assessment, integrated curriculum, and technology. It also includes several pages of classroom tested instructional ideas submitted by teachers.

MEMBERSHIPS

International Reading Association
800 Barksdale Road
Newark, Delaware 19714-8139

Phone: (302) 731-1600

The International Reading Association seeks to promote literacy worldwide by improving the quality of reading instruction through the study of the reading process and teaching techniques; serving as clearinghouse for the dissemination of reading research through conferences, journals, and other publications; and actively encouraging the lifetime reading habit. Membership in the organization for elementary teachers includes a subscription to *The Reading Teacher.*

5

Language Arts

Consultant: Dr. Julie M. Jensen
University of Texas
Austin, Texas

Dr. Jensen is Professor of Curriculum and Instruction at The University of Texas at Austin, where she teaches courses in language, literacy, and children's literature. She received her doctorate and master's degree from the University of Minnesota. She has served as an elementary teacher in the Minneapolis, Minnesota Public Schools.

An active member of professional organizations, Dr. Jensen was President of the National Council of Teachers of English and editor of its journal *Language Arts*. She has served as a member of numerous committees of the National Council of Teachers of English, Texas Council of Teachers of English, Central Texas Council of Teachers of English, International Reading Association, and National Conference on Research in English.

Dr. Jensen has authored and edited numerous publications. Most recently she co-edited the National Council of Teachers of English publication, *Adventuring with Books: A Booklist for Pre-K–Grade 6*. Other publications include *Measures for Research and Evaluation in the English Language Arts*, *Developing Children's Language*, *Composing and Comprehending*, *Stories to Grow On*, and *Handbook of Research on Teaching the English Language Arts*.

DOCUMENTS/GUIDELINES/STANDARDS

International Reading Association and National Council of Teachers of English, eds. *Cases in Literacy: An Agenda for Discussion*. International Reading Association and National Council of Teachers of English, 1989. 43 p. ISBN 0-87207-152-9 (IRA, paper); 0-8141-1320-7 (NCTE, paper).

Language Arts

Jointly prepared by the National Council of Teachers of English and the International Reading Association, *Cases in Literacy* is a guide for groups of teachers engaged in discussing literacy-related issues, among them: defining literacy, the values of literacy, teaching, learning, and assessing literacy. Each issue is followed by a background statement, a school-based vignette of "case," and a list of questions intended to focus the issues raised and encourage the expression of diverse viewpoints. Though all eleven cases relate to reading and writing, users may expand the number of applications by broadly defining literacy to include communicating through the use of symbols of all kinds.

International Reading Association and National Council of Teachers of English Joint Task Force on Assessment. *Standards for the Assessment of Reading and Writing*. International Reading Association and National Council of Teachers of English, 1994. 44 p. ISBN 0-87207-674-1 (IRA, paper); 0-8141-0213-1 (NCTE, paper).

For professionals making decisions about assessing the teaching and learning of reading and writing, here is a guide in three parts. Because decision-makers need to understand assessment in ways that take into account current knowledge about language, about learning, and about the complex literacy demands of today's society, introductory sections describe assessment, language, language learning, language assessment, and assessment language. Following are six standards related to the goals of assessment (e.g., to improve teaching and learning) and five standards related to the implementation of assessment (e.g., it should involve multiple perspectives and sources of data). Each standard is elaborated by a rationale and by implications; some are illustrated, additionally, by a case study. Concluding is a detailed glossary of assessment terms.

National Council of Teachers of English and International Reading Association. *Standards for the English Language Arts*. National Council of Teachers of English, 1996. 132 p. ISBN 0-8141-4676-7 (hardcover).

Representing over three years of research and discussion among teachers, parents, and administrators, this book presents standards designed to equip all K–12 students with a literacy education encompassing the use of print, oral, and visual language. The work addresses six English language arts: reading, writing, speaking, listening, viewing, and visually representing. This work is intended to complement other national, state, and local standards for English language arts.

KEYSTONE WORKS

Britton, James. *Language and Learning: The Importance of Speech in Children's Development*. 2nd ed. Boynton Cook, 1993. 298 p. ISBN 0-86709-335-8 (paper).

Though speech is most readily thought of as a means of communication, the focus here is not on the importance of speech to listeners, but to speakers themselves. Conveying his principal learnings and teachings to readers who want to listen to children with greater understanding, Britton outlines the theory underlying the book: People use language as a means of organizing their representation of the world, that representation constituting the world they operate in, and forming the basis of all predictions by which they set the course of their lives.

Chukovsky, Kornei. *From Two to Five*. Ed. and trans. by Miriam Morton. University of California Press, 1971. 170 p. ISBN 0-520-00238-5 (paper).

Born in 1882, Chukovsky was a scholar of adult literature, a celebrated poet for children, an analytic observer and loyal admirer of children, and an advocate of children's rights to savor all kinds of experiences and literary fare, particularly nonsense verse and fairy tales. Believing children's language is a window on their thought processes, he observed and recorded for four decades the verses of two- to five-year-olds, publishing them first in 1925. In chapters titled "A Linguistic Genius" and "The Tireless Explorer," Chukovsky shows through a wealth of examples the vast, varied, and complex mental effort young children expend in the process of learning their native language.

Moffett, James. *Teaching the Universe of Discourse*. Boynton Cook Publishing, 1983. 215 p. ISBN 0-86709-181-9 (paper).

This companion book to *Student-Centered Language Arts, K–12,* outlines a pedagogical theory of discourse pertinent for anyone rethinking education in the native language. Moffett recommends teaching the universe of discourse, not by having students analyze language, but by creating opportunities for students to use language realistically and in all its dimensions. He reminds readers that languages are symbol systems, not content subjects, and that learning symbol systems means learning how to manipulate them. Students learn to manipulate symbols through involvement in discourse of all kinds, with the sequence of involvement, Moffett argues, reflecting levels of abstraction that characterize intellectual growth. His goal is students who can "play freely the whole symbolic scale."

Vygotsky, L. S. *Thought and Language*. The M.I.T. Press, 1962. 168 p. ISBN 0-262-72-001-9 (paper).

Russian-born Vygotsky died in 1934 at age thirty-eight, leaving behind eighty unpublished manuscripts of which *Thought and Language* is his last. Through ten years of experiments and observations of children learning to talk and to solve problems, Vygotsky pursued his theme of interrelations between thought and the spoken word. In seven chapters he discusses his methods, analyzes related theories of Piaget and Stern, traces the genetic roots of thought and language, reports stud-

Language Arts

ies of the development of word meanings and concepts during childhood, and, finally, sets forth a theory of intellectual development, which is at once a theory of education.

CULTURAL AND LINGUISTIC DIVERSITY

•Au, Kathryn H. *Literacy Instruction in Multicultural Settings.* Harcourt Brace College Publishers, 1993. 208 p. ISBN 0-03-076847-0 (paper).

Au helps teachers to think through issues they face when they teach reading and writing to students with diverse cultural and linguistic backgrounds. Eleven chapters provide research findings and practical examples of effective instruction for children of African American, Asian American, Hispanic American, and Native American heritage. Topics include the nature of literacy, constructivist approaches to instruction, classroom organization, cultural differences, language differences, multi-ethnic literature, and the process approach to writing.

Dyson, Anne Haas, and Celia Genishi, eds. *The Need for Story: Cultural Diversity in Classroom and Community.* National Council of Teachers of English, 1994. 250 p. (ISBN 0-8141-2953-6 (paper).

Everyone needs to organize important experiences into stories. But if listeners do not appreciate the ways stories are created or the experiences they reflect, the storyteller can be silenced. Stories flourish in classrooms where they are allowed, where there is playfulness with language, and where there are diverse story models, appreciative listeners, and reflective talkers. Through stories teachers come to know their students' cultures, experiences, and connections to others. And, through sharing both child-written and professionally written stories, teachers and children build new connections among themselves. Sixteen articles aim to help teachers to listen more sensitively to and to exploit the power of the stories their students tell.

Heath, Shirley Brice. *Ways with Words: Language, Life and Work in Communities and Classrooms.* Cambridge University Press, 1983. 421 p. ISBN 0-521-25334-9 (hardcover); 0-521-27319-6 (paper).

Between 1969 and 1978 Heath lived, worked, and played with children and their families and friends in two small, working-class communities near the textile mills of the Piedmont Carolinas. "Roadville's" residents were white; nearby "Trackton's" were black. Her central interest was in the question: What are the effects of a home and community environment on the learning of language needed in classroom and job settings? In her answer, which documents profound cultural differences in the communities' "ways with words," Heath raises important questions about the nature of language development and about the sources of communication problems in schools and workplaces.

Rigg, Pat, and Virginia G. Allen, eds. *When They Don't All Speak English.* National Council of Teachers of English, 1989. 156 p. ISBN 0-8141-5693-2 (paper).

This compilation of essays sets down important principles for teachers to know about language learners and language learning, then develops applications of those principles for the classroom. Written for teachers who are almost certain to have English-as-a-second-language (ESL) students in their classes, and who are almost equally certain not to have any formal ESL training, this book offers information particularly focused on how to integrate new speakers of English into a classroom. Among the chapter topics are: how the first language develops, the variety of students in ESL programs, the characteristics of a quality program, and classroom teachers working cooperatively with ESL teachers.

Taylor, Denny, and Catherine Dorsey-Gaines. *Growing Up Literate: Learning from Inner-City Families.* Heinemann, 1988. 234 p. ISBN 0-435-08457-7 (paper).

Black children living with extraordinary economic hardships, who are perceived by their parents as successfully learning to read and write, are the subjects of this study of family literacy. Chapters present ethnographic portraits of families, then describe and interpret the literate lives of the children both at home and at school. Concluding that sex, race, economic status, and setting are not significant correlates of literacy, the authors hope to alter the image of the urban poor family-as-educator, and to provide ways to bring the strengths of home learning into the classroom.

EMERGENT LITERACY

•Allen, JoBeth, and Jana M. Mason, eds. *Risk Makers, Risk Takers, Risk Breakers: Reducing the Risks for Young Literacy Learners.* Heinemann, 1989. 351 p. ISBN 0-435-08483-6 (paper).

Reflective of widespread interest in the early stages of literacy learning and in "at-risk" students, this compilation is devoted to reducing risks for young literacy learners. Four sections reflect a framework which emphasizes the interaction among children, teachers, families, and policy-makers. In Section 1, "Learning with Children," three authors provide detailed accounts of the learning of individual children. Section 2, entitled "Learning with Teachers," examines teachers and classroom learning environments in detail. Authors address home/school connections in Section 3, "Learning with Families." Finally, while all sections address policy issues, Section 4 focuses exclusively on literacy policies by setting agendas and outlining steps toward ensuring growth in literacy for all young learners.

•Clay, Marie M. *What Did I Write? Beginning Writing Behavior.* Heinemann, 1975. 78 p. ISBN 0-435-01120-0 (paper).

Clay observed five-year-olds, collected examples of their work from classrooms and from homes, and interpreted those samples in order to help teachers to become better observers of children's writing efforts. Believing that writing samples are a rich source of information about children's development, Clay illustrates through numerous examples some of the insights children gain during early contacts with the arbitrary conventions of writing, as well as some of the points of confusion. Dating and saving work in folders is recommended because it allows for comparisons, and it chronicles children's growing awareness of the conventions of print.

Dyson, Anne Haas. *Multiple Worlds of Child Writers: Friends Learning to Write.* Teachers College Press, 1989. 317 p. ISBN 0-8077-2972-8 (hardcover); 0-8077-2971-X (paper).

Inspired by three years of observing in an urban, culturally diverse classroom in which five- to eight-year-olds had frequent opportunities to write and talk and draw their own thoughts, Dyson offers a way of thinking about the beginning and end goals of writing in school. In doing so she tells how one teacher and her students formed a supportive community, then looks in detail at four children and how they grew—through writing—as classmates, as artists, and as creators of imaginary worlds. Placing learning to compose within a context of learning how to symbolize experiences and form relationships with others, the book provides insight into the developmental challenges children face as writers and the resources they lean on for support.

Harste, Jerome C., Virginia A. Woodward, and Carolyn L. Burke. *Language Stories and Literacy Lessons.* Heinemann, 1984. 252 p. ISBN 0-435-08211-6 (paper).

Throughout a program of research related to literacy before schooling, the authors collected stories from children which highlighted important aspects of their language learning. From that collection grew this book, intended to guide teachers to experience literacy learning from a child's perspective. Each story yields literacy lessons—lessons that enhance our knowledge by using the child as a theoretical and curricular informant. Taken together, the stories allowed the authors to identify and explain language and language learning principles that support sound reading and writing instruction.

•Holdaway, Don. *The Foundations of Literacy.* Ashton Scholastic, 1991. 232 p. ISBN 0-590-02306 (paper).

Once a teacher of New Zealand Maori children, Holdaway calls his book "a child-watcher's guide to literacy." Among the lessons children taught him: (1) literacy can develop out of song and change, (2) art experiences can flower into language, and (3) fascination with stories leads more directly to reading and writing their prepared lessons in word recognition. The author demonstrates great admiration for children, respect for their learning potential, and belief that they can teach themselves within a properly supportive environment. He describes programs, techniques, and styles of teaching collectively known as "shared-book experience," which were developed in a ten-year effort to respond to the observation that many children who learn to speak with ease and joy face failure and frustration when learning to read and write.

Paley, Vivian Gussin. *Wally's Stories: Conversations in the Kindergarten.* Harvard University Press, 1981. 223 p. ISBN 0-674-94593-X (paper).

Wally is a five-year-old. Paley is a kindergarten teacher, an observer, and a recorder of her students' conversations, stories, and playacting. During the school year Wally and his classmates make up stories, read published stories, and discuss a variety of topics, allowing Paley to showcase the nature of their thinking about magic, about science, about seemingly everything. As the children speak for themselves, readers can bring into focus a supportive teacher who is captivated by the range of interests and points of view of young children.

•Strickland, Dorothy S., and Lesley Mandel Morrow, eds. *Emerging Literacy: Young Children Learn to Read and Write.* International Reading Association, 1989. 161 p. ISBN 0-87207-351-3 (paper).

Applicable to a range of audiences and settings, the ideas compiled here aim to help caregivers and teachers to encourage and support literacy growth from infancy through the early school years. Contributing authors, reflecting current research and theory, view literacy learning as a continuous process, beginning in infancy with talk, oral reading, and writing. Chapters examine young children's learning about reading and writing, relationships between oral language and literacy development, shared book experiences, links with parents, assessment, school literacy environments, and policy directions.

Wells, Gordon. *The Meaning Makers: Children Learning Language and Using Language to Learn.* Heinemann, 1986. 235 p. ISBN 0-435-08247-7 (paper).

What is required for children to be able to extend their command of language to include reading and writing? Do some preschool experiences prepare children more effectively than others for learning to write? What school experiences best help children to make up for what they missed at home? In a search for answers to these questions, Wells followed thirty-two students from their first words through their final year of elementary education. Observations, tests, assessments by teachers, and interviews with parents, teachers, and the children enabled the identification of major linguistic influences on children's educational achievement and made possible this story of active learners constructing an internal model of the world together with a linguistic system for communicating about it.

LANGUAGE

Cazden, Courtney B. *Classroom Discourse: The Language of Teaching and Learning.* Heinemann, 1988. 230 p. ISBN 0-435-08445-3 (paper).

In her study of language use in the classroom, Cazden wears the hats of primary grade teacher and university researcher in psychology, educational anthropology, and applied linguistics, but, additionally, leans on insights from all behavioral sciences and cites examples from a range of educational levels, ethnic groups, and English-speaking countries. Since the basic purposes of school are achieved through communication, her general goal is to improve education through better understanding of its communication system. Her specific goals are to find out: (1) how patterns of language use affect what counts as "knowledge," and what occurs as learning, (2) how these patterns affect equality of educational opportunity, and (3) what communicative competence these patterns presume and/or foster.

Dyson, Anne Haas. *Social Worlds of Children Learning to Write in an Urban Primary School.* Teachers College Press, 1993. 263 p. ISBN 0-8077-3296-6 (hardcover); 0-8077-3295-8 (paper).

Dyson observed six urban, African American children, kindergarteners through third graders, in one classroom, along with each child's friends as they used various oral and written language forms and traditions to construct and participate in the complicated social relationships of school. The interrelated aims of her longitudinal study include: (1) documenting how children build literacy tools from social and language resources, (2) illustrating the sociocultural intelligence of young composers, (3) demonstrating the link between composing a test and composing a place in the social world, and (4) sharing the successes and challenges faced by teacher and children as they construct a shared world.

Jaggar, Angela, and M. Trika Smith-Burke, eds. *Observing the Language Learner.* International Reading Association and National Council of Teachers of English, 1985. ISBN 0-87207-890-6 (paper).

Seventeen skilled observers of children's language help teachers to become effective "kidwatchers" because they believe that "by listening carefully to what children say and watching what they do, we can learn a great deal about their concepts of oral and written language, their stages of development, their strategies for processing language, and their uses of language." Abundant knowledge about children's language and literacy development is synthesized, then illustrated with specific ways teachers can observe and interpret children's oral and written language behavior in the classroom and beyond.

Lindfors, Judith Wells. *Children's Language and Learning*. 2nd ed. Prentice-Hall, 1987. 497 p. ISBN 0-13-131962-0 (hardcover).

Lindfors' philosophy of children and language and learning sees: (1) children as shapers of their own knowing, their own language, (2) children's development of language as a creative construction process they carry out in their constant and continuing experience in a social world, and (3) children's learning in all areas as an active sense-making process—necessary and inevitable and individual. Teaching, then, becomes a sensitive and supportive response to the powerful learning processes of children. Five dimensions of language form five sections of the book: language structure, language acquisition, language and learning, language use in social contexts, and language variation. Each is devoted to building sensitivity through understanding.

READING AND WRITING

Bissex, Glenda L. *Gnys at Wrk: A Child Learns to Write and Read*. Harvard University Press, 1990. 223 p. ISBN 674-35485-0 (hardcover); 674-35490-7 (paper).

Gnys at Wrk (genius at work) is a landmark, in-depth case study of one child, the author's son Paul, learning to write and read between the ages of five and eleven. Readers see him becoming a fluent writer (using systems of his own invention which gradually merge with conventional written English) before he becomes a fluent reader. Most important, they see reading and writing developing inseparably. Bissex's intent is not to offer generalizations about language development to be applied to other children, but to offer encouragement to look closely at individuals in the act of learning.

Calkins, Lucy McCormick. *Living Between the Lines*. Heinemann, 1991. 315 p. ISBN 0-435-08538-7 (paper).

Contributing to a continuing dialogue about the teaching and learning of reading and writing, this book grew from years of reading, writing, and talking among educators in a writing project. Setting out to challenge, revise, and extend earlier ideas which put "heart and soul, rigor and direction" into the teaching of writing, the author also takes stock of professional progress, for example, viewing writing as "life-work" instead of "deskwork," and establishing reading and writing workshops not just to help children write well, but to live well.

•Hansen, Jane. *When Writers Read.* Heinemann, 1987. 242 p. ISBN 0-435-08438-0 (paper).

In twenty-two chapters Hansen brings reading and writing instruction together by demonstrating that recent approaches in the teaching of writing are useful in the teaching of reading. Drawing on several years of her own classroom-based research, she explores how principles of a response approach to writing instruction, which encourages students to take control of their own learning, can be useful in reading instruction. Hansen writes in the interest of helping teachers to create classrooms where children read extensively and look forward to reading, classrooms where both reading and writing instruction are consistent with knowledge about how children learn language.

————, Thomas Newkirk, and Donald Graves, eds. *Breaking Ground: Teachers Relate Reading and Writing in the Elementary School.* Heinemann, 1985. 211 p. ISBN 0-435-08219-1 (paper).

Groundbreakers are teachers, sometimes beginners, who have convictions, who are willing to challenge tradition, and who believe in risk-taking by both teachers and students. Groundbreakers, further, see the conflict between reading instruction taught with basals and worksheets and using reading across the curriculum, creating a predictable environment in which students can be independent decision-makers, talking about good books, and working together as one cohesive literacy community. The writing process approach led many teachers in this book to evaluate their teaching of reading, to explore relationships between reading and writing, and finally, to show through their own published writing how principles of the process approach now inform their teaching of reading.

Harste, Jerome C.; with Kathy Short, and Carolyn L. Burke. *Creating Classrooms for Authors: The Reading–Writing Connection.* Heinemann, 1988. 403 p. ISBN 0-435-08465-8 (paper).

Helping students understand how reading and writing relate to reasoning and learning is the purpose of the curricular framework presented here. In this curriculum, reading and writing are seen as composing, composing as a form of learning, and learning as a kind of authorship. Initial chapters, summarizing the theoretical base, explaining how to begin and to keep going an "authoring cycle," and describing an appropriate classroom context, are followed by full lesson plans written by teachers. Both this book and a videotape series entitled *The Authoring Cycle: Read Better, Write Better, Reason Better* are curricular applications of research on the evolution of literacy reported in *Language Stories and Literacy Lessons.*

Wilde, Sandra. *You Kan Red This!: Spelling and Punctuation for Whole Language Classrooms, K–6.* Heinemann, 1992. 208 p. ISBN 0-435-08595-6 (paper).

This comprehensive handbook for K–6 teachers demonstrates how spelling and punctuation fit into student-centered classrooms where authentic reading and writing experiences form the core of the curriculum. Theory, research, teaching ideas, sample lessons, and stories of how children learn to spell and punctuate are blended in order to explicate themes related to predictable developmental patterns seen in young writers, their active construction of knowledge, and the contributions of the classroom climate to children's growth in spelling and punctuation.

RESEARCH/REFERENCE WORKS

Flood, James, Julie Jensen, Diane Lapp, and James R. Squire, eds. *Handbook of Research on Teaching the English Language Arts.* Macmillan, 1991. 888 p. ISBN 0-02-922382 (hardcover).

With the goal of better informed instruction, the National Council of Teachers of English and the International Reading Association co-sponsored this comprehensive examination of research in the teaching of the English language arts. Four editors invited prominent scholars to compile and summarize findings, as well as to assess the significance of research, evaluate new developments, find relationships to scholarship in related fields, examine current conflicts, controversies, and issues, and identify tomorrow's priorities for English language arts teaching. Their work appears in five sections: (1) theoretical and historical bases, (2) methods of research, (3) research on language learners, (4) environments for teaching, and (5) research on specific aspects of the English language arts curriculum.

Hudelson, Sarah J., and Judith Wells Lindfors, eds. *Delicate Balances: Collaborative Research in Language Education.* National Council of Teachers of English, 1993. 148 p. ISBN 0-8141-1077-0 (paper).

Eight stories help to bring collaborative research into focus—enough to uncover characteristics that transcend all, enough to reveal the range of possibilities evident in diverse topics, kinds of expertise, roles, processes, and final products. While collaborators were encouraged to tell their stories in their own ways, all were asked to explain the research, to describe the nature of the collaboration, to summarize the findings, and to reflect on the experience. "Delicate balances" lie in the relationships among collaborators—continually negotiated blends of individual and social, autonomous and affiliated.

Purves, Alan C., ed. *Encyclopedia of English Studies and Language Arts.* Scholastic, 1994. 1338 p. (2 vols.) ISBN 0-590-49268-3 (hardcover).

Intending to explain English teaching to "the world at large," seven hundred authors created three hundred alphabetically arranged entries of three thousand words, bound into two comprehensive volumes. Subjects beginning with "Abridgment" and ending with "Young Adult Literature" are categorized into eleven topic areas: assessment, composition, curriculum, drama, general, language, learning and teaching, literature, media, reading, and technology. Preparing these non-technical introductions to aspects of English, its study, and its pedagogy, which span all levels of education, was a project of the National Council of Teachers of English.

TEACHING THE LANGUAGE ARTS

Dyson, Anne Haas, ed. *Collaboration Through Writing and Reading: Exploring Possibilities.* National Council of Teachers of English, 1989. 284 p. ISBN 0-8141-0737-0 (paper).

By talking, reading, and writing among themselves, the book's contributors aim to advance efforts to integrate the language arts in classrooms. They explore possibilities, rather than present solutions, thus acknowledging complex relationships among the language arts which are affected by the who, what, where, when, and why of the language user. Further, they recognize that accomplishing an infusion of writing, reading, and talking throughout the curriculum requires information, time, space, and support. Chapters explore historical perspectives on writing and reading instruction, writing and reading in the community, the problem-solving processes of readers and writers, writing and reading in the classroom, and writing and reading relationships.

Galda, Lee, Bernice E. Cullinan, and Dorothy S. Strickland. *Language, Literacy and the Child.* Harcourt Brace College Publishers, 1993. 478 p. ISBN 0-15-500024-1 (hardcover).

This book about teaching and learning the English language in kindergarten through eighth grade classrooms focuses first on developing the reader's knowledge about language, then on examining the ways teachers can teach and children can learn about language. Though individual chapters highlight listening, speaking, reading, or writing, the authors stress the interrelatedness of them all as children become proficient language users. Because another theme permeating the book is the importance of literature as a support to language arts teaching and learning, a rationale for literature-based instruction is included, along with ways of organizing and implementing it.

Jensen, Julie M., ed. *Stories to Grow On: Demonstrations of Language Learning in K–8 Classrooms.* Heinemann, 1989. 183 p. ISBN 0-435-08482-8 (paper).

Humane, learner-centered, inquiring, risk-taking, and highly interactive classrooms are the wish of these teacher/authors for today's language learners. They met for three weeks at a conference of the Coalition of English Associations, where they discussed a vision of the kind of schooling needed for children for today and tomorrow. United in the view that K–8 classrooms can have environments that are in harmony with knowledge about how children learn language, they set down their conclusions in report format. Then, eight of them wrote stories for their fellow teachers about language learning in their own classrooms. Each story is an invitation to build connections, and to be inspired to grow professionally.

Moffett, James, and Betty Jean Wagner. *Student-Centered Language Arts, K–12*. 4th ed. Boynton Cook Publishers/Heinemann, 1992. 437 p. ISBN 0-86709-292-0 (paper).

This comprehensive and detailed handbook for teachers at all levels sets forth a rationale and suggests practices appropriate in an individualized, interactive, and integrative classroom learning environment. When the first edition appeared in 1968 it broke ground, presenting many ideas which seem commonplace today. Using their currently popular names, those ideas include: whole language, reading in the content areas, writing across the curriculum, cooperative learning, process writing and process reading, writing response groups, peer editing, portfolio assessment, and teacher-student conferencing.

•Routman, Regie. *Invitations: Changing as Teachers and Learners K–12*. Heinemann, 1994. 502 white p. plus 256 blue p. ISBN 0-435-08836-X (paper).

As a primary classroom teacher, Routman wrote *Transitions* in 1988 to lend support to fellow teachers who were beginning to move from basal texts and worksheets to more meaning-centered and student-centered approaches. Now, as a language arts resource teacher who assists others in their transitions to whole language, she has written *Invitations* to encourage K–12 teachers in their further transitions—self-reflection, risk taking, greater understanding of language learning, and closer ties between theory and practice. This long, detailed, and practical book is organized for sampling, particularly the concluding "Blue Pages" which include annotated professional books and journals, recommended literature for children, and numerous other resources for teachers.

Watson, Dorothy J., ed. *Ideas and Insights: Language Arts in the Elementary School*. National Council of Teachers of English, 1987. 244 p. ISBN 0-8141-2259-0 (paper).

An Environmental Print Walk, Epitaphs: Graveyard Images, Mailboxes, and Science Logs are among the best ideas of teachers in the United States, Canada, and Australia. Organized into five sections—(1) reading, (2) writing, (3) language across the curriculum, (4) kids helping kids and bringing home and classroom together, and (5) assessment—each idea is then presented in four parts: (1) Why, (2) Who (intended audience), (3) How, and (4) What Else (follow-up). Placing particular importance on Why, the editor includes preambles written by Leland Jacobs on literature, Kenneth Goodman on reading, and Donald Graves on writing and stresses in her introduction that these are not skill, drill, fill-in-the-blank exercises, but rather theoretically anchored experiences based on a whole language approach to learning.

WRITING

Atwell, Nancie, ed. *Coming to Know: Writing to Learn in the Intermediate Grades.* Heinemann, 1990. 233 p. ISBN 0-435-08500-X (paper).

Third- through sixth-grade teachers illustrate how the philosophy and methods of workshop approaches to teaching can be applied across the curriculum. Recurring subjects are connecting reading and writing with each other and with all subject matter areas, and the role of children's literature in content area teaching. Two kinds of writing are highlighted: report writing in all content areas that is meaningful and personal, and the informal writing in learning logs that can stimulate thinking in any field of study.

Graves, Donald H. *A Fresh Look at Writing.* Heinemann, 1994. 408 p. ISBN 0-435-08824-6 (paper).

Graves' widely read *Writing: Teachers and Children at Work* (Heinemann, 1993) discussed writing instruction that contributes to lasting learning, listening to children and learning from them, allowing children to choose their own topics, conferences, revision, and publishing children's work. So does *A Fresh Look at Writings.* But, emboldened by new knowledge about the essentials of teaching writing, this book is more assertive about when to step in, when to teach, and when to expect more of students. Chapters include numerous Actions, or experiments in learning for teachers. Graves observes that teachers of writing have so little time, they are obliged to use that time well—to decide what endures.

Newkirk, Thomas. *More Than Stories: The Range of Children's Writing.* Heinemann, 1989. 228 p. ISBN 0-435-08490-9 (paper).

Young children can write lists, labels, signs, jokes, riddles, badges, letters, menus, captions, descriptions, explanations, arguments, dialogues, complaints, invitations—not just stories. Through more than a hundred examples of writing and drawing produced by children under age seven, Newkirk illustrates the range of their writing, thereby challenging the common assumption that narrative writing is for young children, while analytical writing experiences are to be reserved for more mature students. In support of the evolving competence of versatile writers, the book is an argument for elementary school classrooms where a range of writing possibilities is open to students.

———, and Nancie Atwell, eds. *Understanding Writing: Ways of Observing, Learning, and Teaching K–8.* 2nd ed. Heinemann, 1988. 312 p. ISBN 0-435-08441-0 (paper).

Thirty articles, most set in a classroom, written by a skilled classroom teacher, and filled with examples of student work, are grouped into six sections: beginnings, collaborative learning, writing and reading, assessment, programs and process, and reflections. The book's subtitle is rooted in the editors' belief that without informed observation, process approaches to writing become just another mindless school routine. Hence, these authors are observers, learners, and teachers. They observe their students, their teaching, and their own learning. Their purpose here is to help other teachers to see, to respond, and to reflect.

Smith, Frank. *Writing and the Writer.* 2nd ed. Lawrence Erlbaum Associates, 1994. 287 p. ISBN 0-8058-1421-3 (hardcover); 0-8058-1422-1 (paper).

Smith likens his book to a sandwich. The thick filling describes attributes achieved by a fluent writer: getting started and keeping going, putting meaning into words, understanding differences between spoken and written language, having a sense of audience, mastering conventions of writing, and using tools—primarily computers. The rather thin-sliced bread is Smith's reflections on his process of writing the book, then creating this revised edition a dozen years later. Typical of Smith, writing coexists with learning, thinking, language, and other language arts, particularly reading. Both filling and bread help teachers to think about writing in both theoretical and practical ways.

JOURNALS

Language Arts. National Council of Teachers of English. ISSN 0360-9170.

Language Arts is a national professional journal devoted to the teaching and learning of all facets of the language arts during the pre-school through middle school years. Each of the eight annual issues has a theme, supplemented by recurring features which profile authors and illustrators and review juvenile trade books as well as address topics of ongoing interest such as the role of technology and recent research. A subscription to *Language Arts* is purchased as part of a membership in its sponsoring organization, the National Council of Teachers of English (NCTE). For information write: NCTE, 1111 W. Kenyon Road, Urbana, IL 61801.

Primary Voices K–6. National Council of Teachers of English. ISSN 1068-073X.

Published since April 1993 by the National Council of Teachers of English, each issue of *Primary Voices K–6* includes five articles unified by a theme or concept—inquiry-based instruction, writing to learn, authentic assessment. The first article explores theoretical aspects of the topic; the next three illuminate the topic through classroom portraits; and the final article is a reflection upon the first four. Taken together, they are intended not to offer solutions, but to consider possibilities and to start conversations. Each quarterly issue is edited by a different "literacy community," an NCTE Affiliate, a Writing Project, a school team, or other group submitting a successful proposal. For subscription information write: NCTE, 1111 W. Kenyon Road, Urbana, IL 61801-1096.

MEMBERSHIPS

National Council of Teachers of English
1111 West Kenyon Road
Urbana, Illinois 61801-1096.

Phone: (217) 328-3870
Fax: (217) 328-0977

The mission statement for NCTE states: "The Council promotes the development of literacy, the use of language to construct personal and public worlds and to achieve full participation in society, through the learning and teaching of English and the related arts and sciences of language." NCTE publications for English language arts educators in grades K–6 include *Primary Voices K–6* and *Language Arts*. NCTE members also receive NCTE's official newspaper, *The Council Chronicle*.

6

Children's Literature

Consultant: Dr. Richard F. Abrahamson
University of Houston
Houston, Texas

Dr. Richard F. Abrahamson is Professor of Literature for Children and Adolescents in the College of Education at the University of Houston. A graduate of the College of William and Mary, he received an M.A. from the University of Maine and his Ph.D. from the University of Iowa.

Dr. Abrahamson has been a member of the editorial board of the National Council of Teachers of English and the editorial advisory board of *The Reading Teacher*. He currently serves on the International Reading Association's review board for new books to be published by the Association and is a member of the editorial review board for *English Journal*. An author of over one hundred professional articles, he has had his own column on juvenile literature in both *English Journal* and the *Journal of Reading*. His books include *Books for You* and *Nonfiction for Young Adults: From Delight to Wisdom*, both coauthored with Dr. Betty Carter. In addition, he is an author of the *Harcourt Brace Treasury of Literature*.

Dr. Abrahamson has won the Education Press Association Award for Excellence in Educational Journalism and is listed in *Who's Who in American Education*. He is the recipient of the Texas State Reading Association's Literacy Award, the Texas Council of Teachers of English Outstanding Language Arts Educator Award, and the University of Houston's Teaching Excellence Award.

KEYSTONE WORKS

Rosenblatt, Louise M. *Literature as Exploration*. 5th ed. Modern Language Association, 1995 (First pub. 1938). 319 p. ISBN 0-87352-568-X (paper).

Rosenblatt's classic 1938 text provides much of the basis for today's "response" movement and how we teach literature and reading in elementary school classrooms. In it she writes about the personal experience of reading literature and that this reading is a dynamic interaction between the text and the reader whether we are reading for information or find ourselves swept up with the emotions and adventures of the book and its characters.

INFORMATION ABOUT AUTHORS AND MEDIA ADAPTATIONS OF BOOKS

Collier, Laurie, and Joyce Nakamura. *Major Authors and Illustrators for Children and Young Adults.* 6 vols. Gale Research, 1993. 2700 p. ISBN 0-8103-7702-0 (hardcover).

Educators and young readers are often in need of biographical information about an author or illustrator. Many professional collections cannot afford to buy the highly acclaimed *Something About the Author* series with its more than seventy volumes. Keeping that in mind, the editors of this six-volume series have updated and revised "sketches on nearly eight hundred of the most widely read authors and illustrators appearing in Gale's *Something About the Author* series." Here you'll find home addresses for many of the authors or their agents. There is a section on their careers, another on their awards, a listing of the books they have written, and a section on media adaptations of their books. Most importantly, you'll find pages of interesting detail about the lives of these creative people. Patrons will refer to this fine series over and over again.

Moss, Joyce. *From Page to Screen: Children's and Young Adult Books on Film and Video.* Gale Research, 1992. 443 p. ISBN 0-8103-7893-0 (hardcover).

You're planning a unit on Judith Viorst's books. You want to know if any have been made into videos. Are they any good? How much do they cost? Where can I purchase/rent them? This reference shows that there is a film, video, and laser disc version of the two Alexander books. It lists costs, provides reviews of the media versions, and mentions awards the products have won. You'll also discover videos of *The Goodbye Book, I'll Fix Anthony,* and *The Tenth Good Thing About Barney.* This time-saver includes more than 750 books that have been made into films, videos, and laser discs.

INSTRUCTION AND ACTIVITIES

Bauer, Caroline Feller. *Presenting Reader's Theater: Plays and Poems to Read Aloud.* H. W. Wilson, 1987. 241 p. ISBN 0-8242-0748-3 (hardcover).

Bauer offers educators an enthusiastic introduction to reader's theater from informal classroom presentations to PTA program formality. Most importantly, she provides over fifty read-aloud scripts ready for classroom presentation. The works of Byars, Lobel, Kipling, Cleary, Viorst, Andersen, Grimm, and dozens of other children's literature luminaries are the quality sources for Bauer's adaptations. She writes in her introduction, "I thought that if there was a plentiful source of ready-to-use scripts, perhaps Reader's Theater would become a 'do it today' activity instead of a 'someday' activity."

———. *This Way to Books.* H. W. Wilson, 1983. 363 p. ISBN 0-8242-0678-9 (hardcover).

If you are looking for hundreds of ways to get young readers and books together, Bauer is the master magician at pulling reading motivation activities out of her hat. Her emphasis is on practicality and enjoyment whether she is showing how to make crafts or invent games using children's books, presenting poetry, giving booktalks, or developing holiday programs around Jacob Grimm's or Johnny Appleseed's birthday.

Chatton, Barbara. *Using Poetry Across the Curriculum: A Whole Language Approach.* Oryx, 1993. 214 p. ISBN 0-89774-715-1 (hardcover).

Chatton has chosen specific poems and collections and tied them to areas of the elementary school curriculum. In the Poetry and Science section there are lists of poems about spiders, trees, rocks/stones, and changes in nature. Poems to go with physical education, health, art, music, language arts, math, and social studies classes are selected as well. Chatton's book will be helpful if you are developing cross-curricular thematic units or if you simply believe that poetry shouldn't be relegated only to the language arts classroom. While the actual poems aren't printed, the author provides a solid reference work so that you can find the poems on your own.

Hall, Susan. *Using Picture Storybooks to Teach Literary Devices.* Oryx, 1990, vol. 1. ISBN 0-89774-582-5 (paper); 1994, vol. 2. ISBN 0-89774-849-2 (paper).

You're looking for books to help children understand onomatopoeia. Hall offers a definition along with an example. What follows are nine books that use the literary device, from *The Tale of Peter Rabbit* to Yashima's *Umbrella.* Examples of onomatopoeia from each book are quoted along with sections on each picture book's art style, other literary devices employed, and curriculum tie-ins. From allusion to hyperbole, from parody to understatement, these two volumes offer educators motivating resources to use in teaching literary devices.

SELECTION AIDS—GENERAL

Colborn, Candace. *What Do Children Read Next? A Reader's Guide to Fiction for Children.* Gale Research, 1994. 1135 p. ISBN 0-8103-8886-3 (hardcover).

Children's Literature 75

Colborn's book is a terrific help in matching young readers in grades one through eight with specific fiction titles. Each of the two thousand books in this work are summarized. In addition, the titles are classified according to recommended age range, subject, time period, locale, and major characters (names and descriptions). Entries showing where reviews of the book can be found are listed along with awards won and other books written by that author. Most importantly, for each of the two thousand titles included, five other books are listed and annotated under the heading Other Books You Might Like.

•Jensen, Julie M., and Nancy L. Roser, eds. *Adventuring with Books: A Booklist for Pre-K–Grade 6.* 10th ed. National Council of Teachers of English, 1993. 603 p. ISBN 0-8141-0079-1 (paper).

This tenth-edition booklist, made up of eighteen hundred quality books published between 1988 and 1992, features a more visually appealing, larger format with bigger print, more white space, and pictures of the covers from some of the books selected. With the paragraph-length annotations is a recommended age level for each book. Besides sections devoted to the standard genres of children's literature, the editors have included chapters containing books dealing with science and mathematics, social studies, and language arts/reading. These curriculum-based chapters will be useful to educators looking for tradebooks to use in literature-based classrooms.

•Lima, Carolyn W., and John A. Lima. *A to Zoo: Subject Access to Children's Picture Books.* 4th ed. Bowker, 1993. 1158 p. ISBN 0-8352-3201-8 (hardcover).

If you are looking for children's picture books about a specific subject, this is a fine reference listing of over fourteen thousand titles cataloged under nearly eight hundred subjects for preschool children through second graders. The book also includes indexes of the picture books listed by title, author, and illustrator. *A to Zoo* is especially useful for developing story hours or literature-based teaching units focused on almost any subject from aardvarks to zookeepers.

Lipson, Eden Ross. *The New York Times Parent's Guide to the Best Books for Children.* Rev. ed. Times Books, 1991. 508 p. ISBN 0-8129-1889-4 (paper).

The children's book editor of the *New York Times* has selected and annotated some seventeen hundred "best" books from the world of children's literature. Her recommendations are grouped under six categories: wordless books, picture books ("principally for preschool children"), story books ("suited for children in the early grades"), early reading books ("for children who are learning to read"), middle reading books, and young adult books. With wide margins and illustrations from various selected books, this reference is designed for easy browsing and includes indexes listing the books by title, author, illustrator, subject, age-appropriateness, and suitability for reading aloud.

SELECTION AIDS—SPECIFIC

Carroll, Frances Laverne, and Mary Meacham. *More Exciting, Funny, Scary, Short, Different, and Sad Books Kids Like About Animals, Science, Sports, Families, Songs, and Other Things.* American Library Association, 1992. 192 p. ISBN 0-8389-0585-4 (paper).

What makes this collection of annotated bibliographies unique is that they are aimed at children and are grouped according to the ways youngsters ask for books. Consequently, there are bibliographies by such titles as "Do You Have Any Books like The Baby-Sitters Club?," "Do You Have Any Books about Aliens?," "I Want a Skinny Book," or "I Have to Read a Biography at Least 150 Pages Long." Each list gives children and educators a good place to start looking when someone asks "Do You Have Any Books like Shel Silverstein's?"

Children's Book Council, ed. *Children's Books: Awards and Prizes.* The Children's Book Council, 1992. 404 p. ISBN 0-933633-01-7 (hardcover); 0-933633-020-5 (paper).

Here is one-stop shopping for the person who wants to know what books have won awards. Part I is a listing of juvenile books that have won U.S. awards selected by adults, such as the Caldecott, Newbery, and Wilder awards. Part II includes winning titles selected by children for awards like the Texas Bluebonnet, the Kentucky Bluegrass, and the Pacific Northwest Young Readers' Choice Award. Part III provides lists of award winners from Australia, Canada, New Zealand, and the United Kingdom. A paragraph describing the history and criteria for each award precedes the winning titles and year that each book won.

Day, Frances Ann. *Multicultural Voices in Contemporary Literature: A Resource for Teachers.* Heinemann, 1994. 244 p. ISBN 0-435-08826-2 (paper).

Day's well designed book "celebrates the lives and works of thirty-nine inspiring multicultural authors and illustrators." The chapter on African American author/illustrator Pat Cummings, for example, provides an address for writing to her, her birth date, a list of published works, and a biographical sketch. What follows is a section that focuses on each of nine books done by Cummings. A plot summary is accompanied by "Suggestions for the Classroom." Appendices include a list of additional multicultural authors/illustrators, an assessment plan for a multicultural education program, and a multicultural calendar.

Freeman, Judy, ed. *Books Kids Will Sit Still For: The Complete Read-Aloud Guide.* 2nd ed. Bowker, 1990. 660 p. ISBN 0-8352-3010-4 (hardcover).

Freeman's book on reading aloud is more comprehensive than Jim Trelease's handbook. If you are working with parent volunteers or teacher/library aides,

Children's Literature

you'll appreciate the chapters on tricks of the trade for reading aloud as well as the specific chapters and short stories she has culled from children's books for quick read-alouds. The bulk of the book (over five hundred pages) is made up of annotated lists of good books for reading aloud to children. The fiction books are divided by grade level and precede chapters on traditional literature, poetry, and nonfiction and biography. Also consider Freeman's sequel, *More Books Kids Will Sit Still For,* published in 1995.

Gillespie, John T., and Corinne J. Naden. *Middleplots 4: A Book Talk Guide for Use with Readers Ages 8–12.* Bowker, 1994. 434 p. ISBN 0-8352-3446-0 (hardcover).

Now that Judy Blume's *Fudge-a-mania* has made it to television, let's assume you want to introduce this book to fourth graders. The authors provide a detailed plot summary and let you know this is the second sequel to *Tales of a Fourth Grade Nothing.* In the Book Talk section you are given specific pages that make good read-aloud excerpts. Six related titles are briefly annotated, and there is a section listing where the book has been reviewed and where you can find out more about the author. Eighty books are given this treatment and grouped into categories by subject or genre.

Helbig, Alethea K., and Agnes Regan Perkins. *This Land is Our Land: A Guide to Multicultural Literature for Children and Young Adults.* Greenwood Press, 1994. 401 p. ISBN 0-313-28742-2 (hardcover).

More than five hundred books published between 1985 and 1993 are carefully annotated and evaluated in twelve chapters. Three sections deal with African Americans: Books of Fiction, Books of Oral Tradition, and Books of Poetry. This same three-chapter organizational structure is used for books dealing with Asian Americans, Hispanic Americans, and Native-American Indians. Age and grade levels accompany standard bibliographic information for each book. The books' strength is the detailed and thoughtful critical appraisals written for each title included.

International Reading Association, ed. *More Kids' Favorite Books: A Children's Choices Compilation.* International Reading Association, 1995. 112 p. ISBN 0-87207-130-8 (paper).

For two decades the International Reading Association and the Children's Book Council have sponsored the Children's Choice project. This annual popularity contest involves five hundred new books that are sent yearly to five test sites across America. Approximately ten thousand youngsters read these books and vote for their favorites. The votes from all sites are tabulated, and the most popular books are listed each year as Children's Choices. This new compilation of yearly lists has over three hundred titles for ages four to thirteen. If you're looking for a taste of what a national sampling of children has selected as favorite books, this is the compilation to consult.

International Reading Association, ed. *Teachers' Favorite Books for Kids.* International Reading Association, 1994. 200 p. ISBN 0-87207-389-0 (paper).

Each year since 1989 seven regional teams of teacher/librarian reviewers field test, in classrooms and libraries, between two hundred and five hundred new books submitted by publishers. The reviewers look for high literary quality books that "might not be discovered or fully appreciated by children without introduction by a knowledgeable adult." This book compiles five years of "Teachers' Choices" titles grouped by grade/age levels. The 150-plus books are annotated and accompanied by teachers' suggestions for curriculum use.

Kobrin, Beverly. *Eyeopeners II: Children's Books to Answer Children's Questions About the World Around Them.* Scholastic, 1995. 305 p. ISBN 0-590-48402-8 (paper).

In a format similar to Jim Trelease's *The Read-Aloud Handbook,* Kobrin writes specifically to parents, teachers, grandparents, and librarians about the importance of nonfiction reading in the lives of children. She offers a list of ten characteristics used to evaluate nonfiction for juveniles and, like Trelease, ends the book by annotating some eight hundred nonfiction books for youngsters grouped under headings from Adoption to Endangered species to Math and counting to Wolves and foxes. Along with these annotations, the author offers tips for using these quality books with youngsters in the elementary school.

Thomas, Rebecca L. *Primaryplots 2: A Book Talk Guide for Use with Readers Ages 4–8.* Bowker, 1993. 431 p. ISBN 0-8352-3411-8 (hardcover).

Primaryplots 2 was designed "to serve as a guide for book talks, story programs, classroom activities, and reading guidance." Thomas has chosen 150 books; divided them into eight chapters such as Exploring the Past or Analyzing Illustrations; and provided a detailed plot summary of each book, a paragraph on thematic material, a section on book talk material and activities, and a section on related titles that could be used with the main book. Whether you're looking for activities to go with McMillan's *Eating Fractions,* or you want to know five other related titles or you simply want to refresh your memory about the plot, *Primaryplots 2* offers the needed information.

Trelease, Jim. *The Read-Aloud Handbook.* 4th ed. Penguin Books, 1995. 387 p. ISBN 0-14-046971-0 (paper).

No other book on reading aloud to children has ever become a million-copy bestseller like this one. With missionary zeal Trelease writes to parents and educators extolling the benefits of reading aloud to children in chapters devoted to Why Read Aloud?; The Dos and Don'ts of Read-Aloud; Television; and Sustained Silent Reading. The book features an extensive Treasury of Read-Alouds that includes annotations of good books to read aloud, suggested grade levels, and other related books for each title. This fourth edition of *The Read-Aloud Handbook* was substantially revised and is the best version yet.

TEXTBOOKS

Cullinan, Bernice E., and Lee Galda. *Literature and the Child.* 3rd ed. Harcourt Brace, 1994. 546 p. ISBN 0-15-500985-0 (hardcover).

In this third edition of a fine children's literature textbook, the authors use the image of a patchwork quilt to "... represent the varied colors and patterns of books and people who inhabit the world of children's literature." In addition to chapters on the various genres of children's literature and criteria for excellence, the book includes sections on multicultural literature, planning a literature curriculum, and children responding to books. Strengths of this text include the boxed teaching ideas and bibliographies of quality children's books on topics such as Poems that Stir Emotions, Types of Folktales from Around the World, and Stories of World War II and the Holocaust.

Huck, Charlotte S., Susan Hepler, and Janet Hickman. *Children's Literature in the Elementary School.* 5th ed. Harcourt Brace, 1989. 866 p. ISBN 0-03-047528-7 (hardcover).

Huck's book is the most comprehensive of all the children's literature textbooks on the market. The authors do a fine job establishing criteria for excellence in each genre of children's literature. Hundreds of quality books that meet these standards of excellence are discussed, and scores of tips for educators called Resources for Teaching can be found throughout this text. In addition to chapters devoted to each genre, Huck offers sections on response to literature, the history of children's books, planning the literature curriculum, and extending and evaluating children's understanding of literature through such things as art, singing, drama, and writing.

Kiefer, Barbara Z. *The Potential of Picturebooks: From Visual Literacy to Aesthetic Understanding.* Macmillan, 1995. 247 p. ISBN 0-02-363535-5 (paper).

Increasingly, teachers and librarians are helping children study and appreciate the illustrations in picture books. Kiefer's book does the best job of teaching all of us about the art in children's books and offering educators classroom connections for teaching youngsters. Part One deals with children's responses to picture books. Part Two examines the art of this genre with a look at its history and an examination of how DePaola, Steptoe, and Hyman create their works. The final section is on picture books in the classroom, with activities on exploring media, bookmaking, and holding a mock Caldecott award. Also worth considering is John Warren Stewig's *Looking at Picture Books.* Highsmith Press, 1995. 269 p. ISBN 0-917846-29-X.

Norton, Donna E. *Through the Eyes of a Child.* 4th ed. Macmillan, 1995. 713 p. ISBN 0-02-388313-8 (hardcover).

Here's a beautifully produced textbook that teachers will consult for years to come. Children's literature is discussed in chapters devoted to genres from poetry to picture books to fantasy and nonfiction. Criteria for excellence in each genre are discussed along with quality titles and authors. Teachers will appreciate the practical methods section that follows each chapter, such as Involving Children with Artists and Their Illustrations. New to this edition is a database disk that accompanies the text. It contains the entire bibliography from the book and enables teachers to construct and print out all kinds of personalized booklists.

JOURNAL

Book Links. Booklist Publications (an imprint of ALA). ISSN 1055-4742.

This colorful, bimonthly magazine was created to help connect books, libraries, and classrooms. It accomplishes that goal admirably. Educators will find each issue filled with author interviews, bibliographies of books developed for all aspects of the elementary and middle school curriculum, tips for teaching specific books, behind the scenes writer/illustrator stories about how their books were created, and articles on the artwork in children's books. *Book Links* is certain to be a magazine you'll refer back to for lesson plans, thematic units, and author studies.

7

Science

Consultant: Dr. James P. Barufaldi
University of Texas
Austin, Texas

Dr. James Barufaldi, Professor of Science Education and Director of the Science Education Center at the University of Texas at Austin, earned a bachelor's degree in the biological sciences from Marietta College in Ohio, a master's degree in biology and education from Kent State University, and a Ph.D. degree in science education from the University of Maryland.

A frequent recipient of state and national awards for service and teaching, he was named the 1988 Outstanding Science Educator of the Year by the national organization, the Association for the Education of Teachers in Science, for his dedication to teaching and his exemplary work in science curriculum development and research, and for his leadership in the education community. At the state level he has received the Outstanding Service Award of the Science Teachers Association of Texas, the University of Texas Excellence in Teaching Award in the College of Education, and the Rebecca Sparks Elementary Science Award by the Texas Council of Elementary Science.

An active member of professional organizations, Dr. Barufaldi has served on the boards of the National Association for Research in Science Teaching and the National Science Teachers Association. He has served as president of the National Association for Research in Science Teaching as well as president of the Association for the Education of Teachers in Science and the Texas Association of Biology Teachers. As a Fellow of the American Association for the Advancement of Science, Dr. Barufaldi was an elected member to the Electorate, section Q. He has presented more than two hundred workshops, papers, and seminars in countries such as Russia, Japan, Israel, Costa Rica, Mexico, Australia, Belize, and Trinidad.

He has authored or co-authored more than fifty articles and book reviews. His most recent authored book is *Teaching Elementary School Science: A Perspective for Teachers*. He has served as editor of monographs and yearbooks published by AETS and the School Science and Mathematics Association.

DOCUMENTS/GUIDELINES/STANDARDS

American Association for the Advancement of Science. *Science for All Americans*. American Association for the Advancement of Science, 1989. 217 p. ISBN 0-87168-341-5 (paper).

This publication is a Project 2061 report of literacy goals in science, mathematics, and technology. It is the first report of Project 2061, a project of the American Association for the Advancement of Science designed to contribute to the attainment of the goal of scientific literacy. The publication is organized into three major parts: Education for a Changing Future, Recommendations of the National Council on Science and Technology Education, and Bridges to the Future. Teachers and curriculum developers will find the set of recommendations by the National Council quite valuable in planning programs for instruction. The recommendations establish a conceptual base for reform in science education by delineating knowledge, skills, and attitudes that all students should acquire as a consequence of their schooling. The recommendations, which are presented in twelve chapters, include categories such as the nature of science, mathematics and technology, the human organism, the human society, the physical setting, the designed world, common themes, and habits of the mind.

Loucks-Horsley, Susan, et al. *Developing and Supporting Teachers for Elementary School Science Education*. The NETWORK, 1989. 95 p. (paper).

This document, a report of the National Center for Improving Science Education, addresses three questions: "What do teachers need to know to be able to teach science well?," "How can they be assisted to learn and continuously renew their learning?," and "What organizational policies and structures can support their teaching?" Readers will find suggestions contained in the report quite helpful in designing strategies to reform the elementary science curriculum, to initiate the kinds of teacher development activities that will most likely influence the knowledge and skills of science teachers, and to improve the organizational contexts within teachers. Eleven recommendations are provided for organizational structures and support and for teacher training and development. This report would be quite useful to elementary teachers and administrators involved in professional development schools.

National Research Council. National Science Education Standards. National Academy Press, 1996. 263 p. ISBN 0-309-05326-9 (paper).

The Standards, statements that can be used to judge quality in science education, were developed as a guideline for all students to achieve scientific literacy. Emphasizing a new way to teach and to learn science, the book focuses on standards for science teaching, professional development for teachers of science, assessment in science education, science content, science education programs, and science education systems. The book describes contemporary teaching practices that lead to an exemplary science classroom and supports the basic belief that learning science should be an active, engaging process, one that initiates and nurtures further inquiry. This book is highly recommended for all interested in the restructuring of science education and will be especially helpful to those designing new frameworks for a contemporary science curriculum. Teachers, administrators, scientists, and science educators will find this book of standards a useful aid in redesigning science education at all educational levels.

ASSESSMENT

Kulm, Gerald, and Shirley M. Malcom, eds. *Science Assessment in the Service of Reform.* American Association for the Advancement of Science, 1991. 400 p. ISBN 0-87168-426-8 (hardcover).

This volume, which contains papers written by curriculum and assessment specialists, researchers, teachers, and psychologists, supports the notion that assessment must inform instruction. Teachers will find the readings quite useful in making assessment a tool for meaningful reform in science education. Part One of the volume focuses on policy issues in science assessment; Part Two discusses issues related to science assessment and the curriculum; and Part Three relates assessment to instruction. The appendices describe various forms of alternative assessments in elementary science, specific examples from the field, and the assessment of collaborative learning. This volume is timely in that it discusses the important topic, assessment in educational reform.

Ostlund, Karen L. *Science Process Skills—Assessing Hands-on Student Performance.* Addison-Wesley, 1992. 138 p. ISBN 201-29092-8 (paper).

Elementary teachers who are committed to an activity-based program will find *Science Process Skills* a helpful tool in providing an effective method for determining student achievement and providing teachers with feedback on student performance. More than sixty appraisal items are introduced at six different levels of development. Assessment items focusing on the basic process skills such as observing, measuring, and inferring are introduced in Level 1 and Level 2. The basic skills are reinforced in Levels 3 through 6, in addition to the integrated process skills such as controlling variables, defining operationally, and investigating. A student response section is included as a guide to indicate trends the teacher may expect from the collected data upon administration of the assessment tasks.

Raizen, Senta A., et al. *Assessment in Elementary School Science Education.* The NETWORK, 1989. 149 p. (paper).

Many science educators, teachers, and parents are concerned about the quality of assessment in science education and wish to initiate and implement change in the system. This document, a report of the National Center for Improving Science Education, provides a strong background on assessment in elementary school education. It begins with information about the importance of assessment and assessment priorities. Issues confronting assessment, assessment of student learning, and assessment of program features provide valuable information to elementary teachers and schools interested in making assessment a meaningful, integral component of curriculum and instruction in the sciences. The publication provides suggestions for constructing an integrated assessment system responsive to educational goals at each level of the system. Recommendations to improve assessment are described throughout the document.

CURRICULUM

American Association for the Advancement of Science. *Benchmarks for Scientific Literacy.* Oxford University Press, 1993. 418 p. ISBN 0-19-508986-3 (hardcover).

This book is designed as a tool for everyone involved in state or local efforts to transform the teaching and the learning of science, mathematics, and technology. It is intended to be used along with the publication *Science for All Americans* (SFAA), a publication of the AAAS in conjunction with Project 2061, a major curriculum reform movement in science, mathematics, and technology education. Teachers will find *Benchmarks* a valuable resource as they embark on improving science learning and instruction at the elementary school level. The book includes statements of what all students should know or be able to do in science, mathematics, and technology by the end of grades 2, 5, 8 and 12; it provides a common core of learning that contributes to the science literacy of all students. The grade designations provide reasonable checkpoints for estimating student progress toward the science goals outlined in *SFAA. Benchmarks* is a practical guide that has the potential to improve the status of science education and prepare students for learning for the 1990s and beyond.

Glatthorn, Allan A. *Developing a Quality Curriculum.* Association for Supervision and Curriculum Development, 1994. 136 p. ISBN 0-87120-234-4 (hardcover).

Curriculum reform in science education at the elementary level is an ongoing process. This research-based book, a "how-to-do-it" publication, is a guide to both understanding and implementing an educationally sound curriculum. The process of curriculum development and implementation is well delineated. Chapters include Getting Started, Organizing and Planning for Curriculum Work, Laying the Foundation for the District Curriculum, Supporting the District Curriculum, Developing the Classroom Curriculum, and Conducting a Curriculum Audit to Ensure Quality. Assessment instruments, criteria for evaluating programs, tables, models, and figures support the text. Specific audit issues for the quality curriculum criteria are described in the appendix. This book serves as a step-by-step guide to quality curriculum development.

Loucks-Horsley, Susan, et al. *Elementary School Science for the '90s.* The National Center for Improving Science Education, 1990. 166 p. ISBN 0-871120-176-3 (paper).

This book, organized by thirteen research findings of the National Center's work on elementary school science, is written for decision makers and all other individuals who share responsibility for the teaching and the learning of elementary school science. A chapter is devoted to each of the recommendations and answers two questions: "What can be done?" and "What is known from research literature and practice experience?" The chapters are organized to respond to questions about inadequacies in curriculum, instruction, and teaching force (What should we teach?), instruction (How should we teach?), and teacher development and support (How can we prepare and support teachers to teach science well?). Chapters deal with conceptual understanding, assessment, science as a basic, instructional models, and effective approaches to staff development. The book is written in a "user friendly style" and discusses "what we know" about a particular topic, taking action on what we know, local roles, state roles, and things to do for the future to improve the quality of science instruction and curriculum.

GENERAL RESOURCES

Champagne, Audrey B., Barbara E. Lovitts, and Betty J. Calinger. *This Year in School Science 1989: Scientific Literacy.* American Association for the Advancement of Science, 1989. ISBN 0-87168-359-8 (paper).

This book, which includes papers from the 1989 AAAS Forum for School Science, attempts to capture the "essence" of scientific literacy, the basic goal of elementary school science. Scientific literacy is difficult to define; the authors of this publication help illuminate some of the reasons for this difficulty. Information presented produces a clearer understanding of what it means to be scientifically literate. One chapter in particular, "Views of Scientific Literacy in Elementary School Science Programs: Past, Present, and Future," will help elementary teachers gain deeper understanding of literacy. The author provides definitions of three forms of literacy: cultural scientific literacy, functional scientific literacy, and true scientific literacy. Teachers will find this book quite valuable as they plan contemporary science curriculum for the classroom.

DeBoer, George E. *A History of Ideas in Science Education: Implications for Practice.* Teachers College, Columbia University, 1991. 269 p. ISBN 0-8077-3054-8 (hardcover); 0-8077-30530-X (paper).

This book is written for all of those interested in science education. It is a historical account of ideas in science education that covers a time frame of approximately one hundred years. Elementary teachers will find the book informative concerning the "roots" of elementary science education. The eleven chapters include topics such as curriculum reform, process and product in science education, educational thought and practice in the nineteenth century, and the reorganization of science education. The author discusses the political, social, and economic pressures that have initiated change in science education through this period of time.

Glynn, Shawn M., Russell H. Yeany, and Bruce K. Britton, eds. *The Psychology of Learning Science.* Lawrence Erlbaum Associates, 1991. 269 p. ISBN 0-8058-0668-7 (hardcover).

The authors of this book—science educators, cognitive scientists, and psychologists—skillfully describe the "state-of-the-art research" and apply it directly to the science classroom. Helpful models, illustrations, and a rich array of scenarios from classrooms will enable the reader to implement ideas garnered from the book into the classroom. The chapters describe a constructivist view of learning, present a research-based learning model to deliver science instruction, discuss students' conceptual frameworks for learning science, and describe conceptual patterns in understanding concepts in astronomy, chemistry, and physics. Elementary teachers will find the chapters dealing with children's biology and their conceptual development in the life sciences useful in planning for instruction. In addition, science activities are discussed in relation to their effect on learning, and arguments are presented to support an activity-based science program. Those becoming more involved in technology will find the information presented on learning in software "microworlds" quite beneficial.

Hazen, Robert M., and James Trefil. *Science Matters: Achieving Scientific Literacy.* Anchor Books-Doubleday, 1991. 194 p. ISBN 0-385-26108-X (paper).

This book is a "must" for those teachers wishing to understand the basic ideas or underpinnings of science. The authors organized this book around the assumption that "the basic ideas underlying all science are simple." They present basic facts and concepts which the authors believe the reader needs to know to understand the scientific issues of the day. Scientific literacy is defined as what constitutes the knowledge one needs to understand public issues. The book focuses on eighteen general principles or big concepts. The authors contend that upon reading this publication, the reader will have "not only a general notion of how the world works, but also specific knowledge you need to understand how individual pieces of it (the earth's surface, for example, or a string of DNA) operate." Topics such as energy, the atom, chemical bonding, nuclear physics, particle physics, ecosystems, the code of life, and astronomy are presented in ways that do not intimidate one with limited science content knowledge. This book would provide a valuable reference for the elementary teacher.

Mallow, Jeffry V. *Science Anxiety—Fear of Science and How to Overcome It.* H & H Publishing, 1986. 175 p. ISBN 0-943202-18-3 (hardcover).

Numerous findings from research have well documented the notion that many elementary school teachers feel uncomfortable and incompetent teaching science to young children. In fact, many teachers exhibit an avoidance behavior toward teaching science. This book explores the phenomenon that many refer to as "the fear of science" and how to overcome it. The author believes that to "cure" what many refer to as a national ailment is to confront and deal with science avoidance and science anxiety directly. The author examines the causes of science anxiety and investigates consequences, both personal and political. Chapters include topics such as science as a liberal art, science teaching and learning, overcoming science anxiety, fighting science anxiety, the role of teachers and parents, and a bibliography of women and science.

INSTRUCTION—ACTIVITIES

Bosak, Susan V. *Science Is: A Source Book of Fascinating Facts, Projects and Activities.* Scholastic Canada, 1991. 515 p. ISBN 0-590-74070-9 (paper).

Science Is . . . is an extensive compendium of hands-on, minds-on investigative experiences and projects that reflect the spirit of elementary school science. The text is arranged into ten subject areas, including plants, living creatures, matter and energy, humans, and discovering science. Forty topics are contained in this resource book; examples include electricity, forces, birds, air, chemical reactions, mammals, stars, and pollution. The author subscribes to a learning cycle of exploration, discussion, and discovery. Numerous innovative activities such as "The Marble Race," "Balancing the Impossible," "Soap Bubble Derby," and "Go Fly a Kite" would surely enhance an existing elementary school science curriculum. *Science Is . . .* is a complete resource book that supports exploration and promotes good inquiry-oriented questions.

Gabel, Dorothy L. *Introductory Science Skills.* Waveland Press, 1993. 423 p. ISBN 0-88133-697-1 (paper).

This book is appropriate for elementary school teachers wishing to develop and improve their science process skills; it is designed to help teachers and students understand the nature of scientific inquiry. The text emphasizes science process skills—observing, classifying, measuring, inferring, predicting, communicating, hypothesizing, problem solving, and model building. Ideas garnered from the book could readily be adapted for use in the elementary school classroom. Twelve comprehensive units include an overview of the skill and inquiry-based investigative experiences emphasizing the particular skills. Black and white figures, tables of information, and diagrams support the text.

Gega, Peter C. *Concepts and Experiences in Elementary School Science.* Macmillan, 1991. 519 p. ISBN 0-02-413405-8 (paper).

This book is a thorough science experience sourcebook that contains hundreds of experiences that reflect the nature of contemporary science education. The author makes the distinction between *activities,* first-hand experiences through which children may learn concepts and the skills of science, and *investigations,* experiences that often include open-ended topics and problems. Each activity is introduced with a discussion of the appropriate science content background. The activities are well designed and include helpful illustrations, lists of materials, procedures, a series of discovery problems, and a teaching comment section. Topics include light, heat, sound, magnetic and electrical energy, simple machines, the environment, the human body, Earth, and weather. The contents of this book may also be found in Gega's *Science in Elementary Education,* 7th edition (Macmillan, 1994).

Lawrence Hall of Science. *Great Explorations in Math and Science (GEMS).* Lawrence Hall of Science/University of California at Berkeley. ISBN 0-912511-72-9 (paper).

GEMS is a series of well-designed science units that include Teacher's Guides, Assembly Presenter's Guides, and Exhibit Guides. The teacher guides promote the guided discovery approach and suggest numerous innovative, creative ancillary science teaching units such as Earthworms, Bubble-ology, Animal Defenses, Liquid Exploration, Fingerprinting, Oobleck, and Crime Lab Chemistry. The guides include student data collection sheets, black and white illustrations, tables, figures, and clearly presented instructional models. This contemporary series of activities will enrich the existing science curriculum.

Levenson, Elaine. *Teaching Children About Science: Ideas and Activities Teachers and Parents Can Use.* Prentice-Hall, 1987. 211 p. ISBN 0-8306-4598-5 (paper).

Science

Teaching Children About Science contains numerous activities to motivate children's natural curiosity about the sciences—earth, life, and physical science. This resource book is a comprehensive guide to many investigative experiences and demonstrations. Each lesson within the units is well organized and includes a description of materials, preparation, and procedure. Appropriate terminology is introduced throughout each lesson. Three basic approaches to organizing a science unit are introduced: moving from the familiar to the less familiar, moving from the beginning of a process to a result with a tangent or two, and arranging information in chronological order. The process skills of science are emphasized and developed in each unit. One unit of study carefully develops the important concept of a *model*. A bibliography includes a listing of many science texts for teachers and science trade books for children.

Poppe, Carol A., and Nancy A. Van Matre. *Science Learning Centers for the Primary Grades*. The Center for Applied Research in Education, 1985. 241 p. ISBN 0-87628-749-6 (paper).

This is a "how to" book for those elementary teachers interested in enriching the teaching of science by implementing science learning centers in the classroom. The management of learning centers, setting up the room environment, and ways to maintain centers are described. Complete instructions for establishing centers such as those for the five senses, the human body, space, plants, and dinosaurs are provided. The text includes reproducible full-page student activity pages, bulletin-board activities, boardwork for related activities, and reproducible illustrated direction pages for mounting on file folders. Numerous black-and-white illustrations provide the teacher with additional information and directions for designing centers. Although the ideas presented in the book are more appropriate for children in the primary grades, the techniques and topics suggested may be easily adapted to use with older children.

Sewall, Susan B. *Hooked on Science: Ready to Use Discovery Activities for Grades 4–8*. The Center of Applied Research in Education, 1990. 202 p. ISBN 0-87628-404-7 (paper).

Hooked on Science is an easy-to-use resource with activities, teacher instructions, worksheets, and handouts for the classroom. The book is organized into six units: Critters and Creatures, Wonders of the Green World, Outdoor Activities and Equipment, Thinking Like Scientists, Recycling, and What Else. The supplemental activities include an overview, procedure, extensions, and list of appropriate resources. Teachers and students will enjoy pursuing innovative ideas such as the spider convention, the great earthworm hunt, food web stamp collecting, underwater viewing bottles, the memory game, and the window of decomposing leaf. Black-and-white illustrations support the text.

Tolman, Marvin N., and James O. Morton. *Science Curriculum Activities Library*. Parker Publishing, 1986. 228 p. ISBN 0-13-536061-7 (paper).

The *Library,* a three-volume series, provides more than five hundred activity-based experiences in the life, earth, and physical sciences. Each activity is "user friendly" and includes a question to investigate, material list, detailed procedure, and special background information for the teacher. A bibliography of professional texts, periodicals, and sources of free and inexpensive materials for the sciences is provided. The series is a rich supplement to the elementary classroom and provides the teacher with a wide selection of meaningful, innovative hands-on activities to support the existing science curriculum.

INSTRUCTION—METHODS

Abruscato, Joseph. *Teaching Children Science.* Allyn & Bacon, 1993. 428 p. ISBN 0-205-13650-8 (hardcover).

This is a well-organized and -designed book that presents science as an ongoing human endeavor. The text is organized into four sections: Planning for Learning; The Earth and the Cosmos—Content and Discovery Activities; The Life Sciences—Content and Discovery Activities; and The Physical Sciences—Content and Discovery Activities. Suggested readings are included in each chapter. Teachers will find the chapter Integrating Science with Other Subjects quite useful when planning for instruction. Discovery learning, cooperative learning and science, technology, and society are emphasized. Appropriate science content for teachers provides the necessary foundation to teach the suggested science units.

Carin, Arthur A. *Teaching Science Through Discovery.* 7th ed. Macmillan, 1993. 332 p. ISBN 0-02-319385-9 (hardcover).

Elementary teachers will find this text a valuable resource and an exemplary addition to their professional library. The book is a rich resource of creative, innovative teaching ideas, sound suggestions to improve the teaching of science, and numerous activities supported with necessary content information that will enable teachers to become more comfortable and competent in delivering science instruction to the young learner. Chapters describing assessment, questioning and listening, planning and classroom management, reaching students with special needs, integrating science across the curriculum, and using science programs and textbooks will enrich the existing elementary science curriculum. A feature, Chart a New Course, offers strategies and ideas from successful teachers throughout the country that may be modified by the classroom teacher to enable children to experience science in a meaningful, hands-on, minds-on way. This resource is an excellent compendium of ideas, methods, and techniques that most elementary teachers will welcome.

Cohen, Herbert G., Frederick A. Staley, and Willis J. Horak. *Teaching Science as a Decision Making Process.* Kendall/Hunt, 1989. 251 p. ISBN 0-8403-5634-X (paper).

Science

The main goal of this book is to help teachers become effective decision makers in dealing with planning, implementation, and assessment of teaching and learning at the elementary school level. The authors model a learning spiral approach which is highly recommended for inquiry and discovery in the classroom. Topics in the book include a thorough description of the decision making process; the role of science in the elementary school curriculum; the learning of science; the relationship of science, children, and teaching; management methods; informal science; and planning and implementing inquiry teaching. Each chapter is organized using the learning spiral approach: introduction, exploration, discussion, summary, and applications. Emphasis is placed on teacher attitudes toward science and children doing science. Appendices include a description of Piagetian tasks, diagrams and explanations to develop and implement learning centers, and a sample thematic science unit.

De Vito, Alfred K., and Gerald H. Krockover. *Creative Sciencing: Ideas and Activities for Teachers and Children.* Scott, Foresman, 1991. 306 p. ISBN 0-673-52008-0 (paper).

Creative Sciencing should be on the shelf in all elementary school classrooms. The book includes more than 160 open-ended, innovative teaching ideas and activities. Innovative activities such as Bubble Trouble, Classifying with Cookie Bars, Skulls and Skins, and Pollution Poetry are presented to engage children in the inquiry processes of science; the teacher will find that the activities will serve as a catalyst or springboard for more creative inquiry. More than thirty "shoestring sciencing" activities enhance this activity book. Teachers will find the design of the table of contents helpful in organizing a science program around specific science subjects or topics and selecting appropriate activities to enhance their science program.

Dunn, Susan, and Rob Larson. *Design Technology: Children's Engineering.* Falmer Press, 1990. 176 p. ISBN 1-85000-590-7 (paper).

The authors state that "design technology is a natural, intellectually and physically interactive process of design, realization, and reflection. Through the consideration of ideas, aesthetics, implications, and available resources, children become imaginative engineers, exploring alternative solutions to contextualized challenges." This book presents a "fresh approach" to education that extends the natural childhood processes of learning. Elementary teachers will find that many innovative ideas in the book encourage children to integrate concepts and skills from all curriculum areas, help them develop their "personalized" evaluation skills, and use their hands and minds in an active manner. Numerous four-color photographs show children actively engaged in the design process. Chapters describe the design process and present a diagram revealing the four major design technology processes: investigation, invention, implementation, and evaluation. Teachers will find the "Framework for the Analysis of Design Technology Components" quite helpful in facilitating science and technology instruction in their respective classrooms.

Esler, William K., and Mary K. Esler. *Teaching Elementary Science.* 6th ed. Wadsworth, 1993. 601 p. ISBN 0-534-17700-X (hardcover).

The purpose of this book is to assist all teachers in acquiring the skills, attitudes, and knowledge that will enable them to improve the teaching and learning of science in the elementary school classroom. The following common characteristics of good science teaching are recognized throughout the book: the ability to relate science to the cognitive and affective development of children; the ability to understand and implement the inquiry technique; the ability to implement didactic teaching techniques; the ability to plan instruction to include both the process and the content of science; the ability to adapt the science program and individualize instruction for both normal and exceptional children in the classroom; the ability to impart knowledge and understanding of some of the major concepts of science; the ability to acquire and use a knowledge of sources of elementary science programs, manipulatives, print, film, and graphic media, including computer applications for science education in the elementary school; and the ability to provide an understanding of the problems confronting our society that result from applications of science and technology. Chapters include topics such as materials and resources for teaching elementary school science, and teaching science by inquiry. Thirteen units of study for elementary school science include ecological relationships, heat and matter, magnetism, plant and animal life, sound, and electricity. This book is an excellent resource for building an exemplary elementary school science program.

Freidl, Alfred E. *Teaching Science to Children—An Integrated Approach.* McGraw-Hill, 1991. 318 p. ISBN 0-07-022423-4 (paper).

Teachers will welcome the hundreds of discrepant events in the book and find them quite valuable in enhancing their science units and lessons. The methods and content of science are integrated throughout the twenty chapters. The author provides many hands on, minds-on activities. A rich array of scientific, discrepant events and pupil investigations are well described and carefully explained within the science context. The processes of science are reinforced and spiraled throughout the text. The book is comprehensive in both science content background and methodologies. The instruction model suggested is one that most elementary teachers will be able to implement with ease. The science content areas—life, earth, and physical science—are well covered and supported with numerous activities, illustrations, and a glossary of important scientific terms.

Gega, Peter C. *How to Teach Elementary School Science.* Macmillan, 1991. 225 p. ISBN 0-02-413411-2 (paper).

Elementary teachers will find this book an excellent resource of teaching strategies and techniques. Each chapter develops a particular teaching competency or a group of teaching skills. The book describes the "place" of science in the elementary school; suggests ways to improve children's thinking; shows how to locate and

Science 93

use a variety of resources, models, and closed-ended and open-ended teaching activities; and presents ways to assess learning outcomes. The appendices include science activities, science supply sources, and an overview of children's thinking in relation to their development. This book is included in the comprehensive volume, *Science in Elementary Education,* 7th edition (Macmillan, 1994).

———. *Science in Elementary Education.* 7th ed. Macmillan, 1994. 713 p. ISBN 0-02-341302-6 (hardcover).

The organization of this book demonstrates a well integrated teaching approach and combines activities, science content, and practical methods on how to teach science to children. The text is arranged in two sections: how to teach elementary school science; and subject matter, investigations, and activities. The methodology section suggests ways to arrange and manage learning centers, projects, and computer centers; provides ways to improve children's thinking; describes ways to organize and assess science teaching; and demonstrates the use of closed-ended and open-ended teaching activities. The second section of the book builds upon the methodology section, describing hundreds of investigative, concrete experiences to use with the young learner and serves as an excellent compendium of ways to improve and enhance the teaching of science. The subject matter component gives appropriate explanations of scientific phenomena that are tied to the investigations and activities. The appendix includes descriptions of contemporary elementary school science programs and a list of commercial suppliers of science materials and equipment.

Hampton, Carol. *Classroom Creature Culture: Algae to Anoles.* National Science Teachers Association, 1994. 96 p. ISBN 0-87355-120-6 (paper).

This resource book, an anthology of activities from *Science and Children,* demonstrates how to take care of living organisms in the elementary school classroom. The skills of science—observing, investigating, classifying, collecting data—are presented in interesting and appropriate ways so as not to intimidate teachers who may be somewhat anxious or skeptical about using living organisms in their science lessons. Elementary teachers will welcome this resource book that "takes the guessing" out of proper ways to care for plants and animals. Throughout this publication, the affective domain is nicely developed and emphasized as children are provided opportunities to appreciate the unique traits and behaviors of living things. Creatures such as lizards, butterflies, turtles, and duckweed are presented with well delineated instructions to care for and nurture the organisms.

Hassard, Jack. *Minds On Science—Middle and Secondary School Methods.* HarperCollins, 1992. 450 p. ISBN 0-06-500019-6 (hardcover).

Although this book is specifically designed for middle and secondary school science teaching, the following chapters are of special importance and value to elementary school teachers. The chapter "Minds on Science: A Reconnaissance" describes the nature of science and teaching science, discusses characteristics of effective science teachers, and provides information about conceptual change teaching, cooperative learning, and interactive teaching. "How Students Learn Science" presents behavioral, social cognitive, and constructivist theories of learning. "The Goals and History of Science Education" will enable the teacher to become familiar with the development of science education. "Models of Science Teaching" will help the elementary teacher to rethink appropriate strategies and techniques that nurture the teaching of science. Additional topics of interest include strategies that foster thinking in the science classroom; science, technology, and society in the classroom; and facilitating learning in the science classroom. The book contains many creative science investigations and inquiry-oriented experiences that the teacher will be able to adapt to acknowledge the unique needs of all children in the elementary school classroom.

Howe, Ann C., and Linda Jones. *Engaging Children in Science.* Macmillan, 1993. 406 p. ISBN 0-675-21186-7 (paper).

Reading and implementing ideas presented in this book will enhance the ability of elementary teachers to construct their own understanding about how children learn science. The book provides a thorough theoretical underpinning of constructivism by describing learning ideas supported by Papert, Kohlberg, Piaget, Bruner, and Vygotsky. The text, a well-written methods book, will aid teachers in the construction of their own knowledge of science processes and help to implement appropriate methods to teach science concepts to children. The book provides numerous examples of planning and presenting both direct-instruction and guided discovery lessons. The integrated or advanced science processes are described and supported with innovative activities such as mystery boxes, hidden circuits, and battery contests. Elementary teachers will find the section "Piaget Tasks" quite valuable in helping to determine the developmental stages of those young learners they teach. Directions for administering the task are carefully described. Instructions include a listing of required materials and stated procedures. The teacher is also provided with suggestions to record and interpret interviews conducted with children. Topics such as integrating science with other subjects, long-term planning, and science topics for the elementary school make this book an excellent resource for the elementary school classroom.

Jacobson, Willard J., and Abby Barry Bergman. *Science for Children: A Book for Teachers.* 3rd ed. Prentice-Hall, 1991. 417 p. ISBN 0-13-795014-4 (hardcover); 0-13-794843-3 (ringbound).

This book is specifically designed for teachers, teacher aides, and others involved in teaching science to children. The eighteen chapters deal with topics such as science and mathematical development; reading, writing, language development, and science; children and plants; science and technology in our lives; science experience for young children; and teaching the nature of science. The chapters provide an exemplary resource for teaching the important skills and content areas in science. The "how we teach" and "what we teach" are presented in a balanced way. Background information in the sciences and an excellent collection of science activities will enable the teacher to enrich the teaching and the learning of science. Specific content related to the concepts and activities developed for the young learner has been carefully selected. The numerous investigative experiences will provide the teacher with the "essence" of contemporary elementary science education. Attention is also given to early childhood education and to children with special needs.

Martin, Ralph E., Colleen Sexton, and Kay Wagner. *Teaching Science for All Children.* Allyn & Bacon, 1994. 622 p. ISBN 0-205-14875-1 (hardcover).

Teaching Science is a comprehensive resource that integrates the ideas, skills, and attitudes in science in a holistic manner. The philosophy that guides the book is one of "promoting the concept of whole science" by ensuring that the skills, knowledge, and attitudes are infused in the experiences that teachers present to the young learners. The well-described activities subscribe to the concept of constructivism. All chapters are introduced with a topic web that teachers will find helpful in organizing their learning experiences. Each chapter focuses on a question which is discussed and answered throughout the development of the text. Hands-on, minds-on activities; helpful diagrams and illustrations; concrete suggestions and ideas; findings from research and implications for teaching and learning science summaries; and an extensive reference section provide the necessary tools and information to present contemporary science experiences to children. Information about safety in the science classroom is a welcome addition. The authors skillfully present and describe the "essence" of elementary school science in a supportive, engaging manner. The text, partially supported by the National Science Foundation, is a quality publication that will help teachers improve science teaching and learning in the elementary classroom.

Martinello, Marian L., and Gillian E. Cook. *Interdisciplinary Inquiry in Teaching and Learning.* Macmillan College Publishing, 1994. 232 p. ISBN 0-02-376502-X (paper).

The overall aim of the book is for children to become creative thinkers. The authors describe the interdisciplinary qualities of the process of inquiry and discuss several modes of thought categorized into three major categories: symbolic, magic, and affective. Numerous concrete examples of the modes and the processes of inquiry are taken from the literary arts, natural and social sciences, mathematics, and the humanities. The reader is provided with guidelines for designing theme studies. Criteria are presented in the form of questions to help determine whether a theme is important enough to warrant children's study. Possible sources of topics and themes are discussed in great detail, including current events, children's common interests, textbook topics, cultural heritage, local sites, teacher's interests or expertise, and children's literature and trade books. Helpful guidelines for designing theme studies are presented. Each guideline is carefully discussed and supported with many appropriate examples. The role of brainstorming, involving thinking fluently and flexibly, is discussed; the authors use the procedure of "webbing" to help redirect how one looks at a theme. This book serves as a valuable tool for those involved in the development of thematic studies across academic disciplines.

Neuman, Donald B. *Experiencing Elementary Science.* Wadsworth Publishing, 1993. 434 p. ISBN 0-534-18822-2 (hardcover).

This well-organized book will help teachers design both a contemporary and an effective science program. Beginning with the development of a frame of reference for elementary school science, the text then discusses the theory and practices of elementary science, ways to organize and implement an activity-centered science program, experiences for children with special needs, and science units that may be used to further the development of science lessons. The appendices include information about safety in the science classroom, resources for teachers, suppliers of science equipment, and special resources.

Stepans, Joseph. *Targeting Students' Science Misconceptions: Physical Science Activities Using the Conceptual Change Model.* Idea Factory, 1994. 224 p. ISBN 1-885041-00-4 (paper).

This book has filled a void in elementary science methodology by providing teachers with a resource of ideas for using the conceptual change strategy as applied to physical science topics. The conceptual change model for instruction encourages students to confront their own preconceptions and those of their classmates, moving them toward resolution of the concept and conceptual change. The six-stage instructional model is applied to activity-based lessons focusing on topics such as matter, density, air pressure, liquids, heat waves, sound, forces, work, and machines. Each topic includes a background information section for the teacher, the identification of the particular concept to be developed, an overview of representative student misconceptions, a review of sources of students' confusion and misconceptions, and teaching notes. The activities provide an exemplary, contemporary learning-cycle model for concept development and instruction. This book is an excellent resource, one that would help elementary teachers develop educationally and scientifically sound science lessons for the young learner.

MULTICULTURAL EDUCATION AND THE SCIENCES

Atwater, Mary, K. Radizik-March, and M. Strutchens. *Multicultural Education: Inclusion for All.* The University of Georgia, 1994. 297 p. ISBN 0-96248188-2-3 (hardcover).

Teachers and teacher educators will find this book quite useful in gaining a greater understanding of the issues of ethnicity, culture, gender, and class in science and mathematics classrooms. The authors emphasize the point that one can no longer ignore the important facets of educating students in highly diversified American classrooms. The book begins with a discussion of the history and inadequacies of American teacher education and emphasizes that the key to transforming education lies within the philosophy, knowledge base, and teaching practices of teacher education. The role of family involvement in empowering students in classrooms is discussed, and various classroom intervention programs are described. Specific proposals on how schools can meet the needs of linguistically and culturally diverse students and their families are provided. This book would be of great value to elementary teachers and administrators who are involved in field-based teacher preparation programs and who wish to improve the quality of education.

Barba, Roberta H. *Science in the Multicultural Classroom: A Guide to Teaching and Learning*. Allyn & Bacon, 1995. 426 p. ISBN 0-205-15105-1 (hardcover).

The focus of this methods book is to provide ways for teachers to meet the needs of all children by proposing culturally affirming instructional strategies. The book is enriched with numerous vignettes, case studies, field-based examples, and a summary of literature related to the specific topic. The author addresses topics such as equity in science education, "ways of knowing" among culturally diverse children, those who are bilingual/bicultural and bidialectic, basic science processes, assessing knowledge, computer technology, the integration of science and mathematics, and science/technology/society in the multicultural classroom. A classroom practice section includes many well designed, manageable, contemporary science activities. Elementary teachers will find this book an excellent resource for planning instruction and developing a well-articulated science curriculum that reflects the needs of all children.

RESEARCH

Gabel, Dorothy L., ed. *Handbook of Research on Science Teaching*. Macmillan, 1994. 598 p. ISBN 0-02-897005-5 (hardcover).

Many elementary teachers are becoming involved in "action research" in their respective classrooms. This type of research usually involves a collaborative partnership with classroom teachers, researchers from a university, staff members from an agency or organization, and school district personnel. The *Handbook* is an exemplary publication, sponsored by the National Science Teachers Association, that provides a comprehensive review of science education research studies over a seventy-year period of time. In addition, several chapters provide specific recommendations and guidelines for practice in the science classroom. The *Handbook* comprises nineteen chapters and is organized into five major sections: Teaching, Learning, Problem Solving, Curriculum, and Context. The chapters examine topics such as cultural diversity, problem solving at the elementary level, assessment, goals of the science curriculum, and affective dimensions of learning. The editor of the *Handbook* has noted that this publication should serve as a "springboard for science education research into the twenty-first century."

Lawrenz, Frances, et al., eds. *Research Matters . . . To the Science Teacher.* National Association for Research in Science Teaching, 1992. n.p. (paper).

The Association publishes a series of monographs with direct application to the science classroom. A recent volume includes articles focusing on instructional strategies designed to teach science, authentic assessment, pupil motivation and achievement in science, and conceptual change teaching and science learning. Numerous research-based practical suggestions are described in each article.

SELECTION AIDS FOR LOCATING SCIENCE RESOURCES

Eisenhower National Clearinghouse for Mathematics and Science Education. Columbus: The Ohio State University.

The Eisenhower National Clearinghouse for Mathematics and Science Education is funded by the U.S. Department of Education and housed at Ohio State University. The purpose of the Clearinghouse is to improve access to mathematics and science resources available to teachers and students. The Clearinghouse is currently creating the most comprehensive listing of mathematics and science curriculum materials in the nation. A catalogue will include materials available in print, video, audio, software, other graphics, and CD-ROM. Users will be able to gain access through the database to other materials, including the complete text of many items, in addition to demonstration sites where users can learn about various technologies. Online discussion groups and access to a permanent repository where Clearinghouse users may examine materials are also part of the services. For more information contact: Eisenhower National Clearinghouse for Mathematics and Science Education, The Ohio State University, 1929 Kenny Road, Columbus, Ohio 43210-1079, (614) 292-7784, e-mail: info@enc.org.

National Science Resources Center. *Science for Children: Resources for Teachers.* National Academy Press, 1988. 176 p. ISBN 0-309-03934-7 (paper).

Science for Children is a comprehensive resource guide designed to assist and encourage elementary school teachers to infuse contemporary activities into the existing curriculum. The materials described provide support for designing an effective hands-on, minds-on elementary school science program and reflect the spirit of contemporary science education. Bibliographic entries for curriculum materials; annotated listings of resources for the teacher; and lists of institutional resources, material suppliers, and publishers are presented.

National Science Teachers Association. *NSTA Science Education Suppliers.* National Science Teachers Association.

This pamphlet, an annual supplement to the journals published by the National Science Teachers Association, provides a listing of suppliers in each of the following categories: program and resource materials, science equipment, computer software, trade book publishers, textbook publishers, and media producers. Each category includes a description, address, and telephone number for each supplier.

JOURNALS

Journal of Research in Science Teaching. John Wiley & Sons. ISSN 0022-4308.

This publication, the official journal of the National Association for Research in Science Teaching, is published monthly except June and July. The journal includes both qualitative and quantitative research-based articles dealing with cutting-edge issues confronting science education. Teachers involved in classroom action research would find the readings quite beneficial as they pursue their research goals.

Journal of Science Teacher Education. Association for the Education of Teachers in Science. ISSN 1046-560X.

Each issue, published quarterly, serves as a forum for presentation and discussion of issues, problems, and concerns related to professional development in science teaching. Elementary teachers involved in the preparation of teachers would find the articles in the journal quite useful in assisting them to remain on the "cutting edge" of reform in science teacher education.

NSTA Reports. National Science Teachers Association.

NSTA Reports, published six times a year, is an exemplary source of news and information for and about science teachers. The publication provides updates on teaching materials and programs, opportunities for science teachers at all education levels, and information about activities of the Association. This publication is timely, especially during this era of educational reform in science education.

School Science and Mathematics. School Science and Mathematics Association. ISSN 0036-6803.

Each issue, published monthly by the Association, contains informative articles dealing with the improvement of science and mathematics education. Regular features of the journal include *SS Miles: School Science and Mathematics Integration Lessons,* book reviews, and a problem section. Recent articles have dealt with the use of manipulative devices, equity issues in science and mathematics, and identifying student outcomes.

Science & Children. National Science Teachers Association. ISSN 0036-8148.

Each issue, published monthly except June, July, and August, includes numerous practical ideas to improve the teaching and the learning of elementary school science. Issues focus on topics such as assessment, the integration of science skills, weather, and animal behavior.

Science Education. John Wiley & Sons. ISSN 0036-8326.

Published six times yearly, this journal includes the results of research findings from all areas in science education. The journal would be of particular interest to teachers involved in classroom action research and to those interested in improving instruction through research.

MEMBERSHIPS

National Science Teachers Association
1840 Wilson Boulevard
Arlington, Virginia 22201

Phone: (703) 243-7100

The National Science Teachers Association, an organization of science education professionals, has as its purpose the stimulation, improvement, and coordination of science teaching and learning. NSTA is an affiliate of the American Association for the Advancement of Science. Membership benefits for elementary teachers include a subscription to *Science and Children* and *NSTA Reports.*

8

Math

Consultant: Dr. Paul Trafton
University of Northern Iowa

Dr. Paul Trafton is Professor of Mathematics Education at the University of Northern Iowa. He is also Fellow in the Regents' Center for Early Developmental Education. At the University of Northern Iowa Dr. Trafton serves as co-director of the graduate program in teaching mathematics for grades 4–8 teachers. The program is built on a professional development model that links university study with classroom practice. He also serves as co-director of Primary Mathematics Project, a collaborative, shared-expertise teacher development program for primary grades teachers which is funded by the Eisenhower Grant. He holds a Ph.D. from the University of Michigan and a master's degree from Northern Illinois University.

As an active member of the National Council of Teachers of Mathematics, Dr. Trafton has been a member of the NCTM Commission on Standards for School Mathematics and is currently on the NCTM Board of Directors.

His most recent publications include coauthoring *Moving Into Mathematics, Grades K–3* (MIMOSA Publications, 1990, 1993) as well as being a contributor to six *National Council of Teachers of Mathematics Yearbooks*. He was editor of *New Directions in Elementary School Mathematics,* the 1989 Yearbook of NCTM (1987–1989).

DOCUMENTS/GUIDELINES/STANDARDS

National Council of Teachers of Mathematics. *Assessment Standards for School Mathematics.* National Council of Teachers of Mathematics, 1995. 102 p. ISBN 87353-419-0 (paper).

This third set of NCTM standards for school mathematics complements the curriculum and teaching standards by discussing standards for assessing students' progress. The document presents six standards to be used as criteria for judging assessment practices, together with four board categories of purposes for assessing student performance. The book also discusses four phases of the processes of assessing learning and includes several classroom vignettes. It provides a foundation for contemporary assessment practices and provides strong support for them.

―――. *Curriculum and Evaluation Standards for School Mathematics.* National Council of Teachers of Mathematics, 1989. 258 p. ISBN 0-87353-273-2 (paper).

The NCTM standards for curriculum and evaluation are the definitive resource for school mathematics reform. This influential document articulates an ambitious, forward-looking vision through curriculum standards that describe the mathematics that students need to learn and how they should learn it and evaluation standards that present criteria for measuring learning. The curriculum standards address four broad components of all mathematics learning in addition to specific content areas. The discussion and numerous classroom examples make this a readable document.

―――. *Professional Standards for Teaching Mathematics.* National Council of Teachers of Mathematics, 1991. 196 p. ISBN 0-87353-307-0 (paper).

The *Professional Standards for Teaching Mathematics,* the second NCTM school reform document, consists of four sets of standards that address the mission, work, evaluation, and professional development of teachers. The section on Standards for Teaching Mathematics presents the framework for classroom mathematics teaching. These six standards focus on four critical aspects of teaching—selecting worthwhile mathematical tasks, teaching through discourse, establishing an appropriate classroom learning environment, and engaging in ongoing analysis of teaching and learning. Teachers will find the set of annotated vignettes that describe instructional episodes from actual classrooms to be particularly helpful.

National Research Council. *Everybody Counts: A Report to the Nation on the Future of Mathematics Education.* National Academy Press, 1989. 114 p. ISBN 0-309-03977-0 (paper).

Powerful arguments for the need to change mathematics programs at all levels are presented in this short treatise, together with a portrait of the kind of teaching and curriculum that is required in order to meet the challenges of the current technological era. The compelling writing style and well-reasoned arguments enable the book to communicate effectively to a wide audience. It is a valuable resource for teachers, administrators, and parents who are attempting to understand the reasons for and the direction of change in school mathematics programs.

EXPERIENCES AND ISSUES IN IMPLEMENTING CHANGE

Ohanian, Susan. *Garbage Pizza, Patchwork Quilts, and Math Magic: Stories about Teachers Who Love to Teach and Children Who Love to Learn.* W. H. Freeman, 1992. 248 p. ISBN 0-7167-2360-3 (hardcover).

The author describes her experiences in primary classrooms across the country that were involved in the Exxon K–3 Mathematics Specialist Project. She vividly captures the exciting and profound experiences she witnessed in her year-long travels. The book is a tribute to the capabilities and insights of young children and their teachers who are exploring new frontiers in mathematics. It also provides insights into the process of change, the struggles teachers face as they implement change, the role of administrators, and the reactions of parents. This vision of school mathematics will appeal to teachers, administrators, and parents.

Parker, Ruth E. *Mathematical Power: Lessons From a Classroom.* Heinemann, 1993. 229 p. ISBN 0-435-08339-2 (paper).

This book tells the dynamic story of implementing a program that reflects the vision and goals of the NCTM Standards in one fifth-grade classroom. It provides insights into planning, decision-making, and dilemmas related to a major shift in goals and teaching strategies and helpful guidance for building a collaborative learning environment, using menus as a teaching strategy, and assessing mathematical understanding through journals, portfolios, and the use of rubrics. The opening and closing chapters provide a conceptual framework and address significant issues related to implementing change. Teachers will find this book to be readable, practical, and provocative.

Sawyer, Ann. *Developments in Elementary Mathematics Teaching.* Heinemann, 1995. 176 p. ISBN 0-435-08371-6 (paper).

Experiences and case studies of British teachers in implementing their National Curriculum are the focus of this powerful book, which offers much to all teachers. The notion of Math Trails, planned field trips that allow children to apply mathematics and collect data for extended tasks, will be particularly interesting. Other chapters address the use of Logo, calculators and computers, themes that connect mathematics with other curriculum areas, and alternative approaches to assessing learning. The rich and carefully documented classroom examples and descriptions of how change can occur offer guidance and encouragement to teachers, administrators, and parents.

Schifter, Deborah, and Catherine Twomey Fosnot. *Reconstructing Mathematics Education: Stories of Teachers Meeting the Challenge of Reform.* Teachers

College Press, 1993. 216 p. ISBN 0-8077-3206-0 (hardcover); 0-8077-3205-2 (paper).

This book is a probing, in-depth examination of the changes that elementary teachers undergo when they commit themselves to a constructivist approach to teaching mathematics. The experiences and growth patterns of a small number of teachers are carefully documented using a case-study approach and numerous examples. The narratives illustrate what is possible in teaching mathematics; they also highlight the significant complexities of inventing new practices and reconstructing one's teaching. Most importantly, this work establishes the compelling need for a serious commitment to teacher development that occurs over an extended period of time and provides ongoing support for teachers.

RESEARCH

Jensen, Robert J., ed. *Research Ideas for the Classroom: Early Childhood Education.* Macmillan, 1993. 374 p. ISBN 0-02-895794-6 (paper).

This initial volume in a research interpretation project provides readable, practical discussions of major research findings in school mathematics and their implications for teachers. The book, which addresses primary grades mathematics, is organized around the themes of learning, processes and content, and teaching, with each chapter coauthored by a researcher and a teacher. The writing style is informal and conversational, with numerous classroom examples and ideas for teachers to try. The breadth of topics included and the applied focus make this a very valuable and useful resource.

Kamii, Constance; with Linda Leslie Joseph. *Young Children Continue to Reinvent Arithmetic—Second Grade: Implications of Piaget's Theory.* Teachers College Press, 1989. 203 p. ISBN 0-8077-2958-2 (hardcover); 0-8077-2957-4 (paper).

This work extends the author's earlier research on learning mathematics and is built on a classical Piagetian constructivist perspective of children's learning. The four sections of the book deal with the theoretical foundation of the work, the goals and objectives of arithmetic, classroom activities that support the theoretical framework, and evaluation of children's learning. Kamii's research reinforces and provides additional insights on the perspective that is reflected in several other books that have been included in this chapter.

Owens, Douglas T., ed. *Research Ideas for the Classroom: Middle School Mathematics.* Macmillan, 1993. 350 p. ISBN 0-02-895792-X (hardcover); 0-02-895795-4 (paper).

Like its counterpart for early childhood educators, this second volume in a research interpretation project provides readable, practical discussions of major research findings in school mathematics and their implications for teachers. The book, which addresses intermediate and middle grades mathematics, is organized around the themes of learning, processes and content, and teaching, with each chapter coauthored by a researcher and a teacher. The writing style is informal and conversational, with numerous classroom examples and ideas for teachers to try. This is a valuable and useful resource.

Wood, Terry, Paul Cobb, Erna Yackel, and Deborah Dillon, eds. *Rethinking Elementary School Mathematics: Insights and Issues.* National Council of Teachers of Mathematics, 1993. 122 p. ISBN 0-87353-362-3 (paper).

This monograph presents the investigation of a constructivist, problem-centered approach to learning mathematics in a second-grade classroom. The research study, which is connected to a multi-year project, provides insights into the mathematics learning of individual children; it also examines the significant role of the social interaction that occurred as children worked in pairs to solve problems and shared their strategies in whole-class discussions. The book presents powerful evidence on the value of allowing children to develop their own strategies and has strong implications for the way mathematics is taught and curriculum is organized.

TEACHER RESOURCES AND REFERENCES

Atkinson, Sue, ed. *Mathematics with Reason: The Emergent Approach to Primary Maths.* Heinemann, 1992. 176 p. ISBN 0-435-08333-3 (paper).

The premise of this book is that young children possess naturally developed and powerful mathematical insights, understandings, and reasoning strategies prior to entering school and that schools need to build mathematics on this rich and substantial foundation. The opening section establishes the rationale for this position and is followed by several brief chapters that provide interesting examples of classroom activities and children's work. The final section suggests ways of implementing the new approach. The conversational style and brief discussions are a major strength of the book, together with the way the numerous examples are woven into the discussions.

Bickmore-Brand, Jennie, ed. *Language in Mathematics.* Heinemann, 1993. 115 p. ISBN 0-435-08340-6 (paper).

This provocative book, originally published by the Australian Reading Association, examines the language approach to teaching and learning mathematics. The nine brief essays provide a theoretical framework for examining the relationship between recent language arts research and mathematics learning. The chapters are clear and readable, contain numerous classroom examples to illustrate the points, provide valuable insights into the contributions of language to learning mathematics, and warn of the pitfalls of superficially following trends. The book helps teachers build a firmer foundation for their activities and develop a broader perspective on current efforts in this area.

Countryman, Joan. *Writing to Learn Mathematics: Strategies that Work, K–12.* Heinemann, 1992. 101 p. ISBN 0-435-08329-5 (paper).

This is a practical, applied guide that offers numerous suggestions for teachers at all levels about an important new emphasis for promoting learning and mathematical reasoning. Multiple ways of incorporating writing into the mathematics classroom are discussed. The author, a classroom teacher, addresses many forms of writing, including journals, learning logs, and autobiographies. The numerous examples provide rich connections to real classrooms and make the book a useful resource. While the majority of the examples are drawn primarily from the upper grades, the ideas are applicable to all levels.

National Research Council. *Measuring Up: Prototypes for Mathematics Assessment.* National Academy Press, 1993. 166 p. ISBN 0-309-04845-1 (paper).

This book addresses using alternatives to conventional assessment procedures to assess learning. It presents thirteen prototypical mathematics assessment tasks that represent what nine- to eleven-year-old children might be expected to demonstrate under a contemporary curriculum. Each task describes the background that children should have, presents suggestions for introducing the task, and describes the assessment activity. Suggestions also are offered about how the task might be varied and scored. The tasks and the sample children's responses will be interesting to teachers and cause them to want to try the tasks with their own classes.

Payne, Joseph N., ed. *Mathematics for the Young Child.* National Council of Teachers of Mathematics, 1990. 306 p. ISBN 0-87353-288-0 (hardcover).

A professional reference work for teachers of children, preschool through fourth grade, this book presents a comprehensive treatment of the content and methodology of primary grades mathematics. Nine themes form the basis of the discussion of content chapters dealing with number concepts, problem solving, basic facts, geometry, measurement, and fractions. Each chapter incorporates recent relevant research and thoughtful discussion on the topic and is accompanied by numerous practical teaching suggestions and instructional activities. This is a useful resource that will guide teachers toward sound practice and decision making.

Stenmark, Jean Kerr, ed. *Mathematics Assessment: Myths, Models, Good Questions, and Practical Suggestions.* National Council of Teachers of Mathematics, 1991. 67 p. ISBN 0-87353-339-9 (paper).

Here is a comprehensive and useful presentation of contemporary approaches to assessment. A discussion of the case for changing assessment practices sets the stage for an inviting survey of what performance assessment is and suggestions for implementing new approaches. The sections that follow present suggestions for assessing learning through teacher observations, interviews, and conferences; for the use of mathematics portfolios; and for implementing various assessment modes. This valuable resource offers a tremendous amount of practical guidance, supported by multiple classroom examples, in a few pages, while also effectively addressing the philosophical framework for the approach.

Stoessiger, Rex, and Joy Edmunds. *Natural Learning and Mathematics.* Heinemann, 1992. 113 p. ISBN 0-435-08328-7 (paper).

Engaging and provocative, this book poses the question, "What if mathematics were taught in the same way as language arts in a classroom where natural learning processes are respected and celebrated?" The authors explore the theoretical framework for a natural-learning approach to K–6 mathematics, share their work with teachers in implementing it, and provide numerous classroom examples. They offer a vision and practical suggestions for teachers who wish to involve children actively in their own learning. The book is delightful to read, but will challenge readers to examine their own teaching as a result.

Theissen, Diane, and Margaret Matthias, eds. *The Wonderful World of Mathematics: A Critically Annotated List of Children's Books in Mathematics.* National Council of Teachers of Mathematics, 1992. 241 p. ISBN 0-87353-353-4 (paper).

This valuable reference lists over five hundred children's books for preschool through grade 6 in which mathematics concepts are a primary emphasis. Each citation indicates the grade levels for which the book is likely to be appropriate, rates the book in terms of its usefulness in teaching mathematical concepts, and provides a description of the book together with observations on its use. There are four major sections—early number concepts, number-extensions and connections, measurement, and geometry and spatial sense—with several subsections under each one. This is a readable, useful resource for all teachers.

Thornton, Carol A., and Nancy S. Bley, eds. *Windows of Opportunity: Mathematics for Students with Special Needs.* National Council of Teachers of Mathematics, 1994. 466 p. ISBN 0-87353-374-7 (hardcover).

This is a comprehensive professional resource for regular classroom and special education teachers who work with students with disabilities in mathematics, as well as those students who are talented. It vividly demonstrates how contemporary approaches to mathematics instruction apply to the full spectrum of students. Chapters devoted to teaching various mathematical content areas and examples of promising practice are a primary focus. These chapters, co-written by professors and classroom teachers, provide an exciting vision of what mathematics can be for *every* student. The classroom examples and teaching vignettes provide practical guidance, as well as hope and inspiration.

Trafton, Paul, ed. *New Directions for Elementary School Mathematics: 1989 Yearbook*. National Council of Teachers of Mathematics, 1989. 245 p. ISBN 0-87353-272-4 (hardcover).

The 1989 NCTM Yearbook provides valuable perspectives on the ideas of the NCTM curriculum standards. Several chapters clarify important aspects of change such as problem solving, communication and reasoning, and a revised view of computation, as well as discussion of issues of change. The chapters devoted to discussions and examples of specific content areas will be particularly helpful, as will the chapters on children's thinking and the implications of this for teaching and curriculum planning. Teachers will find this to be a valuable resource that provides guidance and teaching ideas.

Webb, Norman, ed. *Assessment in the Mathematics Classroom: 1993 Yearbook*. National Council of Teachers of Mathematics, 1993. 248 p. ISBN 0-87353-352-6 (hardcover).

In the minds of many mathematics educators, assessment is integral to the reform efforts in mathematics education, for they believe that curriculum reform cannot occur unless assessment also changes. Thus, the 1993 NCTM Yearbook is devoted to assessment. The twenty-seven chapters address several aspects of assessment, ranging from assessment issues to explanation of assessment techniques. Fourteen chapters are devoted to assessment at the primary and middle grades levels. The yearbook is a strong resource, as it provides a good perspective on the topic and offers practical suggestions for teachers.

Whitin, David, and Sandra Wilde. *Read Any Good Math Lately?: Children's Books for Mathematical Learning, K–6*. Heinemann, 1992. 206 p. ISBN 0-435-08334-1 (paper).

This comprehensive guide to the use of children's literature in teaching mathematics offers teachers help as it engages them in its narrative. The opening chapter establishes a compelling case for incorporating children's literature into mathematics programs. Succeeding chapters, which are organized by mathematical topic, discuss selected books related to the topic, share examples of teachers' experiences with the books, give examples of additional exploration, and list additional books on the topic. The many classroom episodes and samples of children's work are particularly valuable features of the book.

TEACHING AND ASSESSMENT ACTIVITIES

Burns, Marilyn. *Math and Literature (K–3)*. The Math Solutions Publications, 1992 (available through Cuisenaire Corporation of America). 73 p. ISBN 0-941355-07-1 (paper).

Hundreds of teachers have been introduced to using children's literature as a context for exciting and challenging lessons through this book. The book presents several examples of the way a specific book was used in a classroom. Each lesson is richly illustrated with samples of children's work, including written explanations and drawings. In addition, there are brief sketches on twenty-one other books with suggestions for how they might be used. The book is very effective in inspiring teachers to try these ideas with their own classes. A second volume was published in 1994.

—―――, et al. *A Collection of Math Lessons: From Grades 1 Through 3; From Grades 3 Through 6;* and *From Grades 6 Through 8*. The Math Solutions Publications, 1988; 1987; 1990 (available through Cuisenaire Corporation of America). 73 p. for grades 1–3; 193 p. for grades 3–6; 174 p. for grades 6–8. ISBN 0-941-35501-2 for grades 1–3; 0-941-35500-4 for grades 3–6; 0-941-35503-9 for grades 6–8.

The three books in this series present appealing, thoughtful, classroom-tested lessons on a variety of topics with the intent that teachers will try these lessons. The lessons have a problem-solving focus, address important mathematics, emphasize oral and written communication, and promote working in small groups. Each episode tells how the authors taught the lesson and includes sample questions and responses, teacher observations, and students' work. The inviting presentation and level of detail encourage teachers to want to try these lessons for themselves. The books are a wonderful beginning point for trying new instructional approaches.

Leiva, Miriam A., series editor. *Curriculum and Evaluation Standards for School Mathematics, Addenda Series, Grades K–6*. National Council of Teachers of Mathematics, 1991–93. 11-book set. *Kindergarten Book,* 1991. 24 p. ISBN 0-87353-310-0; *First Grade Book,* 1991. 24 p. ISBN 0-87353-311-9; *Second Grade Book,* 1992. 32 p. ISBN 0-87353-312-7; *Third Grade Book,* 1991. 32 p. ISBN 0-87353-313-5; *Fourth Grade Book,* 1992. 32 p. ISBN 0-87353-314-3; *Fifth Grade Book,* 1991. 32 p. ISBN 0-87353-315-1; *Sixth Grade Book,* 1992. 32 p. ISBN 0-87353-316-X; *Geometry and Spatial Sense,* 1993. 56 p. ISBN 0-87353-317-8;

Number Sense and Operation, 1992. 48 p. ISBN 0-87353-319-4; *Patterns*, 1992. 53 p. ISBN 0-87353-320-8.

This set of eleven books provides classroom examples, activities, and investigations to supplement and extend the Curriculum and Evaluation Standards for School Mathematics. There is a short booklet for each grade, K through 6, and topical booklets on geometry, data, number sense and operations, and patterns. A companion set of six topical books was developed for grades 5–8. These publications offer classroom-tested ideas that can easily be used by teachers and provide additional insight into the recommendations of the curriculum standards. They are an important and useful adjunct to the core document, as well as popular with teachers.

NONPRINT MATERIALS

Burns, Marilyn. *Mathematics: Teaching for Understanding*. Cuisenaire Company of America, 1992. ISBN 0-938587-5. Videos.

The three twenty-minute videotapes in this series for K–6 teachers present lesson segments and activities that show how teachers can implement the goals of the NCTM Standards. The tapes address teacher-directed lessons, groups of students working on menu activities, and communication in math classes, including assessment. The lesson segments are thoughtful and engaging and will give teachers ideas for their classrooms. The discussion guide provides summaries of vignettes, suggests inservice activities using the tapes, and supplies blackline masters for the activities. This excellent series is highly effective in promoting discussion and interest in new approaches.

———. *What Are You Teaching My Child?* Scholastic, 1994. Video.

This twenty-minute video production is a powerful and compelling presentation of the need for a new approach to school mathematics and the importance of emphasizing problem-solving, collaborative learning, manipulatives, and mathematical reasoning. It features classroom episodes, interviews with working professionals, and parent comments. One particularly effective segment shows several adults struggling to make sense of an intriguing problem. It is a highly effective way to introduce parents to changes in mathematics and also is effective as part of inservice programs. It is available in English and Spanish editions.

JOURNALS

Mathematics Teaching in the Middle School. National Council of Teachers of Mathematics. ISSN 1072-0839.

Mathematics Teaching in the Middle School is a new journal of the National Council of Teachers of Mathematics that is currently published quarterly. The journal is a resource for teachers in Grades 5 through 9. It focuses on intuitive, exploratory approaches to mathematics that help build students' mathematical reasoning and develop a strong conceptual mathematical foundation. The highly readable, attractively designed journal features a mix of articles, special features, classroom activities, and reviews of books and products.

Teaching Children Mathematics. National Council of Teachers of Mathematics. ISSN 1073-5836. (Formerly entitled *Arithmetic Teacher.*)

Teaching Children Mathematics is a journal of the National Council of Teachers of Mathematics that is published monthly from September through May. The journal presents ideas, activities, and teaching strategies for pre-K through Grade 6 mathematics. It includes new developments in curriculum, teaching, learning, and teacher education, as well as relevant research findings. The journal, which is designed to appeal to classroom teachers, features articles, special features, and reviews of books and products. A focus issue each year is devoted to a specific topic.

MEMBERSHIPS

National Council of Teachers of Mathematics
1906 Association Drive
Reston, Virginia 22091

Phone: (703) 620-9840

The primary organization for elementary teachers in mathematics is the National Council of Teachers of Mathematics. The organization has 125,000 individual and institutional members and is growing. It focuses on K–12 school mathematics. The mission of the NCTM is to provide vision and leadership in improving the teaching and learning of mathematics so that every student is ensured an equitable standards-based mathematics education and every teacher of mathematics is ensured the opportunity to grow professionally. The organization's publications include *Teaching Children Mathematics* and *Mathematics Teaching in the Middle School.*

9

Social Studies

Consultant: Dr. Dorothy Skeel
Peabody College
Vanderbilt University
Nashville, Tennessee

Dr. Dorothy Skeel, Professor Emerita of Vanderbilt University, was Professor of Social Studies in the Department of Teaching and Learning until her retirement in 1995. She received her D.Ed. from Pennsylvania State University.

As an active member in the National Council for the Social Studies, she served as editor of the elementary section of *Social Education.* She has chaired the NCSS Task Force on Social Studies for Early Childhood/Elementary School Children—Preparing for the Twenty-first Century. Additionally, she served as a committee member of the NCSS Early Childhood/Elementary Committee and as a board member of the College and University Assembly of NCSS. Other professional activities related to social studies include the following: Fellow of the Longview Foundation for Education in World Affairs and International Understanding; State Coordinator for the "We the People—The Citizen and the Constitution" program; member of the Teacher Education Board of the Special Youth Committee on Citizenship Education of the American Bar Association; Director of the Peabody Center on Economic and Social Studies Education; and recipient of the Excellence in Education Award presented by the College of Education of Pennsylvania State University.

Dr. Skeel has authored elementary social studies textbooks, method texts, curriculum books, and numerous articles and chapters on social studies topics. Her most recent text is *Elementary Social Studies: Challenges for Tomorrow's World* (Harcourt Brace College Publishers, 1995).

Social Studies

DOCUMENTS/GUIDELINES/STANDARDS

Center for Civic Education. *National Standards for Civics and Government.* Center for Civic Education, 1994. 179 p. ISBN 0-89818-155-0 (paper).

These standards for civics and government meet the goal for the civic mission of schools to ensure that the citizens of the United States are prepared with the knowledge and skills to become competent participating citizens. The content standards are organized around a series of questions including: What is government and what should it do? What are the basic values and principles of American democracy? What are the roles of the citizens in American democracy? What is the relationship of the United States to other nations and to world affairs? How does the government established by the Constitution embody the purposes, values, and principles of American democracy? Intellectual and participatory skills are incorporated within the content standards and are identified for grades K–4, 5–8, and 9–12.

The National Center for History in the Schools. *Standards for United States History and World History.* The National Center for History in the Schools, 1994 (paper).

Since history should not be confined to facts, dates, names, and places, these standards have been developed around five fields of historical thinking: historical chronology, historical comprehension, historical analysis and interpretation, historical issues analysis and decision-making, and historical research. Standards for grades K–4 are organized around topics, while those for 5–12 are defined by eras.

National Council for Geographic Education. *Geography for Life: National Geography Standards 1994.* National Council for Geographic Education, 1994. 272 p. ISBN 0-7922-2775-1 (paper).

Geography for Life specifies the essential knowledge, skills, and perspectives of geography that students should possess to be informed and effective citizens. There are eighteen standards organized around seeing the world in spatial terms, places and regions, physical systems, human systems, environment and society, and the uses of geography. There are content and performance standards for grades K–4, 5–8, and 9–12. Geographic skills are presented in such a way that students will develop an appreciation for and an understanding of geographic modes of inquiry. The skills include: asking geographic questions, acquiring geographic information, presenting geographic information, analyzing geographic information, and developing and testing geographic generalizations. The standards are beautifully illustrated with photographs.

National Council for the Social Studies. *Curriculum Standards for the Social Studies.* The National Council for the Social Studies, 1994. Bulletin 89, 178 p. ISBN 0-87986-065-0 (paper).

The NCSS found it necessary to articulate an integrated set of curriculum standards for social studies, since the individual disciplines of history, geography, and civics and government had developed separate sets of standards. NCSS standards are based on ten thematic strands designed to achieve excellence in social studies. The ten strands are correlated with performance expectations at three grade levels: early, middle, and high school. These themes include culture; time, continuity, and change; people, places, and environments; individual development and identity; individuals, groups, and institutions; power, authority, and governance; production, distribution, and consumption; and science, technology, and society. An overview of essential skills for social studies and a discussion of democratic beliefs and values are included in the Appendices.

Special Committee on Youth Education for Citizenship. *Essentials of Law Related Education: A Guide for Practitioners and Policy Makers.* American Bar Association, 1995. 12 p. ISBN 1-57073-141-1 (paper).

Law related education is an integral part of social studies. It fosters the knowledge, skills, and values that students need to function effectively in our pluralistic, democratic society based on the rule of law. The document outlines the skills, values, concepts, attitudes, and practices that are essential to understanding the law, the legal process, and the legal system, and the fundamental principles and values on which they are based.

EXPERIENCE AND ISSUES IN IMPLEMENTING CHANGE

•Davidman, Leonard; with Patricia T. Davidman. *Teaching With a Multicultural Perspective: A Practical Guide.* Longman, 1994. 241 p. ISBN 0-8013-0835-6 (paper).

The diversity within our schools forces us to consider how best to provide an effective instructional program with a multicultural perspective. This volume provides background information as well as practical applications for the classroom, including creating a multicultural curriculum with integrated social studies and science-based units of instruction and creating a multicultural curriculum with content that links environmental, global, citizenship, and multicultural education. The appendices provide resources for equity-oriented teaching and a text evaluation form that are invaluable.

Ross, E. Wayne, ed. *Reflective Practice in Social Studies.* National Council for the Social Studies, 1994. Bulletin 88, 89 p. ISBN 0-87986-063-4 (paper).

This bulletin encourages curriculum improvement through reflective practices among beginning and experienced teachers. Teachers are viewed as curriculum creators and theorizers, and as leaders of change. Descriptions of projects that are instituted within the framework of reflection at the elementary, middle, and high school levels are included.

Stahl, Robert J., and Ronald L. Van Sickle, eds. *Cooperative Learning in the Social Studies Classroom: An Invitation to Social Study.* National Council for the Social Studies, 1992. Bulletin 87, 62 p. ISBN 0-87986-061-8 (paper).

Cooperative learning is viewed as a viable alternative approach to teaching social studies. This volume introduces the concept, philosophy, and practice of cooperative learning. Research findings focus on the evidence that relates specific cooperative learning approaches and academic achievement, affective growth, and interpersonal and social interaction skills. Teachers describe their experiences in implementing cooperative learning in their classrooms. Johnson and Johnson give practical ideas on how to implement cooperative learning in social studies classrooms. Also included is a description of a group of teachers as they experience the transition of becoming cooperative learning teachers.

Tye, Kenneth A., ed. *Global Education From Thought to Action.* Association for Supervision and Curriculum Development. 1991 Yearbook, 184 p. ISBN 0-87120-171-2 (hardcover).

Global education is explained and its importance in schools is identified. Ideas for how it works and can be implemented are provided. Possibly the most important aspect of this volume is the potential of global education to promote improvements in the schools, including interdisciplinary planning and teaching, the development of critical thinking abilities, the use of the community as a learning laboratory, cooperative learning, and intrinsic motivation of student learning.

FOUNDATIONS FOR REFORM

National Council for the Social Studies. *Social Studies Curriculum Planning Resources.* Kendall/Hunt Publications, 1990. 120 p. ISBN 084-03-63796 (paper).

This guide is a valuable resource when attempting to revise a social studies curriculum. It provides criteria for evaluating a social studies program to determine its quality and gives suggested scope and sequence statements. The NCSS position statement on curriculum is included, and an annotated bibliography provides additional resources.

Parker, Walter. *Renewing the Social Studies Curriculum.* Association for Supervision and Curriculum Development, 1991. 124 p. ISBN 0-87120-177-1 (paper).

This book has been written for local social studies curriculum deliberation. It is intended to spark "home-grown" curriculum reform. This type of reform should come from those people who work with the children and who actually implement the curriculum. The book outlines a process for curriculum deliberation from the contexts of renewal to thoughtful learning and authentic assessment. The appendices contain valuable documents, including "In Search of a Scope and Sequence for Social Studies," "Designing a Social Studies Scope and Sequence for the Twenty-first Century," and "Social Studies Within a Global Education."

RESEARCH

Atwood, Virginia A., ed. *Elementary School Social Studies: Research as a Guide to Practice.* National Council for the Social Studies, 1986. Bulletin 79, 176 p. ISBN 0-87986-054-5 (paper).

After a discussion of elementary social studies, chapters relate what research says about children learning social studies. Each chapter focuses on a different aspect of social studies, including citizenship and law related education, international and multicultural education, geography, history, economics, anthropology and sociology, and learning and instruction. Several chapters are devoted to related topics, including teacher education and certification, parent involvement, and advocating early childhood social studies.

Cornbleth, Catherine, ed. *An Invitation to Research in Social Education.* National Council for the Social Studies, 1986. Bulletin 77, 138 p. ISBN 0-87986-051-0 (paper).

As the title indicates, the individual is invited to participate in the research process. Research is identified as a means of looking "carefully at something or looking at something in a different way in order to describe and explain it." The guide explains alternative research methodologies and encourages teachers to become researchers. One teacher's view of research is presented.

TEACHER RESOURCES AND REFERENCES

Center for Research and Development in Law-Related Education (CRADLE). *We, the People of the World.* Center for Research and Development in Law-Related Education, 1991. 236 p. ISBN 1-879953-04-8 (hardcover).

This publication is a compilation of lesson plans for law-related education for K–12 that has been written and tested by classroom teachers. The lessons are designed to teach about different cultures and laws, from the comparing and contrasting of constitutions of different countries, including Cuba, France, and Japan, to learning about the Islamic system of justice. There are also lessons about the U.S. Constitution.

Drum, Jan, Steve Hughes, and George Otero. *Global Winners: 74 Activities for Inside and Outside the Classroom.* Intercultural Press, 1994. 209 p. ISBN 1-87864-18-8 (hardcover).

A valuable resource book that contains seventy-four activities to increase students' understanding of global issues, including environmental, demographic, intercultural, economic, social, and political. These activities are organized under six themes: state-of-the-planet awareness, developing perspective consciousness, valuing diversity, living responsibly with others, understanding issues and trends, and building the capacity for change. The goals of global education to help students open themselves to positive change and to value diversity are emphasized.

Gallagher, Arlene F., ed. *Acting Together: Reader's Theatre Excerpts from Children's Literature on Themes from the Constitution.* Social Science Education Consortium, 1991. 115 p. ISBN 0-89994-363-2 (paper).

This book is designed to provide opportunities for teachers to integrate the study of the Constitution into their existing curriculum. Reader's Theatre is a strategy that allows students to take on a particular role and view a problem or conflict from that perspective. The selection of folk tales from literature promotes the integration of literature, language skills, and the principles of the Constitution to help students make connections among subject areas. Being actively involved when studying the Constitution helps reach the goal of citizenship education. Teachers field tested these activities.

Gay, Geneva. *At the Essence of Learning: Multicultural Education.* Kappa Delta Pi, 1994. 164 p. ISBN 0-912099-14-3 (paper).

Gay gives a comprehensive view of the principles of multicultural education, including the debate among the critics. Chapters include discussions of the general principles of education, human growth and development, democratic citizenship, and pedagogy. There are reflections and applications sections at the end of each chapter. The applications provide suggested activities to improve understanding of and competence in multiculturalism. All chapters underline that the meaning and intent of general education and multicultural education are the same.

National Council on Economic Education. *Master Curriculum Guides in Economics Teaching Strategies: K–2, 3–4.* National Council on Economic Education, 1994. ISBN 1-56183-470-X (hardcover); 1-56183-471-8 (paper).

The two guides provide a framework of objectives and concepts for teaching of economics in grades K–4. They are divided into a Teacher Resource Manual and activity pages. There is a set in blackline master of exciting activities to connect economics to reading and language arts, mathematics, children's literature, and the community. Detailed lesson plans are provided in the resource manual.

•Seefeldt, Carol. *Social Studies for the Preschool-Primary Child.* 4th ed. Merrill, 1994. 312 p. ISBN 0-02-408451-4 (paper).

An excellent resource for planning and implementing social studies instruction for the preschool and primary age child. It provides the theoretical and research base for understanding the importance of starting early to provide a foundation for citizenship education. Individual chapters discuss concept formation, history, geography, economics, current topics, and cross-cultural education and give examples of lessons to be taught.

Selwyn, Douglas. *Arts and Humanities in the Social Studies.* National Council for the Social Studies, 1995. Bulletin 90, 66 p. ISBN 0-87986-064-2 (hardcover).

This bulletin adds another dimension to the teaching of social studies, by the use of drama, creative writing, and literature. Lesson plans are provided to actively involve students in social studies through the arts. Even though the lessons are intended for high school age, elementary teachers can adapt them for their students. The author presents mock trials, debates, simulation, journal writing, and storytelling.

Skeel, Dorothy J. *Elementary Social Studies: Challenges for Tomorrow's World.* Harcourt Brace College Publishers, 1995. 277 p. ISBN 0-15-501100-6 (hardcover).

Social studies education is introduced through the description of the diversity among children, teachers, classrooms, schools, and conceptions of the subject. Particularly helpful chapters discuss curriculum development and planning for instruction. Examples of daily and unit lesson plans integrated with language arts, math, science, art, music, and physical education are presented. A chapter on map and globe skills gives extensive examples of lessons based on the five themes of geography. Evaluation/assessment strategies are presented.

———. *Small Size Economics: Lessons for the Primary Grades.* Scott, Foresman, 1988. 29 p. ISBN 0-673-18768-3 (paper).

Lesson plans are provided to integrate economic concepts into the ongoing curriculum for grades K–3. Concepts are identified to be taught within the particular curriculum context for that grade level. Different teaching strategies are utilized, including role play, simulation, inquiry, and valuing. Evaluation strategies are presented for each lesson.

•Tiedt, Pamela, and Iris M. Tiedt. *Multicultural Teaching: A Handbook of Activities, Information, and Resources.* 4th ed. Allyn & Bacon, 1995. 427 p. ISBN 0-205-15488-3 (paper).

This book develops the foundation for teaching from a multicultural perspective. It gives a comprehensive view that includes planning, the teacher's role, promoting self esteem, linguistic diversity, and multicultural education across the curriculum. This book is filled with an abundance of learning experiences to be implemented in the classroom.

Zarnowski, Myra, and Arlene F. Gallagher, eds. *Children's Literature and Social Studies: Selecting and Using Notable Books in the Classroom.* Kendall/Hunt, 1993. 88 p. ISBN 084-03-89515 (hardcover).

The editors have selected children's literature books from the list of Notable Children's Trade Books to be incorporated into the social studies program. They give teachers criteria to use in selecting children's books as well as demonstrating how to integrate them into their social studies instruction.

JOURNALS

Social Education. National Council for the Social Studies. ISSN 0037-7724.

The official journal of NCSS provides background information on trends and current issues being discussed in the field. Sections include reports on the latest research, books, classroom teacher's ideas, and instructional technology. The April/May issue carries the list of Notable Children's Trade Books for use with social studies topics. The journal is published seven times a year.

Social Studies and the Young Learner. National Council for the Social Studies. ISSN 1056-0300.

This journal was initiated specifically for elementary social studies teachers. Published quarterly, it is intended to stimulate thinking about social studies in the elementary school classroom. In addition to articles on diverse topics related to teaching social studies, special departments include curriculum concerns, children's literature, teacher resources, and a media corner.

MEMBERSHIPS

National Council for the Social Studies
3501 Newark Street NW
Washington, D.C. 20016-3167

Phone: (202) 966-7840
Fax: (202) 966-2061

NCSS serves as an umbrella organization for elementary, secondary, and college teachers of history, geography, economics, political science, sociology, psychology, anthropology, and law-related education. The organization engages and supports educators in strengthening and advocating social studies and works toward a better understanding of the social studies and their importance in developing responsible participation in social, political, and economic life. The organization publishes two journals of particular interest to elementary educators: *Social Education* and *Social Studies and the Young Learner.*

10

Music

Consultant: Dr. Cornelia Yarbrough
Louisiana State University
Baton Rouge, Louisiana

Dr. Cornelia Yarbrough is Professor of Music and Coordinator of Music Education at Louisiana State University and A & M College, Baton Rouge. She received the Bachelor's in Music Education degree from Stetson University and Master's in Music Education and Ph.D. degrees from Florida State University.

Her public school teaching experience includes eight years as a vocal/choral specialist, K–12, in Georgia. She joined the faculty at Syracuse University in 1973 as dual professor of music and education. During her thirteen years at Syracuse University, she was founder and director of the Syracuse University Oratorio Society, the chorus-in-residence of the Syracuse Symphony Orchestra. She also served as Director of the School of Music and Assistant Dean for the College of Visual and Performing Arts. In the spring of 1986, she received Syracuse University's highest academic award, the Chancellor's Citation for Exceptional Academic Achievement. She joined the faculty at Louisiana State University in the fall of 1986.

Dr. Yarbrough is coauthor with Clifford K. Madsen of the book *Competency-based Music Education* (Prentice-Hall, 1980) and has contributed numerous research articles to a variety of refereed scholarly journals. She served as a member of the editorial board of the *Journal for Research in Music Education* and chair of the National Society for Research in Music Education.

She has been cited as one of the top twenty most eminent and productive researchers in music education (Standley, 1984). More recently, she was cited as one of the eighteen most eminent scholars in music education (Kratus, 1993). Two recent studies cite her as one of the top seven most productive scholars in music education (Hedden, 1991) and cite two of her published articles as ranking ten and twenty-three, respectively, among the most cited articles in music education, competency-based music education, research techniques, and conducting/rehearsal techniques throughout the United States, Canada, and Europe (Schmidt and Zdzinski).

DOCUMENTS/GUIDELINES/STANDARDS

•Consortium of National Arts Education Associations. *National Standards for Arts Education: What Every Young American Should Know and Be Able to Do in the Arts.* Music Educators National Conference, 1994. 142 p. ISBN 1-56545-036-1 (paper).

The National Standards for Arts Education were developed by the Consortium of National Arts Education Associations under the guidance of the National Committee for Standards in the Arts. The Standards were prepared under a grant from the U.S. Department of Education, the National Endowment for the Arts, and the National Endowment for the Humanities. They are written for all students. The Standards affirm that a future worth having depends on being able to construct a vital relationship with the arts, and that doing so, as with any subject, is a matter of discipline and study. The Standards spell out what every young American should know and be able to do in the arts.

Overby, Lynette Young, ed. *Early Childhood Creative Arts.* National Dance Association and Association of the American Alliance for Health, Physical Education, Recreation, and Dance, 1991. 264 p. ISBN 0-88314-522-7 (paper).

This document comprises the proceedings of the December 1990 International Early Childhood Creative Arts conference, which was cosponsored by the Music Educators National Conference and the National Dance Association. Section One, titled General Sessions, provides the reader with theoretical material in the areas of curriculum development, arts assessment, and child development. Section Two, titled Specific Arts Instruction, contains many practical activities as well as theoretical discourses in music, art, dance, and drama. Section Three, titled Model Programs, describes three well-developed arts programs. Section Four, titled Multicultural/International, includes information about creative arts programs of various countries and a multicultural perspective for program development.

BOOKS

Adair, Audrey J. *Ready-To-Use Music Activities Kit.* Parker Publishing, 1984. 291 p. ISBN 0-13-762295-3 (paper).

Contains 204 different music activities which provide a variety of highly motivating, ready-to-use activities to spark children's involvement in music while reinforcing basic music skills and concepts. Each activity is a written exercise to be performed by the individual student, emphasizing one specific area of music education or skill. Each is confined to a single page, is designed to be completed within a typical class period, and can be photocopied as many times as needed for classroom use. The written exercises are presented in a diversity of formats, including anagrams, crossword puzzles, word finders, illustrations, word and symbol matching, and others. A Teacher's Guide and Answer Key at the end of each section of the kit provides complete answers, background information, and teaching suggestions.

Anderson, William M., intro. *Teaching Music with a Multicultural Approach.* Music Educators National Conference, 1991. 104 p. ISBN 0-940796-91-0 (paper).

Based on the Symposium on Multicultural Approaches to Music Education, sponsored by the Music Educators National Conference in collaboration with the Smithsonian Institution's Office of Folklife Programs, the Society for Ethnomusicology, and the MENC Society for General Music, this book is intended to be used with four videotapes, one each for Native American, Hispanic American, African American, and Asian American music. The book contains chapters on each of these musics. Each chapter contains information, lesson plans, and lists of selected resources.

———, and Patricia Shehan Campbell, eds. *Multicultural Perspectives in Music Education.* Music Educators National Conference, 1989. 91 p. ISBN 0-940796-63-5 (paper).

This book can be used by teachers of upper elementary grades and high school. It contains chapters on the following: North America, featuring music of the Southern Appalachian Mountains, Native Americans of the Southwest, and African Americans; Latin America and the Caribbean; Europe; Sub-Saharan Africa; the Middle East; South Asia, particularly India; East Asia, featuring Japan and China; and Southeast Asia, featuring Cambodia (Kampuchea), Laos, Thailand, and Vietnam. Each chapter contains information, lesson plans, and lists of selected resources. A glossary at the end of the book provides pronunciations and definitions of terms used in the book. An index is also included.

Campbell, Patricia Shehan, and Carol Scott-Kassner. *Music in Childhood: From Preschool through the Elementary Grades.* Schirmer Books-Macmillan, 1995. 416 p. ISBN 0-02-870552-1 (hardcover).

This text draws from the most current findings in music education to create a practical and comprehensive guide to enhance the musical development of children. It includes a rich diversity of both Western and World Music sources and addresses such contemporary topics as music technology, the needs of the special learner, and multicultural education. There are chapters demonstrating: (1) musical and instructional approaches suited to the perceptual-cognitive, physical, and affective development of children; (2) children's singing, listening, movement, play, and creativity; (3) educational development, educational opportunities and difficulties associated with the curriculum, technology, multiculturalism, and the special learner; (4) current technology and repertoire; and (5) real-world advice for prospective and practicing teachers on educational methods, lesson planning, curriculum design, student evaluation, and developing a personal style of teaching. It provides current lists of professional organizations and instrument suppliers.

Hackett, Patricia. *The Melody Book: Three Hundred Selections from the World of Music for Autoharp, Guitar, Piano, Recorder, and Voice.* 2nd ed. Prentice-Hall, 1992. 378 p. ISBN 0-13-574427-X (paper).

This is an anthology of three hundred songs for autoharp, guitar, piano, recorder, and voice. Songs included represent a wide variety of styles, including folk music of the world, children's game songs, and themes from symphonic literature, jazz, and contemporary music. Brief historical, stylistic, and biographical descriptions accompany some of the music. Game and dance directions are included for many of the songs. An Appendix presents reference material for music notation, scales and sol fa syllables, key signatures, meter signature, rhythm syllables, musical terms and signs, lead sheet, and transposition. A comprehensive classified index lists music by suitable instrument, voice, modal and pentatonic scale, limited rhythm durations, rhythm and meter, dances/games/percussion, accompaniments/dramatizations, holidays and special occasions, and Western music by style period. It concludes with biographical and historical information.

Palmer, Mary, and Wendy L. Sims, eds. *Music in Prekindergarten Planning and Teaching.* Music Educators National Conference, 1993. 72 p. ISBN 1-56545-017-5 (paper).

Designed to assist prekindergarten teachers, music specialists, and others working with young children in their efforts to help every child reach his or her full musical potential, this work includes chapters on long-range goals for prekindergarten music; guidelines for music activities and instruction; music for children with special needs; developing music concepts and vocabulary; and observing, interpreting, and evaluating music behaviors. It includes practical music activities with tips and examples for immediate use.

Wiggins, Jackie. *Synthesizers in the Elementary Music Classroom: An Integrated Approach.* Music Educators National Conference, 1991. 55 p. ISBN 1-56545-005-1 (hardcover).

The purpose of this book is to help teachers feel comfortable with new technology. Synthesizers can be most useful in the elementary music program for improving performance and listening skills and for nurturing creativity. The first section of this book examines some available equipment, reviews the teacher education necessary to use it, and provides information that will help familiarize teachers with the functions and capabilities of the instruments. The second section presents an overview of a variety of uses in the classroom. The third section, Introducing Synthesizers to Children, offers suggestions for using electronic instruments in all aspects of the music curriculum and provides lesson plans.

Wirth, Marian, Verna Stassesvitch, Rita Shotwell, and Patricia Stemmler. *Musical Games, Fingerplays, and Rhythmic Activities for Early Childhood.* Parker Publishing, 1983. 224 p. ISBN 0-13-607085-X (paper).

This is a book written specifically for classroom teachers who want to use music to enrich their teaching of other subject areas. The format of the book is consistent throughout, offering suggestions for appropriate age levels for each song and illustrations which help the teacher and children follow directions. Guitar, piano, and autoharp chords are notated for all music (most songs have no more than two or three chords, and tunes are notated in comfortable ranges).

MULTI-MEDIA PACKAGE

The Music Connection: Teacher's Edition. 7 vols. *Kindergarten,* 410 p. ISBN 0-382-26189-5; *Book 1,* 448 p. ISBN 0-382-26190-9; *Book 2,* 340 p. ISBN 0-382-26191-7; *Book 3,* 370 p. ISBN 0-382-26192-5; *Book 4,* 374 p. ISBN 0-382-26193-3; *Book 5,* 410 p. ISBN 0-382-26194-1; *Book 6,* 412 p. ISBN 0-382-26196-8.

This series offers a teacher's edition, a student book, and compact discs for each grade level. The teacher's editions contain detailed lesson plans, listening guide transparencies, and a comprehensive reference bank. Reference banks for each grade level include music references, curriculum planners, sections on meeting individual needs, instructions on how to play the autoharp (also tuning instructions) and recorder, a glossary of terms, and indexes. Each grade level's curriculum is divided into three sections: Concepts, Themes, and Reading. Musical concepts are grade level appropriate and based on the National Standards for Music Education. Themes are selected for age level interest: for example, My World of Pretend for kindergartners; Music of Other Cultures for first grade; Making Friends for second grade; a theme musical play, This Beautiful Land We share, for the third grade; How People Work and Play for fourth grade; America's Many Voices for fifth grade; and Bands Around the World for sixth grade. Music Reading sections are sequenced to reinforce the recognition and understanding of musical notation.

NONPRINT MATERIALS

Music Educators National Conference. *Bring Multicultural Music to Children.* Music Educators National Conference, 1992. ISBN 1-56545-009-4. Video, 26.5 minutes.

At recent MENC conferences and symposia, respected music educators have offered innovative ways to teach young students about the music of other cultures. This videotape contains portions of these educators' presentations and gives new ideas for your classroom. It features songs and chants from Africa, China, and Jamaica; music from Native Americans, the Maori of New Zealand, and African Americans. It includes teaching demonstrations and remarks by Rene Boyer-White, Patricia Shehan Campbell, Han Kuo-Huang, David P. McAllester, and Marvelene C. Moore. Suitable for upper elementary grades.

———. *Sing! Move! Listen! Music and Young Children.* Music Educators National Conference, 1993. ISBN 1-56545-00904. Video, 18 minutes.

Filmed during a special conference day on Music and Young Children and presented by the Music Educators National Conference, this work includes ideas and examples to add to and improve music experiences for children. Demonstrations and remarks by David G. Woods, Mary P. Pautz, June Hinckley, Susan Tarnowski, Louise Patrick, and Sandra L. Stauffer are also included. The material is suitable for teachers of first grade and younger children.

———. *Teaching Music of African Americans.* Music Educators National Conference, 1990. ISBN 0-940796-092-9. Video, 26 minutes.

This video, based on the Symposium on Multicultural Approaches to Music Education, sponsored by the Music Educators National Conference in collaboration with the Smithsonian Institution's Office of Folklife Programs, the Society for Ethnomusicology, and the MENC Society for General Music, features illustrations, information, and music with remarks by Bernice Johnson Reagon, Luvenia A. George, and Daniel E. Sheehy. It features authentic performances of Afro-Cuban music and African American religious and work songs, and explanations of the meaning behind the music. Suitable for upper elementary grades. Lesson plans for this video are available in *Teaching Music with a Multicultural Approach* by William M. Anderson (see annotation of this book).

———. *Teaching Music of Asian Americans.* Music Educators National Conference, 1990. ISBN 0-940796-94-5. Video, 27 minutes.

This video is based on the Symposium on Multicultural Approaches to Music Education, sponsored by the Music Educators National Conference in collaboration with the Smithsonian Institution's Office of Folklife Programs, the Society of Ethnomusicology, and the MENC Society for General Music. It features illustrations, information, and music with remarks by Kuo Huang-Han and Patricia Shehan Campbell. It contains a historical survey of Chinese music and thought and an explanation of the most important Chinese instruments and their origins, incorporating authentic performances on stringed, wind, and percussion instruments. This video is suitable for upper elementary grades. Lesson plans for the video are available in *Teaching Music with a Multicultural Approach* by William M. Anderson (see annotation of this book).

―――. *Teaching Music of Hispanic Americans*. Music Educators National Conference, 1990. ISBN 0-940796-95-3. Video, 26 minutes.

Based on the Symposium on Multicultural Approaches to Music Education, sponsored by the Music Educators National Conference in collaboration with the Smithsonian Institution's Office of Folklife Programs, the Society for Ethnomusicology, and the MENC Society for General Music, this work features illustrations, information, and music with remarks by Dale A. Olsen, Linda O'Brien-Rothe, and Daniel E. Sheehy. It provides a look at the intricacies of Andean raft-pipe music and a demonstration and explanation of the instruments and rhythms used in mariachi music. Suitable for upper elementary grades. Lesson plans for this video are available in *Teaching Music with a Multicultural Approach* by William M. Anderson (see annotation of this book).

―――. *Teaching Music of the American Indian*. Music Educators National Conference, 1990. ISBN 0-940796-93-7. Video, 37 minutes.

Based on the Symposium on Multicultural Approaches to Music Education, sponsored by the Music Educators National Conference in collaboration with the Smithsonian Institution's Office of Folklife Programs, the Society for Ethnomusicology, and the MENC Society for General Music, this work offers illustrations, information, and music with remarks by David P. McAllester and Edwin Schupman. Containing performances of dances, songs, and flute music, this is suitable for upper elementary grades. Lesson plans for this video are available in *Teaching Music with a Multicultural Approach* by William M. Anderson (see annotation of this book).

MEMBERSHIPS

Music Educators National Conference
1806 Robert Fulton Drive
Reston, Virginia 22091-4348

Phone: (703) 860-4000
Fax: (703) 860-4826

MENC is the only national organization that addresses all aspects of music education. From elementary general music to music teacher education, at all levels from preschool to college, MENC works to ensure that every student has access to a well-balanced, comprehensive, and high-quality program of music instruction.

11

Visual Arts

Consultant: Dr. Eldon Katter
Kutztown University
Kutztown, Pennsylvania

Dr. Katter is Professor of Art Education at Kutztown University, where he has taught art education courses for over twenty years. He holds a Ph.D. in art education from Pennsylvania State University, with a master's degree in art education from the University of Minnesota. Dr. Katter taught at various levels in the public schools for over ten years and has extensive experience in teaching children with special needs. A former Peace Corps volunteer in Africa, he has a particular interest in multicultural issues.

Dr. Katter coauthored the MELD series of art education games and was the writer for the *Getty Center's Multicultural Art Print Series II*. He is currently the editor of *School Arts Magazine*.

DOCUMENTS/GUIDELINES/STANDARDS

Arnheim, Rudolf. *Thoughts on Art Education (Occasional Paper 2)*. The Getty Center for Education in the Arts, 1989. 61 p. ISBN 0-89236-163-8 (paper).

The author provides teachers with a clear argument of the importance of the perception and creation of visual art as primary agents in the development of the mind. The gist of Arnheim's message is that vision itself is a function of intelligence, that perception is a cognitive event, that interpretation and meaning are an indivisible aspect of seeing, and that the education process can thwart or foster such human abilities.

Broudy, Harry S. *The Role of Imagery in Learning (Occasional Paper 1)*. The Getty Center for Education in the Arts, 1987. 55 p. ISBN 0-89236-145-X (paper).

This monograph proposes a theoretical basis for advocating a program of visual arts education as an integral part of general education. The author makes a case for the centrality of aesthetic perception of images in everyday experience, in learning, and in the formation of the educated mind.

Gardner, Howard. *Art Education and Human Development (Occasional Paper 3)*. The Getty Center for Education in the Arts, 1990. 63 p. ISBN 0-89236-179-4 (paper).

The author surveys the principles that govern the development of human beings, with a special focus on those studies that suggest principles at work in the artistic area and on studies that hold lessons for educators in the arts.

NAEA Task Force. *Purposes, Principles, and Standards for School Arts Programs*. National Art Education Association, 1994. 33 p. ISBN 0-937652-27-X (paper).

This publication is directed toward the promotion and recognition of educationally sound visual art programs in elementary, middle/junior, and high schools. It is designed as a self-assessment evaluation of seven program components: organization, curriculum, personnel, scheduling, facilities, materials/equipment, and budgets.

Perkins, David N. *The Intelligent Eye: Learning to Think by Looking at Art (Occasional Paper 4)*. The Getty Center for Education in the Arts, 1994. 812 p. ISBN 0-89236-274-X (hardcover).

This volume focuses on the importance of art in developing a disposition to thinking and building the mind. The author presents arguments for the value of art in the general education of all students that can be persuasive in presentations to parent groups and school boards. It's an important book for the professional library.

Rollins, Jean. *The National Visual Arts Standards*. National Art Education Association, 1994. 36 p. ISBN 0-937652-65-2 (paper).

Prepared in response to the *Goals 2000: Educate America Act,* this document lists what every student should know and do in the visual arts. It includes six content standards for grades K through 12. Standards are organized K–4, 5–8, and 9–12. Knowledge of these standards is essential for all teachers, as they are the nationally recommended framework for curriculum design and instruction for all grade levels.

KEYSTONE WORKS

Chapman, Laura. *Approaches to Art in Education*. Harcourt Brace, 1978. 444 p. ISBN 0-15-502896-0 (hardcover).

Visual Arts

This classic art education text serves to broaden the scope of art teaching in elementary and junior high schools. Insisting that art is essential rather than supplementary to education, the author suggests a three-part curriculum framework by which children can heighten personal artistic expression and response, increase their awareness of artistic heritage, and develop an understanding of the relationship of art to society. The author offers many lesson ideas for the teaching of art at the elementary level.

Hurwitz, Al, and Michael Day. *Children and Their Art: Methods for the Elementary School.* Harcourt Brace, 1991. 596 p. ISBN 0-15-507295-1 (hardcover).

The title refers not only to what children create and express with art media, but also to their understanding from the broader perspectives of art history, art criticism, and aesthetics. Suggested activities for a broad-based art education are presented at levels appropriate for children's abilities. Attention is given to the needs of gifted children and of handicapped and special learners.

Lowenfeld, Viktor, and W. Lambert Brittain. *Creative and Mental Growth.* Macmillan, 1987. 510 p. ISBN 0-02-372110-3 (hardcover).

This book focuses primarily upon developmental changes in how children draw and paint, while it aims at an understanding of how cognitive development relates to creative and artistic expression. The making of products is not the concern of this book, but rather the process of art and the value of these experiences to children's learning. Now in its eighth edition, this book is one of the classic texts for art education.

AESTHETICS

Eaton, Marcia Muelder. *Basic Issues in Aesthetics.* Wadsworth Publishing, 1988. 154 p. ISBN 0-534-08256-4 (paper).

The purpose of this book is to introduce teachers to the branch of contemporary philosophy that deals with the nature and value of aesthetic objects. The author's prose is free of jargon, which makes this book very accessible to novices in the field of aesthetics. The text is organized around components of an aesthetic situation: objects, artists, audience, critics, and social context. The book should provide insight into the relationship between art and the quality of life.

Lankford, E. Louis. *Aesthetics: Issues and Inquiry.* National Art Education Association, 1992. 106 p. ISBN 0-937652-60-1 (paper).

The author sets out in this book to familiarize the reader with the major topics and issues in aesthetics, thus creating a handbook for teachers wishing to incorporate aesthetics in their instructional program. This book moves from a comprehensive look at what aesthetics is to a brief view of human development in relation to art learning and then on to a complete system for introducing aesthetics to elementary students. The book aims to address the practical concerns of the classroom educator who is interested in moving students progressively toward more complex forms of aesthetic inquiry.

Moore, Ronald, ed. *Aesthetics for Young People.* National Art Education Association, 1995. 127 p. ISBN 0-937652-73-3 (hardcover).

This book, a key resource for any staff development program, provides explicit instructional strategies and learning outcomes for the teaching of aesthetics in the elementary classroom. A major purpose of the book is to dispel the myth that aesthetics is too hard for kids or too esoteric for the K–12 art curriculum. The articles provide many examples of classroom techniques that illustrate how aesthetics can be approachable, interesting, and worthwhile for all children.

Parsons, Michael, and H. Gene Blocker. *Aesthetics and Education.* University of Illinois Press, 1993. 186 p. ISBN 0-252-01988-1 (hardcover); 0-252-06293-0 (paper).

The authors have written this book to help educators integrate aesthetics into the study of art in the school curriculum at all levels. The authors introduce some of the philosophical problems and questions in art, encouraging teachers to form a personal outlook on these issues. The last chapter, which is devoted to aesthetics in the classroom, suggests appropriate content of aesthetics for students of art at different age levels.

ART CRITICISM

Barrett, Terry. *Criticizing Art: Understanding the Contemporary.* Mayfield Publishing, 1994. 200 p. ISBN 1-55934-147-5 (paper).

The primary purpose of this book is to help teachers understand the world of contemporary art. It is written to enable readers to talk about art better than they now can. Teachers will find this book very useful when planning experiences for children to write and talk about art. The book is based on the assumption that art criticism is a careful and engaging argumentation that furthers dialogue about art and life.

Cromer, Jim. *History, Theory and Practice of Art Criticism in Art Education.* National Art Education Association, 1990. 93 p. ISBN 0-937652-50-4 (paper).

This work traces the history and development of art criticism from ancient Greek civilization to the present time, with sample instructional units relating art criticism, art history, and art production.

Visual Arts

ART HISTORY

Addis, Stephen, and Mary Erickson. *Art History and Education.* University of Illinois Press, 1993. 220 p. ISBN 0-252-01970-9 (hardcover); 0-252-06273-6 (paper).

This book asks and answers three simple questions: Why should we study and teach art history? Is it necessary or useful for the education of our children? Why not leave this area of the curriculum to the `experts'? The answers to these questions are especially helpful in demonstrating how art history can be incorporated into the education of children. Curriculum guidelines and lesson plans for the teaching of art history at all levels are offered.

Fitzpatrick, Virginia L. *Art History: A Contextual Inquiry Course.* National Art Education Association, 1992. 78 p. ISBN 0-937652-59-8 (paper).

The author addresses topics such as methods of historical inquiry, the history of instruction in art history, research on the teaching of art history, and current practices and recommendations. The book includes suggested activities for five levels of child development from preschool to high school, with sample lessons for all levels. Guidelines for correlating and integrating art history with other subjects and with other art areas are provided along with suggestions for implementing an art history component in the school curriculum.

ART STUDIO

Brown, Maurice, and Diana Korzenik. *Art Making and Education.* University of Illinois Press, 1993. 208 p. ISBN 0-252-02007-3 (hardcover); 0-252-06312-0 (paper).

This is not a "how-to-do-art" book, but it is essential reading for teachers who involve students in the art making process. Because the authors discuss the role of art making in the curriculum, with particular emphasis on what the process of making art entails, the book might change the way teachers approach the teaching of art. Readers gain insight into the real significance and importance of experiences with studio art materials.

Schuman, Jo Miles. *Art from Many Hands: Multicultural Art Projects.* Davis Publications, 1981. 251 p. ISBN 0-87192-150-2 (paper).

From *pysanky* (Ukrainian Easter Eggs) to African weaving and batik, this book covers basic craft processes adaptable to a wide age group from elementary through middle school. Step-by-step instructions with numerous illustrations serve to provide teachers with the necessary information to guide students in creative art expression and understanding of diverse cultural heritages.

Topal, Cathy Weisman. *Children and Painting.* Davis Publications, 1992. 160 p. ISBN 0-87192-241-X (hardcover).

The content of this book includes approaches to painting, subjects for painting, alternative approaches and aesthetics, thinking about the painting process, and supply needs. Strategies for teaching painting through the themes that excite children as well as the elements of design are provided along with step-by-step techniques. Over forty painting activities are coordinated with a typical elementary curriculum.

———. *Children, Clay and Sculpture.* Davis Publications, 1983. 128 p. ISBN 0-87192-145-6 (hardcover).

Traditional hand building techniques for creating basic sculptural forms, reliefs, animals, heads, faces, and figures are presented to help children explore and appreciate three-dimensional art. Suggestions for individual and group activities adaptable for a single class or a series of lessons are provided, along with practical suggestions for student and teacher evaluations, exploratory exercises, and building the art vocabulary. Historical and contemporary examples of sculpture from many cultures are represented.

CONTENT REFERENCE

Hobbs, Jack, and Richard Salome. *The Visual Experience: Teacher's Edition.* Davis Publications, 1995. 330 p. ISBN 0-87192-291-6 (hardcover).

Designed as a teacher's guide for a high school textbook, this book provides teachers at any level with the basic information needed to help their students see art, artists, and the world around them with an informed perspective. It is a useful "one source" reference for elementary teachers for a survey of global art history, exercises and methods for teaching art criticism and aesthetics, and clear explanations of art materials and processes that can be adapted to the needs of the elementary student.

Marantz, Kenneth, Pat Howard, Melissa Wilson, Jeff Shaw, Mary Hammond, and Myrna Packard. *The Picturebook: Source and Resource for Art Education.* National Art Education Association, 1994. 83 p. ISBN 0-937652-68-7 (paper).

The combined efforts of six authors, telling their stories in five chapters, serve to provide the reader with many examples of the use of the picturebook as a resource for teaching art and integrated concepts in the elementary classroom. The annotated bibliographies of children's picturebooks and pop-up-books are especially helpful for teachers.

Visual Arts

CURRICULUM

Armstrong, Carmen L. *Designing Assessment in Art.* National Art Education Association, 1994. 216 p. ISBN 0-937652-71-7 (hardcover).

An in-depth study of art assessment, this book integrates assessment of student learning with curriculum and art instruction. The author provides multiple examples, sample formats, and suggestions for implementation. She presents and discusses what can be assessed in art; various kinds of assessment instruments; alternatives to traditional assessment; and administering, scoring and reporting results. Various means of observing and recording evidence of student art learning are presented.

Chapman, Laura H. *Adventures in Art, Teacher's Edition.* Davis Publications, 1994. 6 vols. *Level 1.* ISBN 0-87192-257-6 (spiral); *Level 2.* ISBN 0-87192-258-4 (spiral); *Level 3.* ISBN 0-87192-259-2 (spiral); *Level 4.* ISBN 087192-260-6 (spiral); *Level 5.* ISBN 0-87192-261-4 (spiral); *Level 6.* ISBN 0-87192-262-2 (spiral).

Designed as teacher's guides for a student textbook series, these wraparound teacher's editions will stand alone as valuable resources and reference for elementary teachers. In each of the grade-level editions for grades 1 through 6, sixty art lessons are divided into four instructional units. Creative expressions, art history, art criticism, and aesthetic perception are reinforced with thoughtful questions, multicultural comparisons, art vocabulary, and colored reproductions. Comprehensively organized for management ease, the wraparound teacher's editions include overviews of lesson preparation, teaching techniques, evaluations, enrichments, and extensions into other disciplines and cultures.

Cornia, Ivan, Charles Stubbs, and Nathan Winter. *Art is Elementary.* Gibbs Smith, 1994. 400 p. ISBN 0-87905-138-8 (hardcover).

Subtitled "Teaching Visual Thinking Through Art Concepts," this book offers a total art program for preschool through middle school in a single manual. Concepts such as shape, color, texture, etc., are developed progressively with other concepts from one level to the next. Lists of common art projects that can be used as devices for teaching a specific concept make this book a useful resource for the classroom teacher. Steps for evaluation are also included.

Henley, David R. *Exceptional Children/Exceptional Art: Teaching Art to Special Needs.* Davis Publications, 1992. 288 p. ISBN 0-87192-238-X (hardcover).

This book offers techniques for adapting studio experiences to the teaching of exceptional children and makes suggestions for structuring the classroom to integrate students with special needs into the instructional environment. The book's content includes a review of special needs, dealing with behavior, structuring the art process, assessment, child development, and a chapter on each art medium.

Herberholz, Barbara, and Lee Hanson. *Early Childhood Art*. 5th ed. Brown and Benchmark, 1995. 321 p. ISBN 0-697-12524-6 (paper).

The authors provide a well-balanced presentation of theoretical and practical information grounded in the four content areas of art production, aesthetics, art criticism, and art history. Developmentally appropriate, innovative, and enriching art activities, in both responding to art and making art, are presented for teachers, with substantive references to methodology and resources.

London, Peter, ed. *Exemplary Art Education Curricula: A Guide to Guides*. National Art Education Association, 1994. 128 p. ISBN 0-937652-72-5 (hardcover).

Prepared by a task force of art educators, this book presents an in-depth review of art curriculum guides written for K–12. The book includes twenty-six criteria for exemplary art curriculum guides and commentary on current needs in art curricula. The major portion of the book consists of sample pages from the guides with critical discussion of their content, format, and visual impact.

Wachowiak, Frank, and Robert Clements. *Emphasis Art: A Qualitative Art Program for Elementary and Middle Schools*. 5th ed. HarperCollins, 1993. 296 p. ISBN 0-06-500603-8 (hardcover).

The author offers a lucid description of a proven, dynamic program for teachers who seek continuing challenges, new techniques, and classroom-tested art projects for their instructional repertoire. Projects based on universal art principles with lesson objectives in design and composition, art history, art criticism, and aesthetics are presented along with evaluation procedures in a developmentally sequenced curriculum.

POLICY

The Getty Center for Education in the Arts. *Beyond Creating: The Place for Art in America's Schools*. The Getty Center for Education in the Arts, 1985 (paper).

An important, ground-breaking report on art education, this volume serves to inform educators, school policy makers, and parents of the issues that need to be addressed in order to effect lasting change in the content and quality of visual arts education.

Levi, Albert W., and Ralph A. Smith. *Art Education: A Critical Necessity.* University of Illinois Press, 1991. 254 p. ISBN 0-252-06185-3 (paper).

The authors provide a philosophical rationale for the idea of discipline-based art education that features a humanities-based interpretation of teaching and learning in the visual arts. They discuss topics ranging over both the public and private aspects of art, the disciplines of artistic creation, art history, art criticism, and aesthetics.

Smith, Ralph A., ed. *Discipline-based Art Education: Origins, Meanings, and Development.* University of Illinois Press, 1987. 267 p. ISBN 0-252-06085-7 (paper).

The first four articles in this collection chronicle the antecedents of discipline-based art education. The central article presents a framework for defining discipline-based art education. Another set of four articles, written by an art critic, an art historian, an artist, and an aesthetician, present the basic tenets of each of the disciplines and the relationships that exist among them. The final piece, written by a developmental psychologist, argues for the need to balance views of universal child development with an understanding of individual development.

THEORY

Johnson, Andra, ed. *Art Education: Elementary.* National Art Education Association, 1992. 222 p. ISBN 0-937652-61-X (paper).

This anthology on art education for grades K–6 addresses the needs of today's elementary art education. It's practical, confronting real problems; it's visionary, pointing to relevant solutions; and it's daring, offering suggestions for change and restructuring. Chapter topics include the integration of students experiencing disabilities, the movement toward multiculturalism, improving public relations within the school system, aesthetics, evaluating student progress, and art criticism.

JOURNALS

Arts and Activities. Publisher's Development Corporation. ISSN 0004-3931.

A monthly (except July and August) magazine covering art education at levels from preschool through college, this is written for educators and therapists engaged in arts and crafts education and training. Articles range from how-to-do classroom activities to opinions on art education practices. Each issue includes a clip-and-save centerfold art reproduction.

School Arts. Davis Publications. ISSN 0036-6463.

Published monthly, September to May, this journal serves professional art and classroom teachers, K–12. Written by and for teachers, the articles range from ready-to-use classroom tested activities to high-interest opinion features. Lesson plans, instructional strategies and techniques, and other features support and expand the monthly theme. The magazine includes many pull-out-and-use pages, including a large full-color art reproduction centerfold, complete with necessary information to build an entire unit.

MEMBERSHIPS

National Art Education Association
1916 Association Drive
Reston, Virginia 22091-1950

Phone: (703) 860-8000
Fax: (703) 860-2960

The national organization for art educators is the National Art Education Association. The mission of NAEA is to further art education through professional development, service, advancement of knowledge, and leadership. Membership includes subscriptions to *Art Education* and *NAEA News.*

12

Theatre

Consultant: Kim A. Wheetley
University of Tennessee
Chattanooga, Tennessee

Mr. Wheetley is Director of the Southeast Institute for Education in Theatre at the University of Tennessee at Chattanooga, which provides an inservice training program in discipline-based theatre education for K–12 teachers and administrators. He previously served for ten years as theatre specialist at the Texas Education Agency. He holds a B.F.A. from the University of Texas at Austin and an M.A. from Schiller College in Berlin, West Germany, and has enjoyed a variety of teaching experiences, including teaching at high schools in California and Texas. He also taught at the International School in Bangkok, Thailand, as well as at Allan Hancock College in Santa Maria, California, and the University of Texas at Austin. Mr. Wheetley worked for several seasons in repertory theatre at the Pacific Conservatory of the Performing Arts in Santa Maria.

He chaired a national task force that developed a comprehensive *Model Drama/Theatre Curriculum,* has written numerous theatre curriculum documents, and has served as a consultant for several states engaged in developing theatre education programs. Mr. Wheetley was on the Coordinating Council for the Consortium of National Arts Education Association and served as a member of the writing team for the new *National Theatre Education Standards.*

Mr. Wheetley is the Immediate Past–President of the American Alliance for Theatre and Education and a past president of the Texas Educational Theatre Association. He was selected by the Citizen Ambassador Program of People to People International to lead a delegation of theatre educators on a cultural visit to the People's Republic of China in 1993.

DOCUMENTS/GUIDELINES/STANDARDS

American Alliance for Theatre and Education. *A Model Drama/Theatre Curriculum: Philosophy, Goals and Objectives.* Anchorage Press, 1987. 106 p. ISBN 0-87602-027-9 (paper).

This model curriculum is designed to provide guidance for developing curricular and co-curricular theatre programs based upon the individual needs of learners. It presents a rationale for educating students of all ages in the discipline of theatre, and details goals and objectives upon which to build a series of sequential learning experiences. The goals; the component skills, attitudes, and understandings; the broad objectives; and numerous resulting student expectancies are organized developmentally for grades K–12 and presented in chart form. Also included are definitions of terminology and a bibliography.

•Consortium of National Arts Education Associations. *National Standards for Arts Education: What Every Young American Should Know and Be Able to Do in the Arts.* Music Educators National Conference, 1994. 148 p. ISBN 1-56545-036-1 (paper).

The National Standards for Arts Education present a rationale and explanation of arts education, affirming that a future worth having depends on being able to construct a vital relationship with the arts, and that doing so, as with any subject, is a matter of discipline and study. These voluntary guidelines and benchmarks, which were developed by educators from professional associations in arts education, represent a consensus view of educators and administrators, leaders in government and the private sector, and lay persons from around the country about what constitutes a good education in the arts. The Standards address learning in three states—K–4, 5–8, and 9–12—across four arts disciplines: dance, music, theatre, and the visual arts. Both content standards (what students should know) and achievement standards (what students should be able to do) are provided in narrative and chart form.

ANTHOLOGIES

Harris, Aurand. *Six Plays for Children by Aurand Harris.* Edited by Coleman A. Jennings. The University of Texas Press, 1986. 377 p. ISBN 0-292-77568-7 (paper).

The plays of Aurand Harris, one of America's most produced children's theatre playwrights, represent a variety of dramatic form. Included in the collection are

Androcles and the Lion, Rags to Riches, Punch and Judy, Steal Away Home, Peck's Bad Boy, and *Yankee Doodle.* Also included is an analysis of theme, plot, character, dialogue, song, and spectacle as well as a biographical study of the playwright.

Jennings, Coleman A., and Aurand Harris, eds. *Plays Children Love, Vol. II.* St. Martin's Press, 1988. 560 p. ISBN 0-312-01490-2 (hardcover); 0-312-07973-7 (paper).

The twenty plays and excerpts in this work, presented in two sections as "Plays for Adult Performers" and "Plays for Children to Perform," were published between 1945 and 1986 and represent a range of styles. Included are the following plays: *Charlotte's Web, The Wizard of Oz, Treasure Island, The Best Christmas Pageant Ever, Jim Thorpe All American, The Wind in the Willows, Just So Stories, Plays From African Folktales, The Chinese Cinderella, Story Theatre, Who Laughs Last?, Golliwhoppers,* and *The Forgotten Door.* An introduction details the special needs of producing plays for children and provides instructions for helping children get the most out of producing plays themselves.

———, and Gretta Berghammer, eds. *Theatre For Youth: Twelve Plays With Mature Themes.* The University of Texas Press, 1986. 512 p. ISBN 0-292-78081-8 (hardcover); 0-292-78085-0 (paper).

These twelve plays cover a range of topics generally considered taboo for younger audiences: problems of aging, death and dying, conformity, sexuality, and moral judgment. The plays were chosen for their professional integrity, the delicacy with which they handle their subject matter, and their respect for their intended audience. Included are: *The Honorable Urashima Taro, Courage, The Odyssey, Noodle Doodle Box, The Arkansas Bear, The Boy Who Stole the Stars, The Boy Who Talked to Whales, My Days as a Youngling—John Jacob Niles, The Code Breaker, Broken Heart—Three Tales of Sorrow, Doors,* and *The Martian Chronicles.* Also included are introduction and summary paragraphs for each script, and an annotated list of plays for further reading or viewing.

White, Melvin R. *Mel White's Readers Theatre Anthology: 28 All-Occasion Readings for Storytellers.* Meriwether Publishing, 1993. 352 p. ISBN 0-916260-86-0 (paper).

A variety of stories by classical and contemporary writers, journalists, and playwrights have been adapted for reader's theatre performance. The twenty-eight selections are divided into six categories: comedy, mystery, Christmas specials, folklore, children's classics, and the human spirit. Sample titles include *The Tooth Fairy Who Didn't Have Any Teeth, The Taming of the Shrew, The Wind in the Willows,* and *Where Have All the Flowers Gone?* There is also a section defining reader's theatre as a performance art.

Zeder, Suzan. *Wish in One Hand, Spit in the Other: A Collection of Plays by Suzan Zeder.* Edited by Susan Pearson-Davis. Anchorage Press, 1990. 600 p. ISBN 0-87602-029-5 (hardcover).

Suzan Zeder's award-winning plays for young people range from comedy to drama, realism to fantasy, uniquely blending styles and themes. This collection of her first works for the stage includes *Wiley and the Hairy Man, The Play Called Noah's Flood, Step on a Crack, Ozma of Oz, Doors, Mother Hicks, In a Room Somewhere,* and *The Death and Life of Sherlock Holmes.* Each play is accompanied by an introduction and critical essay.

CREATIVE DRAMA

Bissinger, Kristen, and Nancy Renfro. *Leap Into Learning! Teaching Curriculum Through Creative Dramatics and Dance.* Nancy Renfro Studios, 1990. 201 p. ISBN 0-931044-18-9 (paper).

A variety of activities, games, and exercises illustrate how to interrelate creative drama and movement with instruction in language arts, social studies, science, and math. Teaching tips address control mechanisms, movement, pantomime, voice, props, and characterization.

Cottrell, June. *Creative Drama in the Classroom, Grades 1–3.* National Textbook Company, 1987. 242 p. ISBN 0-8442-5496-7 (hardcover).

This book's theoretical background, practical ideas, and examples of creative drama experiences are based on child development theory and pedagogical practices. Teaching goals and objectives, sample lesson plans, and assessment strategies are organized to parallel children's physical, cognitive, emotional, and aesthetic development. Topics include creative drama as an educational tool, the teacher as drama leader, creative drama skills, integrating drama with content areas, mass entertainment, and writing unit and lesson plans. Appendices suggest resource books and anthologies.

———. *Creative Drama in the Classroom, Grades 4–6.* National Textbook Company, 1987. 277 p. ISBN 0-8442-5497-5 (hardcover).

This companion volume to the previously noted text is designed for use with students in grades 4–6.

Cranston, Jerneral. *Transformations Through Drama: A Teacher's Guide to Educational Drama, Grades K–8.* University Press of America, 1991. 335 p. ISBN 0-8191-7994-9 (paper).

Theatre

Focusing on affective and psychomotor learning, this book addresses topics that include learning and the brain, creating dramas, the teacher in role, questioning, drama elements, cooperative learning, and writing. Lesson plans for twenty-one dramas consider the historical and social problems of war, homelessness, oppression, pollution, and addiction. There is also an appendix of music, a bibliography, and a glossary.

Heinig, Ruth Beall. *Creative Drama for the Classroom Teacher.* 4th ed. Prentice-Hall, 1993. 312 p. ISBN 0-13-189663-6 (hardcover).

This classic guide emphasizes children's literature as the basis for classroom drama. Practical, progressive techniques for learning and teaching creative drama focus on teaching methods and materials rather than theories or history. Step-by-step explanations are provided for a variety of activities that gradually become more challenging for both students and instructors. Topics include basics of creative drama instruction, working in groups, narrative pantomime, verbal activities, improvisation, story dramatization, leader-in-role and role drama, and planning drama lessons. There is also an anthology of stories, poetry, and books for dramatization.

———. *Creative Drama Resource Book for Grades K–3.* Prentice-Hall, 1993. 271 p. ISBN 0-13-189-3254 (hardcover).

This user-friendly resource guide presents a clear overview and practice guidelines for creative drama. There is an abundance of theatre games, activities for learning self-control, narrative pantomime activities, verbal activities and improvisations, circle and segmented stories for dramatization, ideas for puppetry and masks, information about theatre conventions and etiquette, ideas for encouraging creative work, and suggestions for extended lesson planning. Sample lesson plans and annotated bibliographies of children's literature are interspersed throughout the text.

———. *Creative Drama Resource Book for Grades 4–6.* Prentice-Hall, 1987. 323 p. ISBN 0-13-189333-5 (hardcover).

This companion volume to the previously noted text is designed for use with students in grades 4–6.

———. *Improvisation With Favorite Tales: Integrating Drama Into the Reading/Writing Classroom.* Heinemann, 1992. 136 p. ISBN 0-435-08609-X (paper).

Basic drama exercises and methods of teaching are presented for nineteen traditional tales. Numerous activities extend beyond the basic story line to create opportunities for exploring the characters, plot lines, and themes. The activities are grouped into categories of pantomime and verbal modes, and then further grouped according to solo, paired, and group playing. A final set of extension activities for each tale focuses on writing, art, and music. The stories include: *The*

Three Bears, The Three Billy Goats Gruff, The Three Little Pigs, Little Red Riding Hood, The Gingerbread Boy, Hansel and Gretel, Cinderella, Jack and the Beanstalk, Rumpelstiltskin, The Frog Prince, King Midas, Snow White, Sleeping Beauty, Beauty and the Beast, Fool of the World and The Flying Ship, The Jolly Tailor Who Became King, The Nightingale, The Pied Piper of Hamelin, and *The Search for Thor's Hammer.*

Kase-Polisini, Judith. *The Creative Drama Book: Three Approaches.* Anchorage Press, 1989. 233 p. ISBN 0-87602-028-7 (hardcover).

What is creative drama? How does it work? Why does it work? The fundamentals and basic procedures of teaching improvisational drama are followed by an introduction to three major approaches: Winifred Ward's playmaking approach, the theatre games method as developed by Viola Spolin, and Dorothy Heathcot's educational drama techniques. Descriptions of the philosophy and techniques for each approach and examples of typical lessons are complemented by an analysis of the advantages and disadvantages of each method. The relationship between the creative process and the creative drama process is also examined.

McCaslin, Nellie. *Creative Drama in the Classroom.* 5th ed. Longman, 1990. 520 p. ISBN 0-8013-0380-X (hardcover); 0-88734-604-9 (paper).

This classic guide to initiating dramatic activities in the classroom covers how to plan simple activities and adapt material for use in theatre and language arts programs. Creative drama is first presented as an art and then as a tool for teaching in other subject areas. Topics include imagination, play, movement and pantomime, improvisation, puppetry and maskmaking, dramatic structure, building plays from stories and other sources, speech-related activities, working with the special child, sharing work with an audience, and attending theatre. Appendices include an overview of student evaluation, sample lessons, and a comprehensive annotated bibliography.

———. *Creative Drama in the Intermediate Grades.* Longman, 1987. 346 p. ISBN 0-88734-605-7 (paper).

This companion volume to the following text is designed for use with students in grades 4–6.

———. *Creative Drama in the Primary Grades.* 6th ed. Addison-Wesley, 1996. 276 p. ISBN 0-8013-1585-9 (paper).

Methods and theories of teaching creative drama are followed by numerous lessons that include objectives, step-by-step instructions, and follow-up questions. Topics include imagination, movement, mime, improvisation, story dramatization, and applications with poetry, puppetry, and masks. There are also chapters on working with the special child, the theatre-viewing experience for young audiences, and pupil evaluation. A glossary and annotated bibliography are included.

Neelands, Jonothan. *Structuring Drama Work: A Handbook of Available Forms in Theatre and Drama.* Edited by Tony Goode. Cambridge University Press, 1990. 84 p. ISBN 0-521-37635-1 (paper).

A range of theatrical conventions to initiate, focus, and develop dramatic activities are presented as an active inquiry process for learning about and through theatre. A sampling of the conventions includes sound tracking, role-on-the-wall, simulations, mantle of the expert, hot-seating, montage, role-reversal, ritual, and thought tracking. A description of each convention is supported by references to cultural connections, learning opportunities, and examples of its use.

Salisbury-Wills, Barbara. *Theatre Arts in the Elementary Classroom, Volume One: Kindergarten Through Grade Three.* 2nd ed. Anchorage Press, 1995. 326 p. ISBN 0-87602-024-4 (hardcover).

Open-ended lesson plans for specific grade levels include concepts, objectives, materials, procedures, and related explanatory comments. There are activities for getting started and for expressively using the body and voice, along with a variety of creative drama lessons. Scope and sequence charts show the sequential development of dramatic concepts from kindergarten through grade six. A special chapter deals with using drama as an instructional technique in other subject areas and with special populations. Detailed evaluation strategies and criteria checklists are provided, along with an appendix of children's literature representing Africa, Asia, Latin America, and Native America.

———. *Theatre Arts in the Elementary Classroom, Volume Two: Fourth Grade Through Sixth Grade.* 2nd ed. Anchorage Press, 1995. 392 p. ISBN 0-87602-025-2 (hardcover).

This companion volume to the previously noted text is designed for use with students in grades 4–6.

Schwartz, Dorothy, and Dorothy Aldrich, eds. *Give Them Roots . . . and Wings! A Guide to Drama in the Elementary Grades.* 2nd ed. Anchorage Press, 1985. 223 p. ISBN 0-87602-022-8 (paper).

The introductory chapters of this series of lessons created by master teachers identify goals and objectives of drama in elementary education, explain the relation of creative drama to other disciplines, illustrate daily processes and procedures, and suggest practical evaluation techniques. Primary and intermediate lessons cover the various components of drama: movement and pantomime, senses and feelings, characterization, vocalization, and dramatic form. The lessons may be used as they are or serve as models in the preparation of similar activities. A glossary and annotated bibliography are included.

Stewig, John Warren, and Carol Buege. *Dramatizing Literature in Whole Language Classrooms.* 2nd ed. Teachers College Press, 1994. 224 p. ISBN 0-80773-307-5 (paper).

Focusing on the role that drama plays in the development of children's language skills, the text demonstrates how improvised drama helps children attain important social, intellectual, and emotional goals. Topics include basic concepts and terminology, initiating a program, the leader's role, motivating techniques, dealing with problems, evaluating sessions, and linking drama to other subjects. A creative drama sequence for kindergarten and primary grades is outlined with suggested poems, stories, and non-story motivations for dramas.

Swartz, Larry. *Drama Themes: A Practical Guide for Teaching Drama.* Heinemann, 1988. 128 p. ISBN 0-435-08509-3 (paper).

Based on the premise that teachers can structure drama activities around themes that arise from the interests of the students, curriculum guidelines, and literature, practical lessons are arranged in ten thematic units: humor, mystery, fantasy, relationships, animals, folklore, the community, the past, the future, and multiculturalism. Each theme includes goals, games, dramatic activities, improvisations, and extensions.

Tarlington, Carole, and Patrick Verriour. *Role Drama: A Teacher's Handbook.* Heinemann, 1991. 128 p. ISBN 0-435-08599-9 (paper).

Role drama is presented as a powerful mode of learning across the curriculum, empowering students to appreciate moral dilemmas common to everyone, to consider the consequences of their actions, and to take responsibility for their decisions. Guidelines for planning and detailed descriptions of successful drama experiences illustrate how to set up imagined situations which students and teachers can enter together, in role, to explore events, issues, and relationships. The role dramas, which spring from literature, social studies, family life, and environmental issues, encourage students to work cooperatively questioning assumptions, exchanging ideas, and solving problems.

PLAYWRITING

Chapman, Gerald. *Teaching Young Playwrights.* Edited and developed by Lisa A. Barnett. Heinemann, 1991. 129 p. ISBN 0-435-08212-4 (paper).
Role-playing and improvisation are presented as the basis for actively engaging students in the playwriting process. Activities are grouped under four headings: reading, both aloud and silently; talking, in discussion and in improvisation; writing, in-

dividually and collaboratively; and analyzing, as individuals and as groups. There is also information about dramatic action, point of view, characterization, the form of playwriting, topic choice, and evaluation and rewriting.

Cooper, Patsy. *When Stories Come to School: Telling, Writing, and Performing Stories in the Early Childhood Classroom.* Teachers & Writers Collaborative, 1993. 144 p. ISBN 0-915924-77-3 (paper).

By placing stories at the center of the early childhood curriculum, this book suggests a natural way to help preschool and kindergarten children begin to read and write. This personal narrative discusses the pedagogical and developmental roles that stories can play and provides a practical guide to having children tell their own stories and perform them with their classmates. Also available is a companion videotape, *The Classroom Lives of Young Readers, Writers, and Actors,* showing teachers and children engaged in the creative activities described in the book.

Sklar, Daniel Judah. *Playmaking: Children Writing and Performing Their Own Plays.* Teachers & Writers Collaborative, 1991. 184 p. ISBN 0-915924-34-X (hardcover); 0-915924-35-8 (paper).

This account of a fifth grade class learning to write, direct, and perform their own plays is not only a manual for using creative drama in the classroom, but also a guide to developing plays and children's imaginations. Each lesson plan includes a discussion between the classroom teacher and the artist-in-residence who conducts the lesson, and the artist's reflections on how the lesson and discussion fit into a larger picture. There is also a glossary of theatre terms and an annotated bibliography.

PUPPETRY AND MASKS

Freericks, Mary, and Joyce Segal. *Creative Puppetry in the Classroom.* New Plays Books, 1979. 144 p. ISBN 0-932720-15-3 (paper).

Techniques for creating original student productions are accompanied by suggestions for using puppetry to teach creative writing, social studies, nutrition, science, and mathematics. Included are detailed instructions and diagrams for making imaginative puppets out of inexpensive materials, illustrated staging and production tips, supply lists, and a bibliography.

Hunt, Tamara, and Nancy Renfro. *Celebrate: Holidays, Puppets and Creative Drama.* Nancy Renfro Studios, 1987. 208 p. ISBN 0-931044-09-X (paper).

Activities for storytelling and puppetry, as well as creative drama, are suggested for Christian and Jewish holidays and various ethnic holidays from around the world. Patterns are provided for finger puppets, story aprons, hand and string puppets, and box theatres. Also included are stories and poems to act out and recommended related children's literature.

———. *Puppetry and Early Childhood Education.* Nancy Renfro Studios, 1982. 264 p. ISBN 0-931044-04-9 (paper).

With an emphasis on process rather than product, creative ideas for making simple and inexpensive puppets are combined with numerous suggestions for using them throughout the preschool curriculum. There are full-size patterns, illustrations, and photographs.

Nobleman, Roberta. *Mime and Masks.* New Plays Books, 1979. 152 p. ISBN 0-932720-46-3 (paper).

An introduction to mime and pantomime is followed by suggestions for creating occupational, character, animal, and abstract mimes. The introduction to mask work is accompanied by ideas for working with character masks, monster masks, animal masks, abstract masks, and body masks, as well as the classic masks of clowns and the Commedia dell'Arte. There are also scenarios and suggestions for performing mime plays.

VanSchuyver, Jan. *Storytelling Made Easy With Puppets.* Oryx Press, 1993. 147 p. ISBN 0-89774-732-1 (paper).

Step-by-step instructions for using puppets with literature for children ages two to eight are enhanced with scripts, follow-up activities to puppet presentations, and solutions to common problems. Related children's literature is arranged by theme, and there is a bibliography of puppetry books, organizations, and sources for purchasing puppets.

SPECIAL POPULATIONS

Bailey, Sally D. *Wings to Fly: Bringing Theatre Arts to Students with Special Needs.* Woodbine House, 1993. 352 p. ISBN 0-933149-58-1 (paper).

Beginning with an overview of physical and developmental disabilities including Down's syndrome, Tourette syndrome, blindness, cerebral palsy, and attention deficit, the text goes on to suggest specific adaptations for improvisational acting, creative drama, puppetry, and script development. Practical issues such as mainstreaming, behavior management, requirements of a physical space, working with teaching personnel, and ways to use drama as a tool to teach other subjects are also addressed.

STORYTELLING

Barton, Bob, and David Booth. *Stories in the Classroom: Storytelling, Reading Aloud and Roleplaying With Children.* Heinemann, 1990. 194 p. ISBN 0-435-08527-1 (paper).

Folktales, picture books, story poems, and novels are used to illustrate how to find, choose, and use stories to build classroom communities of storytellers. Topics include the power of story, the oral tradition, a story inventory, and working with stories. A variety of follow-up activities include basic story talk, retellings, readings of similar stories, writing new versions and entirely original stories, thematic art projects, and dramatizations.

Cassady, Marsh. *Creating Stories for Storytelling.* Resource Publications, 1991. 157 p. ISBN 0-89390-205-5 (paper).

Excerpts from twenty stories illustrate ideas for creating the right story for various audiences. Based on the premise that analysis is the key, topics include audience and purpose, discovering and developing ideas, creating characters, plotting the story, exposition and description, narration and point of view, theme and organization, and using the voice and body.

———. *Storytelling Step by Step.* Resource Publications, 1990. 156 p. ISBN 0-89390-183-0 (paper).

Easy-to-follow techniques are presented for choosing, analyzing, adapting, developing, learning, introducing, and delivering stories. There are suggestions for the use of voice, gesture, and props to enhance the storytelling. Twenty-three stories are presented as learning examples, accompanied by activities for finding the theme, changing the point of view, and adapting the stories for different audiences.

Cooper, Pamela J., and Rives Collins. *Look What Happened to Frog: Storytelling in Education.* Gorsuch Scarisbrick Publishers, 1992. 183 p. ISBN 0-89787-345-9 (paper).

This guide explores why people tell stories and why stories are, or should be, at the heart of the teaching/learning process. Topics addressed include the values of storytelling, choosing stories for telling, taming stories for telling, finding your own voice, story dramatization, and profiles of a variety of storytellers. There is an extensive offering of storytelling activities and lessons. Suggested readings and videos for each topic are also included.

TECHNICAL THEATRE

Asher, Jane. *Jane Asher's Costume Book.* Open Chain Publishing, 1993. 142 p. ISBN 0-932086-31-4 (paper).

Ideas and instructions for making over one hundred unusual or humorous costumes, ranging between easy-to-make items constructed from paper to elaborate sewn garments. The book is most useful if approached as a springboard for students' own ideas for costumes that they can make out of found and recycled objects.

Black, Kaye. *Kidvid: Fun-damentals of Video Instruction.* Zephyr Press, 1989. 96 p. ISBN 0-913705-44-6 (paper).

This practical learning program is designed to help young students understand and use video. A general introduction to video and basic equipment is followed by an explanation of terminology and skills, including preproduction planning with scripts and storyboards, lighting, and working with the camera. A sequence of nine lessons begins by inviting students to evaluate commercial television shows and concludes with evaluation of their own video productions. The appendix includes a glossary, sample forms, references, and information on how to prepare instructional material for the classroom.

Concannon, Tom. *Using Media for Creative Teaching.* New Plays, 1979. 76 p. ISBN 0-932720-85-4 (paper).

Classroom-tested projects show how to use cameras, films, tape recorders, and copying machines to capture children's imaginations, develop new skills, and provide new outlets for their creative development. Topics include available media, television and film utilization, storyboarding, learning with sound, and mixed media happenings. There are practical ideas for making overhead projections, slides with and without a camera, hand-drawn films, animated films, videotapes, and inflatable plastic environments.

Miller, James Hull. *Self-Supporting Scenery for Children's Theatre . . . and Grown-ups', Too.* 5th ed. Meriwether Publishing, 1992. 128 p. ISBN 0-916260-15-1 (paper).

Designs, directions, and illustrations are provided for creating compact, economical, flexible free-standing scenery for use in classrooms and on the stage.

THEATRE GAMES

Poulter, Christine. *Playing the Game.* Macmillan, 1987. 150 p. ISBN 0-88734-611-1 (paper).

Simple step-by-step instructions and diagrams are provided for over one hundred theatre games designed to develop observation, imagination, self-confidence, and social and theatrical skills. Exercises are grouped as warm-up games, observation games, encounter games, improvisation games, and word and story games.

Rawlins, George, and Jillian Rich. *Look, Listen and Trust: A Framework for Learning Through Drama.* Macmillan, 1989. 182 p. ISBN 0-88734-618-9 (paper).

This structured progression of theatre games and exercises aims to harness the natural desire to play as a driving force for learning. The objectives of the games and extension activities are to increase personal and social confidence, develop observation and listening skills, and enhance the ability to communicate and work with others.

Spolin, Viola. *Theater Games for the Classroom: A Teacher's Handbook.* Edited by Arthur Morey and Mary Anne Brandt. Northwestern University Press, 1986. 233 p. ISBN 0-8101-4003-9 (hardcover); 0-8101-4004-7 (paper).

Adapted from Viola Spolin's classic *Improvisation for the Theatre,* this collection of theatre games and exercises is intended to help students develop imagination and intuition, become responsive to their fellow players, explore a variety of performance skills, and learn basic rules of storytelling, character analysis, and literary criticism. Concise step-by-step directions are illuminated by sidebar notations and side-coaching examples. Contents include a rationale and process for bringing theatre games into the classroom, a bibliography, and an index cross-referencing games by subject area.

JOURNALS

Stage of the Art. American Alliance for Theatre and Education. ISSN 1080-7268.

This quarterly publication is intended for educators and theatre artists working with and for young people. Regular features include teaching strategies, lesson plans, applied research, resource lists, play and book reviews, columns, and interviews. Topics include advocacy, theatre in education, model programs, national standards, curriculum, computers, puppetry, diversity issues, professional training, and assessment.

Youth Theatre Journal. American Alliance for Theatre and Education. ISSN 0892-9092.

This annual journal is dedicated to advancing the study and practice of theatre for youth as both education and art. Topics include pedagogy, curriculum design, cultural diversity, learning, personal and social development, aesthetic development, artistic interpretation, audience reception theory, and performance theory.

MEMBERSHIPS

American Alliance for Theatre and Education
Department of Theatre
Arizona State University
Box 873411
Tempe, Arizona 85287-3411

Phone: (602) 965-6064

The American Alliance for Theatre and Education is a national association of classroom teachers, theatre teachers, and artists who serve the needs of children and adolescents in grades K–12. The mission of AATE is to promote standards of excellence in theatre and drama/theatre education by providing the theatre artist and the theatre educator with a network of resources and support, a base for advocacy, and access to programs and projects that focus on the importance of drama in the human experience. The major publications of the organization include *Stage of the Art, Youth Theatre Journal,* and *AATE Newsletter.*

13

Health and Physical Education

Consultant: Dr. George M. Graham
Virginia Tech
Blacksburg, Virginia

Dr. George Graham is Professor of Physical Education at Virginia Tech and Executive Director of the U.S. Physical Education Association. He also serves as co-founder and Director of Curriculum and Instruction of the American Master Teacher Program. Earlier in his career he was a physical education teacher and coach in the public schools of California and Oregon.

Among his many honors, Dr. Graham has served as chair of the National Association for Sports and Physical Education Council on Physical Education for Children, and in 1989 he was highlighted in a featured segment on *CBS in the Morning*.

A frequent presenter at meetings across the United States, Dr. Graham has been keynote speaker at over fifteen state, regional, and national conferences and has presented at over one hundred meetings in thirty-four states, Canada, and Italy. He has also served as a consultant in children's physical education and teacher effectiveness in over sixty school districts throughout the United States.

Over fifty of his articles related to teaching physical education and sports skills have appeared in professional journals, and he has authored or co-authored eleven books and monographs.

DOCUMENTS/GUIDELINES/STANDARDS

Council on Physical Education for Children (COPEC). *Developmentally Appropriate Physical Education Practices for Children.* National Association for Sports and Physical Education, 1992. 21 p. (paper).

This document explains developmentally appropriate and inappropriate practices of various aspects of physical education, such as: curriculum, development of movement concepts and motor skills, cognitive development, affective development, concepts of fitness, physical fitness tests, calisthenics, fitness as punishment, assessment, regular involvement for every child, active participation for every child, dance/rhythmical experiences, gymnastics, games, rules governing game play, forming teams, gender directed activities, number of children on a team, competition, success rate, class size, days per week/length of class time, facilities, equipment, PE and recess, and field days.

National Association for Sports and Physical Education Committee. *Outcomes of Quality Physical Education Programs.* National Association for Sports and Physical Education, 1992. 22 p. (paper).

This document is a nationally endorsed guide that gives direction to the development of standards for student achievements. It provides a definition and outcomes of the physically educated person. The document also provides "benchmarks" for every other grade level from K through 12th grade, amplifying the definition of a physically educated person. They provide guidance for *what* students are able to learn and also *when* it is reasonable to expect that students learn particular skills, concepts, or ideas.

GENERAL WORKS

Dauer, Victor P., and Robert P. Pangrazi. *Dynamic Physical Education for Elementary School Children.* 11th ed. Macmillan, 1991. 694 p. ISBN 0-02-327821-8 (hardcover).

This book is a resource for elementary physical education specialists, preservice teachers, and classroom teachers. The text emphasizes physical development and the achievement of personal fitness goals through participation in movement activities. It includes chapters on developing the physical education curriculum, children with disabilities, incorporating physical fitness into the curriculum, and implementing the sports program. There are also lesson plans available to supplement the book.

Graham, George, Shirley Holt/Hale, and Melissa Parker. *Children Moving: A Reflective Approach to Teaching Physical Education.* 3rd ed. Mayfield, 1993. 553 p. ISBN 1-55934-130-0 (hardcover); 1-55934-226-9 (paper).

This text describes the "skill theme approach" to teaching children's physical education. It begins with a section describing the importance of physical education for

Health and Physical Education 155

children and developmentally appropriate physical education. Part 2 focuses on the specific teaching skills (discipline, motivation, feedback) used by effective teachers. Parts 3 and 4 contain activity lesson ideas for teaching the various movement concepts (space awareness, effort and relationships) and skill themes (throwing, kicking, balancing). The book concludes with dreams about the future of physical education for children.

Hopple, Christine J. *Teaching for Outcomes in Elementary Physical Education: A Guide for Curriculum and Assessment.* Human Kinetics, 1994. 232 p. ISBN 0-87322-712-3 (spiral).

Teaching for Outcomes in Elementary Physical Education provides elementary physical education teachers and district supervisors with practical guidelines for the planning, instruction, and assessment of an outcomes-related curriculum. The book includes an introduction, more than one hundred examples of performance assessments (as well as ready-to-use worksheets) and how to use them, and a progression of twenty-three teaching cues for fitness and movement concepts.

Mohnsen, Bonnie. *Using Technology in Physical Education.* Human Kinetics, 1994. 168 p. ISBN 0-87322-661-5 (paper).

This text provides information on how to use current technology to improve the quality of physical education classes. It provides comprehensive information and practical classroom applications for fitness testing equipment, videocassette and laser disk players, camcorders, computers, telecommunication hardware and software, computer-assisted instructional software, and multimedia systems. The text explains how to evaluate and select from the many technological innovations on the market and provides advice and dozens of illustrations to help teachers apply the various technologies to physical education. Throughout, the language is not highly technical.

Pate, Russell, and Richard Hohn, eds. *Health and Fitness Through Physical Education.* Human Kinetics, 1994. 240 p. ISBN 0-87322-490-6 (paper).

In this text, thirty authorities on health-related fitness make a case for restructuring school-based physical education programs to emphasize lifelong fitness and health. Part one explores the foundations of health-related physical education, including such topics as the status of fitness programming in our nation's schools, the relationship between exercise and health, and determinants of physical activity behavior in children. Part two describes specific physical education curriculum methods designed to enhance fitness in children and promote health habits they will carry into adulthood. Part three presents case studies of fitness programs used in physical education at five elementary schools.

Redican, Kerry, Larry Olsen, and Charles Baffi. *Organization of School Health Programs*. 2nd ed. Brown & Benchmark, 1993. ISBN 0-697-13129-7 (hardcover).

This college text is divided into five parts. Part I focuses on the foundations of school health (school and community health councils), Part II on the environment (the physical plant and maintenance), Part III on services (health appraisals, emergency care), and Part IV on instruction (planning and evaluating). Appendix C includes a listing of textbooks for children in grades K–8.

TEACHING

Foster, Emily R., Karyn Hartinger, and Katherine A. Smith. *Fitness Fun*. Human Kinetics, 1992. 112 p. ISBN 0-87322-384-5 (paper).

This text provides eighty-five different ideas for activities and games for children. Each activity has been field tested and is coded according to which fitness component it helps develop: cardiorespiratory fitness, muscular strength, muscular endurance, or flexibility. In addition, each activity lists equipment needed, how to perform the activity, and any additional benefits. Many of the activities also include safety tips, illustrations, and variations. Each activity is labeled for the most appropriate grade level.

Glover, Donald R., and Daniel W. Midura. *Team Building Through Physical Challenges*. Human Kinetics, 1992. 99 p. ISBN 0-87322-359-4 (paper).

Team Building Through Physical Challenges is for physical educators, classroom teachers, and recreation leaders. Outward Bound tasks are presented that require students to work together to achieve a common goal. Cards that explain each challenge to the students are contained in the text; simply copy and laminate them and they are ready to use. The activities require equipment that is readily available—tumbling mats, ropes, balance beam, cage ball, tires, etc.

Kirchner, Glenn, and Graham Fishburne. *Physical Education for Elementary School Children*. 9th ed. Brown & Benchmark, 1995. 620 p. ISBN 0-697-15248-0 (hardcover).

Physical Education for Elementary School Children is designed for the elementary physical education and the classroom teacher. It is divided into seven parts. Part 1 describes the meaning and purpose of physical education. Part 2 discusses Laban's four elements of movement: locomotor, nonlocomotor, manipulative skills, and motor learning. Parts 3 and 4 are concerned with curriculum design. The last three parts of the book contain separate resource sections for games, dance, and gymnastic activities.

Health and Physical Education

Nichols, Beverly. *Moving and Learning: The Elementary School Physical Education Experience.* Times Mirror/Mosby College Publishing, 1990. 580 p. ISBN 0-8016-5801-2 (hardcover).

Moving and Learning is a resource for elementary physical education teachers and preservice physical educators. The book focuses on physical education content, planning, and teaching. It includes individual activities, educational games and team sports lead-ups, dance and rhythmic activities, and extracurricular opportunities.

TEXT, MANUAL, LESSON PLAN PACKAGE

Thomas, Jerry R., Amelia M. Lee, and Katherine Thomas. *Physical Education for Children: Concepts Into Practice.* Human Kinetics, 1988. 256 p. ISBN 0-87322-175-3 (hardcover).

This text is part of a package that includes two other books, *Daily Lesson Plans* and *Instructor's Manual* (see annotations below). *Physical Education for Children: Concepts Into Practice* provides information on how to teach lessons that combine ordered movement experiences to enhance motor development, match activities to the developmental level of each class, measure and improve children's physical fitness, and formulate yearly instruction plans. This text provides the background needed to teach the lessons presented in the *Daily Lesson Plans.*

———. *Physical Education for Children: Daily Lesson Plans.* Human Kinetics, 1989. 1088 p. ISBN 0-87322-176-1 (ringbound).

This notebook is part of a package that includes two other books, *Concepts Into Practice* and *Instructor's Manual* (see annotations above and below). *Physical Education for Children: Daily Lesson Plans* provides teachers with three hundred seventy-six lesson plans, more than one for every day of the school year. The plans are ready to use with activities included. The notebook is divided into four developmental levels, from K through 8, and within each level the lesson plans are presented in sequence of difficulty and subdivided into four activity areas: fitness, games and sports, rhythmic activities, and gymnastics.

———. *Physical Education for Children: Instructor's Manual.* Human Kinetics, 1988. 72 p. ISBN 0-87322-177-X (paper).

This text is part of a package that includes two other books, *Concepts Into Practice* and *Daily Lesson Plans* (see annotations above). The *Instructor's Manual* presents plans for using the two other books in planning and conducting a university physical education course for elementary teachers and physical education specialists. The manual is free if you buy the other two books.

TEXTBOOKS AND ACCOMPANYING VIDEOS

Belka, David E. *Teaching Children Games: Becoming a Master Teacher.* Human Kinetics, 1994. 131 p. ISBN 0-87322-481-7 (paper and companion video).

This work is part of the American Master Teacher Program Content Series. The series is designed to help teachers gain experience and confidence in teaching the five curriculum areas integral to a complete program: movement concepts and motor skills, games, gymnastics, dance, and fitness. *Teaching Children Games* details the how and why of teaching children this content area. It presents twenty-three practical, child-tested examples of game activities that are appropriate for Grades 1 through 6, divided into five game categories: tag, target, net and wall, invasion, and fielding. The companion videotape shows three condensed lessons that provide real-world examples of teaching children games.

Buschner, Craig A. *Teaching Children Movement Concepts and Skills: Becoming a Master Teacher.* Human Kinetics, 1994. 160 p. ISBN 0-87322-480-9 (book); 0-87322-702-6 (companion video, 31 minutes).

Teaching Children Movement Concepts and Skills provides strategies for teaching children fundamental movements they can use for a lifetime. The text presents twenty-three practical, child-tested examples of movement activities called Learning Experiences that are suitable for grades pre-K through 6. The Learning Experiences are divided into four categories: body and space awareness, effort and relationship concepts, locomotor and nonlocomotor patterns, and manipulative patterns. The companion video, *Teaching Children Movement Concepts and Skills Video*, shows three condensed lessons that provide real-world examples of effectively teaching children movement concepts and skills.

Graham, George. *American Master Teacher Program Pedagogy Course Study Guide,* and *Self Study Video.* Human Kinetics, 1993. 88 p. ISBN 0-87322-407-8 (study guide); 0-87322-416-7 (companion video, 60 minutes).

This study guide is a companion to the text *Teaching Children Physical Education: Becoming a Master Teacher* (see annotation below). It presents exercises and activities that go hand-in-hand with the text and give individuals an opportunity to apply the information from the text to their personal teaching experiences. The accompanying *Self-Study Video* was filmed during actual physical education lessons. It shows examples of master teachers using the skills and techniques described in *Teaching Children Physical Education.*

———. *Teaching Children Physical Education: Becoming a Master Teacher.* Human Kinetics, 1992. 179 p. ISBN 0-87322-340-3 (paper).

Health and Physical Education

This text focuses on effective teaching skills used by master teachers. It integrates research-based information with first-hand experience to describe the decision-making processes used by these teachers. The chapters cover topics such as successful teaching, planning to maximize learning, creating an atmosphere for learning, minimizing off-task behavior and discipline problems, getting the lesson started, instructing and demonstrating, motivating children to practice, observing and analyzing, developing the content, providing feedback, questioning and problem solving, building positive feelings, assessing children's progress, and continuing to develop as a teacher. The text is part of a package that includes a study guide and a self-study video (see annotation above).

Purcell, Theresa M. *Teaching Children Dance: Becoming a Master Teacher.* Human Kinetics, 1994. 126 p. ISBN 0-87322-479-5 (paper and companion video).

This work is part of the American Master Teacher Program Content Series. *Teaching Children Dance* details the why and how of teaching children in this content area. It presents seventeen practical, child-tested examples of dance activities, called Learning Experiences, for grades pre-K through 6. The Learning Experiences are divided into four elements of movement: body awareness, space awareness, effort, and relationships. The companion video shows three condensed lessons that provide examples of teaching children dance concepts.

Ratliffe, Thomas, and Laraine Ratliffe. *Teaching Children Fitness: Becoming a Master Teacher.* Human Kinetics, 1994. 128 p. ISBN 0-87322-478-7 (paper); 0-87322-706-9 (companion video, 30 minutes).

Teaching Children Fitness details the why and how of teaching children physical fitness activities, called Learning Experiences, that are suitable for grades pre-K through 6. The Learning Experiences are divided into five categories: basic fitness concepts, cardiorespiratory endurance, muscular strength and endurance, flexibility, and health habits and wellness. The companion video, *Teaching Children Fitness Video,* shows three condensed lessons that provide real world examples of effectively teaching children fitness.

Werner, Peter H. *Teaching Children Gymnastics: Becoming a Master Teacher.* Human Kinetics, 1994. 145 p. ISBN 0-87322-477-9 (paper and companion video).

This book is part of the American Master Teacher Program Content Series, the first set of resources specifically designed to provide preservice and inservice teachers with developmentally appropriate practices for teaching elementary physical education. *Teaching Children Gymnastics* details the how and why of teaching children this content area. It presents twenty-four practical, child-tested examples of gymnastics activities that are ideal for pre-K through Grade 6. The activities are divided into three skill themes: traveling, statics, and rotation. The companion video shows three condensed lessons that provide real-world examples of teaching children gymnastics.

NONPRINT MATERIALS

A.D.A.M.: The Inside Story. A.D.A.M. Software.

This CD-ROM is an excellent resource for teachers to use to brush up on human anatomy for their own professional development as well as to use in their classrooms. It uses an interactive multimedia format to teach about the various systems of the human body. The Family Scrapbook contains several hours of narration by two animated characters named Adam and Eve who tell about the human body in a story format. For example, the Scrapbook shows exactly what happens when you get stung by a bee, burn your hand, or get a sunburn. It also includes a section on skin color. It is available from Tiger Software (1-800-238-4437).

HEALTH JOURNALS

Journal of Health Education. American Alliance for Health, Physical Education, Recreation and Dance. ISSN 1055-6699.

Journal of Health Education, published six times a year, is the journal of the Association for the Advancement of Health Education, which is under the AAHPERD umbrella. The journal focuses on both school and community health issues and is geared toward teachers and health practitioners. Each issue includes a section on teaching ideas for various health issues.

Journal of School Health. American School Health Association. ISSN 0022-4391.

Journal of School Health is published ten times a year. The journal is not particularly geared toward teachers, but offers articles and research papers on various school health issues with information that teachers can implement into their teaching. Sample articles include overviews of school safety belt incentive programs, formative evaluation of the American Cancer Society's nutrition education curriculum, HIV education, health education in the United States, and celebrities as health educators.

University of California at Berkeley Wellness Letter. Health Letter Associates. ISSN 0748-9234.

This newsletter on nutrition, fitness, and stress management summarizes current research and gives tips and advice for healthy living. Although it is not written especially for teachers, it provides information they may want to include in their lessons. The newsletter is written in straightforward language. Sample sections include a buying guide, quizzes, wellness tips, and a question-and-answer section entitled "Ask the Experts."

PHYSICAL EDUCATION AND FITNESS JOURNALS

Journal of Physical Education, Recreation and Dance. American Alliance for Health, Physical Education, Recreation and Dance. ISSN 0730-3084.

The *Journal of Physical Education, Research and Dance* is published monthly except in July, with the May and June and November and December issues combined. Articles include issues related to physical education, leisure, dance, and health. The typical journal length is one hundred pages, with articles varying from one to ten pages.

Strategies. American Alliance for Health, Physical Education, Recreation and Dance. ISSN 0892-4562.

Strategies, published eight times a year, is designed to provide teachers and coaches with practical ideas and suggestions. Sample topics of articles include ways to motivate students, teaching cues for a variety of motor skills, and coping with teacher burnout. The typical journal length is thirty pages, with articles varying from one to five pages, including photographs and diagrams.

Teaching Elementary Physical Education. Human Kinetics. ISSN 1045-4853.

Teaching Elementary Physical Education (*TEPE*), published six times a year, is a publication of the United States Physical Education Association, distributed by Human Kinetics. *TEPE* is designed to provide a place for teachers to give and receive practical ideas and suggestions. Sample topics include teaching critical thinking through child-designed games, alternative forms of assessment, multiculturalism, and technology.

MEMBERSHIPS

American Alliance for Health, Physical Education, Recreation and Dance
1900 Association Drive
Reston, Virginia 22091

Phone: (703) 620-6091

United States Physical Education Association
P.O. Box 5076
Champaign, Illinois 61825-5076

Phone: (800) 373-USPE

14

Early Childhood Education

Consultants: Dr. Shirley C. Raines
University of Kentucky
Lexington, Kentucky
(Literacy)

Dr. Shirley Raines is Dean of the College of Education at the University of Kentucky. Prior to this position, she was Professor and Department Chairperson for Early Childhood/Language Arts/Reading at the University of South Florida. She completed her Ed.D. at the University of Tennessee, where she specialized in early childhood education. Before becoming a teacher educator, she was a classroom teacher, and she has also served as director of a child care center as well as a Head Start program.

Dr. Raines was member-at-large for the Executive Board of the Association for Childhood Education International. Her research focuses on young children's interest in books and case method in teacher education.

She is the author of numerous books and articles on early childhood education. Her books include the popular series of teacher resource books, *Story S-t-r-e-t-c-h-e-r-s: Activities to Expand Children's Favorite Books; Story S-t-r-e-t-c-h-e-r-s for the Primary Grades;* and *More Story S-t-r-e-t-c-h-e-r-s for the Primary Grades* from Gryphon House. She has written with her husband, Dr. Robert J. Canady, *The Whole Language Kindergarten,* published by Teachers College Press, and with Dr. Rebecca Isbell *Stories: Children's Literature in Early Education,* published by Delmar. Her latest book, *Whole Language Across the Curriculum: Grades 1, 2, 3* was released by Teachers College Press in 1995.

Dr. Pamela O. Fleege
University of South Florida
Tampa, Florida
(Math and Science)

Dr. Fleege is Assistant Professor of Early Childhood Education at the University of South Florida, where she teaches courses in integrated mathematics and science, cognitive development, integrated social sciences, and assessment. She received her Ph.D. from Louisiana State University. With over ten years of experience in public and private schools, she has also worked in many states as an early childhood consultant.

An active member of various professional organizations, Dr. Fleege has presented papers on portfolios, teacher beliefs, interpreting observations, and integrated mathematics and science curricula.

Her publications have addressed a variety of topics, including developmentally appropriate practices, effects of standardized testing on young children, stress, teacher beliefs, and math science activities for the early childhood classroom. Her research interests include developmentally appropriate practices in the primary grades, alternative assessment, and children's understanding of science concepts.

Dr. Susan Gomez
California State University
Sacramento, California
(Creative Expression)

Dr. Susan Gomez is Assistant Professor of Child Development at California State University at Sacramento, where she teaches courses in creative expression, program practices, and intellectual development. She received her Ed.D. degree from the University of New Orleans, where she also completed a master's in education with a specialization in early childhood education. An experienced classroom teacher, Dr. Gomez has taught in public and private preschools and kindergartens. She has also worked with schools in Louisiana and Florida as a consultant and curriculum developer.

An active member of various professional organizations, she has presented papers on classroom literacy environments, teacher belief, holistic assessment, and early childhood programs. She has published on the topics of at-risk children and the application of chaos theory to classroom literacy practices. Her research interests include creative experiences for young children, emergent literacy, teacher development, alternative assessment, and naturalistic research methods.

KEYSTONE WORKS

Allen, K. Eileen, and Lynn Marotz. *Developmental Profiles: Prebirth through Eight.* 2nd ed. Delmar, 1994. 192 p. ISBN 0-8273-5814-8 (paper).

The authors of this text have examined children's development in such areas as growth and physical development and motor, perceptual, cognitive, speech and language, and personal-social skills. The chapters examine these topics in age ranges such as prebirth, infant, toddler, preschooler, and kindergarten/primary. There is also a chapter on when to seek help and resources. An extensive appendix includes developmental checklists, growth charts, health history forms, and an annotated bibliography for additional information. This book would be especially helpful for parents, as well as educators.

Berk, Laura. *Child Development.* 3rd ed. Allyn & Bacon, 1994. 650 p. ISBN 0-205-12682-0 (hardcover).

Although designed primarily as a text for undergraduate courses, this book serves as an excellent resource on child development. Major sections discuss theory and research, foundations of child development, cognition and language, personality and social development, and contexts which influence development. The author's perspective defines development as integrated in all domains and across contexts and cultures, and the study of development as blending theory, research, and practice. Features of each chapter such as introductions and summaries, theme boxes, interim summaries, and numerous tables and illustrations promote ease of use.

Bredekamp, Sue. *Developmentally Appropriate Practice in Early Childhood Programs Serving Children from Birth through Age Eight.* National Association for the Education of Young Children, 1987. 92 p. ISBN 0-935989-11-0 (paper).

This expanded edition presents the National Association for the Education of Young Children's position statements on developmentally appropriate practices for young children from birth through age eight. The book includes individual chapters which provide in-depth descriptions of practices for programs serving infant/toddler, 3-year-olds, 4- and 5-year-olds, and 5- through 8-year-olds. Recommendations set forth by the NAEYC in this text represent an attempt to set standards for practice in the field of early childhood and are based on a consensus of current research and theory.

———, and Teresa Rosegrant. *Reaching Potentials: Appropriate Curriculum and Assessment for Young Children, vol. 1.* National Association for the Education of Young Children, 1992. 169 p. ISBN 0-935989-53-6 (paper).

This first volume of a two-part series addresses the application of professional guidelines for developmentally appropriate curriculum and assessment in programs serving children from birth through age eight. Initial chapters provide a historical overview of curriculum and assessment, the position statement of guidelines, and in-depth descriptions for applying the guidelines to practices in curriculum and assessment. The chapters that follow articulate strategies for reaching potentials of children with special needs and those from culturally and linguistically diverse populations. The concluding section discusses the processes of implementing the guidelines in two primary school settings.

Cuffaro, Harriet K. *Experimenting with the World: John Dewey and Early Education.* Teachers College Press, 1995. 125 p. ISBN 0-8077-3372-5 (hardcover); 0-8077-3371-7 (paper).

Cuffaro offers a detailed account of how the educational philosophy of John Dewey may be translated into the everyday life of the classroom. Particular attention is given to "learning from experience"—a fundamental concept in early education—and the complexities involved in experiential learning. The book also invites the reader to examine the process of developing one's own philosophy of education and chronicles Dr. Cuffaro's examination of what it means to be a teacher of young children.

Elkind, David. *The Hurried Child: Growing Up Too Fast Too Soon.* Addison-Wesley, 1981. 210 p. ISBN 0-201-07397-8 (paper).

This keystone text examines the phenomenon of children who are compelled by society to take on adult physical, psychological, and social roles before they are capable of doing so. Children of younger ages are being pushed into a more structured environment which includes organized sports, exposure to more sex and violence, and dressing and responding in more adult-like ways. This results, according to the author, in children being under an increasing amount of stress. Accordingly, society is seeing an increase in children who experience problems in school, commit acts of delinquency, and report chronic psychosomatic complaints.

———. *Miseducation: Preschoolers at Risk.* Alfred A. Knopf, 1987. 221 p. ISBN 0-394-75634-7 (paper).

The purpose of this book is to provide parents, teachers, administrators, and health care professionals with an understanding of the risks of inappropriate educational practices for young children. The author argues that the influx of academically oriented instruction in early childhood programs creates extraordinary pressures for young children and their families. Elkind discusses characteristics of healthy educational environments and also addresses questions commonly asked by parents.

Gardner, Howard. *Frames of Mind: The Theory of Multiple Intelligences.* Basic Books, 1983. 440 p. ISBN 0-465-02510-2 (paper).

Part I of this text presents an overview of the definition of intelligence and Gardner's Theory of Multiple Intelligences. This is followed in Part II by an in-depth discussion of linguistic, musical, logical/mathematical, spatial, bodily/kinesthetic, and personal intelligences. Part III of the text concludes with a description of the educational system and outlines suggestions for how practitioners might alter environments so that they are more supportive of the development of multiple intelligences.

Snyder, Agnes. *Dauntless Women in Childhood Education 1856–1931*. Association for Childhood Education International, 1972. 405 p. ISBN 0-87173-021-9 (paper).

The Association for Childhood Education International published *Dauntless Women in Childhood Education 1856–1931* as a tribute to the significant accomplishments of many of its early leaders in education. The leaders were members of the International Kindergarten Union and the National Council of Primary Education, the two organizations that merged in 1931 to become the Association for Childhood Education. The book presents the leadership qualities of those women who helped shape education and whose steadfast beliefs and classroom practices are largely ignored in today's historical texts. Some of the women and issues included are: Margarethe Schurz, Elizabeth Palmer Peabody, Susan E. Blow, Kate Douglas Wiggin, and Elizabeth Harrison on the Froebelian influences; and Alice Temple, Patty Smith Hill, Ella Victoria Dobbs, and Lucy Gage on the changes and challenges in early education through 1931. The epilogue provides a glimpse into the future, with many predictions which have proved accurate. While not written as a feminist publication, the book gives insights into the difficulties of the teaching profession and the power struggles for women to be leaders.

APPROACHES

Barbour, Nita H., and Carol Seefeldt. *Developmental Continuity Across Preschool and Primary Grades: Implications for Teachers*. Association for Childhood Education International, 1993. 93 p. ISBN 0-87173-128-2 (hardcover).

Developmental continuity often refers to eliminating artificial barriers, such as grade or group placement, as well as finding ways to make smooth transitions between preschool, kindergarten, and primary grades. The authors discuss nongraded units, special state projects such as Project Construct from Missouri, and national projects such as "Right from the Start" from the National Association of School Boards. A restructured kindergarten/primary unit is reviewed with discussions of management team, grouping, scheduling, promotion, class size, staff, reporting progress, and organization. Teachers are given guidance in creating the learning environment and reviewing the curriculum content.

Edwards, Carolyn, Lella Gandini, and George Forman, eds. *The Hundred Languages of Children: The Reggio Emilia Approach to Early Childhood Education*. Ablex Publishing, 1993. 324 p. ISBN 089391-927-6 (hardcover); 0-89391-933-0 (paper).

Over the past thirty years, educators in Reggio Emilia, Italy, have evolved a distinctive, innovative approach that fosters children's intellectual development through a systematic focus on symbolic representation. Young children from birth to age six are encouraged to explore their environment and express themselves through many "languages," or modes of expression, including words, movement, drawing, painting, sculpture, shadow play, collage, and music. The book brings together the reflections of the Italian educators and the North American educators who studied there. This comprehensive introduction covers the history and philosophy of the approach, its curriculum and methods, its school and system organization, its use of space and physical environment, and adult roles.

Kasten, Wendy C., and Barbara K. Clarke. *The Multi-Age Classroom: A Family of Learners*. Richard C. Owen Publishers, 1993. 84 p. ISBN 1-878450-35-2 (paper).

Kasten and Clarke introduce multi-age classrooms through glimpses into teacher Joni Ramer's family of learners. In a brief but effective presentation, they include chapters on Understanding the Multi-Age Model, Benefits, The Classroom as a Community, and Implementing the Multi-Age Models. The final chapter is one of the most helpful to administrators, teachers, and parents—Questions Teachers and Parents Most Frequently Ask.

Katz, Lilian G., and Sylvia C. Chard. *Engaging Children's Minds: The Project Approach*. Ablex Publishing, 1989. 185 p. ISBN 0-89391-534-3 (hardcover); 0-89391-543-2 (paper).

Katz and Chard are guided by a view of young children as thinkers. As the title implies the child's mind is engaged, and children are engaged with each other as they learn. They thereby develop social and intellectual competence. The authors profile the project approach, highlight the research and principles of practice which guide the approach, and describe such features of the approach as teacher planning, getting started, continuing with projects, and consolidating the projects or culminating them.

ART, MUSIC, AND PLAY

Frost, Joe. *Play and Playscapes*. Delmar, 1992. 356 p. ISBN 0-8273-4699-9 (paper).

The author presents a comprehensive discussion of play and its relationship to play environments, with specific emphasis on outdoor playgrounds. The initial chapters provide an overview of theories of play, developmental characteristics of children's play, and related issues such as gender, television, and aggression. Chapters five through nine examine in depth the design and implementation of outdoor playgrounds. Three additional chapters deal with adapting playgrounds for infant/toddler and special needs populations. Black and white photographs and extensive tables and charts summarize important information. Appendices include extensive resources for designing and using outdoor play spaces.

Isenberg, Joan P., and Mary Renck Jalongo. *Creative Expression and Play in the Early Childhood Curriculum.* Merrill, 1993. 389 p. ISBN 0-02-359945-6 (paper).

This text presents an integrated approach to creative experiences for young children in the areas of music, art, play, and drama. The initial chapters provide a definition of creativity and its role in children's play. Succeeding chapters deal in more depth with art, music, movement, and creative drama. The book closes with a discussion of the role of assessment, guidance, and professional development in fostering children's creative experiences. Each chapter begins with a case study and objectives, and includes strategies for integrated activities founded upon a research framework. The authors incorporate ways to support special populations along with field observation and writing exercises at the end of each chapter.

Schiller, Pam, and Thomas Moore. *Where is Thumbkin?: Five Hundred Activities to Use with Songs You Already Know.* Gryphon House, 1993. 252 p. ISBN 0-87659-164-0 (paper).

Schiller and Moore have compiled a collection of over five hundred activities for teachers based upon familiar children's songs. The activities were designed to be used within an integrated curriculum. Most of the songs selected were appropriate for use with children ages three to six; the authors have also provided a section of songs for toddlers. Each song is accompanied by suggestions for class discussion, and ways to thematically integrate children's literature and related records and tapes. Also included are specific curriculum activities for areas such as math, science, art, dramatic play, cooking, and motor development. An excellent collection for the nonmusician in the classroom.

Young, Jane F., Stephen E. Klesiu, and Hubert A. Hoffman. *Meaningful Movement: A Developmental Theme Approach to Physical Education for Children.* 2nd ed. Kendall/Hunt Publishing, 1994. 314 p. ISBN 0-8403-90998 (hardcover).

The authors establish a set of guiding principles for physical education for children. They provide integration of information and methods (why and how we teach) and content (the learning experiences used in physical education) toward the development of desirable student behaviors. They then take those principles and use a developmental theme approach for six themes: becoming aware, becoming independent, accepting responsibility, acting cooperatively, improving quality of response, and drawing relationships. While written for the physical education teacher, the movement ideas, learning principles, and curriculum development concepts are also excellent resources for the classroom teacher.

ASSESSMENT

Beaty, Janice J. *Observing Development of the Young Child.* 3rd ed. Merrill, 1994. 416 p. ISBN 0-02-307741-7 (paper).

This text, written for pre- and inservice teachers, focuses on developing observation and documentation techniques for two- to six-year-olds. Background and observation techniques for self-identity, prosocial behavior, large and small motor development, spoken language, literacy, art, imagination, and mathematical concepts of classification, seriation, number, time, and space are discussed. An overview of National Association for the Education of Young Children developmentally appropriate assessment guidelines and children's literature is included.

Grace, Cathy, and Elizabeth F. Shores. *The Portfolio and Its Use: Developmentally Appropriate Assessment of Young Children.* Southern Early Childhood Association, 1991. 60 p. ISBN 0-942388-10-0 (paper).

This book presents practical information for classroom teachers, administrators, and parents on portfolio assessment. Although designed primarily for use in preschool and kindergarten, the principles presented are applicable to early elementary grades. The five chapters cover steps in designing and implementing portfolios, from defining purposes through communicating with parents. An extensive set of appendices provides examples of portfolio documentation systems for record keeping, as well as an overview of assessment instruments commonly used with young children.

Kamii, Constance. *Achievement Testing in the Early Grades: The Games Grownups Play.* National Association for the Education of Young Children, 1990. 182 p. ISBN 0-935989-32-3 (paper).

This book presents a collection of fourteen essays which discuss the detrimental effects of standardized achievement testing on children, teachers, and the curriculum. The chapters are written by concerned professionals, including researchers, teachers, and administrators. Specific chapters deal with the influence of standardized achievement testing on literacy and mathematics development, followed by discussions of more appropriate means of assessment. Other sections discuss issues related to achievement testing at the state and school district levels.

CULTURAL DIVERSITY AND SPECIAL NEEDS

•Au, Kathryn H. *Literacy Instruction in Multicultural Settings.* Harcourt Brace, 1993. 208 p. ISBN 0-03-076847-0 (paper).

This text, designed for preservice teachers, is intended to foster their understanding of issues involved in teaching literacy to culturally and linguistically diverse student populations. The book presents an approach to language and literacy development in young children. Both discussions of research and strategies for classroom implementation are included in each chapter; topics range from classroom organization to patterns of interaction, language differences, the writing process, and using children's literature. Individual chapters open with a purpose statement, and include both specific activities along with suggested resources.

Byrnes, Deborah, and Gary Kiger. *Common Bonds: Anti-Bias Teaching in a Diverse Society.* Association for Childhood Education International, 1992. 109 p. ISBN 0-87173-125-8 (hardcover).

The authors integrate theory, research, and practice in this discussion of issues related to cultural diversity in elementary school classrooms. The text is designed to describe aspects of cultural diversity in today's school settings and provide teachers with strategies for implementing inclusionary practices in the classroom. Diversity topics include religion, race, ethnicity, gender, culture, economic class, language, and ability. The final chapter consists of an excellent checklist for educators to evaluate their own classroom with respect to valuing diversity in the areas of environment, materials, teaching strategies, and classroom interaction.

Derman-Sparks, Louise, and the A.B.C. Task Force. *Anti-Bias Curriculum: Tools for Empowering Children.* National Association for the Education of Young Children, 1989. 149 p. ISBN 0-935989-20-X (hardcover).

This resource book focuses on how to develop and implement a bias-free early childhood curriculum. The text presents a discussion of the importance of an antibias curriculum along with chapters related to racial, gender, and cultural similarities and differences. Other chapters address stereotyping, activism, disabilities, and working with parents. Rather than provide a pre-designed curriculum, the book's focus is more philosophical and encourages teachers to use principles presented to develop a curriculum which best suits the diversity needs of their own classrooms. Appendices include adult resources and appropriate children's literature.

Paul, James L., and Rune J. Simeonsson. *Children with Special Needs: Family, Culture, and Society.* 2nd ed. Harcourt Brace, 1993. 316 p. ISBN 0-03-055743-7 (hardcover).

This collection of essays explores the development of special needs children and their families from an ecological perspective. Individual essays are grouped into five sections which address: changes in understandings about families of the disabled, aspects of family contexts affecting disabled children, the influence of cultural contexts and diversity, societal factors, and issues and trends. The editors have made considerable revisions which reflect the expansion and redefinition of families of the disabled. More specifically, the changes afford a broader focus which encompasses more recent interpretive research and which presents a more diverse and pluralistic view of families.

Wolery, Mark, and Jan S. Wilbers. *Including Children with Special Needs in Early Childhood Programs.* National Association for the Education of Young Children, 1994. 230 p. ISBN 0-935989-61-7 (paper).

This collection of essays discusses the design and implementation of full inclusion programs for children with special needs. Topics addressed include working with families, working with members of other disciplines, assessment, classroom environments, teaching strategies, and transitions between programs. The text should serve as a good reference for teachers who are beginning to serve children with a variety of needs in the regular education setting.

CURRICULUM

Hamilton, Darlene Softley, Bonnie Mack Flemming, and JoAnne Deal Hicks. *Resources for Creative Teaching in Early Childhood Education.* 2nd ed. Harcourt Brace, 1990. 672 p. ISBN 0-15-576652-X (paper).

This comprehensive resource book provides teachers and parents with abundant strategies for designing and implementing curriculum. The first section previews program planning, guidance, and the use of centers; it features tips for props and recipes for art materials along with an annotated resource bibliography. The second section contains forty thematic chapters grouped into categories such as families, seasons, and transportation. The format for these chapters consists of basic concepts, facts, and vocabulary; incorporating themes into learning centers (music, art, dramatic plan, books, language); grouptime, stories, games, and motor activities. Teacher resources for each theme include books, films, videos, and community resources.

Taylor, Barbara J. *A Child Goes Forth: A Curriculum Guide for Preschool Children.* 8th ed. Macmillan, 1991. 333 p. ISBN 0-02-419282-1 (paper).

Covering ages two through five years, Taylor's eighth edition continues to be a quality publication, with updates that satisfy the profession's definition of developmentally appropriate practices. Chapters include Good Environments for Young Children, The Value of Play, Planning the Curriculum, and six curriculum chapters. Also critical to the early years classroom is the information on transition activities, food, nutrition, and health, as well as guidance techniques. The helpful appendix materials include an overview of characteristics of young children, curriculum topics, lesson plans, recipes, and sources for children's books and materials.

Trostle, Susan L., and Thomas D. Yawkey. *Integrated Learning Activities for Young Children.* Allyn & Bacon, 1990. ISBN 0-205-12077-6 (paper).

This collection of integrated curriculum activities spans five units—Myself and Others, Playing to Learn, Language Expressions, The World Around Me, and Out of Doors—along with an introductory unit describing how to use the text. Each thematic unit contains three or four chapters with activities designed to promote the cognitive and social development of children from ages two through eight. Individual activities are presented in lesson plan format, with key concepts and objectives, materials, vocabulary and procedures, and levels of difficulty. An index which indicates curriculum area and skill level for all the activities is provided.

GUIDANCE AND PARENTING

Gestwicki, Carol. *Home, School and Community Relations: A Guide to Working with Parents.* Delmar, 1992. 397 p. ISBN 0-8273-4561-5 (paper).

The author promotes a philosophy of working with parents as partners and provides techniques for positive communication and parent involvement. She also addresses the diversity of families and the type of situations which often cause problems for teachers. The book contains reviews of legislative initiatives, and such common concerns as sick children. Issues are reviewed through case studies.

Hildebrand, Verna. *Guiding Young Children.* 5th ed. Macmillan, 1994. 443 p. ISBN 0-02-354521-6 (hardcover); 0-02-354518-6 (paper).

Hildebrand clearly describes the infant through preprimary child and recommends appropriate guidance practices and applications to the curriculum. She describes the goals of guidance, direct and indirect methods to help children with self-direction, and self-esteem. Specific guidance situations include introducing a child to a new group, scheduling, toileting routine, eating, sleeping, dressing and undressing, and playground behavior. The chapters Knowing Children as a Basis for Guidance and Communicating with Parents provide foundational information, and there are also four curriculum chapters.

Marion, Marian. *Guidance of Young Children.* 4th ed. Macmillan, 1995. 227 p. ISBN 0-02-376061-3 (paper).

This book is targeted at pre- and inservice teachers who work with young children, as well as parents and community and health care professionals. The text consists of three units of several chapters each, which discuss theoretical frameworks for guidance programs, the author's suggested guidance approach, and issues such as discipline, aggression, self-esteem, and prosocial behavior. Individual chapters have an overview and objectives section, and conclude with a summary, observation activities for the reader, and a brief reference list. The author includes numerous charts and tables which summarize the information presented.

KINDERGARTEN

Fromberg, Doris Pronin. *The Full-Day Kindergarten.* Teachers College Press, 1987. 267 p. ISBN 0-8077-2833-0 (hardcover); 0-8077-2821-7 (paper).

Fromberg's book helps kindergarten teachers design an effective full-day program. The author reviews kindergarten children's learning characteristics and makes the case for combining academic instruction and the creation of a nurturing environment. The chapters are rich with descriptions of practical activities, case histories, observations, sample schedules, and anecdotes. The curriculum is integrated, and the influences of comprehensive program planning are clear. The author recommends much child choice and effective periods of teacher direction, while helping the reader see the value of play.

Raines, Shirley C., and Robert J. Canady. *The Whole Language Kindergarten.* Teachers College Press, 1990. 273 p. ISBN 0-8077-3049-1 (paper).

Teachers interested in transforming their traditional kindergartens into child- and experience-centered whole language classrooms will find a model in this book. Play, cultural awareness, and creative expression fuse with "emerging literacy." Activities within the classical content areas of reading, writing, science, art, music, and mathematics are presented with ways to make the curriculum more whole language. Clear suggestions are provided on how to interest children in books and print, how to structure grouptime to emphasize whole language, and how parents can reevaluate their roles. The text links statements from National Association for the Education of Young Children on Developmentally Appropriate Practices and from International Reading Association on pre-first grade reading.

LANGUAGE AND LITERACY

Bauer, Caroline Feller. *New Handbook for Storytellers: With Stories, Poems, Magic, and More.* American Library Association, 1993. 550 p. ISBN 0-839-0613-3 (hardcover).

The twenty-six chapters of the book are divided into four parts: Getting Started, Sources for Storytelling, Multimedia Storytelling, and Programs. Bauer, a renowned storyteller, speaks directly with the reader, as she would an audience for her oral presentations. The book is also a collection of stories, some told in their

Early Childhood Education

entirety, and rich resource lists for other stories. A variety of genres, methods, and curriculum ideas are laced throughout this well-organized resource. Teachers will find the puppetry, magic, and music sections particularly helpful. Teachers can stretch their imaginations for story possibilities through creative dramatics, pantomime, book parties, and reader's theatre. In part four, programs for preschool and primary grades are discussed. Booklists abound throughout the book.

•Clay, Marie M. *What Did I Write? Beginning Writing Behavior.* Heinemann, 1975. 78 p. ISBN 0-435-01120-0 (paper).

Based upon her numerous observations in schools, Clay provides an account of the development of writing in young children. The bulk of the text consists of writing samples from children accompanied by the author's discussion of the writing process as it unfolds in early childhood. The author presents a number of principles of writing development related to the concepts of letter, word, alphabet, punctuation, and sentence generation. Also included is a discussion of links between early reading and writing, as well as a rating scale for observing and evaluating children's writing.

Dailey, Sheila, ed. *Tales as Tools: The Power of Story in the Classroom.* The National Storytelling Press, 1994. 213 p. ISBN 1-879991-15-2 (hardcover).

Each chapter of the book is a collection of articles and stories linked together by a topic. For example, Chapter 1, The Teacher as Storyteller has contributions by four authors. Parts of the chapter include: The Sage's Gift, Daring to Tell, Storytelling in a Country School, Making Time for Stories, The Moral of the Story, and Tips for Using a Simple Tale. Other chapters highlight storytelling in teaching reading, writing, history, and science. Multicultural education and children's sense of their responsibilities for the environment are also topics. Tips are given for using puppets, flannel boards, and props, as well as organizing storytelling troupes and festivals.

•Holdaway, Don. *The Foundations of Literacy.* Ashton Scholastic, 1991. 232 p. ISBN 0-590-02306 (paper).

Holdaway's book on beginning literacy provides a developmental level perspective on how children learn to read and write. He synthesizes ideas from researchers and practitioners. Perhaps best known for his use of "Big Books" or the "Shared Book Experience," the author also provides glimpses into children's literacy learning before entering school. Holdaway does not neglect the basics, but rather refocuses the reader's attention on basic reading strategies, rather than skills. Memory of text, unison activities, enlarged texts, and controlling task difficulty are discussed, along with a developmental perspective of first, second, and third year programs.

Morrow, Lesley Mandel. *Literacy Development in the Early Years: Helping Children Read and Write.* 2nd ed. Allyn & Bacon, 1993. 399 p. ISBN 0-205-14043-2 (paper).

Morrow's book is designed to help teachers, undergraduate students, parents, and administrators understand the development of writing and reading in young children. The text presents a wealth of specific instructional strategies for early childhood and elementary school settings based upon recent research and theory, including the author's own studies. Chapter topics consist of a theoretical framework; the role of the home in literacy development; areas of literacy including oral language, reading, and writing; and organizing classroom literacy environments. Each chapter contains focus questions, classroom ideas, and activities. Appendices list selected children's literature as well as teacher and parent resources.

Raines, Shirley C., and Robert J. Canady. *Story S-t-r-e-t-c-h-e-r-s: Activities to Expand Children's Favorite Books* (4 books in series). Gryphon House, 1989. 251 p. ISBN 0-87659-119-5 (paper).

Using eighteen curriculum themes, such as Families, Friends, Seasons, and Transportation, the authors selected five children's books for each theme. Each of the ninety books has a suggested way to present the book during circle time, followed by five extension activities. *Story S-t-r-e-t-c-h-e-r-s* are teaching ideas based on children's favorite books. The first *Story S-t-r-e-t-c-h-e-r* and *More Story S-t-r-e-t-c-h-e-r-s* were written for preschool and kindergarten teachers. *Story S-t-r-e-t-c-h-e-r-s for the Primary Grades* and *450 More Story S-t-r-e-t-c-h-e-r-s for the Primary Grades* have more science units, as well as literature units on poetry, folktales, and author studies.

―――, and Rebecca T. Isbell. *Stories: Children's Literature in Early Education.* Delmar, 1994. 416 p. ISBN 0-8273-5509-2 (hardcover).

The authors explain the connections between language, literacy, and the use of children's literature to assist in making developmentally appropriate literature selections for infants through grade three. Featuring practical information, such as how to design an inviting classroom environment for young children, the authors also present effective ways of involving parents. Different genres are presented, with extensive bibliographies of books for each development age. Multicultural children's literature appears throughout the book. Brief teaching cases allow readers to identify ways to make the early childhood classroom a more effective literacy environment and foster children's appreciation of good literature.

Schickendanz, Judith A. *More than the ABCs: The Early Stages of Reading and Writing.* National Association for the Education of Young Children, 1986. 145 p. ISBN 0-912674-95-4 (hardcover).

The author presents suggestions and ideas for helping children develop writing and reading from infancy and toddlerhood into the early school years. Schickendanz helps parents and teachers understand the natural and meaningful ways in which literacy emerges. Chapters provide strategies for sharing books with toddlers and preschoolers, fostering children's writing, and organizing supportive literacy

Early Childhood Education

environments in both the home and the classroom. Appendices discuss how parents can help children learn about reading, suggest appropriate books, and present position statements of professional early childhood and literacy organizations regarding reading practices before first grade.

MATHEMATICS, SCIENCE, AND SOCIAL STUDIES

Baratta-Lorton, Mary. *Mathematics Their Way.* Addison-Wesley, 1976. 398 p. ISBN 0-201-04320-3 (paper).

This text presents a suggested mathematics curriculum for kindergarten through second grade. The instructional approach advocated is based on the use of hands-on, manipulative activities in individual and small- and large-group formats. Materials needed for completion of the activities are inexpensive and easy to obtain. Chapter topics include free exploration, sorting and classifying, counting, graphing, patterning, place value, and number concepts. Activities are presented in lesson plan format, with skills, materials, and suggested teaching strategies accompanied by clear photographs and illustrations. The text also provides blackline masters needed to prepare some of the materials.

―――. *Workjobs: Activity Centered Learning for Early Childhood.* Addison-Wesley, 1972. 225 p. ISBN 0-201-04331-4 (spiral).

In nine chapters, this text presents hands-on activities for preschool and kindergarten in the areas of language and mathematics. The workjobs are activities designed to be used by children independently and feature materials common to the lives of children and readily available in any preschool setting. The lesson plan format highlights concepts presented, procedures, materials, and ideas for follow-up. Black-and-white photographs accompany each activity for illustration purposes. Specific areas of language activities include perception, matching, classification, and sounds and letters; for mathematics, topics consist of sets, number sequences, combining and separating groups, and relationships.

Charlesworth, Rosalind, and Karen K. Lind. *Math and Science For Young Children.* 2nd ed. Delmar, 1995. 664 p. ISBN 0-8273-5869-5 (paper).

This book, targeted for pre- and inservice teachers, features seven easily readable sections. It offers a comprehensive and sequential approach to creating an appropriate mathematics and science curriculum for preschool through primary children. An explanation of how the concepts develop, as well as developmentally appropriate activities and assessment techniques, are incorporated. The extensive appendices include sequential developmental assessment tasks, children's books, songs, and fingerplays.

Holt, Bess-Gene. *Science with Young Children*. Rev. ed. National Association for the Education of Young Children, 1989. 232 p. ISBN 0-935989-28-5 (hardcover).

This book is intended to help parents and teachers develop and implement a science curriculum for children from preschool through early elementary grades. The book opens with a discussion of the importance of science for young children and the role of both teacher and children in the curriculum. The author then presents an overview of curriculum content, which is based primarily on an ecological perspective that draws heavily on children's personal life experiences. Individual chapters give an overview of strategies teachers can use to adapt the curriculum to their own classrooms. Appendices include information about the metric system and about plants.

•Seefeldt, Carol. *Social Studies for the Preschool-Primary Child*. 4th ed. Macmillan, 1993. 312 p. ISBN 0-02-408451-4 (paper).

Although designed in part as a text, this book also serves as a resource for classroom teachers. The first section presents information on planning and resources for a social studies curriculum for preschool through third grade. The second section deals with curriculum content in the areas of history, geography, economics, current topics, and multiculturalism. The final section discusses the development of skills, attitudes, and values. Individual chapters open with a listing of key concepts and conclude with resources, references, and ideas for projects.

Williams, Robert A., Robert E. Rockwell, and Elizabeth A. Sherwood. *Mudpies to Magnets: A Preschool Science Curriculum*. Gryphon House, 1987. 157 p. ISBN 0-87659-112-8 (paper).

This collection of activities for the classroom takes an integrated approach to the science curriculum. Activities are designed to promote exploration of concepts and materials and the development of thinking and observational skills. The opening section contains tips on choosing materials, science centers, instructional strategies, and resources. Activities are divided into nine sections, which range from center activities and construction to outdoor science, art, and nutrition. Suggestions for materials, concepts and vocabulary, procedures, and follow-up ideas are all provided.

NUTRITION

Wanamaker, Nancy, Kristin Hearn, and Sherill Richarz. *More Than Graham Crackers: Nutritional Education and Food Preparation with Young Children*. National Association for the Education of Young Children, 1979. 93 p. ISBN 0-912674-69-5 (paper).

Early Childhood Education

This guide for teachers and parents presents ways to help children learn about nutrition and cooking. The opening three chapters describe principles of nutrition and how to involve children in food preparation activities. Four chapters then present specific recipes and activities for fruits and vegetables, breads and cereals, dairy products, and the meat group. An additional chapter addresses the problem of junk food. Recipes provide a list of ingredients and step-by-step instructions, as well as reviewing skills needed to complete the recipe and supporting activities.

TECHNOLOGY

Wright, June L., and Daniel D. Shade. *Young Children: Active Learners in a Technological Age.* National Association for the Education of Young Children, 1994. 196 p. ISBN 0-935989-63-3 (paper).

This book is an outgrowth of a symposium on the use of computers with young children sponsored by Wheelock College. Based on those discussions, the text examines how children use computers, how to structure experiences with computers, and how staff development can support computer implementation. Information is also provided on selecting appropriate software. The appendices include information about integrating computer use with thematic units, networking, and suggested software currently available. The authors also provide a glossary of terms for the novice computer user and a resource list of organizations and readings.

NONPRINT MATERIALS

Kunesh, Linda, and Sue Bredekamp. *Developmentally Appropriate First Grade: A Community of Learners.* National Association for the Education of Young Children in conjunction with North Central Regional Educational Laboratories, 1994. Video.

NAEYC presents a first-hand look inside a developmentally appropriate first-grade classroom in a rural public school. The film is designed to illustrate how one teacher has taken the principles of developmentally appropriate practices and applied them to his own elementary school classroom by following the class through a typical day. The format consists of a panel of educators interviewing the teacher about his teaching practices, interspersed with clips of interactions in the class. Topics discussed and demonstrated include guidance, role of the teacher, cooperative learning, readers' and writers' workshops, use of children's literature, and assessment.

National Association for the Education of Young Children and South Carolina Educational Television. *Developmentally Appropriate Practice: Birth Through Age 5*. National Association for the Education of Young Children, 1990. Video.

This twenty-seven-minute videotape based on NAEYC's position statement depicts care and teaching practices recommended for use with children from birth through age five. These practices are then contrasted with practices considered to be inappropriate for use with young children. The videotape shows teachers and children actively engaged in developmentally appropriate programs. This would be useful for parents when choosing childcare programs.

———. *Discipline: Appropriate Guidance for Young Children*. National Association for the Education of Young Children, 1990. Video.

Positive guidance of children from birth through preschool is the subject of this twenty-eight-minute videotape. Guidance is viewed from the perspective of child development and typical behavior for a particular age. How to handle difficult situations such as not taking turns, hitting, and temper tantrums is the focus. Parents, caregivers, and anyone who works with young children would find this videotape beneficial.

JOURNALS

Childhood Education. Association for Childhood Education International. ISSN 0009-4056.

Childhood Education is the journal of ACEI, the Association for Childhood Education International. It is published five times per year. Although the majority of its readers are early childhood teachers and administrators, the journal also publishes articles about children and programs from infancy through early adolescence. The journal seeks to stimulate thinking rather than advocate fixed practice. It explores emerging ideas and presents conflicting opinions, supported whenever possible with research. Articles include: innovative practices, reviews of research, statements by leaders in education and allied fields, discussions of timely issues, descriptions of programs beyond the United States' borders, and teacher interest stories.

Dimensions of Early Childhood. Southern Early Childhood Association. ISSN 1068-6177.

This journal addresses the interests of early childhood professionals and paraprofessionals in the field of child development and education. Specifically, the journal's target audience is teachers and administrators from preschool through the primary grades. Along with topical articles, each issue features reviews of children's literature and professional resources. Issues are published in the fall, winter, spring, and summer. Members of SECA automatically receive this journal, and subscriptions are available to nonmembers as well.

Early Childhood Research Quarterly. National Association for the Education of Young Children and Ablex. ISSN 0885-2006.

This quarterly journal consists of articles presenting theory and research in the education of children from birth through age eight. Selections included often reflect NAEYC's commitment to an interdisciplinary perspective in early childhood. One issue each year is devoted to a specific theme; examples of recent themes are kindergarten and Head Start. Subscriptions can be obtained from either NAEYC or Ablex, and are available to both members and nonmembers.

Journal of Research in Childhood Education. Association for Childhood Education International. ISSN 0256-8543.

This journal highlights articles related to theory and research in the education of young children from birth through early adolescence. Along with empirical studies, published selections include theoretical discussions and ethnographic and other naturalistic studies. Issues are published biannually in the fall/winter and spring/summer. Subscriptions are available to both members and nonmembers.

Young Children. National Association for the Education of Young Children. ISSN 0044-0728.

Young Children, the professional journal of NAEYC, is published six times per year. Its purpose is to keep members abreast of the latest developments in early childhood education with its readable yet scholarly approach to research and theory and its emphasis on expert classroom practice. Subjects often include curriculum, administration, child-care through primary-grades programming, guidance, legislation, and parenting.

MEMBERSHIPS

Association for Childhood Education International
11501 Georgia Avenue, Suite 315
Wheaton, Maryland 20901

Phone: (800) 423-3563

ACEI is an international, nonprofit professional organization for those involved in the education of children from infancy through early adolescence. The organization is committed to fulfilling every child's potential and the professional development of the classroom teacher. Membership benefits include professional resources and publications, including the journals *Childhood Education* and *Journal of Research in Childhood Education*. Opportunities for professional development include annual conferences at the national and state levels, along with grants and awards for members. Affiliates beyond the national level include state, local, and student branches.

National Association for the Education of Young Children
1509 16th Street N.W.
Washington, D.C. 20036-1426

Phone: (800) 424-2460

This is a national, nonprofit professional organization for those involved in the education of children from birth through age eight. NAEYC is committed to high-quality programs for children and the professional development of teachers. It also sponsors a national accreditation system for early childhood programs. Membership benefits consist of professional resources and publications such as the journals *Young Children* and *Early Childhood Research Quarterly*. Opportunities for professional development include annual conferences at the national and state levels, along with grants and awards for members.

15

Special Education
Part I—Cross-Categorical Issues and Methods

Consultant: Dr. William L. Heward
The Ohio State University
Columbus, Ohio

Dr. Heward is Professor of Education at The Ohio State University, where he coordinates the doctoral program in special education and applied behavior analysis. He received his doctorate from the University of Massachusetts at Amherst. He was a Visiting Professor in the Psychology Department at Keio University in Tokyo in 1993, and, as a Fulbright Scholar in 1986, he helped train special education teachers in Portugal.

In 1985 he received Ohio State University's highest honor for teaching excellence, the Alumni Association's Distinguished Teaching Award. His current research focuses on improving the effectiveness of group instruction by developing and evaluating methods for increasing the frequency of active participation by each student in the class.

Dr. Heward has published seven books, including *Exceptional Children: An Introduction to Special Education* (Prentice-Hall, 5th edition, 1996), and more than sixty papers in professional journals. He (with Dr. Teresa Grossi) is currently under contract with Prentice-Hall for a publication scheduled for 1997, *A Dozen Common Teaching Mistakes and What to Do Instead*.

ASSESSING STUDENT NEEDS AND DEVELOPING INDIVIDUALIZED EDUCATION PROGRAMS (IEPS)

Giangreco, Michael F., Chigee J. Cloniger, and Virginia S. Iverson. *Choosing Options and Accommodations for Children: A Guide to Planning Inclusive Education.* Paul H. Brookes, 1993. 189 p. ISBN 1-55766-106-5 (spiral).

A field-tested, practical guide showing IEP team members how to select curriculum objectives and learning activities that will produce valued life outcomes for students with disabilities and that can be implemented in general education classrooms. Provides clear and comprehensive instructions for prioritizing families' needs and goals, determining short- and long-term objectives, identifying needed classroom supports, and scheduling and adapting the learning activities within the regular school day. Blank, reproducible forms are provided for each step in the COACH process, which is illustrated by several case examples.

Howell, Kenneth W., Sheila L. Fox, and Mada Kay Morehead. *Curriculum-based Evaluation: Teaching and Decision Making*. 2nd ed. Brookes Cole Publishing, 1993. 526 p. ISBN 0-534-16428-5 (paper).

The authors view evaluation of students as an ongoing process of determining what teachers *can do* to make instruction more effective, not as a method for finding out what students *cannot do*. A direct and sometimes humorous writing style is supported by numerous quotes, tables, charts, and study questions to help the reader "think like an evaluator" instead of just carry out measurement for measurement's sake. Includes flowcharts that guide the teacher in the decision-making route of an evaluator and many "exhibits" of testing materials that can be used to evaluate students. A study guide/workbook is also available.

McLoughlin, James A., and Rena B. Lewis. *Assessing Special Students: Strategies and Procedures*. 4th ed. Macmillan, 1994. 646 p. ISBN 0-02-379492-5 (hardcover).

This is a comprehensive, in-depth examination of the purposes and methods of special education assessment. It reviews the technical quality and provides suggestions for administering, scoring, and interpreting the most widely used standardized tests for intelligence, school achievement, social and classroom behavior, and academic areas. This book will help teachers to: (a) better understand and interpret the results of formal, standardized tests administered by school psychologists, and (b) select, devise, and conduct better assessments in their classrooms. It includes a case history form, sample case report, answers to review questions for each chapter, addresses of test publishers, and a glossary of terminology.

Strickland, Bonnie B., and Ann P. Turnbull. *Developing and Implementing Individualized Education Programs*. 3rd ed. Macmillan, 1993. 511 p. ISBN 0-675-21142-5 (paper).

The Individuals with Disabilities Education Act (IDEA) requires that an individualized education program (IEP) be developed and implemented for every student with disabilities. This book helps educators develop IEPs that meet both the letter and the spirit of IDEA. The books' fourteen chapters are organized into three parts: (1) procedural guidelines for IEP development, (2) the mechanics of IEP development, and (3) implementation of the IEP. Included are numerous examples of completed IEPs, and perforated, reproducible blank IEP forms and curriculum checklists. This is comprehensive and detailed enough to serve as a school district's guidebook for IEP development, implementation, and evaluation.

COLLABORATING AND TEAMING WITH COLLEAGUES

Heron, Timothy E., and Kathleen C. Harris. *The Educational Consultant: Helping Professionals, Parents, and Mainstreamed Students.* 3rd ed. PRO-ED, 1993. 559 p. ISBN 0-89079-569-X (paper).

Heron and Harris define consultation as the "voluntary and mutual interaction between two or more parties to prevent or solve problems." They explain the role and duties of an effective educational consultant (who may be a special educator, regular class teacher, bilingual or ESL educator, counselor, school psychologist, or administrator) and outline numerous procedures for using collaborative consultation to solve particular academic and behavioral problems of special students in school and at home. An excellent resource for all educators, this text is especially recommended because the authors rely heavily on methods supported by classroom-based research.

Thomas, Carol Chase, Vivian Ivonne Correa, and Catherine Voelker Morsink. *Interactive Teaming: Consultation and Collaboration in Special Programs.* 2nd ed. Macmillan, 1995. 448 p. ISBN 0-02-420204-5 (hardcover).

Describes the rationale and application of interactive teaming—a problem-solving model based on transdiciplinary consultation and collaboration—as a strategic framework by which teams of teachers and other helping professionals can analyze problems and make decisions involving the educational needs of students with disabilities and those at risk for school failure. Two chapters are devoted to meeting the needs of culturally diverse students in regular and special education. Realistic vignettes that open and close each chapter provide examples of teaming in practice.

EFFECTIVE INSTRUCTION, CLASSROOM ORGANIZATION, AND BEHAVIOR MANAGEMENT

Alberto, Paul A., and Anne C. Troutman. *Applied Behavior Analysis for Teachers: Influencing Student Performance.* 4th ed. Macmillan, 1995. 480 p. ISBN 0-02-301264-1 (paper).

Three decades of classroom-based research have shown that applied behavior analysis has much to offer the practicing teacher. This popular text shows how behavior analysis works by using a sequence of chapters that follow the development of a classroom behavior analysis project. The book describes how to select and define academic and social target behaviors, collect and use student performance data, select and use behavioral procedures (e.g., contingent praise, response prompts), promote generalization and maintenance of behavior changes, and teach students to manage their own behavior. The humorous misadventures of the "fictional" Professor Grundy help illustrate the relevance of the material.

Kameenui, Edward J., and Craig B. Darch. *Instructional Classroom Management: A Proactive Approach to Managing Behavior.* Longman, 1995. 209 p. ISBN 0-8013-0636-1 (paper).

Instead of traditional models of classroom management that react to individual behavior problems as they arise, the authors recommend a proactive, instructional approach for managing social behavior *before* problem behavior occurs. They explain how to carefully and strategically teach students all the information they need in order to behave appropriately and how to arrange numerous opportunities for students to demonstrate and receive reinforcement for their increasing skills as reflective and problem-solving school citizens. Included is a 180-day classroom management plan with specific suggestions and guidelines for each month of the school year. Numerous anecdotes, tablets, and charts illustrate and summarize the recommended strategies.

Smith, Deborah Deutsch, and Diane M. Rivera. *Effective Discipline.* 2nd ed. PRO-ED, 1993. 220 p. ISBN 0-89079-579-7 (paper).

After suggesting ten guiding principles for an effective classroom discipline program (e.g., avoid power struggles, give students choices, anticipate problems), the authors introduce the "intervention ladder," which is designed to help teachers select interventions that match the infraction. The ladder provides the conceptual framework for a hierarchy of tactics in which mild interventions are selected first (prevention serves as the ladder's first rung) and more intrusive interventions are used only when other techniques have proven unsuccessful. This work encourages and shows teachers how to create and maintain a positive learning environment and includes many helpful line drawings, charts and tables, tips for implementation lists, and "practice what you've learned" activities.

Van Houten, Ron. *Learning Through Feedback: A Systematic Approach for Improving Academic Performance.* Human Sciences Press, 1980. 182 p. ISBN 0-87705-424-X (hardcover); 0-87705-440-1 (paper).

Children learn by doing, but they learn better and faster when they receive feedback on what they do. In clear and user-friendly prose, Van Houten shows teachers how to improve students' academic performance by providing feedback that is frequent, immediate, precise, positive, and differential (comparing a student's present performance with her previous efforts). Describes how to set up classroom performance feedback systems that motivate students to try to improve their academic skills more effectively than traditional "star charts" that only recognize perfect papers. Also shows how students can provide their own feedback through self-scoring. Every teacher should read this book.

FOUNDATIONS, CONTEMPORARY ISSUES, AND PERSPECTIVES

Heward, William L. *Exceptional Children: An Introduction to Special Education.* 5th ed. Prentice-Hall/Merrill, 1996. 680 p. ISBN 0-13-366756-4 (hardcover).

A comprehensive introduction to the field of special education. Part I (three chapters) explains key terminology, concepts, laws, practices, and societal influences. Part II (nine chapters) describes definitions, characteristics, methods and issues related to assessment and instruction, and current issues related to specific categories of exceptionality (e.g., mental retardation, visual impairments, gifted and talented). Part III (three chapters) examines working with parents and families, early intervention, and transition to adulthood. Includes Profiles and Perspective boxes (personal stories of and by exceptional persons and teachers), Teaching and Learning boxes (instructional tactics), a comprehensive glossary, and more than one thousand two hundred references to the special education literature.

Kauffman, James M., and Daniel P. Hallahan. *The Illusion of Full Inclusion: A Comprehensive Critique of a Current Special Education Bandwagon.* PRO-ED, 1995. 362 p. ISBN 0-89079-612-2 (paper).

Proponents of full inclusion contend that all students, regardless of the nature or severity of their disabilities, should be educated in regular education classrooms within a single system of education. (Several of the books annotated under the Mainstreaming and Inclusion subcategory describe the philosophy and methods of inclusion.) This book's eighteen chapters—authored by well-known special educators who caution against wholesale adoption of what the book's editors call the full inclusion "bandwagon"—are organized in three parts: Historical Context, Policy Analyses and Commentary, and Disability-Specific Issues.

Turnbull, H. Rutherford. *Free Appropriate Public Education: The Law and Children with Disabilities.* 4th ed. Love, 1993. 413 p. ISBN 0-89108-225-5 (hardcover).

PL 94-142, passed by Congress in 1975, mandates that every child with disabilities is entitled to a free and appropriate public education. All educators should understand the underlying rationale and the procedural requirements of the law—now called the Individuals with Disabilities Education Act (IDEA). Rud Turnbull—an attorney, nationally recognized expert on special education law, and the father of a son with severe disabilities—provides an in-depth but very readable explanation of the IDEA's six basic principles (such as least restrictive environment, nondiscriminatory testing). Other federal laws and major court cases affecting the education of individuals with disabilities (Americans with Disabilities Act, Section 504 of the Rehabilitation Act) are also examined.

Ysseldyke, James E., Bob Algozzine, and Martha L. Thurlow. *Critical Issues in Special Education.* 2nd ed. Houghton Mifflin, 1992. 436 p. ISBN 0-395-59694-7 (paper).

This provides an in-depth examination and analysis of current issues in special education. Especially good are the chapters exploring various perspectives and debates on major issues in general education (school reform and restructuring, school choice, the move toward outcomes-based education and national testing) that are having an impact on the education of students with disabilities. It also examines issues specific to special education such as assessment, instruction, early intervention, economic and legal issues, and the future of special education.

MAINSTREAMING AND INCLUSION

Lewis, Rena B., and Donald H. Doorlag. *Teaching Special Students in the Mainstream.* 4th ed. Macmillan, 1995. 602 p. ISBN 0-02-370502-7 (hardcover).

This widely adopted text includes individual chapters devoted to basic mainstreaming skills for the regular classroom teacher (adapting instruction, promoting social acceptance, arranging the classroom environment) and methods for mainstreaming students with specific types of disabilities (learning disabilities, behavioral disorders, mental retardation, physical and health impairments, sensory impairments). A full chapter is devoted to helping students who are at risk for school failure in the regular classroom. Special features throughout the book include Tips for Teachers (answers to frequently asked questions), For Your Information (highlighting latest research findings), and Spotlight on Technology (showing how current technology can aide mainstreaming). Highly recommended.

Stainback, Susan, and William Stainback, eds. *Curriculum Considerations in Inclusive Classrooms: Facilitating Learning for All Students.* Paul H. Brookes, 1992. 275 p. ISBN 1-55766-078-6 (paper).

This widely cited book contains fourteen chapters by well-known leaders in the "inclusive schools movement" in the United States and Canada. The goal of inclusive schools is to ensure that all students, regardless of the nature or severity of their disabilities, are accepted and included as equal and valued members of the school community. Strategies for promoting inclusive education by designing, adapting, and delivering curriculum in general education classrooms are explained.

Thousand, Jacqueline S., Richard A. Villa, and Ann I. Nevin. *Creativity and Collaborative Learning: A Practical Guide to Empowering Students and Teachers.* Paul H. Brookes, 1994. 420 p. ISBN 1-55766-158-8 (paper).

This seventeen-chapter book is based on the premise that once "the barriers created by traditional instruction are removed," all children—regardless of their intellectual ability—are capable of helping one another learn. It presents the rationale and methods for creating a variety of collaborative learning opportunities among students that capitalize on their individual differences in order to promote the academic and social development of every student. Several chapters describe methods for preventing and dealing with behavioral disruptions, designing peer tutoring and partner learning activities, and building and maintaining peer connections and supports for students with disabilities. Case examples and nearly one hundred pages of sample group lesson plans are included.

Wood, Judy W. *Adapting Instruction for Mainstreamed and At-Risk Students.* 2nd ed. Macmillan, 1992. 404 p. ISBN 0-675-21421-1 (paper).

Wood states that the physical integration of students with disabilities in regular classrooms does not guarantee their success in the mainstream; the instructional process must be modified as well. This twelve-chapter book is organized around the author's four-part mainstreaming model: (a) Overview and Assessment, (b) Adapting the Environment, (c) Adapting Planning and Teaching, and (d) Adapting Evaluation and Grading Procedures. Content of special interest to practicing teachers includes a standard format that can be used to adapt lesson plans in any subject area and the two chapters on alternative testing and grading procedures.

WORKING WITH PARENTS AND FAMILIES

Kelley, Mary Lou. *School Home Notes: Promoting Children's Classroom Success.* Guilford Press, 1990. 198 p. ISBN 0-89862-356-1 (hardcover); 0-89862-235-2 (paper).

Parent involvement can often be the key to helping children who are experiencing academic or behavioral difficulty in school. Case examples show how to develop and use school-home notes as the basis for an ongoing communication program in which teachers and parents work as a team to help children improve their classroom performance. Common miscommunications between teachers and parents that can impede problem solving and interfere with the child's adjustment at home and school are highlighted in tables. Includes a variety of easily duplicated handouts and sample school-home notes.

Turnbull, Ann P., and H. Rutherford Turnbull. *Families, Professionals, and Exceptionality: A Special Partnership.* 2nd ed. Macmillan, 1990. 485 p. ISBN 0-675-21207-3 (paper).

The Turnbulls—special educators and the parents of a son with severe disabilities—explain, in a style that is both scholarly and personal, the impact of exceptionality on the roles and functions of family members. Their "family systems" perspective provides professionals with a meaningful context for establishing and maintaining a strong parent-professional partnership by improving parent-teacher communication, coordinating parent involvement in the referral and evaluation process, increasing parent participation in the IEP process, and resolving conflicts in compliance with the due process requirements of federal special education law.

Turnbull, H. Rutherford, and Ann P. Turnbull. *Parents Speak Out: Then and Now.* 2nd ed. Macmillan, 1985. 287 p. ISBN 0-675-20404-6 (paper).

Here is a collection of powerful first-person accounts of parents' efforts to obtain educational and other services for their children with disabilities. It provides a unique perspective in that most of the contributors are not only parents or relatives of someone with a disability but also professionals who serve people with disabilities. The authors not only document with candor and eloquence the frustrations and challenges posed by living with and caring for a family member with disabilities, they dispel the notion held by many professionals that a child with disabilities is "invariably a burden and cause for family distress." *Parents Speak Out* should be required reading for every teacher.

Part II — Curriculum Content and Disability Areas

Consultant: Dr. Teresa A. Grossi
University of Toledo
Toledo, Ohio

Dr. Grossi is Assistant Professor in the Department of Special Education at the University of Toledo in Toledo, Ohio. She received her doctorate from The Ohio State University in Special Education and Applied Behavior Analysis. Dr. Grossi prepares teachers and practitioners to work with students and adults with developmental and multiple disabilities. Her research interests include developing effective instructional strategies for the classroom and community, self-management strategies, and transitioning students from school to adult life and supported employment. She (with Dr. William Heward) is currently under contract with Prentice-Hall for a publication scheduled for 1997, *A Dozen Common Teaching Mistakes and What to Do Instead*.

ACADEMIC CONTENT AREA

Gable, Robert A., and Jo M. Hendrickson, eds. *Assessing Students with Special Needs: A Sourcebook for Analyzing and Correcting Errors in Academics*. Longman, 1990. 174 p. ISBN 0-8013-0177-7 (paper).

The authors describe a set of effective strategies for identifying and remediating students' errors in tool skills—reading, arithmetic, spelling, handwriting, written language, and subject matter content areas. Error analysis focuses on the learner's academic response pattern as the "unit of analysis" and is essential for making effective instructional decisions. An expert group of contributing authors offers a step-by-step guide to informal assessment and a comprehensive presentation of error analysis procedures. Numerous tables and charts illustrate practical solutions to commonly encountered error patterns.

Lovitt, Thomas C. *Tactics for Teaching*. 2nd ed. Macmillan, 1995. 359 p. ISBN 0-02-371813-7 (paper).

Teachers often complain that educational research can never be applied to the classroom. Lovitt solves this concern by providing teachers with research-based tactics and ideas for increasing learners' academic and social skills. *Tactics of Teaching* describes 105 tactics categorized into six sections: reading, writing, spelling, mathematics, classroom management, and self-management. Each tactic is presented in the same format: a description of the tactic, the pupils with whom the tactic would be most appropriate, and procedures for implementing and evaluating the technique. This book shows teachers how to put the findings of research immediately into practice in their classroom. *Tactics* is a resource every teacher should have.

Mercer, Cecil D., and Ann R. Mercer. *Teaching Students with Learning Problems.* 4th ed. Macmillan, 1993. 705 p. ISBN 0-02-380561-7 (paper).

One of the most widely used texts in special education, this book provides research-based methods that improve teacher effectiveness and student achievement. Focused on students with mild disabilities, grades K–12, the book offers over three hundred fifty teaching activities, fifty self-correcting instructional materials, seventy-five instructional games, and reviews of one hundred fifty commercial programs and aids. Techniques are provided to show a teacher how to set up and maintain instructional programs for large groups, small groups, and individual learners. Best practices in collaborative consultation, cooperative learning, peer tutoring, and ideas for homework practices, class size, grading, and adaptation of materials are covered.

Polloway, Edward A., and James R. Patton. *Strategies for Teaching Learners with Special Needs.* 5th ed. Macmillan, 1993. 545 p. ISBN 0-02-396021-3 (paper).

This easy-to-read text describing a broad scope reflects a selection of proven approaches to promote educational success. It presents a cross-categorical approach of teaching methods and strategies for learners with special needs. In addition to the chapters on curriculum design and academic content areas, a helpful feature is a section on critical skills covering topics such as study skills, social skills instruction, classroom management, and behavior change strategies. The authors make it clear throughout the book that while teaching methods are rarely category-specific, differences among learners must be reflected in their instructional programming.

CURRICULUM CONTENT

Agran, Martin, Nancy E. Marchand-Martella, and Ronald C. Martella, eds. *Promoting Health and Safety: Skills for Independent Living.* Paul H. Brookes, 1994. 221 p. ISBN 0-55766-135-9 (paper).

Current best practice for students with moderate and severe disabilities emphasizes community-based instruction of functional daily living, recreation/leisure, and work skills. This resource book addresses responsibilities and risks faced by individuals with disabilities when working and living in the community. A broad range of topics is covered, including first aid, crime deterrence, home and job safety, fire safety, nutrition and food preparation, and the prevention of substance abuse and HIV/AIDS. Case studies are included to demonstrate effective behavioral-instructional strategies for teaching personal safety and health skills.

Block, Martin H. *A Teacher's Guide to Including Students with Disabilities in Regular Physical Education.* Paul H. Brookes, 1994. 276 p. ISBN 1-55766-156-1 (paper).

An increasing number of students with disabilities are being included in regular classrooms as well as regular physical education classes. This practical guide for including students of all ages and abilities in regular physical education programs is based on an ecological approach to program planning. The author describes a systematic process for developing and implementing inclusive physical education programs that emphasizes preplanning and training support personnel. Numerous practical examples and applications illustrate the recommended instructional and curricular strategies. Forms and checklists are provided to assist in program planning.

Brolin, Donn E. *Career Education: A Functional Life Skills Approach.* 3rd ed. Macmillan, 1995. 528 p. ISBN 0-02-315062-9 (hardcover).

Career education—introducing children to the world of work—is seldom mentioned when elementary curriculum is discussed. However, for students with disabilities who need more than the standard academically oriented curriculum, early exposure to and instruction on work-related attitudes and skills is critical. This book details a comprehensive functional, life-skills model of career education for students in grades K–12. General guidelines and specific steps for integrating career education with the academic curriculum as well as other functional living skills are included.

Carnine, Douglas, Jerry Silbert, and Edward J. Kameenui. *Direct Instruction Reading.* 2nd ed. Macmillan, 1990. 467 p. ISBN 0-675-21014-3 (hardcover).

Over a decade of research with beginning and remedial readers led to the development of *Direct Instruction Reading.* The Direct Instruction model is designed to produce the maximum amount of learning in the shortest possible time by incorporating carefully chosen teaching examples, high rates of student response, and corrective feedback into fast-paced, teacher directed lessons. The book covers beginning reading, decoding, and comprehension, with the largest part devoted to beginning reading. Related research findings, application exercises, and specific suggestions are provided for solving reading problems frequently encountered in the classroom.

Lewis, Rena B. *Special Education Technology: Practical Applications.* Brookes Cole Publishing, 1993. 552 p. ISBN 0-534-20286-1 (paper).

This is a practical book on ways teachers can use computers and other technologies to improve the education of students with disabilities. The first section presents an overview of classroom applications of technology and offers strategies for adapting computers and selecting software for students with special needs. The core of the book shows teachers how to integrate technology into the classroom to support students with disabilities across the curriculum. The final three chapters tell how technology can enhance the quality of life for individuals with disabilities by helping them overcome communication, physical, and sensory barriers.

Phelps-Teraski, Diana, and Trisha Phelps-Gunn. *Teaching Competence in Written Language: A Systematic Program for Developing Writing Skills.* PRO-ED, 1988. 35 p. (paper).

Intended for teachers who help students with special needs to learn how to write competently. This systematic, individualized, and highly structured program allows the student to move in a step-by-step fashion from idea, to sentences, to paragraphs. Competence in written language expression is developed by giving students practice in the different uses and kinds of writing. Teachers are provided with all the necessary steps, techniques, and materials to implement this program.

Silbert, Jerry, Douglas Carnine, and Mary Stein. *Direct Instruction Mathematics.* 2nd ed. Macmillan, 1990. 508 p. ISBN 0-675-21208-1 (paper).

Teachers frequently request guidance on how to deal with students having difficulty learning mathematics. This text explains the inadequacies of some instructional programs and provides teachers with the information needed to modify the programs. The book is organized into two parts: (1) Perspectives, describing the philosophy and techniques of direct instruction; and (2) Skills and Concepts, discussing math skills (counting, symbol identification, place value). Special features include procedures for teaching major skills; procedures for evaluating, selecting, and modifying mathematics programs; and techniques for effectively presenting lessons. Teachers will find this book extremely practical and directly applicable to the classroom.

DISABILITIES

Barrage, Natalie C., and Jane N. Erin. *Visual Handicaps and Learning.* 3rd ed. PRO-ED, 1992. 213 p. ISBN 0-89079-515-0 (paper).

A major objective of this book is to present a new way of thinking about individuals with visual impairments so that they are viewed as participating members of a "seeing world" despite their reduction in visual functioning. This book gives general and special education teachers an overview of visual impairments and strategies to enhance academic achievement and independence for the student with visual impairments. Special chapters of interest to teachers include: tactual, auditory, and visual development and learning; assessment and evaluation; and curricular adaptations and media.

Batshaw, Mark L., and Yvonne M. Perret. *Children with Disabilities: A Medical Primer.* Paul H. Brookes, 1992. 664 p. ISBN 1-55766-102-2 (paper).

An excellent resource book for teachers and other professionals on the needs of children with physical disabilities and health-related conditions. This easy-to-read book offers clear explanations of essential information concerning the causes and effects of various disabling conditions and diagnostic and intervention strategies. Topics such as what happens before, during, and after birth to cause a developmental disability, cerebral palsy, seizure disorders, prenatal exposure to alcohol and cocaine, HIV/AIDS, spina bifida, and traumatic brain injury are discussed. Each chapter presents information through case studies and the use of illustrations, charts, and graphs. Appendices include a guide to related resources and a glossary of terminology.

Beirne-Smith, Mary, James R. Patton, and Richard Ittenbach. *Mental Retardation.* 4th ed. Macmillan, 1994. 636 p. ISBN 0-02-307883-9 (hardcover).

This text, widely used in teacher training programs, provides a thorough, highly researched, and up-to-date examination of the many facets of mental retardation. Coverage includes causes and prevention, assessment, learning and behavior characteristics of the different levels of mental retardation, and educational programming issues across the life span. Changes that have occurred in the area of mental retardation are presented from a historical perspective, with highlights of recent developments such as community-based instruction, transition planning, supported employment, and inclusion. Each chapter includes short vignettes and personal stories which enrich and broaden certain topics.

Bigge, June L. *Teaching Individuals with Physical and Multiple Disabilities.* 3rd ed. Macmillan, 1991. 636 p. ISBN 0-675-21017-8 (hardcover).

Educators seeking background and in-depth knowledge to assist students with physical and multiple disabilities will find this informative book resourceful and very helpful. The first five chapters provide general information, information on conditions which frequently result in physical and multiple disabilities, and services required. Discussion of special health care needs and avenues to physical participation (e.g., position and seating, environmental control, and assistive technology) will be of particular interest to teachers. The remaining chapters describe curriculum and instructional adaptations and focus on preparation for life management and optimizing independent living. Several chapters feature sections on computer applications. An appendix of technology sources is included.

Ford, Alison, Roberta Schnorr, Luanna Meyer, Linda Davern, Jim Black, and Patrick Dempsey, eds. *The Syracuse Community-referenced Curriculum Guide for Students with Moderate and Severe Disabilities.* Paul H. Brookes, 1989. 404 p. ISBN 1-55766-027-1 (hardcover).

This highly regarded curriculum guide is based on the premise that every student, no matter how severe his or her disabilities, is capable of living, working, and recreating in the community. The field-tested curriculum consists of four major community living areas: self-managers/home living, vocational, recreation/leisure, and general community functioning. It also covers functional academics and embedded social, communication, and motor skills. Numerous examples of instructional programs are provided throughout the book. Includes a wide variety of reproducible forms and charts for data collection, parent communicators, and IEPs.

Kaufman, James M. *Characteristics of Emotional and Behavioral Disorders of Children and Youth.* 5th ed. Macmillan, 1993. 579 p. ISBN 0-02-362141-9 (hardcover).

This overview of the field of emotional and behavioral disorders interprets recent research in psychology and special education for use by the classroom teacher. Comprehensive discussion of causal factors, types of emotional and behavioral disorders, procedures and problems in screening assessment and classification, and educational intervention is presented. A special section on the facets of disordered behavior includes topics such as attention and activity disorders, overt aggression and covert antisocial behavior, delinquency, and substance abuse. Each of the chapters is relevant for both regular and special educators.

Koegel, Robert L., and Lynn Kern Koegel. *Teaching Children with Autism: Strategies for Initiating Positive Interactions and Improving Learning Opportunities.* Paul H. Brookes, 1995. 352 p. ISBN 1-55766-180-4 (paper).

A comprehensive text on state-of-the-art strategies for helping children with autism participate successfully in school and community life, this research-based text presents practical information in an easy-to-read format. Three important goals of intervention are highlighted: motivating children with autism to respond to social and environmental stimulation, teaching children with autism to respond to complex multiple cues, and providing education in inclusive settings. Four chapters are devoted to the impact of the child with autism on the family and the importance of including the child's parents and family as valued participants in program planning and implementation.

Lerner, Janet W., Barbara Lowenthal, and Sue R. Lerner. *Attention Deficit Disorders: Assessment and Teaching.* Brookes Cole Publishing, 1995. 259 p. ISBN 0-534-25044-0 (paper).

A resource guide for teachers and other professionals working with children who have attention deficit disorders (ADD), this is an easy-to-read book offering practical strategies for making accommodations in the regular classroom as well as teaching methods to be used by regular and special educators. Each chapter begins with a brief case vignette and a section summarizing important points. In-depth coverage of assessment, medication, and the challenges parents face offers teachers and parents practical ideas and solutions for helping children with ADD. Several appendices provide useful resources for teachers and parents.

Mercer, Cecil D. *Students with Learning Disabilities.* 4th ed. Macmillan, 1991. 677 p. ISBN 0-02-380540-4 (hardcover).

Students with learning disabilities comprise one-half of all students who receive special education services. This comprehensive and widely used text reflects the latest developments and trends in learning disabilities, including implications across the life span, recent teaching technology, and current issues concerning identification, assessment, and where the student with learning disabilities should be served. A perspective on what research indicates are the best practices is presented throughout the book. Of special interest to teachers is the coverage on learning strategies, social skills training, collaborative teaching, and effective assessment and teaching practices in the academic areas. An appendix with a list of publishers of books, tests, and materials is included.

Paul, Peter V., and Stephen P. Quigley. *Language and Deafness.* 2nd ed. Singular Publishing Group, 1994. 374 p. ISBN 1-56593-362-1 (hardcover); 1-56593-108-4 (paper).

According to the authors, the present state of the education of deaf children "can be characterized as one of creative confusion." Creative, because new approaches are being tried; confusing, because there is too little research to guide the development of effective practices. Following an in-depth analysis of the impact of deafness on language development, the authors conclude that the extent of English literacy attained by a deaf student is "inextricably related to the mode of communication which is used initially" (e.g., oralism, total communication, American Sign Language) and that a "first language" should be developed at as early an age as possible.

Simpson, Richard L., and Paul Zionts. *Autism: Information and Resources for Parents, Families, and Professionals.* PRO-ED, 1992. 179 p. ISBN 0-89079-538-X (paper).

Numerous questions have surrounded autism and for some of them, there are answers. For others, there are no definite answers. This easy-to-read book provides scientifically valid information in a question-answer format. Common questions about autism were selected for family members and professionals wanting to learn more. Without going into great depth, this book presents an overview of concepts and characteristics of autism; background on the disorder; and alternatives, considerations, and strategies for obtaining education, treatment, and support. A resource guide is included in the appendix.

Snell, Martha E., ed. *Instruction of Students with Severe Disabilities.* 4th ed. Macmillan, 1993. 639 p. ISBN 0-02-413751-0 (hardcover).

An expert group of contributing authors gives a comprehensive and in-depth examination of state-of-the-art teaching practices for students with severe disabilities. Functional skill development is emphasized with five major curriculum areas: self-care, functional academics, daily living and community living, leisure and recreation, and vocational. Case studies are presented to relate the text concepts to the classroom practices and challenges. This widely regarded text is an excellent resource for any educator who wants to help students with severe disabilities function more independently in integrated settings.

Sternberg, Les, ed. *Individuals with Profound Disabilities: Instructional and Assistive Strategies.* 3rd ed. PRO-ED, 1994. 546 p. ISBN 0-89079-557-6 (hardcover).

This comprehensive book presents issues, concerns, and strategies that relate to working with profound disabilities, from birth to adulthood. Numerous experts contribute to this text, presenting critical information on a wide range of topics including biomedical causes of profound disabling conditions, assessing levels of state and arousal, special health care interventions, curricular designs, and behavioral and instructional interventions. Case examples, assessment guides, and administrative forms are provided throughout the book. This work will benefit teachers, service providers, and others working with individuals with profound disabilities.

Walker, Hill M., Geoff Colvin, and Elizabeth Ramsey. *Antisocial Behavior in School: Strategies and Best Practices.* Brookes Cole Publishing, 1995. 481 p. ISBN 0-534-25644-9 (paper).

Children are becoming involved in violent behavior at an ever younger age. This book is written for the educator or practitioner who must cope with students who either have or are at high risk for developing antisocial behavior patterns. The material in this book is designed to enhance a professional's understanding of the nature, origins, and causes of antisocial behavior. Based on an ecological social-learning perspective, information on the best available practices, interventions, and model programs for preventing and remedying the most destructive behavior disorders in school is presented. Developing a partnership between schools, families, and social agencies is essential to addressing the complex needs of the antisocial student.

Wolery-Allegheny, Mark, Melinda Jones Ault, and Patricia Munson Doyle. *Teaching Students with Moderate to Severe Disabilities: Use of Response Prompting Strategies.* Longman, 1992. 252 p. ISBN 0-8013-0491-1 (paper).

Trial and error learning—difficult and frustrating at best for students without disabilities—is often a waste of time for students with severe disabilities. Instead of waiting for a correct response, the teacher provides an extra cue that virtually ensures a correct response ("say 'danger'"). If these response prompts are gradually and systematically withdrawn over a series of learning trials, control of the student's correct responding transfers to the instructional item (the printed word 'danger'). The coauthors, who have contributed much of the applied research on which the procedures are based, describe their rationale, procedural details, and multiple examples for using response prompting.

SOCIAL SKILLS

Cartledge, Gwendolyn, and James Kleefeld. *Taking Part: Introducing Social Skills to Children.* American Guidance Service, 1991. 168 p. ISBN 0-88671-421-4 (guide); 0-88671-420-6 (program).

Most children often learn social skills through imitating others or by making a mistake and receiving correction or a reprimand from an adult. For many children, however, specific social skills instruction is needed. This training program is for children in regular and mainstreamed classrooms, preschool through grade three. *Taking Part* consists of six units: (1) making conversation, (2) communicating feelings, (3) expressing oneself, (4) cooperating with peers, (5) playing with peers, and (6) responding to aggression and conflict. Each unit contains five to seven specific skills, with step-by-step descriptions of all activities. An activity kit is provided that includes materials required for the lessons, puppets, skill posters, blackline masters, and stickers.

―――. *Working Together: Building Children's Social Skills Through Folk Literature.* American Guidance Service, 1994. 275 p. ISBN 0-8867-11487 (guide); 0-8867-11665 (program).

Working Together is a social skills training program for children in regular and mainstreamed classrooms, grades three through six. The activities provided in this curriculum can either be used alone or to extend or supplement language arts or social studies lessons. A teacher's guide and kit provide a step-by-step description of all activities and materials needed for each activity. Each of the five units contains four to eight specific skills covering topics such as making conversation and expressing feelings, cooperating with peers, playing with peers, responding to conflict and aggression, and performing in the classroom.

Cartledge, Gwendolyn, and JoAnne Fellows Milburn. *Teaching Social Skills to Children and Youth.* 3rd ed. Allyn & Bacon, 1995. 308 p. ISBN 0-205-16073-5 (hardcover); 0-205-16507-9 (paper).

Teachers are increasingly assuming more responsibility for teaching appropriate social and behavior skills to their students. This book is intended for both regular and special educators and clinicians working in various settings. Emphasis is placed throughout the book on building prosocial, adaptive, and new behaviors with the belief that social behaviors should be taught specifically as part of the school curriculum. A directive teaching model serves as the framework for this book. Special features include topics covering programming for aggressive children, training needs for individuals with developmental disabilities, and implications of multicultural understanding for social skills instruction.

Sargent, Laurence R. *Social Skills for School and Community: Systematic Instruction for Children and Youth with Cognitive Delays.* Council for Exceptional Children, 1991. 308 p. ISBN 0-685-52087-0 (hardcover).

This social skills program is designed for use with children who spend a portion or all of their day in regular education classrooms. Over one hundred examples of proactive social skills instruction across the K–12 continuum are included. The social skills lessons were developed along age-related concepts such as getting along with teachers and school officials, getting along with peers, getting along in the community, and getting along on the job. The lessons are based on a direct instruction model and contain a six-step procedure: (1) establish the need, (2) identify skill components, (3) model the skill, (4) role-play, (5) practice, and (6) generalize.

Walker, Hill M., Scott McConnell, Deborah Holmes, Bonnie Todis, Jackie Walter, and Nancy Golden. *The Walker Social Skills Curriculum: The ACCEPTS Program.* PRO-ED, 1988. 154 p. ISBN 0-936104-30-9 (paper).

One of the leading social skills curricula in special education, the ACCEPTS curriculum is designed for use with primary and intermediate grade students with mild and moderate developmental delays. Twenty-eight skills are grouped into five major content areas: (1) classroom skills, (2) basic interaction skills, (3) getting along, (4) making friends, and (5) coping skills. The program uses a direct instruction and competency-based approach to ensure student mastery. Instruction, which can take place in the classroom or natural settings (e.g., the cafeteria, the playground), is carried out in a small-group format. Involving the target child with nondisabled peers is recommended.

JOURNALS

Exceptional Children. Council for Exceptional Children. ISSN 0014-4029.

Publishes original research, position papers, debates, and reviews of the literature related to contemporary issues concerning the education of exceptional children.

Designed to assist all professionals who work with exceptional children, including school psychologists, counselors, and administrators. Occasional special issues on thematic topics are published (e.g., bilingual special education, African-American youth in special education, educating children with attention-deficit disorder).

Teaching Exceptional Children. Council for Exceptional Children. ISSN 0040-0599.

TEC is a practitioner's journal designed to assist both regular and special education classroom teachers of children with disabilities as well as those who are gifted and talented. Most articles feature practical methods and materials for classroom use. Also includes a teacher idea exchange, reviews of books and instructional materials, descriptions of selected materials from the ERIC Clearinghouse on Disabilities and Gifted Education, and information on national meetings and inservice training opportunities.

MEMBERSHIPS

Council for Exceptional Children
1920 Association Drive
Reston, Virginia 22091-1589

Phone: (800) 845-6232
Fax: (703) 264-9494

The worldwide mission of the Council for Exceptional Children is "to improve educational outcomes for individuals with exceptionalities. The organization accomplishes its mission by advocating for appropriate governmental policies; by setting professional standards; by providing continuing professional development; and by helping professionals achieve the conditions and resources necessary for effective professional practice." The two official journals of the CEC are *Exceptional Children* and *Teaching Exceptional Children.* Several of CEC's seventeen divisions publish journals that focus on specific disability categories or service delivery concerns.

16

Gifted and Talented Education

Consultant: Dr. Karen L. Westberg
University of Connecticut
Storrs, Connecticut

Dr. Karen Westberg is Assistant Professor in the Department of Educational Psychology at the University of Connecticut, where she is one of the principal investigators for the National Research Center on the Gifted and Talented and teaches graduate coursework in gifted education and research methodology. Dr. Westberg received her master's degree and Ph.D. degree in Gifted Education from the University of Connecticut. Before joining the faculty at the University of Connecticut, she was an elementary classroom teacher, a teacher of the gifted, and coordinator of a gifted program in Minnesota.

In addition to her varied teaching and research experiences, Dr. Westberg has conducted workshops for educators throughout the country on several topics in education, including creative thinking skills, the Schoolwide Enrichment Model, and talent development.

Among her publications, Dr. Westberg has coauthored monographs based on her research on the gifted and talented. These monographs can be ordered from the National Research Center on the Gifted and Talented (Storrs, CT). They include the following: *An Observational Study of Instructional and Curricular Practices Used With Gifted and Talented Students in Regular Classrooms* (Research Monograph 93104, 1993); *Regular Classroom Practices With Gifted Students: Results of a National Survey of Classroom Teachers* (Research Monograph 93102, 1993); and *Why Not Let High Ability Students Start School in January? The Curriculum Compacting Study* (Research Monograph 93106, 1993).

DOCUMENTS/ GUIDELINES/ STANDARDS

U.S. Department of Education. *National Excellence: A Case for Developing America's Talent.* U.S. Department of Education, 1993. 33 p. ISBN 0-16-04298-5 (hardcover); Gordon Press, ISBN 0-8490-8586-1 (hardcover).

This federal document on the status of gifted and talented education in the country replaces the previous national report which was published over twenty years ago. The report focuses on the national interest in gifted education and contains suggestions on how to improve the education of our nation's most talented students. The report includes an updated, federal definition of who these top students are. It should be noted that the terms "outstanding talent" and "talent development" are used to reflect current knowledge about the existence and development of cognitive abilities.

ACCELERATION

Southern, Thomas W., and Eric D. Jones, eds. *The Academic Acceleration of Gifted Children.* Teachers College Press, 1991. 242 p. ISBN 0-8077-3069-6 (hardcover); 0-8077-3068-8 (paper).

The editors of this volume compiled information about the various forms of acceleration, including grade skipping, early admission, and curriculum acceleration, and the major views on the acceleration of bright children. In addition to the various acceleration options, the authors discuss the major issues and concerns on this topic held by educators such as school readiness, affective development, and placement procedures. The information provides practitioners with guidance for assessing, implementing, and evaluating acceleration options. The book is an up-to-date reference on a topic that is frequently misunderstood.

CREATIVITY

Davis, Gary A. *Creativity is Forever.* 3rd ed. Kendall/Hunt Publishing, 1992. 352 p. ISBN 0-8403-66-911 (paper).

In a highly entertaining and playful style, this book provides general information about creativity; namely, what it is, what hinders its expression, characteristics of creative people and products, stages in the creative process, techniques for stimulating creativity, and methods for assessing creativity. One chapter is devoted to creativity as it applies to gifted education. While the book is based on solid research and theory, it presents practical information that is worthwhile and easily understood. Individuals learn a great deal about creativity from this book.

Starko, Alane Jordan. *Creativity in the Classroom: Schools of Curious Delight.* Longman Publishers, 1995. 342 p. ISBN 0-8013-1230-2 (paper).

This book is written for teachers who have an interest in enhancing students' creative thinking skills and abilities. Information about various theories and models of creativity and creativity within content areas, as well as how to teach for the development of creative thinking, are discussed. For example, several divergent thinking strategies (attribute listing, creative problem solving) are explained. Issues related to the assessment of creativity and the organization of classrooms for stimulating creativity are also included. Sidebars entitled "Thinking about the Classroom" are included throughout the book to encourage teachers to relate the material to their own teaching situations.

Treffinger, Donald J., Marion R. Sortore, and Mary C. Tallman. *The Creative Problem Solver's Guidebook.* Center for Creative Learning (4152 Independence Court, Suite C-7, Sarasota, FL 34234), 1992. 54 p. (paper).

This guidebook contains a set of twenty-three reproducible "templates" designed to help adults or students who are learning the six stages in the Creative Problem Solving method. The templates, or forms, are used for gathering and recording information when individuals are involved in discussions or exercises at each stage. For example, open-ended "brainwriting," "SCAMPER" checklists, and "morphological matrix" forms are included for the Idea-Finding stage. This booklet would be used best if accompanied by Treffinger and Isaksen's guidebook, *Creative Problem Solving: An Introduction,* annotated below.

Treffinger, Donald J., and Scott G. Isaksen. *Creative Problem Solving: An Introduction.* Center for Creative Learning (4152 Independence Court, Suite, C-7, Sarasota, FL 34234), 1985. 100 p. ISBN 0-943456-05-3 (hardcover).

This guidebook is a concise, easy-to-understand discussion of the importance of creative and critical thinking skills and an updated overview of the six stages of the Creative Problem Solving (CPS) method which was developed originally by Osborn and further elaborated upon by Parnes and Treffinger. The six stages of the CPS process are: Mess-Finding, Data-Finding, Problem-Finding, Idea-Finding, Solution-Finding, and Acceptance-Finding. The authors provide several guidelines and techniques for helping students engage in convergent and divergent thinking at each stage of the CPS process.

CURRICULUM DEVELOPMENT

Maker, C. June. *Curriculum Development for the Gifted*. PRO-ED, 1982. 393 p. ISBN 0-89079-130-9 (hardcover).

The author proposes that integrating a variety of strategies may be the best approach to use when developing an effective gifted education program. The first section of the book discusses how to make content, process, product, and learning environment modifications for gifted students. This is followed by recommendations and a step-by-step plan for developing curriculum at the local level. In the final section, Maker provides examples of approaches to educating gifted students in different settings, including an elementary resource room program.

Renzulli, Joseph S. *The Enrichment Triad Model: A Guide for Developing Defensible Programs for the Gifted and Talented*. Creative Learning Press, 1977. 88 p. ISBN 0-936386-01-0 (paper).

This is the original book in which Renzulli presented his enrichment model for the education of gifted students, which has been cited by *Phi Delta Kappan* and the *New York Times* as the most widely used model in the country. The model contains three enrichment types which emphasize providing students with opportunities, resources, and encouragement to pursue individual interests. Type I Enrichment provides students with exposure experiences designed to develop potential interests. Type II Enrichment focuses on developing cognitive and affective processes. Type III Enrichment provides students with an opportunity to pursue real world problems in independent projects.

Van Tassel-Baska, Joyce. *Comprehensive Curriculum for Gifted Learners*. Allyn & Bacon, 1994. 415 p. ISBN 0-205-15412-3 (hardcover).

Teachers who are responsible for the development of a challenging curriculum for gifted students may be interested in this book, which focuses exclusively on curriculum development at several grade levels. Three curriculum models are emphasized throughout the book: a content model emphasizing acceleration through the curriculum, a process/product model focusing on independent problem solving experiences, and an epistemological model examining the major themes and concepts in an area of study. Chapters are also devoted to the major content areas and the development of thinking skills, the humanities, the arts, affective development, and leadership skills.

GENERAL BACKGROUND

Clark, Barbara. *Growing Up Gifted*. 4th ed. Macmillan, 1992. 587 p. ISBN 0-02-322680-3 (hardcover).

Clark's book, now in its fourth edition, has been widely used as an introductory text and reference book on gifted education. She integrates theory, research, and practice in each chapter and deals with all of the major topics in gifted education, from conceptions of giftedness to the evaluation of services for gifted learners. What sets this comprehensive book apart from other introductory texts is her interest in and emphasis on brain functioning. What makes this text particularly useful is the Questions Often Asked section included at the end of each chapter.

Colangelo, Nicholas, and Gary A. Davis, eds. *Handbook of Gifted Education.* Allyn & Bacon, 1991. 463 p. ISBN 0-205-12652-9 (ringbound).

As a comprehensive book about gifted education, this is often viewed as a "must have" for individuals who have an interest in the field. Thirty-one chapters, written by the top leaders in the field, provide information about theory, research, and practices in gifted education. Topics include problems and promising practices in identification, instructional models for gifted learners, ability grouping, counseling gifted students, ethnic and cultural issues, and future directions for the field. The book is a good reflection of the accumulated knowledge about the education of the gifted and talented.

Davis, Gary A., and Sylvia B. Rimm. *Education of the Gifted and Talented.* 3rd ed. Allyn & Bacon, 1994. 494 p. ISBN 0-205-14806-9 (hardcover); 0-13-236605-3 (ringbound).

This book provides readers with a general understanding of topics in the field of gifted education. The eighteen chapters are easy to understand and are in-depth enough to provide a thorough understanding of topics, including definitions of giftedness, identification procedures, instructional strategies, and evaluation of both students and programs. With regard to enrichment and acceleration options, the authors discuss over fifteen specific strategies. The importance of grouping gifted students for advanced instruction is also discussed. Issues of special interest include underachievement, gifted females, parenting the gifted, and provisions for gifted students with handicapping conditions.

Gallagher, James J., and Shelagh A. Gallagher. *Teaching the Gifted Child.* 4th ed. Allyn & Bacon, 1994. 468 p. ISBN 0-205-14828-X (hardcover).

This text, now in its fourth edition, has been widely used in introductory gifted education courses for the past thirty years. The book contains three major sections: (1) definitions and identification of gifted students, (2) curriculum modifications in the major subject areas, and (3) the development of process skills such as problem finding and creative thinking. In this edition, the authors elaborate on the relationship between the teaching practices developed in gifted education and many of the educational reforms that have been proposed recently for students to perform at the highest levels within the industrialized world.

Piirto, Jane. *Gifted Children and Adults: Their Development and Education.* Macmillan, 1994. 648 p. ISBN 0-02-395775-1 (paper).

Piirto approaches the study of giftedness from a developmental perspective, emphasizing the evolution of talents from birth to adulthood. She presents various conceptions of giftedness and intelligence and the importance of identifying a wide range of intellectual and creative behaviors. Then she discusses how giftedness evolves throughout the life span, placing particular emphasis on cognitive and personality factors. In the final section, she provides suggestions on how to develop curriculum and how to use counseling strategies to meet the needs of students who have a variety of talents and potentials.

Renzulli, Joseph S., ed. *Systems and Models for Developing Programs for the Gifted and Talented.* Creative Learning Press, 1986. 484 p. ISBN 0-936386-44-4 (paper).

Chapters in this book are written by leaders in gifted education who each describe their system or model for meeting the needs of gifted and talented students. The authors provide a rationale for their system or model, describe the strategies for implementing the system or model, and explain the research that supports the effectiveness of their work. Included among the chapters are the Purdue Three Stage Elementary Model (by Feldhusen and Robinson), the Enrichment Triad/Revolving Door Model (by Renzulli and Reis), the Talents Unlimited Model (by Schlichter), and the Independent Learner Model (by Treffinger).

Shore, Bruce, Dewey Cornell, Ann Robinson, and Virgil Scott. *Recommended Practices in Gifted Education: A Critical Analysis.* Teachers College Press, 1991. 367 p. ISBN 0-8077-3084-X (hardcover).

This seminal book presents the background information and the supporting evidence, and lack of supporting evidence, for one hundred and one recommended practices in gifted education. Topics addressed include curriculum and program policies such as acceleration, thinking skills, and career education for girls; advice to educators on such concerns as individualized reading, creative abilities, and independent study; and social and emotional adjustment issues such as the development of leadership ability, the encouragement of broadened interests, and the development of positive self-concepts. Although the book focuses on a research base, it is directed toward a practitioner audience.

Sternberg, Robert J., and Janet E. Davidson, eds. *Conceptions of Giftedness.* Cambridge University Press, 1986. 460 p. ISBN 0-521-26814-1 (hardcover); 0-521-31879-3 (paper).

What is "giftedness"? While there has been no consensus on this issue throughout history, and there has been only partial agreement among school personnel with regard to how giftedness should be viewed, commonalities among theories are emerging. This book presents a scholarly discussion about contemporary conceptions of giftedness by seventeen prominent and distinguished educators and psychologists. In the concluding chapter, the editors synthesize the various theories and suggest avenues for further research on this topic. This book is a significant contribution to the gifted education literature that appeals to scholars and practitioners.

GUIDANCE

Genshaft, Judy, Marlene Bireley, and Constance Hollinger, eds. *Serving Gifted and Talented Students: A Resource for School Personnel.* PRO-ED, 1995. 440 p. ISBN 0-89079-605-X (hardcover).

Serving Gifted and Talented Students: A Resource for School Personnel, a joint effort by the publisher and the National Association of School Psychologists, was designed to alert school psychologists, counselors, and other personnel to the unique academic and psychosocial needs of gifted students. Identification, evaluation, and the affective development of gifted students are often assigned to specialists; however, few have an adequate background in providing for the needs of gifted students. The six parts of the book deal with important issues such as identification, intervention strategies, and how gifted education can be a key element in the reform movement.

Schmitz, Connie C., and Judy Galbraith. *Managing the Social and Emotional Needs of the Gifted: A Teacher's Survival Guide.* Free Spirit Publishing, 1985. 156 p. ISBN 0-915793-05-9 (hardcover).

As pointed out in this book, being bright is not necessarily associated with being happy, secure, and socially adept, nor is it associated with being overly sensitive, difficult, or socially inept. The book is designed to help teachers and counselors understand and deal with the varied social and emotional characteristics of gifted, talented, and creative students. It provides background research and practical strategies for helping students with several issues, including stress management, peer relationships, and high expectations. Sample discussion questions for dealing with various issues in classroom situations or support groups are also included.

Silverman, Linda Kreger, ed. *Counseling the Gifted and Talented.* Love Publishing, 1993. 372 p. ISBN 0-89108-227-1 (hardcover).

This book addresses a special aspect of gifted education, the provision of counseling services to gifted students. Three general areas of counseling are examined. The first area addresses specific aspects of schooling for which counseling services are appropriate, including academic issues, career options, and the development of social and leadership qualities. The second area is related to meeting the counseling needs of special populations, including students who are underachievers, learning disabled, or from minority cultures. The third area addresses counseling issues related to the family, including the home environment, peer relationships, and parental recognition of early signs of giftedness.

Van Tassel-Baska, Joyce L., and Paula Olezewski-Kubilius, eds. *Patterns of Influence on Gifted Learners: The Home, The Self, and the School.* Teachers College Press, 1989. 250 p. ISBN 0-8077-2938-8 (hardcover); 0-8077-2937-X (paper).

"How do institutions like the family and the school act as agents of the talent development process?" "What personal characteristics are most critical for students to possess in the talent development process?" (p. 1). The editors' purpose was to provide answers to these questions. The book is separated into three sections dealing with the influence of the family, personal characteristics, and the role of effective schooling. The book contains chapters written by experts in the field of gifted education who provide a variety of perspectives on these three issues.

PROGRAM DEVELOPMENT

Maker, C. June, ed. *Critical Issues in Gifted Education: Defensible Programs for the Gifted.* PRO-ED, 1986. 357 p. ISBN 0-89079-194-5 (vol. I, hardcover); 0-89079-184-8 (vol. II, hardcover).

The unique feature of this book is that it presents differing views on issues in gifted education which focus on the meaning of the term, "qualitatively differentiated." Each chapter is followed by another chapter or two in which responses or alternative views are given. The chapters are organized in five major sections: definitions of giftedness, curriculum, enrichment and acceleration, evaluation of gifted programs, and defending gifted programs. Chapter titles include "Giftedness: The Mistaken Metaphor" by William Foster and "What Happens to the Gifted Girl?" by Linda Silverman.

Renzulli, Joseph S. *Schools for Talent Development: A Practical Plan for Total School Improvement.* Creative Learning Press, 1994. 379 p. ISBN 0-936386-65-7 (hardcover).

Renzulli's most recent book, this represents the accumulation of his work directed at developing educational programs that help students realize their talent; therefore, it is an extension of *The Enrichment Triad, The Revolving Door Identification Model,* and *The Schoolwide Enrichment Model.* Using the gifted pedagogy described in his previous books, revisited and refined in the current book, he explains how to apply these practices to improve the education of all students. "Enrichment clusters," a newer concept and service delivery component, is of special interest.

Renzulli, Joseph S., and Sally Reis. *The Schoolwide Enrichment Model: A Comprehensive Plan for Educational Excellence.* Creative Learning Press, 1985. 522 p. ISBN 0-936386-34-7 (paper).

This book extends the information on flexible identification and programming in *The Enrichment Triad* and *The Revolving Door Identification Model* by presenting detailed procedures for delivering curricular and program services to high-achieving students. The book contains several charts and forms, such as overviews of the three Triad enrichment types, announcement of program activities, and lists of enrichment resources. The sixteen Simsits (simulation situations) that were designed for staff development purposes are particularly unique and useful. For example, "What Should We Do For Joanie" is a brief simulation designed to assist classroom teachers with curriculum compacting.

———, Sally Reis, and Linda H. Smith. *The Revolving Door Identification Model.* Creative Learning Press, 1981. 248 p. ISBN 0-936386-16-9 (paper).

Although published several years ago, and updated since, this book is an important and useful reference for educators using Renzulli's enrichment education model in their schools. This was the first major publication in which Renzulli and his colleagues outlined procedures for the flexible identification of, and programming for, "student talent" as opposed to "students." Practitioners may be especially interested in the book's sample forms used for various program activities, such as nomination forms, student questionnaires, and independent study management plans, as well as the sample materials in the appendices such as identification and program evaluation instruments.

Sorenson, Juanita, ed. *The Gifted Program Handbook: Planning, Implementing, and Evaluating Gifted Programs with a Special Model for Small School Districts.* Dale Seymour Publications, 1988. 159 p. ISBN 0-86651-477-5 (hardcover).

This book is useful for school personnel who intend to plan, implement, evaluate, or modify a program to meet the needs of gifted students in their districts. It includes an overview of the characteristics of gifted and talented students, various identification procedures, the major programming models, and strategies for differentiating the curriculum, as well as suggestions for staff development programs and evaluation procedures. A unique feature of the handbook is a section on how to develop a gifted program in a small school district.

PROGRAM MODELS

Maker, C. June. *Teaching Models in Education of the Gifted.* PRO-ED, 1982. 475 p. ISBN 0-89079-186-4 (hardcover).

Gifted and Talented Education 211

This book provides an analysis of ten models that have been developed and advocated for educating gifted students. These models include The Enrichment Triad Model by Renzulli, the Structure of the Intellect Model by Guilford, the Multiple Talent Approach by Taylor, and the Moral Dilemmas Model by Kohlberg. A general description of each model is provided, followed by a sample curriculum unit based on each model. Maker presents an analysis of each model and lists additional resources for readers interested in studying the models in greater detail.

RESEARCH

Cox, June, Neil Daniel, and Bruce O. Boston. *Educating Able Learners: Programs and Promising Practices.* University of Texas Press, 1985. 243 p. ISBN 0-292-70386-4 (hardcover); 0-292-70387-2 (paper).

The authors report the results of a study commonly referred to as the Richardson Study, which consisted of a survey of schools' identification and programming practices for gifted learners, follow-up visits to a few schools with differing types of programs, and a few mini-conferences throughout the country. The book includes descriptions of the various program types that were visited, such as specialized schools and enrichment programs. In addition to the research findings, the authors provide a rationale and description of the schooling they believe is needed to meet the needs of capable learners.

Kulik, James A. *An Analysis of the Research on Ability Grouping: Historical and Contemporary Perspectives.* National Research Center on the Gifted and Talented, 1992. 56 p. [Document #9204].

This is an extremely comprehensive and scholarly examination of the literature on ability grouping and its effects on students, with particular attention directed at understanding the effects on high achieving students. After studying the meta-analyses of over fifty years of research on this topic, Kulik arrived at several conclusions. One of the most salient findings was as follows: when a differentiated and accelerated curriculum is provided to gifted students, there appear to be substantial gains in the ability-grouped programs.

Robinson, Ann. *Cooperative Learning and the Academically Talented Student.* National Research Center on the Gifted and Talented, 1991. 38 p. [Document #9106].

Cooperative learning is a major grouping strategy used by teachers in elementary classrooms; however, little attention has been directed to the benefits and drawbacks of cooperative learning with high-ability students. Robinson summarizes various types of cooperative learning, presents findings from research on cooperative learning conducted exclusively with gifted students, and provides recommendations for using cooperative learning with academically talented students. For example, if a school is committed to cooperative learning, models which encourage access to materials beyond grade level are preferable for academically talented students, and the student achievement disparities within the group should not be too severe.

Rogers, Karen. *The Relationship of Grouping Practices to the Education of the Gifted and Talented Learner.* National Research Center on the Gifted and Talented, 1991. 65 p. [Document #9101].

What forms of grouping are most appropriate for gifted learners? Rogers addresses this by reporting findings based on a major analysis of thirteen research syntheses of over one thousand studies which have examined ability grouping. This analysis resulted in several conclusions, including: (1) gifted students should be provided with enrichment and acceleration options that extend the regular curriculum, (2) gifted and talented students should spend the majority of the school day working with students of similar academic abilities and interests, and (3) cooperative learning should be used sparingly with gifted students, perhaps only for social development.

SPECIAL POPULATIONS

Kerr, Barbara A. *Smart Girls, Gifted Women.* Ohio Psychology Publishing, 1985. 194 p. ISBN 0-910707-07-3 (paper).

This book addresses issues related to the realization and fulfillment of gifted girls' academic potential. Kerr explains the special pressures, conflicts, and barriers to achievement that bright girls face, such as the "Cinderella Complex" and the "Impostor Phenomenon." In addition, she discusses the factors that influence girls' academic achievement, such as time alone to obtain a sense of self, career counseling, and female role models. Kerr includes guidelines for providing support and encouragement to girls at various stages of development.

TEACHING STRATEGIES

Burns, Deborah E. *Pathways to Investigative Skills: Instructional Lessons for Guiding Students from Problem Finding to Final Product, Grades 3–9.* Creative Learning Press, 1990. 83 p. ISBN 0-936386-54-1 (ringbound).

Gifted and Talented Education

This comprehensive guidebook provides teachers and students with step-by-step guidelines and materials for investigating and completing independent projects. It includes lessons that guide students from the problem-finding stage to completion of the final product. The guidebook, which is in a three-ring binder format, includes materials for students such as sample interest inventories and problem focusing worksheets. Specific materials for teachers, such as sample scripts for discussing aspects of the research process with students and actual slides of completed student projects, are also included. This guidebook was designed to help teachers improve the quality of students' investigations.

Parke, Beverly N. *Gifted Students in Regular Classrooms.* Allyn & Bacon, 1989. 271 p. ISBN 0-205-11736-8 (hardcover).

Parke's book offers a comprehensive approach for addressing the needs of gifted students within regular classrooms. She provides background information to help teachers recognize the needs of their students and provides specific information about accommodations for addressing these needs. The accommodations include how to (1) make adjustments in the pace of learning, (2) vary the depth of learning, (3) accommodate individual interests, and (4) create a classroom environment for self-directed learning. This book successfully translates the best practices for gifted learners into a comprehensive and "teacher-friendly" book.

Reis, Sally M., Deborah E. Burns, and Joseph S. Renzulli. *Curriculum Compacting: The Complete Guide to Modifying the Regular Curriculum for High Ability Students.* Creative Learning Press, 1992. 170 p. ISBN 0-936386-63-0 (paper).

This is a "how to" book for teachers on how to use a curricular modification strategy entitled curriculum compacting. Curriculum compacting refers to a process in which a teacher preassesses the skills and content previously mastered by above-average students and modifies the curriculum for these students. A rationale and step-by-step procedures for accomplishing this task are described. A unique feature of the book is that every chapter contains a "compacted version" of the information presented within the chapter.

Winebrenner, Susan. *Teaching Gifted Kids in the Regular Classroom.* Free Spirit Publishing, 1992. 161 p. ISBN 0-915793-47-4 (paper).

Written with the classroom teacher in mind, the author explains and illustrates several specific strategies that can be incorporated quite easily and immediately into the classroom to address the needs of high-achieving students. Among these strategies are curriculum compacting, learning contracts, independent study, cooperative learning, and cluster grouping. Several sample forms designed to help teachers manage modifications for students within the regular classroom, such as independent study contracts, are included. The author also uses case scenarios and question-and-answer sections to help teachers be more comfortable with the strategies.

NONPRINT MATERIAL

Tomlinson, Carol Ann, and ASCD. *Challenging the Gifted in the Regular Classroom.* Association for Supervision and Curriculum Development, 1994. [ASCD stock #4-94057]. Video and 150-page guidebook.

This video and facilitator's guidebook prepared by Tomlinson and produced by ASCD present experts' suggestions for instructional and curricular provisions that should be made for capable students in regular classrooms. Seven specific strategies for providing appropriate experiences are presented: questioning techniques, tiered assignments, flexible skills grouping, learning centers and interest centers, curriculum compacting, independent study projects, and interest grouping. In addition to receiving information about these seven techniques, viewers see case scenarios of teachers actually using them in their classrooms. The accompanying guidebook describes how to use the video in a workshop and includes a list of references for further study.

JOURNALS

Challenge: Reaching and Teaching the Gifted Child. Good Apple. ISSN 0745-6298.

Challenge contains articles and materials that are designed to help teachers provide academic "challenges" to high-ability, preschool to grade 8 students. Each issue contains ideas for stimulating gifted students in the regular classroom and includes many ready-to-use reproducible activity pages for a variety of curriculum areas. Articles by experts in the field of gifted education that focus on practical applications, as opposed to discussions of theory and research, are also included.

Gifted Child Quarterly. National Association for Gifted Children. ISSN 0016-9862.

The *Gifted Child Quarterly* was the first professional journal published in gifted education and is viewed widely as the major scholarly publication in the field. The journal publishes articles on recent research and developments in the field of gifted education. Issues often focus on special topics such as Teachers and Talent Development and Alternative Assessment. While most of the articles report research findings, a sidebar entitled Putting the Research to Use is included with every article.

Gifted and Talented Education

Gifted Child Today. Prufrock Press. ISSN 0892-9580.

Gifted Child Today is a "teacher-friendly" magazine that provides information on programming options, current issues, and practical suggestions for educating gifted students. The articles, written by classroom teachers, gifted education specialists, and university personnel, are non-technical and discuss various aspects of gifted education. The magazine appeals to classroom teachers and gifted education personnel.

Journal for the Education of the Gifted. The Association for the Gifted, a Division of the Council for Exceptional Children. ISSN 0162-3532.

Journal for the Education of the Gifted publishes theoretical, descriptive, and research articles directed toward meeting the needs of gifted students. Issues are often devoted to special themes such as Curriculum in Special Schools and Mathematics for Gifted Learners. Many of the articles report original research studies that have implications for practice in schools. Reviews of literature on areas of interest, book reviews, and articles that describe innovative programming and instructional practices for gifted and talented students are also included.

MEMBERSHIPS

National Association for Gifted Children
1155 15th Street N.W., Suite 1002
Washington, D.C. 20005

Phone: (202) 785-4268

The major gifted and talented organization in the United States is the National Association for Gifted Children. It has been responsible for advocacy efforts for gifted education programs and practices for over twenty-five years. During the past couple of years, the NAGC Board of Directors has approved position papers on major topics (e.g., Competencies Needed by Teachers of Gifted and Talented Students, Differentiation of Curriculum and Instruction, Grouping Practices for Gifted Students) that provide guidance to schools and teachers about appropriate programs and practices for high-achieving students. Membership includes the *Gifted Child Quarterly* journal, the *Communique* newsletter, discounts on materials, annual convention fees, and a free information service.

17

Multicultural Education

Consultant: Dr. Andrea B. Bermúdez
University of Houston–Clear Lake
Houston, Texas

Dr. Bermúdez is Professor of Multicultural Education and Director of the Research Center for Language and Culture at the University of Houston–Clear Lake. She holds an Ed.D. in Foundations of Education from the University of Houston, with an M.A. in Spanish Literature and Linguistics from the University of Virginia.

Dr. Bermúdez has written numerous chapters, monographs, and articles related to multicultural and bilingual education. As the author of seven books, her most recent publication is *Doing Our Homework: Engaging Hispanic Parents in the Schools* (ERIC Clearinghouse for Urban Small Schools, 1994). She was Senior ESL Consultant for three textbooks: *Literature and Language, Grades 9–12* (McDougal, 1992), *Literature and Language, Grades 6–8* (McDougal, 1994), and *Transitions to English* (McGraw-Hill, 1992).

She has served as editor of the *Bilingual Research Quarterly* and is a member of the editorial boards of *Journal of Educational Issues of Language Minority Students* and *Compendium of Readings in Bilingual Education*. An active member of various professional organizations, Dr. Bermúdez is a frequent presenter of her research at conferences throughout the world.

GENERAL RESOURCES

Banks, James A. *Multiethnic Education: Theory and Practice.* 3rd ed. Allyn & Bacon, 1994. 330 p. ISBN 0-205-14745-3 (hardcover); 0-205-11791-0 (paper).

This source is designed to facilitate the development of a personal philosophical stance in preservice and inservice educators regarding multiethnic education. This process would enhance the quality of its implementation as well as ensure its institutionalization. The book, divided into five major sections, deals with a broad range of concerns, including terminology, definitions, historical background, goals, philosophical positions, strategies, and curriculum as they relate to the presence of diversity in the schools and its impact on practices and programs. The fifth section addresses prejudice reduction and also presents a summary of the key issues discussed throughout. The appendix contains a checklist to assist educators in examining the extent to which their institutions represent diversity.

―――. *Teaching Strategies for Ethnic Studies.* Allyn & Bacon, 1991. 576 p. ISBN 0-205-12756-8 (paper).

This text includes an overview of major ethnic groups living in the United States. Its purpose is to generate knowledge, skills, and resources to develop an inclusive curriculum that addresses the needs of all students. The book is divided into six major sections: part one discusses goals, concepts, and instructional planning; parts two through five deal with concepts and strategies for understanding and educating African Americans, European Americans, Hispanic Americans, and Asian Americans living in the U.S.; and part six discusses multicultural units and strategies. Five appendices follow, including a historical overview as well as a list of additional instructional resources.

―――, and Cherry A. McGee Banks. *Multicultural Education: Issues and Perspectives.* 2nd ed. Allyn & Bacon, 1993. 368 p. ISBN 0-205-14044-0 (hardcover); 0-205-11791-0 (paper).

This collection of essays contains a view of multiculturalism and diversity across race, ethnicity, gender, social class, religion, and exceptionality. A section of the book discusses the impact of these complex issues on school reform. The book is aimed at preservice and inservice educators in need of information regarding multicultural nomenclature, research, and educational paradigms which will equip them with the skills and sensitivity required to be an effective and responsible professional in a pluralistic classroom. Resources and a glossary are included in the appendices.

Bennett, Christine. *Comprehensive Multicultural Education: Theory and Practice.* 3rd ed. Allyn & Bacon, 1995. 452 p. ISBN 0-205-15024-1 (hardcover).

This book explores the relationship between multiculturalism and global issues in education. It addresses a rationale for multicultural education; implications for teaching, learning, and curriculum reform; basic concepts related to multiculturalism; major ethnic minorities in the U.S.; and teaching strategies, guidelines, and lesson plans. Vignettes depicting teacher-student interactions are used to describe how the conceptual framework impacts classroom practice. The book is aimed at pre- and inservice teachers. An instructor's manual with copy masters, sample course syllabi, and test items accompanies this edition.

• Davidman, Leonard, with Patricia T. Davidman. *Teaching with a Multicultural Perspective: A Practical Guide.* Longman, 1994. 241 p. ISBN 0-8013-0835-6 (paper).

This text is aimed at training programs for elementary and middle-school teachers to be used by content area instructors charged with infusing multicultural education in their discipline. A knowledge base on multicultural education issues, as well as practical applications, is offered through its five chapters, emphasizing: (a) definitions and examples of multicultural teaching, (b) equity activities and lessons, and (c) curriculum. Several appendices appear in the text, including ones on multicultural teaching typology, observation forms, position papers, and other resources.

Gollnick, Donna M., and Philip C. Chinn. *Multicultural Education in a Pluralistic Society.* 4th ed. Merrill, 1994. 355 p. ISBN 0-02-344491-6 (paper).

The authors present an overview of the various cultures represented in most public school classrooms. According to the authors, educators must also achieve an understanding of their own culture in order to be effective in a pluralistic environment. Diversity is explained in very comprehensive terms as it not only includes racial and ethnic differences but also diversity of gender, class, disability, religion, language, and age. The book also includes strategies for implementing multicultural education. An instructor's manual accompanies the text, with suggested activities and test items for each chapter.

Grossman, Herbert. *Teaching in a Diverse Society.* Allyn & Bacon, 1995. 340 p. ISBN 0-205-16247-9 (paper).

Part of developing sensitivity and understanding of culturally diverse environments is to recognize lack of equality in education. Large numbers of students fail because the educational system has not integrated diversity in their instruction, assessment, and classroom management. This text is designed for the preservice teacher in need of information which helps close the gap between the student and the learning environment. Chapters address disparities between various cultural groups and the mainstream; explore their intrinsic and extrinsic causes; discuss contextually, communicatively, and gender-appropriate educational approaches; and offer valuable insights on instruction and assessment.

Richard-Amato, Patricia, and Marguerite Ann Snow, eds. *The Multicultural Classroom: Readings for Content-Area Teachers.* Longman, 1992. 413 p. ISBN 0-8013-0511-X (paper).

The authors indicate that the text was developed principally for inservice and preservice mainstream practitioners who are unfamiliar with theoretical explanations and effective practices concerning second-language acquisition and learning. There are twenty-six readings incorporated into four sections highlighting: (a) theory (language proficiency, collaboration, and cooperative learning); (b) culture (relationship between language, thought, and culture; culturally sensitive feedback; and home-school language incongruity); (c) instruction and materials (cognitive and affective strategies, content modification, and development of writing skills); and (d) readings in specific content areas (model lessons for elementary school teachers with potential for adaptation to higher levels).

Skutnabb-Kangas, Tove, and Jim Cummins, eds. *Minority Education: From Shame to Struggle.* Multilingual Matters, 1988. 410 p. ISBN 1-85359-004-5 (hardcover); 0-85359-003-7 (paper).

The authors in this collection of studies examine the challenges of minority students' education in an international setting. Each author represents a minority perspective on related issues. Minority education is represented as a power struggle against racist societal institutions that deny these students equal educational rights. The topics cover four main areas: (a) sociopolitics (multilingualism, language policies, programs and goals); (b) experiential perspectives (identity, bicultural and bilingual living); (c) community struggles (educational rights, parental involvement); and (d) the global context (language for empowerment).

Sleeter, Christine E., and Carl A. Grant. *Making Choices for Multicultural Education: Five Approaches to Race, Class, and Gender.* Edited by Linda A. Sullivan. 2nd ed. Macmillan, 1994. 253 p. ISBN 0-02-411563-0 (paper).

In addition to presenting an argument for empowering culturally diverse groups through multicultural education, this source presents a clarification of what multicultural education is and should be to promote effective implementation of its basic principles. The text is divided into seven chapters organized around the concept of five major approaches followed by educators' comments regarding the teaching of racial, class, and gender diversity. These approaches include: (a) assimilation or "catching up" with the mainstream, (b) improving social interactions and self-concept, (c) concentrating on a single group, (d) addressing multicultural education as a reform movement, and (e) focusing on social justice and empowerment. The last chapter contains an explanation of the authors' favored choice, which involves educational and social reform and change.

Spring, Joel. *The Intersection of Cultures: Multicultural Education in the United States.* McGraw-Hill, 1995. 172 p. ISBN 0-07-060559-9 (hardcover).

This book is designed for teachers who encounter daily the intersection of diverse cultures in their classrooms. It is divided into two parts: (a) foundations of multicultural education, and (b) teaching perspectives. Part one includes a discussion of the multicultural debate and lays the framework for Part two. This section comprises examples on teaching about racism, sexism, linguistic diversity, ethnocentrism, cultural tolerance, and empowerment. Each chapter is accompanied by thought-provoking questions which promote reflection and understanding of the issues presented.

•Tiedt, Pamela L., and Iris M. Tiedt. *Multicultural Teaching: A Handbook of Activities, Information, and Resources.* 4th ed. Allyn & Bacon, 1995. 427 p. ISBN 0-205-15488-3 (paper).

Two important foci characterize this selection: (a) the presentation of information on key issues and concepts related to multicultural education and (b) learning activities for culturally diverse students in kindergarten through eighth grade. The text is divided into ten chapters covering: (a) survival skills and basic understandings for living in a multiculture, (b) information necessary to prepare multicultural instruction, (c) student strengths, (d) student belongingness, (e) student empowerment, (f) linguistic and cultural diversity, (g) the multicultural curriculum, and (h) future directions in multicultural education.

SPECIALIZED RESOURCES—LANGUAGE

Faltis, Christian J. *Joinfostering: Adapting Teaching Strategies for the Multilingual Classroom.* Merrill, 1992. 179 p. ISBN 0-675-21326-6 (paper).

This work is aimed at preservice and inservice teachers who will be dealing with students proficient in other language(s) and in the process of developing English proficiency. The concept of Joinfostering relates to creating classrooms with sufficient interaction between the teacher and students and among the students, fostering social integration of second-language students with native English-speaking students in all aspects of classroom learning, integrating second-language acquisition principles with content instruction, and ensuring full involvement and participation of these students in all aspects of learning. The book presents the experiences of dealing with a multilingual/multicultural classroom through an examination of a teacher's multiple challenges. The author includes corresponding theoretical explanations for these challenges as well as strategies to address the challenges effectively, including parental inclusion in the educational process. Historical and political overviews of programs aimed at this student population are also included.

Fishman, Joshua A. *Reversing Language Shift: Theoretical and Empirical Foundations of Assistance to Threatened Languages.* Taylor & Frances, 1991. 500 p. ISBN 1-85359-122-X (hardcover).

The author emphasizes the central role of families in maintaining home language along with traditional family values. The book is organized around three sections: (a) introductory considerations (the existence of threatened languages, and the process by which they are lost); (b) case studies of threatened languages (Irish,

Basque, Frisian, Navajo, Spanish in the U.S., Yiddish, and Maori); and (c) a final section with chapters on language transmission, challenges to language maintenance, and ways to accomplish minority language revival. Three basic postulates guide the author's discussion: (a) bring linguistic and bilateral assimilation to an end, (b) minority and majority rights are not mutually exclusive, and (c) bilingualism benefits everyone.

Genesee, Fred, ed. *Educating Second Language Children: The Whole Child, the Whole Curriculum, and the Whole Community.* Cambridge University Press, 1994. 365 p. ISBN 0-521-45179-5 (hardcover); 0-521-45797-1 (paper).

The central thread of this book is the transitional nature of language codes. Children are first socialized at home; therefore the native language becomes the medium of communication. Once in school, the child's speech community changes and so does his/her language choice. There are four main sections: (a) General Perspectives, addressing language acquisition processes and the need for empowering students from non-mainstream language backgrounds; (b) The Preschool Years, which looks at several groups of young bilingual children's family interactions, language socialization, and second-language development in preschool programs; (c) The Classroom, incorporating effective teaching and assessment issues and strategies; and (d) Additional Challenges, addressing special education, low-literacy students, and acculturation of immigrant and refugee children.

Oxford, Rebecca L. *Language Learning Strategies: What Every Teacher Should Know.* Heinle & Heinle, 1990. 342 p. ISBN 0-8384-2862-2 (paper).

This book presents a comprehensive discussion of theory-based foreign language (FL) and second language (SL) learning strategies. The resource provides teachers with practical advice on how to help students develop learning strategies which promote language development. Language strategies research and taxonomy as well as strategy instruction and assessment techniques comprise the core of this text. In addition, two versions of the Oxford's Strategy Inventory for Language Learning (SILL), one for FL and one for SL, along with their administration procedures are included.

Perez, Bertha, and Maria Torres-Guzman. *Learning in Two Worlds: An Integrated Spanish/English Biliteracy Approach.* Longman, 1992. 215 p. ISBN 0-8013-0628-0 (paper).

This resource addresses effective transition to Spanish/English biliteracy. It includes topics, materials, and strategies dealing with the development of literacy in first and second languages. The authors present the process of language acquisition as a complex and integrated activity which impacts students' academic success and extends to the development of self worth and socialization skills. The three sections address: (a) the relationship between thought and culture using a framework; (b) the classroom climate and instruction (the classroom should reflect the student's culture, and the language used should spring from the student's home language); and (c) materials and resources for second-language development and assessment. The authors make a special effort to provide an insightful explanation of diversity within the Spanish-speaking communities.

Rodriguez, Rodolfo, Nancy J. Ramos, and Jose Agustin Ruiz-Escalante, eds. *Compendium of Readings in Bilingual Education: Issues and Practices*. Texas Association for Bilingual Education, 1994. 334 p. ISBN 0-205-1478-95 (paper).

This compendium of readings offers an overview of policy, programs, theories, and practices for educators dealing with language minority students. The authors' contributions are organized around six major areas: (a) foundations of bilingual education and related policies, (b) programs and evaluation processes, (c) theory and classroom practices, (d) teacher preparation, (e) teaming, and (f) personal perspectives. Appendices include a glossary of key nomenclature in bilingual education and a directory of resources for bilingual educators.

Scarcella, Robin. *Teaching Language Minority Students in the Multicultural Classroom*. Prentice-Hall, 1990. 271 p. ISBN 013851-8254 (hardcover).

Teaching Language Minority Students in the Multicultural Classroom summarizes recent research in bilingual, ESL, and multicultural education. The book presents important theoretical and practical information for content area teachers working with linguistically and culturally diverse students. Examples, illustrations, and case studies are included to document the author's discussions. This book is not intended to provide all the answers to the challenge of providing "culturally responsive education" (p. viii) for language minority students, but is intended to describe selected principles or guidelines for teaching while providing useful information on diversity profiles, language acquisition, classroom climate, home-school continuity, and unbiased assessment. In presenting a comprehensive view of linguistic and cultural diversity, the book offers an opportunity to reverse academic failure for language minority students.

SPECIALIZED RESOURCES—OTHER

Bermúdez, Andrea B. *Doing Our Homework: How Schools Can Engage Hispanic Communities*. ERIC Clearinghouse on Rural Education and Small Schools, 1994. 82 p. ISBN 1-880785-11-0 (paper).

This work is intended for school personnel interested in improving school relations and services to language minority parents. The recurring theme of this book is that schools must initiate partnerships with non-English speaking parents to promote student academic success. The seven chapters address: (a) historical background of parental involvement in the United States; (b) rationale for parental involvement; (c) barriers impeding the home-school partnership; (d) parental roles, strategies, and programs to promote effective involvement; (e) parent and teacher partnership training; (f) engaging community support and advocacy; and (g) future directions in parent involvement in the schools. The Appendix contains a detailed description of a university's parent education training model.

Bull, Barry L., Royal T. Fruehling, and Virgie Chattergy. *The Ethics of Multicultural and Bilingual Education.* Teachers College Press, 1992. 211 p. ISBN 0-8077-3187-0 (paper).

This book presents three theoretical frameworks (liberal, democratic, and communitarian) to explain the ethical dilemmas posed by multicultural education. Case studies are used to illustrate and analyze the creation of linguistic and cultural tensions within a community, as well as their moral resolution by using each of the three perspectives. The contents of this book are geared to clarify inservice and prospective educators' views of multiculturalism and to promote a deeper understanding of related ethical issues.

Chavkin, Nancy Feyl, ed. *Families and Schools in a Pluralistic Society.* State University of New York Press, 1993. 268 p. ISBN 0-7914-1227-X (hardcover); 0-7914-1228-8 (paper).

The studies contained in this source address the general failure of schools in educating the increasing minority student population, and strongly suggest that the avenue of incorporating parents in the process be urgently explored. The goal of this collection of studies is to impart knowledge to educators about current theory and effective practices related to the involvement of parents in the schools. More specifically, the book addresses the following major areas: (a) overview of parental involvement in the schools, (b) current research, (c) effective practices, and (d) future opportunities for parental involvement in the schools.

Horgan, Dianne D. *Achieving Gender Equity Strategies for the Classroom.* Allyn & Bacon, 1995. 207 p. ISBN 0-205-15459 (hardcover).

An important concern of the author is to give teachers the concepts and skills necessary to ensure gender equity in the classroom. This approach would encourage increased levels of self-confidence as well as academic success for all students. The chapters deal with socialization practices for both genders, strategies for teachers to establish gender-equitable learning environments, and suggestions for dealing with how parents can achieve gender equity for their children. Case studies, examples, a "gender bias audit," and checklists are included.

King, Edith W., Marilyn Chipman, and Martha Cruz-Janzen. *Educating Young Children in a Diverse Society.* Allyn & Bacon, 1994. 223 p. ISBN 0-205-14789-5 (hardcover).

The need for awareness of cultural diversity in the schools has been identified by the authors as a primary exigency for inservice personnel and professionals dealing with early childhood education. The "diversity perspective" is introduced through children's self-portraits as a multicultural classroom project which encourages self-acceptance and the sharing of diverse traits with others. Topics covered within the book's ten chapters include diversity in early childhood, socialization, developmentally appropriate practice, curriculum, gender and ethnic identity, culture, bias, a sociological perspective on the young child, research, and education. Chapters are supplemented with summaries, key concepts, issues and actions, and additional resources.

Kohl, Herbert. *I Won't Learn From You: The Role of Assent in Learning.* Milkweed Editions, 1991. 52 p. ISBN 0-915943-64-6 (hardcover).

This essay advances the thesis that there is a difference between making a choice not to learn ("a will to refuse knowledge," p. 15) and a failure to learn ("a loss of self confidence accompanied by a sense of inferiority and inadequacy," p. 15). The author considers students who are disenfranchised from the educational and social institutions as those who have willfully made the choice not to learn in order to gain control over a system they see as inequitable. Reasons can vary, but one can surmise that seeking an identity by not choosing to learn what others want one to learn may be critical in surviving the system. This book provides educators with an opportunity to understand educational failure as a complex and interdependent set of variables brought to being by social and political realities more so than by personal failure.

Lonner, Walter J., and Roy S. Malpass, eds. *Readings in Psychology and Culture.* Allyn & Bacon, 1994. 317 p. ISBN 0-205-14899-9 (hardcover).

The authors included in this text discuss the various areas in which psychology and culture intersect, and how culture modifies human behavior. There are seven sections addressing the universal nature of diversity and the challenges faced as humans adapt to different environments, as well as the impact of culture on individual and social definitions; social, developmental and psychological processes; everyday modes of functioning; and health psychology. Each section is led by a brief introduction focusing on issues raised in the chapters that follow. An instructor's manual containing supplementary topics and sample syllabi accompanies the text.

•Miller-Lachmann, Lyn, ed. *Our Family, Our Friends, Our World: An Annotated Guide to Significant Multicultural Books for Children and Teenagers.* Bowker, 1992. 710 p. ISBN 0-8352-3025-2 (hardcover).

This reference book contains a collection of over one thousand books for adolescents and children covering minority cultures in the U.S. (e.g., Native Americans, African Americans, Hispanics, Asian Americans), as well as chapters portraying foreign cultures. There is an introductory chapter in which the editor explains the rationale for the selections. Eighteen chapters by the various authors follow; each contains an introduction which includes the standing of children's literature for the particular group represented, selection criteria, and book annotations by grade level.

Siccone, Frank. *Celebrating Diversity: Building Self Esteem in Today's Multicultural Classrooms.* Allyn & Bacon, 1995. 248 p. ISBN 0-205-16175-8 (paper).

This hands-on collection offers seventy-five activities to develop self-esteem. The activities emphasize the responsibilities of accepting and celebrating one's unique cultural heritage, as well as learning how to relate to others in society. The eight chapters address developing self-esteem through: (a) achieving greater personal independence; (b) learning how to get along with others; and (c) attaining individual and social empowerment (accepting oneself, celebrating success, and collaborating with others). The chapters are grouped into four sections, each containing suggested readings, key learnings, and a teacher checklist.

JOURNALS

Bilingual Research Journal. National Association for Bilingual Education. ISSN 0885-5072.

This journal addresses bilingual and multicultural issues, generally within the context of the United States. Published four times a year, it focuses on current research and practices related to various areas of bilingualism, including linguistics, politics, culture, and methodology. In addition, a book review section appears in each issue.

The Journal of Educational Issues of Language Minority Students. Boise State University. ISSN 1077-0550.

Published three times a year, this journal addresses broad issues related to the education of bilingual/bicultural students in the United States. The *Journal* is funded by Title VII of the Elementary and Secondary Education Act through the Office of Bilingual Education and Minority Language Affairs. There is no subscription fee. Requests for copies should be sent to the Editor, *The Journal of Educational Issues of Language Minority Students,* 1910 University Drive, Education Building 215, Boise State University, Boise, Idaho 83725.

Multicultural Education. National Association for Multicultural Education. ISSN 1068-3844.

This quarterly magazine is for educators at all levels. It contains several feature articles, book and film reviews, interviews with significant people in the field, and a lengthy column entitled "Multicultural Resources." To order this journal, contact Caddo Gap Press, 3145 Geary Boulevard, Suite 275, San Francisco, California 94118; or telephone (415) 750-9978.

TESOL Matters. Teachers of English to Speakers of Other Languages. ISSN 1051-8886.

This publication is a newspaper published six times a year under the sponsorship of the Teachers of English to Speakers of Other Languages (TESOL). It contains current discussions on standards and practices regarding English as a second language (ESL). Affiliate news and calls for proposals are announced. An "Interest Section" includes current practices and strategies for effective ESL instruction.

TESOL Quarterly. Teachers of English to Speakers of Other Languages. ISSN 0039-8322.

The *TESOL Quarterly* is dedicated to research in second language development. It includes articles on research perspectives for classroom application, a forum with evaluative comments from readers and responses from authors as well as teaching issues, a section on brief research reports and summaries, book reviews, and book notices.

MEMBERSHIPS

National Association for Multicultural Education
2101-A North Rolfe Street
Arlington, Virginia 22209-1007

Phone: (703) 243-4525

NAME is an organization for all levels of educators who work with multicultural education. Membership includes a subscription to the quarterly magazine, *Multicultural Education*.

18

Instructional Technology

Consultants: Dr. Kent L. Gustafson
University of Georgia
Athens, Georgia

Dr. Gustafson is Professor and Chair of the Department of Instructional Technology at the University of Georgia. He holds a Ph.D. in Instructional Development and Technology from Michigan State University, with a master's degree from the University of Massachusetts. As a former classroom teacher and director of school media services in public schools Dr. Gustafson has enjoyed a wide range of teaching experiences.

Dr. Gustafson is a member of the Association for Educational Communications. He served as president of the national organization in 1994–1995 and continues to take an active part in the organization.

An author of various journal articles as well as chapters and books, Dr. Gustafson's most recent work is *Research for School Library Media Specialists* (Ablex, 1994), coauthored with Jane Bandy Smith. Other recent works include *Instructional Design: Principles and Applications* (Educational Technology Publications, 1991), coedited with Leslie J. Briggs and Murray H. Tillman, and *Instructional Technology: A Systematic Approach to Education* (Holt, Rinehart and Winston, 1986), coauthored with Frederick G. Knirk.

Dr. Melvin M. Bowie
University of Georgia
Athens, Georgia

Dr. Bowie is Associate Professor in the Department of Instructional Technology at the University of Georgia, where she teaches courses in technical services, collection development, and administration of school media programs. She received her Ph.D. in Curriculum and Instructional Media from Iowa State University. A former school library media specialist and public librarian, Dr. Bowie holds a master's degree in Library Science from the University of Illinois at Urbana-Champaign. Dr. Bowie's research interests include collection development and resource-based teaching.

DOCUMENTS/GUIDELINES/STANDARDS

•American Library Association and Association for Educational Communications and Technology. *Information Power: Guidelines for School Library Media Programs.* American Library Association and Association for Educational Communications and Technology, 1988. 171 p. ISBN 0-8389-3352-1 (paper).

This book comprises a set of national cooperation guidelines designed to help in developing sound media programs. It covers the responsibilities of the media specialist to the school's program, the leadership needed to manage and develop effective media center collections, and the role of planning in designing and implementing a strong media program. Emphasis in the guidelines is on the need for cooperation between classroom teachers and media specialists in all levels of K–12 schools.

DIRECTORIES, YEARBOOKS, AND MANUALS

Abrams, A. *Educator's Guide to Macintosh Applications.* Allyn & Bacon, 1995. 294 p. ISBN 0-205-16284-3 (paper).

The author states that the user of this volume will "start from ground zero." Each of the nine chapters is a tutorial in which the computer novice learns basic applications of the Macintosh. The purpose of the book is to get the user up and running in a very short time by offering clear and easy-to-follow instructions on how to use such basic software packages as Microsoft Works, Aldus PageMaker, and PowerPoint. When necessary, the author uses illustrations from menu screens, application screens, and sample products to enhance the text. New terms are presented in bold throughout the text, and there is a comprehensive glossary in the back. A practice disk containing exercises accompanies the book. Anyone who wishes to use the Macintosh in the classroom or who wants to increase their own personal productivity will find this to be a very useful volume.

Directory of Video, Multimedia, and Audio-visual Products. International Communications Industries Association. ISSN 1086-9565 (paper).

It would be difficult to manage an up-to-date school media center or classroom without access to this annual directory. Arranged by type of media, the directory presents specifications for more than two thousand items and pieces of equipment. It is the leading reference work of its kind.

Instructional Technology

Educational Media and Technology Yearbook. Libraries Unlimited. ISSN 8755-2094 (hardcover).

This yearbook presents a year in review about developments in technology, communications, instructional technology programs, and major influences of the federal government on educational programs. There are sections on technology updates, leadership profiles, and graduate programs. Each section is authored by an expert in the field. There is also an annual list of the most recommended books, journal articles, and reference materials concerning the latest in technology and media. This is an excellent reference tool that should be in every professional collection.

Erickson, Fritz, and John A. Vonk. *Computer Essentials in Education.* McGraw-Hill, 1994. 280 p. ISBN 0-07-021242-4 (paper).

Some of the most useful sections of this book are found in the appendices. Here there are discussions and illustrations of the four main platforms presently used in education—Macintosh, MS-DOS, Apple II, and Microsoft Windows. The authors have removed the chaff and gotten to the essentials about each of the systems. Using the appendices, it is possible for a reader to make informed decisions about choosing a system to fit a given need. Information in the remainder of the volume is treated in much the same way, with most attention given to the essentials of computing. The book also contains a glossary and an index.

Goodman, Danny. *Danny Goodman's Computer Concepts: Using the Macintosh.* Glencoe, 1995. 152 p. ISBN 0-02-801051-5 (hardcover).

The page layout and the design in this book make it a joy to read. Page margins are colorfully coded for each chapter, with a single color used throughout a chapter to highlight important information. The text is comfortably large, with very bold headings and subheadings. Drawings and illustrations are simple, in color, and clearly labeled. The book explains the differences between the Macintosh and the IBM PC. Other sections cover software, setting up a network, communications basics, and desktop publishing, and there is a combined glossary/index in the back. This is probably one of the most attractive and easy-to-use volumes on the market.

Norlin, Dennis, Cay Gasque, Christopher Lewis, Ruth O'Donnell, and Lawrence Webster. *A Directory of Adaptive Technologies to Aid Library Patrons and Staff with Disabilities.* American Library Association, 1994. 110 p. ISBN 0-8389-7754-5 (hardcover).

This directory was published to help educators, primarily librarians, comply with the Americans With Disabilities Act (ADA). It is a one-stop resource for finding adaptive technology that is effective, affordable, and appropriate for persons with physical disabilities. There is also a section on how to obtain funding for some of the more expensive and specialized needs.

Sinofsky, Esther R. *A Copyright Primer for Educational and Industrial Media Producers.* 2nd ed. Association for Educational Communications and Technology, 1994. 227 p. ISBN 0-914143-12-3 (hardcover).

Sinofsky lists nine rules of thumb about copyright in the beginning pages of her book. Four of them seem critical for school personnel: (1) Educational use is not fair use; (2) Nonprofit, educational entities may have difficulties claiming fair use; (3) License and contract clauses are negotiable; and (4) It is cheaper to buy a license than settle out of court. What the law says about copyright is explored by providing working definitions of legal, literary, and electronic terms. After a brief history of copyright laws, there are detailed discussions of what can and cannot be copyrighted, what is in the public domain, what constitutes fair use, and how producers should approach the use of characters, scripts, music, and other elements of a multimedia project. Remedies for infringement are succinctly outlined, as are approaches to a search for copyright holders. The appendices contain guidelines for off-air taping, a sample copyright search, and a list of publications from the U.S. Copyright Office. A bibliography of books, articles, documents, and court cases is included. There is also a table of court cases and an index. This is truly one of the most important and comprehensive works dealing with copyright law and its implications for educators.

Whiteley, Sandy, ed. *American Library Association Guide to Information Access: A Complete Research Handbook and Directory.* Random House, 1994, 533 p. ISBN 0-679-75075-4 (paper).

This directory puts over three thousand print and electronic sources at one's fingertips. Arranged by topics, this book is a treasure trove of sources to answer almost any question. For each topic to be searched, the reader is introduced to general works in the field, special handbooks, online journals, resources on CD-ROM, and online bibliographic utilities. This directory is almost a complete reference collection in a single volume.

IMPROVING THE SCHOOLS

Barron, Ann, and Gary W. Orwig. *New Technologies for Education: A Beginner's Guide.* 2nd ed. Libraries Unlimited, 1995. 209 p. ISBN 1-56308-340-X (paper).

Improving the instructional process requires many different approaches and resources. The authors believe that the use of CD-ROMs, interactive video, and local networks all have something to offer in the process. This book can be used as a guide for inservice instruction or as a textbook for those who are engaged in a lengthy study of instructional technology. Each chapter begins with a scenario that

Instructional Technology 231

depicts the use of technology in an educational setting. Settings are both student and teacher problem centered. One of the book's strong points is its discussions of both the advantages and the disadvantages of all technology formats included. For each format presented, the authors provide graphs for configuring during set-up, a glossary, a list of vendors/producers, and a list of sources for further reading. This is a well-designed text and an excellent source for beginners.

•Carson, Ben, and Jane Smith, eds. *Renewal at the Schoolhouse: Management Ideas for Library Media Specialists and Administrators.* Libraries Unlimited, 1993. 156 p. ISBN 0-87287-914-3 (hardcover).

How does one identify and bring together all of the resources inside and outside the school to improve the school's instructional program and set goals for improvement? How does one motivate the players and develop the leaders? These and other important questions are the focus of this book. Answers are provided from two perspectives: that of a former district media supervisor, and that of a state media director. Staff development for a new kind of professional and the use of site-based management are offered as partial solutions. This is a well-written book that should change schools for the better.

Means, Barbara, et al. *Using Technology to Support Education Reform.* Government Printing Office, 1993. ISBN 0-16-042048-2 (hardcover); Gordon Press, 1993. 110 p. ISBN 0-8490-5776-0 (hardcover).

Working from the premise that true school reform cannot be successful with a piecemeal approach, the researchers advocate the use of technology to bring about a complete and fundamental change in the ways schools operate. They believe that authentic challenging tasks should form the core of educational reform and that these tasks should be approached from a number of teacher, administrator, and student vantage points. Classrooms should be completely overhauled, they argue, to form learning cultures in which collaboration, delegation, goal clarification, facilitation, and performance-based assessment can flourish. The authors also maintain that technology should be the vehicle through which students can communicate, explore their world, be tutored and tutor, and engage in problem-solving. The book discusses uses of multimedia, networks, CD-ROMs, and word processors and other writing tools. There is an extensive list of references.

Papert, Seymour. *The Children's Machine: Rethinking School in the Age of the Computer.* Basic Books, 1993. 241 p. ISBN 0-465-01063-6 (paper).

At a time when educators are overwhelmed with identifying specifications for the appropriate computer system for their schools, much of their attention is being directed to using the computer as an instructional delivery tool. Papert maintains that the computer should be viewed as a mind tool for learners, not as a teacher tool. Students need computers to "stretch" their minds and to improve their problem-solving abilities. When viewed from this perspective, the computer becomes an exciting and necessary addition to the learning apparatus of all students. Used in this manner, the computer negates most teacher-directed activities, while control of learning tasks is placed with the student. Papert's book is a collection of fascinating essays that should be read by all who are interested in schools and how children learn.

Reigeluth, Charles, and Robert Garfinkle, eds. *Systemic Change in Education.* Educational Technology Publications, 1994. 172 p. ISBN 0-87778-271-7 (hardcover).

A theory of educational change is presented, followed by a presentation of change models. Examples of how these models are currently being translated into everyday practice are also included. The use of instructional technology in this process is considered in light of school policy, student assessment, and school finance. While classroom teachers might find this volume slow reading, school administrators should be pleased with its whole-school-picture approach to school improvement.

Wishnietsky, Dan, ed. *Assessing the Role of Technology in Education.* Phi Delta Kappa, 1994. 261 p. (paper).

This volume brings together some of the best articles from *The Kappan* over the past five years. The editor states that selection for inclusion was difficult because of the sheer number of articles that had been published on the topic. Each selection was chosen because ". . . it was well written, current, presented important information, and contributed to the volume's purpose." There is an overview of the integration of technology in education that includes looking at technology with an eye on the twenty-first century. The role of teachers and administrators is discussed within the context of leadership and staff development. An important section of the book looks at the impact of technology on students and asks whether computer literacy is a basic skill for all students. Other articles deal with technology and its contributions to the subject areas of science and the humanities. There are also examinations of ethical issues surrounding the use of technology, along with discussions of gender bias, cultural bias, and at-risk students. A piece on planning for the future rounds out this important and scholarly volume.

INSTRUCTIONAL APPLICATIONS

Dewing, Martha. *Beyond TV: Activities for Using Video with Children.* ABC-CLIO Publishers, 1992. 186 p. ISBN 0-87436-601-1 (paper).

This is a source book written for elementary classroom teachers who see television/video as a motivating and viable instructional tool. It contains teaching ideas and themes and topics for children to explore for their own video productions. It also provides suggestions on building a strong video collection that will support the school curriculum. It should be especially appealing to the teacher who wishes to use this technique but needs help in managing the many facets of student-made productions.

Dick, Walter, and Robert Reiser. *Planning Effective Instruction.* Prentice-Hall, 1989. 136 p. ISBN 0-13-679457-2 (paper).

At a time when teachers struggle to design more effective lessons, this book should prove extremely helpful. It is very readable and contains practical models to be used by the teacher who has little time for sorting through scientific and technical flowcharts that are often used in elaborate training programs. There are practical application exercises in each chapter in the book.

Dockterman, David. *Great Teaching in the One Computer Classroom.* 2nd ed. Tom Snyder Productions, 1990. 124 p. (paper).

This is an excellent source of information on how elementary school teachers can make effective use of a single computer in the classroom. Specific examples for both teacher and student use are included. An excellent video accompanies this book.

Heinich, Robert, Michael Molenda, and Jane Russell. *Instructional Media and the New Technologies of Instruction.* 5th ed. Merrill, 1996. 429 p. ISBN 0-02-353070-7 (hardcover).

This well-respected and widely used text is now in its fifth and probably its most comprehensive edition. Starting from a model or plan for effective teaching, the authors take the student and the teacher through techniques for producing and using traditional media (overheads, displays, photographs) and newer media (computers and telecommunications). An important emphasis in the book is on understanding new terminology and how these terms become operational in the execution of an actual lesson or project. There are numerous photographs, line drawings, and charts to help the user with important concepts. This is probably the single best instructional media book in the field.

Kemp, Jerrold, and Don Smellie. *Planning, Producing and Using Learning Technologies.* 7th ed. HarperCollins, 1994. 406 p. ISBN 0-06-500604-6 (hardcover).

This is the classic "how to do it" book for designing and producing a variety of instructional materials, including non-projected visuals, bulletin boards, overhead transparencies, slides, and audio and video productions. It is well illustrated, and step-by-step instructions are often provided. The guidelines for effective visual design and layout are particularly helpful. Templates for various types of visuals are also provided. Utilization tips and ideas on how to incorporate media into lessons are included, and a systematic planning process is presented as well.

Schurr, Sandra L. *Dynamite in the Classroom: How-to Handbook for Teachers.* National Middle School Association, 1989. 140 p. ISBN 1-56090-041-5 (paper).

Middle schools provide assistance in the developmental gap between young children and young adults. Teachers who work with students in this age group (and sometimes younger children) are often strapped when it comes to identifying sound and effective learning activities. This book helps fill this need. It brings together research findings about middle school education and practical classroom applications, centering on methods and activities that lead to the development of important intellectual skills such as propositional thought, reasoning with hypotheses, analysis, and interpretation. Using Bloom's Taxonomy and other tested theories, the author provides a wealth of structured activities that should both delight and motivate learners. Each activity has an accompanying quiz and information on further readings, and there are numerous culminating tests in the back of the volume. There is no index.

Seaver, Alice. *Library Media Skills: Strategies for Instructing Primary Students.* 2nd ed. Libraries Unlimited, 1991. 230 p. ISBN 0-87287-857-0 (paper).

Convinced that finding and using information are processes that should begin early in life, the author presents a planning guide for teachers and library media specialists who work with young children. The book discusses the unique developmental characteristics of primary learners and suggests age-appropriate lesson plans and activities to be used in the classroom and the media center. An Apple Works computer disk that contains activities from the book accompanies the text. The disk can be customized to fit a specific media center collection.

Teague, Fred, Doug Rogers, and Roger Tipling. *Technology and Media: Instructional Applications.* Kendall/Hunt, 1994. 332 p. ISBN 0-8403-8438-6 (spiral).

This very readable text contains discussions of basic instructional media and how they can be used by teachers and students of instructional technology. There is an excellent section on the use of computers for both classroom management and classroom instruction. The guidelines for selection and utilization should prove very helpful.

Turner, Sandra, and Michael Land. *HyperCard: A Tool for Learning.* Wadsworth Publishing, 1993. 372 p. ISBN 0-534-17496-5 (paper).

HyperCard has been around a relatively long time, at least since the mid-1980's, but teachers are still finding new and exciting ways of using it in the classroom. This book will help teachers in designing and creating stacks. One does not need previous experience with the software to create attractive and successful lessons. The authors discuss such topics as preparing the background for a stack, modifying graphics for use in the stack, importing a graphic, creating title cards, and printing out stack reports. There are also chapters that suggest ways of using animation, sound, and other multimedia. The book is well written and easy to use. There are a glossary and an index in the back. An activities disk for use with Macintosh computers accompanies the text.

RESOURCE GUIDES

Brock, Patricia. *Educational Technology in the Classroom.* Prentice-Hall, 1994. 250 p. ISBN 0-87778-269-5 (hardcover).

Written in a question-and-answer format, this reference source for teachers and library media specialists contains extensive lists of references, publishers, producers, and other information sources.

Going the Distance: Distance Learning Comes of Age. ERIC/EDRS, 1992; 1993 supplement.

This annotated bibliography contains unpublished documents on distance learning, available in the ERIC database. Each entry contains the document number, author, title, and publication year and a lengthy abstract. Each document is available from the ERIC Document Reproduction Service for a very small fee.

Harris, Judi B. *The Way of the Ferret: Finding Educational Resources on the Internet.* Rev. ed. International Society for Technology in Education, 1994. 191 p. ISBN 0-685-72762-9 (paper).

The author states in her Preface, "In 5 to 10 years, my hope is that this book will no longer be necessary . . . tools will be developed and distributed that will make Internet resources just 'points and clicks' away. Until then, help is needed with Fetch, TurboGopher, Eudora, and Mosaic." The author uses the term "ferret" in the title because of its connotation of carefully seeking out hidden gems with clever persistence, since that is what using the Internet is all about. The book makes several assumptions for effective use: (1) the user has access to the Internet; (2) the user has a modem hooked to her/his computer; and (3) the user is comfortable with a good word processing package. The book is divided into four sections that cover such topics as electronic mail, file transfers, location tools, and listserv groups. There is a complete chapter that is devoted to activities with telecomputing that can be used by novices. Two appendices that list Telnet and FTP sites and an index round out the book.

Hoffman, Andrea C., and Ann Glannon. *Kits, Games and Manipulatives for the Elementary Classroom: A Source Book.* Garland Publishing, 1993. 605 p. ISBN 0-8240-5342-7 (hardcover).

The authors identify instructional but nonbook materials from which teachers and school media specialists can select to build a classroom or media center collection. The more than fifteen hundred items are arranged by broad subjects, ranging from animals to language to weather. Each entry contains a physical description, learning objective, suggested use, grade level, cost, and name of producer. There is a descriptor or key word index and a directory of producers and vendors.

Krol, Ed. *The Whole Internet User's Guide and Catalog.* Academic edition. O'Reilly & Associates, 1996. 609 p. ISBN 0-53450-674-7 (paper).

While this book is heavily slanted to the UNIX user, it will accommodate users of Macintosh, DOS, or VAX/VMS just as well. It is written for the professional who has a job to do and needs the Internet to get it done. It assumes only one thing—that the user is computer literate. There are twelve chapters that discuss topics such as dial-up connections, needed hardware, domain authority, and finding files. The book's treatment of the World Wide Web is probably one of the most comprehensive available. One of its most compelling features is its discussion of legal constraints placed on users, both private and commercial, along with an excellent discussion on network ethics. The subject-arranged directory in the back makes this book a handy reference tool to be kept on almost every user's desk.

Restructuring America's Schools: A Blueprint for Action. ERIC/EDRS, 1992; 1993 supplement.

This annotated bibliography contains unpublished documents on school reform available in the ERIC database. Each entry contains the document number, author, title, and publication year and a lengthy abstract. Individual documents are available from the ERIC Document Reproduction Service for a nominal fee.

Stevens, Gregory, ed. *Videos for Understanding Diversity: A Core Selection and Evaluation Guide.* American Library Association, 1993. 217 p. ISBN 0-8389-0612-5 (paper).

This guide lists over one hundred documentary and feature videos dealing with diversity and multiculturalism. Each entry contains the title, series, date, producer, rental or purchase information, and an indication of the availability of a study guide or transcript. An evaluation of each video suggests recommended audience and provides information on subject or theme, historical background when available, and how the video can be used to heighten cultural understanding. This book should be especially useful in schools where collections of multicultural materials of all types are in need of improvement.

TELECOMMUNICATIONS, DISTANCE LEARNING, AND THE INTERNET

Dern, Daniel. *The Internet Guide for New Users.* McGraw-Hill, 1994. 570 p. ISBN 0-07-016511-4 (paper).

There are many texts available for those who have had some experience with the Internet, but very few for those who have had none. This book is one of the best for such an audience. From a brief history of this superhighway, the author takes the reader through setting up an account with little money, to the importance of names and addresses, to basic concepts about Unix. From there, the reader is introduced to Internet tools—e-mail, gophers, FTP, etc.—and finally to how to actually use these and other tools. There are chapters on commercial services and a very extensive section on tips and suggestions for troubleshooting. In the appendix there is a very useful list of Internet-related organizations, with their addresses, e-mail addresses, phone numbers, and fax numbers. A bibliography, glossary, and index complete the book.

Levine, John, Margaret Young, and Arnold Reinholt. *The Internet for Dummies.* 2nd ed. IDG Books Worldwide, 1995. 210 p. ISBN 1-56884-977-X (paper).

This book is a beginner's introduction to the Internet. It defines the Internet and discusses its structure, who can use it, and how it is accessed. Its use of simple nontechnical terms with short easy-to-read sentences makes it a useful tool for the educator who wishes to venture onto the superhighway, but is still a little timid. The book is filled with cartoons and other humor that make it enjoyable to read. A subsequent volume provides more advanced information for those who like this style of writing.

Machovec, George. *Telecommunications, Networking and Internet Glossary.* American Library Association, 1993. 124 p. ISBN 0-8389-7697-2 (paper).

When venturing into a new field, everyone needs a handy and useful glossary of terms. This glossary is a greatly expanded edition of an earlier publication of the Library and Information Technology Association in 1990. The volume reflects the emergence of the Internet, NREN, and other technology. The author notes that many of the terms in this volume did not exist in 1990. The glossary contains both proprietary and nonproprietary terminology. There is minor emphasis on terms related to computer technology, library automation, and information technology because the author determined that these could be easily found elsewhere. Terms are entered in all caps, with definitions in lower-case type. The abundant use of cross reference helps the user in understanding the relationships and interdependence among many concepts. There is a list of references on which the definitions in the back of the volume were based.

Willis, Barry, ed. *Distance Education: Strategies and Tools.* Educational Technology Publications, 1994. 334 p. ISBN 0-87778-268-7 (hardcover).

This book examines a variety of issues related to distance education that will be of great value to those contemplating initiating such an endeavor. Using research and experience from around the globe, the editor brings together discussions of research findings, how to conduct needs assessments, how to plan off-site lessons and courses, how to integrate computers and other devices into the instruction, and how to cope with the use of copyrighted materials.

NONPRINT MATERIALS

Global Quest: The Internet in the Classroom. Lorain County Joint Vocational School. Video.

This eleven-minute videotape presents the benefits of using the Internet and urges that all schools have access. The government-sponsored tape is available to all educators and can be copied at no cost at any NASA Teacher Resource Center.

Great Teaching in the One Computer Classroom. Tom Snyder Productions. Video.

This video is a companion to David Dockterman's text, *Great Teaching in the One Computer Classroom* (Tom Snyder Productions, 1990), annotated under the subcategory of "Instructional Applications."

JOURNALS

The Computing Teacher. International Society for Technology in Education. ISSN 0278-9175.

This journal is for people who are interested primarily in the instructional uses of computers and telecommunications. It covers methods of teaching and needs in teacher education, and often discusses the general impact of technology on education. Articles are mostly brief but very practical. The journal is a good source of ideas for teachers who work with remedial students. It does a good job of blending theory and practice in the classroom.

Educational Technology. Educational Technology Publications. ISSN 0013-1962.

This journal is an excellent source of research findings from studies conducted on the use and value of technology in education and training. Its articles are long and comprehensive. While the authors generally come from higher education and/or large corporations, the articles are written so that practicing teachers and school administrators can understand the implications of the research and suggested ideas. The writing is scholarly, with well-documented discussions. There is a section devoted to new developments in the areas of teleconferencing, multimedia, management, and other cutting-edge educational techniques.

Electronic Learning. Scholastic. ISSN 0278-3258.

This journal could be the only subscription to a periodical in educational computing in a school, and it just might meet all the needs of the faculty. It is very strong on practical applications of computers and covers almost everything that one might want to know about computers in the school. Articles are generally brief but informative, covering new products, teacher uses of technology, staff training, and other concerns that teachers might have about instructional technology.

Journal of Educational Multimedia and Hypermedia. Association for the Advancement of Computing in Education. ISSN 1055-8896.

Current applications of multimedia and hypermedia in the various subject areas are the focus of this journal. The articles are research-based and discuss findings from the promotion of multimedia in the various subject matters. Each article contains an introduction, a methodology, and a summary of findings with implications. Reference lists are extensive. This journal is for the educator who is interested in using multimedia and hypermedia and who wants to begin from a sound base of research.

Media & Methods. American Society of Educators. ISSN 0025-6897.

This journal is subtitled "Educational products, technologies & programs for schools & universities." Each issue offers innovative ideas in the use of technology in K–12 schools, four-year colleges, and training programs. The feature articles are not very lengthy but are long enough to provide the reader with details about the topic being presented. Articles are signed and are well written. Authors are recruited from a variety of sources—schools, colleges, businesses, and government. There are also reviews of products and new books. A useful section is called "Products in Action." Here, new products are presented along with a short description and an accompanying picture.

•*School Library Journal.* Cahners. ISSN 0362-8930.

This comprehensive reviewing tool is targeted at school media specialists but could be useful to any educator who is looking for the latest publications for K–12 media centers and classrooms. It reviews books, audiovisual materials, and computer software. Reviewers are generally mainstream practicing media specialists and teachers. There is an editorial page that examines issues concerning the use of different types of materials in the schools. Each issue also contains a calendar of upcoming professional events and a column on the latest resources for professional reading.

The three to four special feature articles examine reading problems, evaluation of materials, technology, and intellectual freedom.

Technology & Learning. Peter Li. ISSN 1053-6728.

Designed for the educator who wants to keep abreast of the latest and effective uses of technology in educational settings. Each issue contains at least one lengthy article on how innovative schools, classrooms, media centers, or educational laboratories are distributing and sharing resources. There are regular announcements of available grants and other opportunities for schools. The November/December issue is devoted to in-depth reviews of awarding-winning computer software for K–12 classrooms. The "What's New" column reviews new software as well as updates of existing packages, management tools, hardware, and other services. Subscribers can use the enclosed "Free Information" cards to send for further information about products and services advertised in a given issue.

TechTrends. Association for Educational Communications and Technology. ISSN 8756-3894.

This journal, the official publication of AECT, is published for the professional growth of its membership. Each issue is divided into three sections: columns, feature articles, and departments. The first section contains opinions and information on copyright, ethics, and other topics surrounding the use of technology. Features can vary each month but often follow a theme. The departments contain reviews of latest products, a date book, news from the Association, recommended resources, and news about festivals and awards.

T.H.E. Journal. Technological Horizons in Education. Information Synergy. ISSN 0192-592X.

This is one of the few journals in the field that offers free subscriptions on a limited basis to subscribers in the U.S. It is an excellent source for keeping up with new management techniques and information about the cost effectiveness of various forms of media and technology. Feature articles are short, generally no more than a single page, and to the point. The journal's many examples of technology at work make it one of the most valuable publications on the market today. Topics of articles range from staff development to effective use of games, kits, and videodiscs.

MEMBERSHIPS

Association for Educational Communications and Technology
1025 Vermont Avenue, N.W., Suite 820
Washington, D.C. 20005

Instructional Technology

Phone: (205) 347-7834
Fax: (205) 347-7839

AECT is an international professional organization of teachers, media directors, instructional designers, production specialists, and researchers. It has eleven divisions, forty-five state affiliates, and some thirty active committees. There are ten categories of membership, covering a broad spectrum of applicants from corporations to international students.

19

Promoting the Professional Collection

In addition to intrinsic excellence, professional resources must gain recognition and acceptance to be useful. A primary concern during the development of the lists for this book was that the materials would be used by teachers. As the experts in the various fields selected items for inclusion from the thousands of professional materials available, they asked the question: "Will this book or nonprint material be truly useful to elementary teachers?" While the consultants focused on intrinsic excellence, other factors also bring useful life to a professional collection.

During the preparation of this book I visited various model professional libraries. One stunning professional center displayed all the window dressings of an exemplary professional library—a separate, attractive room within the school media center, shelves of fully processed books, a well-organized nonprint collection, a computer center, eye-catching bulletin boards, and a comfortable seating area. Yet, after browsing the shelves and examining the wealth of excellent resources on three separate occasions, it became evident that the most important ingredient of any professional library—the users—appeared to be missing! Unless the professional collection is promoted and used, it is of little value.

Engaging teachers in the use of a professional collection is not necessarily a simple matter. The development of an active, frequently used professional center requires four key elements: (1) a commitment to professional development within the school district; (2) a rich, exciting collection of materials that satisfy the professional needs of the educators; (3) easy access; and (4) a library media specialist who markets the collection. Only when schools or districts are responsive to these four elements do teachers take full advantage of what a professional collection has to offer.

Commitment to Professional Development

In schools and districts where professional libraries thrive, a positive disposition concerning the importance of professional development has been established. The commitment of district administrators, principals, library media specialists, and teachers to professional development is apparent in the quality of professional development programs offered, as well as in the collection of resources available to educators. Professional development should be provided on a regular and continual basis with a sequential plan in mind. A true commitment to professional development includes more than disconnected workshops, seminars, or individual speakers. Planned, well-organized, sequential programs with well-defined objectives are essential to sustain professional growth.

While this commitment to ongoing professional growth may be externally emphasized by administrators and supervisors through various workshops based on identifiable goals and expectations, the desire for professional growth must come from educators themselves who recognize the importance of lifelong learning. In addition to continuing to provide teachers with formal professional development activities, the school districts should focus on creating an environment which promotes the notion of constant growth of the learner. Such environments encourage educators to take responsibility for their own professional growth. The professional library supports this idea by offering educators the professional resources and services needed to organize a plan and keep up-to-date with their profession.

Along with the commitment to professional training should come the support of a professional collection at district and school levels, which will in turn enrich and support the inservice training activities. A school district's acknowledgment of the importance of a professional collection comes in a variety of forms: (1) provision of financial support; (2) arrangements for a designated space and staff; and (3) a spirit of enthusiasm for professional development.

Provision of Financial Support. Library media specialists involved in the survey discussed in Chapter 1 emphasized the need for financial support when they were asked: "What do you find is the biggest problem in maintaining professional collections?" Over 65 percent of the library media specialists agreed that funding was the biggest problem they faced (see Appendix). Educators would agree that without specific funding designated for professional materials, school libraries are often unable to provide the professional resources and facilities necessary for ongoing professional growth.

While school district administrators typically allocate funds for professional development, they often overlook the importance of earmarking some of the funds for a professional collection at the school and/or district level to augment the inservice training. In some cases, before funds are made available for a specific resource area such as the professional collection, a need must be perceived. While the children's collection will always remain a priority in any elementary library budget, librarians will want to use a small portion of the budget to begin building a professional collection for teachers. Circulation of the professional materials purchased can be used to illustrate faculty enthusiasm for the collection as well as the need for more resources. Perhaps this data can help librarians gain special funding from the school district for professional resources. It is critical that administrators recognize the essential role a professional collection plays in the support of teachers' professional growth, and that they move toward establishing a professional development center at district level that encompasses both inservice programs and a professional library or teacher center to support the programs.

Arrangements for a Designated Space and Staff. As a school or a district moves toward establishing a clear priority concerning professional growth for teachers, that commitment should become evident through the provision of staff and material support, as well as a designated space for a professional collection. Of course, this commitment is usually directly related to the amount of financial support the district provides for professional growth.

While the ideal is a separate, inviting room within the library devoted to professional materials, many elementary schools cannot afford the extra space required for the separate facility. Therefore, the library media specialist may find it necessary to call upon his or her own creativity to define an existing area for the professional collection. Whether this is inside the library, within the work area, or in a vacant classroom, an innovative library media specialist can create a professional environment by highlighting the area with bulletin boards, comfortable and attractive furnishings, and displays that focus on professional materials and send out the message of professional growth and teacher involvement.

In the very best of worlds, the district's commitment to district-wide professional growth is reflected in the designation of a teacher center at the district level devoted to professional materials and services. Teacher centers at district level make a statement to district personnel and to the community that the school district is committed to professional development.

Interviews with district-level teacher center directors revealed that, besides lack of funding, a major problem involves lack of staff to support the professional libraries. They mentioned that in school districts which visibly support professional development by making a resource-rich teacher center available to teachers, there is often a lack of staff to make the center really work. As one director commented, "What's the purpose of having the latest professional materials if we don't have the staff to get them on the shelves and out to the teachers?" Library media specialists at the school level also voiced concerns about the difficulty of getting the professional materials processed, due to lack of aides or volunteers. So once the district has allotted funds for the facility and the resources that make up the collection, an additional factor that must be considered when developing an exemplary professional library is staffing.

A Spirit of Enthusiasm for Professional Development. While the facility, staffing, and materials indicate the level of commitment by the school or district, the most important element in determining the success of any professional library is the involvement and enthusiasm of the library media specialist. In districts where a strong commitment has not been made by the administration, enthusiastic library media specialists sometimes take on a leadership role by developing a worthwhile collection of professional resources and by providing teachers with activities that support their professional growth. A two-hour workshop for the entire faculty on World Wide Web, a booktalk on *Smart Girls, Gifted Women* (Kerr, 1985), and a mini-workshop for primary teachers on children's reading preferences are just a sampling of the valuable professional activities arranged by school librarians. Each of these activities was supported by resources from the professional collections in the schools.

Teachers and administrators are usually surprised by the wide range of knowledge and skills related to professional development possessed by school librarians. The role of the librarian in professional development is discussed in *Information Power* (ALA and AECT, 1988, p. 34), the national guidelines for school librarians. The document states that the library media specialist should "provide staff development opportunities for teachers and school administrators in the selection, use, evaluation, and production of media resources." By identifying specific areas of need, such as reference skills, computer technology, and literature, librarians can offer activities that update the teacher's knowledge. The appendix to *Information Power* (p. 137) goes a step further and makes recommendations for the allocation of space for a teacher/professional area. In its recognition of the library's role in professional development at the district level, *Information Power* (p. 96) notes that a district library media facility should include "a professional library and teacher center where all types of professional materials and equipment can be housed." The success of a professional collection as well as other professional development activities within the school are dependent on the commitment of the school librarian to professional development.

This commitment should be reflected in statements in acquisitions and procedures policies that specifically address professional collections. Unfortunately, however, Philip Turner reports in *Helping Teachers Teach* (1993, p. 32) that few districts include in their policies any reference to professional collections. Inclusions in policies of explicit statements concerning professional collections is essential if professional libraries are to gain the recognition and funding they deserve.

Development of an Interesting, Rich Professional Collection

In building an exciting collection for children, librarians typically depend on children's preferences, selection aids, and book review sources. The professional collection should be built with these same considerations in mind. *Story S-t-r-e-t-c-h-e-r-s for the Primary Grades* (Raines, 1992), *Science Through Children's Literature* (Butzow and Butzow, 1989), and *Multicultural Teaching: A Handbook of Activities, Information and Resources* (Tiedt and Tiedt, 1995) are just a few of the titles that may whet teachers' appetites for professional materials. Since professional reading is often not required and the desire must come from within each teacher, a librarian's special attention to teacher interests and preferences during the selection process will pay off. A rich and varied collection of materials will keep teachers coming back to use the professional library.

Awareness and Fulfillment of Teacher Interests and Needs. Library media specialists should approach the development of the professional collection with a focus on interests and needs in the same manner that they develop the children's collection. Knowledge of professional resources that teachers frequently check out can prove valuable in developing the collection. Teacher preferences reflected in surveys such as the one described in Chapter 1 and displayed in the Appendix should encourage librarians to include such popular works as *Invitations* (Routman, 1991), *The Read-Aloud Handbook* (Trelease, 1995), and *A to Zoo: Subject Access to Children's Picture Books* (Lima and Lima, 1994) in their collections.

Becoming familiar with teacher needs and interests involves communication between the teachers and librarians. *Information Power* (ALA and AECT, 1988, p. 35) describes the importance of serving on curriculum and grade-level committees as one means of understanding classroom needs and capitalizing on teachers' interests in the various content areas. Knowledge of the curriculum and needs of specific faculty members gained through these

Promoting the Professional Collection

meetings will aid the librarian in ordering the appropriate professional resources as well as the related children's materials. For example, during one grade-level meeting science teachers discussed their plans for developing learning centers in the fall. Because of her awareness of these plans, the school librarian ordered *Science Learning Centers for the Primary Grades* (Poppe and Van Matre, 1985) and made the book available to science teachers at the next meeting. As demonstrated in this case, membership on curriculum and grade-level committees gives the librarian the opportunity to key in on special interests, invite suggestions for professional materials, and keep faculty informed as to what is available in the professional library.

Besides attention to fulfilling professional needs related to classroom lessons and curriculum, librarians should also be aware of the "happenings" across the district and within the community. Knowledge concerning district meetings, workshops, conferences, and university courses can make collection development easier and result in a stronger collection. This knowledge can be gathered in a variety of ways: sending a short questionnaire to faculty each year, attending curriculum meetings, keeping up with notices in district newsletters, and attending local meetings of professional organizations.

Just as a child's needs must be satisfied if he or she is to choose to return to the library, an educator's needs also must be satisfied. Granted, many times the small professional collection will not contain the requested resource. Yet the librarian is often able to fulfill the user's need in other ways, such as referring him or her to another library, ordering the requested material for the collection, or using interlibrary loan privileges. The important thing is that once the professional collection fulfills a real need, the educator will continue to use the collection, and the professional collection has also gained an advocate for its continued support.

Keeping Up With Book Reviews. Librarians routinely consult the reviews of professional materials found in professional journals and other selection aids in updating their professional collections, but they often find that few faculty use the review sources in making requests for professional materials. A book review workshop can be one method of encouraging faculty to request professional materials. While book review workshops typically focus on how to write a good review, one creative librarian puts a different twist on such workshops: she uses them to acquaint faculty with the book review process, as well as the quality review sources in the various content areas. The success of the workshop experience is evident in the increase in teacher requests for professional review sources.

Access to library journals as well as content-area journals is essential to collection development. School librarians can turn to their own journals, such as *School Library Journal* and *Emergency Librarian,* for reviews of professional materials. Additionally, they can browse the book reviews in teacher journals such as *Reading Teacher, Teaching Children Mathematics, Science and Children,* and *School Arts Magazine* for recommended resources to add to the professional collection.

Focus on All Subject Areas Within the School. A balanced collection of professional materials should include materials from the various subject areas. Titles such as *Celebrate: Holidays, Puppets and Creative Drama* (Hunt and Renfro, 1987), *Hooked on Science: Ready to Use Discovery Activities for Grades 4–8* (Sewall, 1990), and *Read Any Good Math Lately? Children's Books for Mathematical Learning, K–6* (Whitin and Wilde, 1992), from the fields of theatre, science, and math, add richness and depth to any professional collection.

Interestingly, the national survey discussed in Chapter 1 indicates that the professional tools that elementary teachers use most frequently focus on literacy and include many selection aids related to children's literature. Three reasons may account for this: (1) Library media specialists may tend to focus on selecting titles of professional works that interest them and meet their own needs; (2) Much of the elementary day is spent on language arts and reading, and therefore, the titles of professional materials most frequently circulated by teachers reflect this; and (3) The whole language approach emphasizes the use of thematic units which can be developed through the use of professional materials and selection aids and related to children's literature. Library media specialists will want to move beyond these interests and consider all content areas when ordering materials for the professional collection.

Easy Access to a Centralized, Well-Organized Collection

Organization. Ideally, the professional collection, like the children's collection, should be centralized. With the materials available for all curriculum areas located in the professional library rather than scattered throughout the school in various departments or grade levels, all teachers within a school have the materials conveniently available to them. Even when materials are checked out to special programs or grade levels for much of the year, teachers will have access to the catalog listing of the resources. The centralized checkout system allows the librarian to know where each item can be found when needed by other faculty members. Besides convenient access to materials, the centralized location saves money by reducing the need for duplication of items, as it encourages a sharing of resources.

Promoting the Professional Collection 249

Interviews and visits to various professional libraries indicated that some professional collections are haphazardly organized, with materials not fully processed. Librarians in these professional libraries may depend on donations and used books to augment their collections or may simply not have time to process the professional books. Organization, usually by Dewey Decimal Classification, is essential. While much of the circulation is based on browsing, it is important that teachers have access to a database or card file that lists the available materials according to author, title, and subject. Unless professional materials are properly processed and entered into the catalog, they will not be used by teachers. If the district or school already enjoys an automated catalog of library materials, including the professional materials in the catalog establishes access for all users of the system.

Flexible Checkouts. Flexibility and creativity in circulation procedures play a key role in increasing the circulation of the collection. The circulation policy should consider the faculty's needs for flexible checkout periods. Even when a checkout period of several weeks or a month is the standard for professional materials, teachers should feel comfortable renewing the materials. As mentioned above, the advantage of a centralized collection is in knowing what exists and where the materials can be found if another teacher requests the item.

Interviews and visits to professional collections underlined the importance of creative circulation arrangements to encourage the use of journals and professional books. As one librarian in the Houston area noted: "Since I made the journals available to teachers in the lounge area, the journal circulation has quadrupled." Another librarian mentioned that the circulation increased when she "began to wheel a cart filled with professional books on specific subject areas into the teachers' lounge." Advertising the collection, along with innovative circulation procedures such as longer checkout periods, will help put the professional materials into the hands of teachers.

Flexible Hours. To provide more opportunities for teachers to browse the professional collection, the library should be open during hours when teachers can use the library most easily, such as thirty minutes before school begins and during the thirty minutes after school.

Visits with directors of teacher centers indicated that they are well aware of the need to provide hours before and after school as well as on Saturdays for teachers to check out professional materials. Yet the directors also admitted that it was impossible to please all teachers with their schedules. Additionally, they made it clear that with cutbacks in funding, after-hours services were often the first ones to go. Maximum flexibility of hours, however, remains a way to promote the professional collection and thus increase the circulation, justifying support for the collection.

Marketing the Collection

A visit to an exemplary elementary school library media center provided a glimpse of the various ways a professional collection can impact the educational programs within a school. The visit was on an inservice day for teachers, and the library was buzzing with small groups of primary teachers designing story aprons for their classrooms. A special guest provided a variety of sample story aprons, demonstrated their use, and shared how to design the aprons. Throughout the session, the teachers were surrounded by a multitude of children's books that could be used in the development of story aprons. Also, the selection aids had been pulled from the professional collection and were made readily available to help the teachers select appropriate children's books to highlight. The story aprons created during this inservice day would be placed in the special materials center of the library, adding additional resources for teachers. This is one example of how a professional library can actively provide professional growth for classroom teachers through special activities and professional materials. When activities such as the story-apron workshop are carried out in the professional library, teachers are encouraged to become involved in professional growth and reminded to call upon the professional library for materials to enrich their professional development activities. Hopefully, these same teachers will continue to return to the professional library for resources.

Advertising. One librarian who was interviewed pointed out: "Letting the teachers know which materials are available is the most important means of promoting the professional collection. After all, without use there is little need to spend the time building a collection." Many of the same practices used in encouraging children to check out books can be used successfully with the professional collection. Comments concerning successful advertising techniques used by enthusiastic librarians include:

"Last week I tucked an article on fractions from *Teaching Children Mathematics* in the math teacher's box."
"I post reviews of the professional books I recently ordered on the bulletin board in the teachers' lounge."
"I display new arrivals for the professional collection at faculty meetings. Some of the faculty have begun to arrive early for meetings just to see the new professional materials."

Promoting the Professional Collection 251

> "My principal has set aside a five-minute period during each faculty meeting for me to highlight several professional works."
>
> "I find that our library newsletter offers an excellent means of promoting the professional collection. A special column featuring resources in our professional collection has increased circulation."
>
> "I tack articles from various professional journals on the bulletin board in the lounge and make the journals available to the faculty for checkout in the lounge."
>
> "Every time I display professional resources on a cart in the faculty lounge area, I find that many of the books are immediately checked out."
>
> "The faculty in my school appreciate bibliographies of professional resources related to topics they are teaching."
>
> "Grade-level meetings give me a chance to share new materials with teachers."

By pushing professional resources at faculty meetings, in the teachers' lounge, at curriculum or grade level meetings, and any place teachers gather, librarians will see circulation of professional tools rise. Sometimes this entails displaying books on a specific topic. Or it may mean discussing new arrivals with teachers, or publicizing them in a newsletter. Then again, it may require developing bibliographies that focus on specific topics. Librarians will want to take advantage of every opportunity to get professional materials into the hands of teachers.

Special Programs That Highlight the Collection. Since the library media specialist's most important role in professional development involves making teachers aware of the available materials and encouraging their use, high visibility and active promotion are important. Special programs, such as the ones shared below, provide an excellent means of attracting users to the professional library at school or district level.

Interviews with elementary librarians proved valuable in compiling the following interesting and practical program ideas that can be used to promote the professional collection.

1. Offer faculty "mini-programs" or "mini-workshops" related to specific professional needs.

A mini-program, which should last no longer than thirty minutes, can provide librarians with the opportunity to zero in on a clearly defined interest or need of a specific group of teachers. Possibilities for program topics are endless. Videotaping, puppetry, the Internet, and folk literature are just a few topics of professional interest that librarians may tackle during a short program. Regardless of the focus, the program offers an opportunity to pull together the professional resources on the topic and promote the professional collection. For example, one library media specialist focused on the third grade teachers' plans to incorporate a weekly storytelling session into the curriculum. With this in mind, the library media specialist developed a thirty-minute program for teachers related to storytelling. After sharing a video that demonstrated storytelling techniques, she highlighted the various storytelling resources available in the professional library. Excited to know about the storytelling resources, faculty returned to the professional library in search of resources for other content areas.

2. Organize a Teachers as Readers group.

Many reading/language arts educators are familiar with the Teachers as Readers program in which librarians, teachers, and other educators meet regularly as a group to discuss their readings. There are no hard and fast rules—participants may all read the same book; they may read different books by the same author; or they may read different books on a specific topic. Oftentimes, the group focuses on children's books, but some librarians use this idea of Teachers as Readers to promote and involve teachers in professional resources. For some of the gatherings, they encourage the teachers in the group to read different professional works and then present booktalks on them. Including principals and school administrators in the group helps publicize the involvement of the library in professional growth activities. (For more information on Teachers as Readers, refer to an editorial by Barbara Elleman in *Book Links,* January 1995, p. 5).

3. Highlight library selection aids.

Library media specialists often take for granted their vast knowledge of library selection aids. Why not share this valuable information with teachers? For example, selection aids such as the popular *Read-Aloud Handbook* (Trelease, 1995), *More Kids' Favorite Books* (International Reading Association, 1995), and *This Way to Books* (Bauer, 1983) can be used to help teachers select outstanding literature for the classroom. While some selection aids support teachers in the development of lists of books to use during thematic units, others include creative ideas for using the literature. Even works that are typically considered librarians' tools, such as *Children's Catalog* and *Elementary School Library Collection,* can be of interest to teachers.

Resources such as *The Collection Program in Schools* (Van Orden, 1995) provide librarians and teachers with a listing of selection aids. Whether such aids are shared individually with teachers or during a mini-program on selection aids, teachers will be coming back to the professional library to use the selection tools.

Promoting the Professional Collection 253

4. Arrange a visit to the district teacher center for the teachers in your school.

One librarian's advertising campaign, "Eye-openers: Teacher Center Close-Up," resulted in half of the faculty signing up for a field trip to the district's teacher center. Recognizing that few teachers take full advantage of the available services and even fewer actually set foot in the teacher center, she arranged the field experience with the teacher center director, who was thrilled to advertise the center and share the various services. The professional collection, production services, and special materials area were just a few of the items on the agenda, and each participant went away with a handout listing the various services.

5. Offer an in-depth library orientation tour to all faculty each fall.

While library tours for new faculty are quite common, returning faculty also need a tour of the school library facility each year. Many library tours, however, give only a passing glance to the professional collection. A focus on this section could prove worthwhile in enticing teachers to use the professional materials. Acquainting classroom teachers with the available resources, services, checkout procedures, and programs will reinforce the message that the collection is available to them. Providing a videotape of the tour to new teachers along with maps of the library allows one more opportunity to focus on the professional library.

6. Try booktalking the professional literature.

Teachers and librarians routinely use booktalks to promote new books with youngsters. Why not consider using booktalks to promote the professional literature as well? Whether the booktalk is presented to a specific grade level or to the entire faculty, it can be used to familiarize faculty with the professional resources available in their professional collection and/or their teacher center collection. Using the same techniques for booktalking as outlined in professional works such as *Middleplots 4* (Gillespie, 1994) and Joni Richards Bodart's *Booktalk!* and *Booktalking the Award Winners* series, the library media specialist can excite teachers about professional books.

7. Provide teachers with packaged and ready-to-go units.

One elementary librarian, fortunate enough to have an aide and several volunteers, offers teachers the special service of pulling together the available children's books and materials on a specific topic. She carries her "Bundles of Books" program one step further by including in the bundle those professional resources that can offer additional support for the classroom unit. For example, for a second grade language arts teacher's unit on pop-up books, the librarian selected the outstanding pop-up books from the collection and tucked a journal article on how to make pop-up books into the bundle. Including this article in the packaged unit added a new dimension to the teacher's knowledge of pop-up books.

8. Host receptions, coffees, luncheons, and special programs in the library media center.

Invite teachers to attend a brown-bag luncheon in the library media center on a teacher inservice day, or host a coffee for teachers one morning before school. During the event display and share the latest professional materials with faculty, or highlight a guest speaker from the local university or school district who has professional materials to share. With more exposure to the library and its professional collection, more usage by teachers can be expected.

9. Include professional resources in the annual book fair or organize a book fair specifically for teachers.

Why devote school book fairs exclusively to children's books? Why not include professional materials for teachers in the fair? Adding new professional resources will give teachers an opportunity to browse the new materials and possibly purchase them or request that the librarian purchase a professional work for the collection.

In addition, if school district policy permits, consider inviting a local bookstore owner to put on a book fair for teachers, one that focuses on professional materials.

10. Develop programs that highlight community resources.

Community resources may encompass people, places, businesses, organizations, and institutions within the community. An ongoing program in one elementary library, entitled "Closer Encounters: Community Resources to Enrich Professional Growth," brings in various community members to present valuable programs related to professional development. Whether it's a visit by the director of a local fitness center or a visit by volunteers from the fine arts museum, participants in the program usually gain some helpful knowledge that can carry over to their elementary classrooms. On a few occasions the faculty may visit the community resources, such as a recent visit to the local university for a presentation by a well-known author of children's books. These visits and field trips give the librarian one more opportunity to display and promote the professional books available on the topic.

The preceding ten programs suggest ways to gain support for professional development. As teachers become exposed to the available profes-

Promoting the Professional Collection

sional materials in the school or teacher center professional library, they also become more involved in professional development. The creative library media specialist is challenged to develop a multitude of appropriate programs that will offer opportunities to promote the professional library, increase circulation of the collection, and perhaps result in more funding for the professional collection.

Beyond the Collection

In addition to the professional collection described in this book, many school libraries and district teacher centers provide other services and materials to support and enrich teaching and professional growth. Based on interviews with teacher center directors and library media specialists in schools with exemplary professional collections, the following resources and services deserve consideration when developing a professional library.

Other Professional Services

Collection of instructional materials to use with students. This book has focused on resources that teachers may use for their own professional growth—materials that help them enrich and update their knowledge, help them develop lessons, and offer ideas for activities to use in the classroom. In addition to these resources, teachers need access to instructional materials they can use with their students in the classroom. Materials such as the following may be included in the instructional materials section of the library:

- Audiovisual and computer software
- Models, kits, dioramas, realia, manipulatives
- Class sets of books for teachers
- Teacher-made materials
- Games
- Maps and globes

Curriculum guides and documents. In addition to the national documents, including national standards, for the various curriculum areas recommended here, some librarians or teacher center directors establish a separate area to highlight state and local documents and curriculum guides.

Bibliographic and selection tools. Some library media specialists choose to put these tools in a special area within the professional library rather than keeping them in the librarian's work area. A few of these bibliographic and selection tools may not be available for circulation due to their constant use.

Reference collection. In addition to the reference tools in the children's collection, educators need reference materials for preparing lessons. While the reference collection for teachers is usually a part of the professional collection, the distinction is that the materials are not circulated. A separate reference collection for teachers should contain frequently used reference items such as dictionaries, encyclopedias, indexes, and atlases. Many of the resources are currently available on CD-ROM and therefore require a computer with CD-ROM capabilities to be available in the professional library.

Collection of resources for parents. A collection of books and pamphlets for parents to borrow or use in the library is an excellent public relations tool, as it reinforces the idea of a partnership between community and school. Discipline, learning disabilities, child development, and the whole-language learning approach are just a few of the topics of interest to concerned parents.

Media production services. While most district teacher centers offer media production services, some school libraries also provide these services for teachers. The provision and amount of these services is usually based on the size of the library staff and the budget. Some libraries provide teachers with a wide range of services such as graphics and lettering, copying tapes, and laminating. The majority of the school libraries have audiovisual and computer equipment available for teachers to check out or use in the library.

Community resources file. The term "community resources" refers to people and places in the community that can support and enrich the educational programs in the school. Community resources can also encompass places that students and teachers may visit to gain more knowledge. A resource file should be made available to teachers in the professional library. The file should list the names, addresses, phone numbers, contact persons, and other useful information concerning museums, libraries, companies, government agencies, institutions, and other organizations within the community. Additionally, the file may include names of community members who have agreed to share special talents, travel and life experiences, and skills with the school.

Resource sharing. Doing more with less is a way of life today. Libraries have long capitalized on the idea of using interlibrary loans to obtain materials not available locally. Sharing professional resources within a school district or among several school districts or public libraries can provide a way to cut expenses. Utilizing new technology, interlibrary loan is now faster and has expanded to include "interlibrary sharing" in many instances. With a computer and modem, electronic resources are literally at our fingertips.

Promoting the Professional Collection

The Internet offers an endless supply of resources which can be tapped, and training in its use is certainly a much needed professional development activity that should be provided by the school district.

Networking proves very helpful to teachers who are in need of specialized journals, books, or other resources to use with students or for their own professional growth. The professional library can provide teachers with access to materials in other collections through printed or electronic catalogs to collections, as follows:

Catalogs for district collections
> Professional libraries at the school level will depend heavily on the resources from the district teacher center and the regional service centers. Teachers must be familiar with what is available in these district collections. Catalogs or computerized databases for these collections should be made available to teachers.

Catalogs for university collections (electronic or print)
Catalogs for public city and county libraries

Computer center. With many indexes, selection aids, and other reference tools available on CD-ROM, teachers need access to a computer with a CD-ROM player and a modem in their school professional libraries. At district level, the computer center should include the computerized reference sources discussed earlier as well as more expensive yet essential resources such as *Educational Resources Information Center* on CD-ROM. Access to the Educational Resources Information Center's database is also available online, as well as on microfiche and in book form. This rich educational resource, sometimes included in the resources at district teacher centers, provides an index and abstracting service to identify educational resources and journal articles on specific topics of interest to educators.

Government documents. Some professional libraries include a special section for government documents.

Professional organizations and memberships. This book provides the names, addresses, and telephone numbers of the national organizations related to education. Librarians may want to contact these organizations and request membership applications to be placed in a special center that focuses on membership in teacher organizations. Membership concerning state and local organizations should also be made available to teachers. Most organizations publish a journal or newsletter related to the specialized educational area.

Bulletins for conferences and courses. A section of the professional library should provide teachers with information and registration forms concerning educational conferences at the local, state, and national levels. With the help of the teachers in the various content areas, librarians can make this information available. Additionally, university catalogs, bulletins, course offerings, and registration forms could be placed in this center to encourage professional growth. Departments of education at local universities will gladly provide semester schedules concerning graduate courses as well as notices of upcoming conferences.

Bibliographic services. A few district teachers center directors interviewed reported that they provide their teachers with bibliographic services whereby the teacher center will perform a search for resources or reference works on specific topics. Additionally, some librarians at district teacher centers noted that with the help of staff, they regularly develop and publish bibliographies on specific topics for teachers.

Collection of textbooks used within the school or district. School libraries as well as teacher centers should establish a collection of textbooks, including teacher editions, that are currently used in the classroom. These textbook collections allow teachers to become familiar with the scope and sequence of the various curriculum areas and can provide teachers with necessary content information and ideas for planning lessons.

Textbooks used in education courses at local universities. To encourage teachers to attend graduate school and to take some of the financial burden off individual teachers, a few district teacher center directors determine the university textbook needs of the teachers in the district and include these textbooks in the teacher center collection.

Review center featuring new books for teachers to review. A few district teacher centers have established book review centers. Publishers send complimentary children's and professional books to the center. In return, the librarians and teachers are asked to review the books and to determine whether they would like to order them. Review forms are available to formalize the process.

When library media specialists move beyond the professional collection to offer additional services such as the ones highlighted above, they will need to promote and advertise these services to make them effective.

For teachers to fully enjoy professional growth, a library serving their professional needs must be given life. This requires an enthusiastic and knowledgeable library media specialist who recognizes the librarian's leadership role in professional development, who is committed to developing an exciting collection of resources and services, and who goes one step further to promote the professional growth tools, thus encouraging educators to continue lifelong learning.

Promoting the Professional Collection

References

American Library Association and Association for Educational Communications and Technology. *Information Power: Guidelines for School Library Media Programs.* Chicago and Washington, DC: American Library Association and Association for Educational Communications and Technology, 1988.

Bauer, Caroline Feller. *This Way to Books.* New York: H. W. Wilson, 1983.

Bodart, Joni Richards. *Booktalk! 2.* New York: H. W. Wilson, 1985.

———, ed. Booktalking the Award-Winners, 1992– . New York: H. W. Wilson, 1993– .

Butzow, Carol, and John Butzow. *Science Through Children's Literature.* Englewood, CO: Libraries Unlimited, 1989.

Children's Catalog. 17th ed. New York: H. W. Wilson, 1996.

Elementary School Library Collection. 18th ed. Williamsport, PA: Brodart, 1992.

Elleman, Barbara. "An Idea Too Good to Die." *Book Links,* 4(January 1995): 5.

Emergency Librarian. Seattle: Rockland Press. Issued five times a year.

Gillespie, John T., and Corinne J. Naden. *Middleplots 4: A Book Talk Guide for Use with Readers Ages 8–12.* New Providence, NJ: Bowker, 1994.

Hunt, Tamara, and Nancy Renfro. *Celebrate: Holidays, Puppets and Creative Drama.* Austin, TX: Nancy Renfro Studios, 1987.

International Reading Association (eds.). *More Kids' Favorite Books: A Children's Choices Compilation.* Newark, DE: International Reading Association, 1995.

Kerr, Barbara A. *Smart Girls, Gifted Women.* Dayton, OH: Ohio Psychology Publishing Company, 1985.

Language Arts. Urbana, IL: National Council of Teachers of English. Issued eight times a year.

Lima, Carolyn, and John Lima. *A to Zoo: Subject Access to Children's Picture Books.* New Providence, NJ: Bowker, 1994.

Poppe, Carol A., and Nancy A. Van Matre. *Science Learning Centers for the Primary Grades.* Englewood Cliffs, NJ: Center for Applied Research in Education, 1985.

Raines, Shirley. *Story S-t-r-e-t-c-h-e-r-s for the Primary Grades.* Beltsville, MD: Gryphon, 1992.

Reading Teacher. Newark, DE: International Reading Association. Issued eight times a year.

Routman, Regie. *Invitations: Changing As Teachers and Learners K–12.* Portsmouth, NH: Heinemann, 1991.

School Arts Magazine. Worcester, MA: Davis Publications. Issued nine times a year.

School Library Journal. New York: Cahners Publishing Company. Issued twelve times a year.

Science and Children. Washington, DC: National Science Teachers Association. Issued eight times a year.

Sewall, Susan B. *Hooked on Science: Ready to Use Discovery Activities for Grades 4–8.* Englewood Cliffs, NJ: Center for Applied Research in Education, 1990.

Teaching Children Mathematics. Reston, VA: National Council of Teachers of Mathematics. Issued nine times a year.

Tiedt, Pamela L., and Iris M. Tiedt. *Multicultural Teaching: A Handbook of Activities, Information, and Resources*. Needham Heights, MA: Allyn & Bacon, 1995.

Trelease, Jim. *Read-Aloud Handbook*. 4th ed. New York: Viking Penguin, 1995.

Turner, Philip M. *Helping Teachers Teach*. 2nd ed. Englewood, CO: Libraries Unlimited, 1993.

Van Orden, Phyllis. *The Collection Program in Schools: Concepts, Practices, and Information Sources*. 2nd ed. Englewood, CO: Libraries Unlimited, 1995.

Whitin, David, and Sandra Wilde. *Read Any Good Math Lately? Children's Books for Mathematical Learning, K–6*. Portsmouth, NH: Heinemann, 1992.

Appendix

The Status of Professional Collections in Elementary Schools: A National Survey of Library Media Specialists

The following tables depict results of data collected during the 1993–1994 national study conducted according to the methodology detailed in chapter 1, where the survey results are also interpreted. The twenty multiple choice items from the survey that were on topics of specific importance to this book are presented, along with the responses expressed as valid percentages based on the actual number of librarians responding to each question. (The remaining multiple choice items were related to processing and circulation procedures.) The tables are arranged according to topics which provide insight into the status of professional collections at school and district levels—availability, importance, general description, location, size, usage, currency, and problems. (Please note that while a total of 516 librarians responded to the survey, the number of respondents answering each question vary, as not all respondents answered every question. Because percentages are rounded off to the tenths places, the total valid percentage does not always equal 100 percent.)

Availability of a Professional Collection

Is there a professional collection for teachers in your elementary school?		
	Frequency	Valid Percentage
YES	496	96.1
NO	20	3.9
Total: 516		

The 496 librarians responding "yes" to the above question were asked to answer the following questions. Their responses are depicted below:

Importance of a Professional Collection

How important do you think it is for you and teachers to have access to a well-organized professional collection?

	Frequency	Valid Percentage
Very important	256	51.9
Important	158	32.0
Moderately important	74	15.0
Not important	3	.6
Other: _____	2	.4
Total:	493	

Description of Professional Collection

Which statement best describes the professional collection within your school?

	Frequency	Valid Percentage
It is an excellent collection and surpasses most of the teachers' needs.	18	3.7
It adequately meets teacher needs	304	62.9
Teachers rarely find what they need in it due to the small size of the collection.	102	21.1
Teachers rarely find what they need in it due to lack of current materials.	49	10.1
Teachers rarely find what they need in it due to lack of organization of collection	10	2.1
Total:	483	

Which phrase best describes the source of the majority of the professional materials other than journals that make up the professional collection?

	Frequency	Valid Percentage
Donated, used textbooks	18	3.6
New materials ordered by SLMS	294	59.4
New materials ordered by a source other than SLMS	38	7.7
Both donated and new	74	15.0
Other: _____	71	14.3
Total:	495	

The Status of Elementary Professional Collections

Location of Professional Collection

Where is the professional collection located?		
	Frequency	Valid Percentage
School library	355	71.9
Teachers' lounge	33	6.7
Work room	20	4.0
Both school library & lounge	69	14.0
Other	17	3.4
Total:	494	

Size of Collection

Excluding journals, approximately how many materials are included in the professional collection at your school?		
	Frequency	Valid Percentage
Over 400	41	8.4
250–400	83	17.0
100–249	152	31.1
50–99	121	24.8
Less than 50	91	18.7
Total:	488	

Approximately how many different professional journal subscriptions do you have for yourself and teachers?		
	Frequency	Valid Percentage
Over 30	11	2.2
20–30	37	7.5
11–19	188	38.1
Less than 10	255	51.6
None	3	.6
Total:	494	

Usage of Professional Collection

Which type of materials do the teachers use the most often from this collection?

	Frequency	Valid Percentage
Journals	217	44.7
Tradebooks	257	52.9
Nonprint media related to professional development	4	.8
Documents and guidelines	7	1.4
Other: _____	1	.2
Total:	486	

Approximately how many total checkouts (including journals) do you have per week from faculty members using professional materials from the collection?

	Frequency	Valid Percentage
More than 15	51	10.4
11–15	60	12.3
6–10	134	27.5
1–5	227	46.5
None	16	3.3
Total:	488	

How often do you use your professional collection to aid yourself in selecting books?

	Frequency	Valid Percentage
Very frequently	245	50.2
Frequently	134	27.5
Sometimes	71	14.5
Seldom	27	5.5
Never	11	2.3
Total:	488	

For what purpose other than book selection do you most often use the professional collection?

	Frequency	Valid Percentage
University course assignment and/or research	22	4.6
Preparation for classes	255	53.6
Gain more knowledge on topics for my personal satisfaction	167	35.1
Preparation for workshop and inservice presentations	32	6.7
Other: _____	0	0
Total:	476	

The Status of Elementary Professional Collections

Aside from book selection, how often do you use the professional collection to meet your own needs?		
	Frequency	Valid Percentage
Very frequently	97	19.9
Frequently	172	35.3
Sometimes	157	32.2
Seldom	55	11.3
Never	6	1.2
	Total: 487	

Currency

Which phrase best describes how up-to-date you consider your professional collection?		
	Frequency	Valid Percentage
Outstanding in regard to currency	43	8.7
Good in regard to currency	151	30.6
Average in regard to currency	177	35.9
Below average in regard to currency	80	16.2
Poor in regard to currency	42	8.5
	Total: 493	

Problems

What do you find is the biggest problem in maintaining professional collections?		
	Frequency	Valid Percentage
Lack of funds to purchase professional materials	319	65.0
Lack of time to maintain collection	61	12.4
Many of the materials do not come fully processed, and I don't have the time to do it	26	5.3
Teachers don't follow proper circulation of materials and materials are often lost	32	6.5
Other: _____	53	10.8
	Total: 491	

Professional Collections at District Level

Is there a professional collection located at the district level within your school district?		
	Frequency	Valid Percentage
YES	284	56
NO	223	44
	Total: 507	

The 284 librarians reporting that they had a professional collection located at the district level were asked to respond to the following questions. (As in the previous section, keep in mind that the valid percentages are based only on the actual number of librarians responding to each question, and the number of respondents to each question vary.)

Which of the following best describes the professional collection at district level?		
	Frequency	Valid Percentage
Excellent	34	12.5
Very good	59	21.6
Good	74	27.1
Adequate	67	24.5
Poor	39	14.3
Total: 273		

For what purposes do you think teachers most often use the professional collection at district level?		
	Frequency	Valid Percentage
University course assignments and/or research	126	48.5
Classroom preparation	82	31.5
Gain more knowledge on topics for personal satisfaction	18	6.9
Preparation for professional presentations	30	11.5
Other: _____	4	1.5
Total: 260		

Approximately how many materials does your professional collection at district level house?		
	Frequency	Valid Percentage
Over 500	112	40.6
301–500	22	7.9
100–300	30	10.9
Less than 100	19	6.9
No idea	93	33.7
Total: 276		

The Status of Elementary Professional Collections

How often do you use the collection at district level to meet your own professional needs?

	Frequency	Valid Percentage
More than 10 times per year	45	15.9
7–10 times per year	23	8.1
3–6 times per year	85	30.0
Rarely	89	31.5
Never	41	14.5
	Total: 283	

Approximately how many teachers from your school use the professional collection at district level to meet their needs each week?

	Frequency	Valid Percentage
More than 10	22	8.3
7–10	15	5.7
4–6	27	10.2
1–3	58	22.0
Teachers rarely use this collection	142	53.8
	Total: 264	

Author and Title Index

The first author only, whether personal or institutional, of each citation is indexed here. Names of consultants and services are included as well as titles of books, videos, and journals.

A.D.A.M.: The Inside Story, 160
A to Zoo: Subject Access to Children's Picture Books, 25
Abrahamson, Richard F., 72
Abrams, A., *Educator's Guide to Macintosh Applications*, 228
Abruscato, Joseph, *Teaching Children Science*, 90
Academic Acceleration of Gifted Children, The, 203
Achievement Testing in the Early Grades: The Games Grownups Play, 170
Achieving Gender Equity Strategies for the Classroom, 223
Acting Together: Reader's Theatre Excerpts from Children's Literature on Themes from the Constitution, 117
Adair, Audrey J., *Ready-To-Use Music Activities Kit*, 122–23
Adams, Marilyn Jager, *Beginning to Read: Thinking and Learning About Print*, 41
Adapting Instruction for Mainstreamed and At-Risk Students, 189
Addis, Stephen, *Art History and Education*, 133
Administering the School Library Media Center, 22
Adventures in Art, Teacher's Edition, 135
Adventuring with Books: A Booklist for Pre-K–Grade 6, 75
Aesthetics and Education, 132
Aesthetics for Young People, 132
Aesthetics: Issues and Inquiry, 131–32
Agran, Martin, *Promoting Health and Safety: Skills for Independent Living*, 192–93
Alberto, Paul A., *Applied Behavior Analysis for Teachers: Influencing Student Performance*, 185–86
Allen, JoBeth, *Risk Makers, Risk Takers, Risk Breakers: Reducing the Risks for Young Literacy Learners*, 52, 60–61

Allen, K. Eileen, *Developmental Profiles: Prebirth through Eight*, 164–65
American Alliance for Health, Physical Education, Recreation and Dance, 161–62
American Alliance for Theatre and Education, 152
  A Model Drama/Theatre Curriculum: Philosophy, Goals and Objectives, 140
American Association for the Advancement of Science
  Benchmarks for Scientific Literacy, 84–85
  Science for All Americans, 82
American Association of School Librarians, 30
  Information Power: Guidelines for School Library Media Programs, 13
American Library Association Guide to Information Access: A Complete Research Handbook and Directory, 230
American Master Teacher Program Pedagogy Course Study Guide, and Self-Study Video, 158
Analysis of the Research on Ability Grouping: Historical and Contemporary Perspectives, An, 211
Anderson, Duncan, *Focus on Research: A Guide to Developing Students' Research Skills*, 18
Anderson, Richard C., *Becoming a Nation of Readers: Report of the Commission on Reading*, 40–41
Anderson, William M.
  Multicultural Perspectives in Music Education, 123
  Teaching Music with a Multicultural Approach, 123
Anti-Bias Curriculum: Tools for Empowering Children, 171
Antisocial Behavior in School: Strategies and Best Practices, 198
Applied Behavior Analysis for Teachers: Influencing Student Performance, 185–86

269

Approaches to Art in Education, 130–31
Arithmetic Teacher. See *Teaching Children Mathematics*
Armstrong, Carmen L., *Designing Assessment in Art*, 135
Arnheim, Rudolf, *Thoughts on Art Education (Occasional Paper 2)*, 129
Art Education and Human Development (Occasional Paper 3), 130
Art Education: A Critical Necessity, 137
Art Education: Elementary, 137
Art From Many Hands: Multicultural Art Projects, 133–34
Art History: A Contextual Inquiry Course, 133
Art History and Education, 133
Art is Elementary, 135
Art Making and Education, 133
Arts and Activities, 137
Arts and Humanities in the Social Studies, 118
Asher, Jane, *Jane Asher's Costume Book*, 150
Assessing Special Students: Strategies and Procedures, 184
Assessing Students with Special Needs: A Sourcebook for Analyzing and Correcting Errors in Academics, 191
Assessing the Role of Technology in Education, 232
Assessment in Elementary School Science Education, 84
Assessment in the Mathematics Classroom: 1993 Yearbook, 108
Assessment Standards for School Mathematics, 101–2
Association for Childhood Education International, 181–82
Association for Educational Communications and Technology, 240–41
Association for Supervision and Curriculum Development, 39
  Making Meaning: Integrated Language Arts Series, 54
At the Essence of Learning: Multicultural Education, 117
Atkinson, Sue, *Mathematics with Reason: The Emergent Approach to Primary Maths*, 105–6
Attention Deficit Disorders: Assessment and Teaching, 196–97
Atwater, Mary M., *Multicultural Education: Inclusion for All*, 97
Atwell, Nancie
  Coming to Know: Writing to Learn in the Intermediate Grades, 69
  In the Middle: Writing, Reading, and Learning with Adolescents, 46
Atwood, Virginia A., *Elementary School Social Studies: Research as a Guide to Practice*, 116
Au, Kathryn H., *Literacy Instruction in Multicultural Settings*, 52, 59, 170–71
Austrom, Liz, *Implementing Change: A Cooperative Approach*, 25

Authentic Reading Assessment: Practices and Possibilities, 44
Autism: Information and Resources for Parents, Families, and Professionals, 197–98

Bailey, Sally D., *Wings to Fly: Bringing Theatre Arts to Students with Special Needs*, 148–49
Banks, James A.
  Multicultural Education: Issues and Perspectives, 217
  Multiethnic Education: Theory and Practice, 216–17
  Teaching Strategies for Ethnic Studies, 217
Baratta-Lorton, Mary
  Mathematics Their Way, 177
  Workjobs: Activity Centered Learning for Early Childhood, 177
Barba, Roberta H., *Science in the Multicultural Classroom: A Guide to Teaching and Learning*, 97
Barbour, Nita H., *Developmental Continuity Across Preschool and Primary Grades: Implications for Teachers*, 167
Barr, Rebecca, *Handbook of Reading Research*, 41
Barrage, Natalie C., *Visual Handicaps and Learning*, 194
Barrett, Terry, *Criticizing Art: Understanding the Contemporary*, 132
Barron, Ann, *New Technologies for Education: A Beginner's Guide*, 230
Barton, Bob, *Stories in the Classroom: Storytelling, Reading Aloud and Roleplaying With Children*, 149
Barufaldi, James P., 81–82
Basic Issues in Aesthetics, 131
Basic Principles of Curriculum and Instruction, 37
Batshaw, Mark L., *Children with Disabilities: A Medical Primer*, 195
Bauer, Caroline Feller
  New Handbook for Storytellers: With Stories, Poems, Magic, and More, 174–75
  Presenting Reader's Theater: Plays and Poems to Read Aloud, 73–74
  This Way to Books, 74
Beaty, Janice J., *Observing Development of the Young Child*, 170
Becoming a Nation of Readers: Report of the Commission on Reading, 40–41
Becoming Literate: The Construction of Inner Control, 44
Beginning to Read: Thinking and Learning About Print, 41
Beirne-Smith, Mary, *Mental Retardation*, 195
Belka, David E., *Teaching Children Games: Becoming a Master Teacher*, 158
Benchmarks for Scientific Literacy, 84–85
Benjamin, Harold, *The Saber-Tooth Curriculum*, 36

Author and Title Index

Bennett, Christine, *Comprehensive Multicultural Education: Theory and Practice,* 217
Berk, Laura, *Child Development,* 165
Bermúdez, Andrea B., 216
  Doing Our Homework: How Schools Can Engage Hispanic Communities, 222–23
Beyond Creating: The Place for Art in America's School, 136
Beyond Storybooks: Young Children and the Shared Book Experience, 49
Beyond TV: Activities for Using Video with Children, 232–33
Bickmore-Brand, Jennie, *Language in Mathematics,* 106
Bigge, June L., *Teaching Individuals with Physical and Multiple Disabilities,* 195
Bilingual Research Journal, 225
Bissex, Glenda L., *Gnys at Wrk: A Child Learns to Write and Read,* 64
Bissinger, Kristen, *Leap Into Learning! Teaching Curriculum Through Creative Dramatics and Dance,* 142
Black, Kaye, *Kidvid: Fun-damentals of Video Instruction,* 150
Block, Martin H., *A Teacher's Guide to Including Students with Disabilities in Regular Physical Education,* 193
Bloom, Benjamin S., *Human Characteristics and School Learning,* 36
Book Links, 80
Book Report and Library Talk editors, *School Library Management Notebook,* 21
Books Kids Will Sit Still For: The Complete Read-Aloud Guide, 76
Bosak, Susan V., *Science Is: A Source Book of Fascinating Facts, Projects and Activities,* 87
Bowie, Melvin M., 227–28
Brainstorms and Blueprints: Teaching Library Research as a Thinking Process, 19
Breaking Ground: Teachers Relate Reading and Writing in the Elementary School, 65
Bredekamp, Sue
  Developmentally Appropriate Practice in Early Childhood Programs Serving Children from Birth through Age Eight, 165
  Reaching Potentials: Appropriate Curriculum and Assessment for Young Children, vol.1, 165–66
Bring Multicultural Music to Children (video), 126
British Columbia Teacher-Librarians' Association, *Fuel for Change: Cooperative Program Planning and Teaching,* 14
Britton, James, *Language and Learning: The Importance of Speech in Children's Development,* 57–58
Brock, Patricia, *Educational Technology in the Classroom,* 235
Brolin, Donn E., *Career Education: A Functional Life Skills Approach,* 193

Broudy, Harry S., *The Role of Imagery in Learning (Occasional Paper 1),* 129–30
Brown, Maurice, *Art Making and Education,* 133
Buchanan, Jan, *Flexible Access to Library Media Programs,* 14–15
Bull, Barry L., *The Ethics of Multicultural and Bilingual Education,* 223
Burns, Deborah E., *Pathways to Investigative Skills: Instructional Lessons for Guiding Students from Problem Finding to Final Product, Grades 3–9,* 212–13
Burns, Marilyn
  A Collection of Math Lessons: From Grades 1 Through 3; From Grades 3 Through 6; and From Grades 6 Through 8, 109
  Math and Literature (K–3), 109
  Mathematics: Teaching for Understanding (video), 110
  What Are You Teaching My Child? (video), 110
Buschner, Craig A., *Teaching Children Movement Concepts and Skills: Becoming a Master Teacher* (book & video), 158
Byrnes, Deborah, *Common Bonds: Anti-Bias Teaching in a Diverse Society,* 171

Calgary Board of Education, *The School Library Program: Teacher-Librarian Resource Manual,* 15
California Media and Library Educators Association, *From Library Skills to Information Literacy: A Handbook for the 21st Century,* 15
Calkins, Lucy McCormick, *Living Between the Lines,* 64–65
Campbell, Patricia Shehan, *Music in Childhood: From Preschool through the Elementary Grades,* 123–24
Canadian Library Handbook: Organizing School, Public and Professional Libraries, The, 24–25
Career Education: A Functional Life Skills Approach, 193
Carin, Arthur A., *Teaching Science Through Discovery,* 90–91
Carnine, Douglas, *Direct Instruction Reading,* 193
Carroll, Frances Laverne, *More Exciting, Funny, Scary, Short, Different, and Sad Books Kids Like About Animals, Science, Sports, Families, Songs, and Other Things,* 76
Carson, Ben, *Renewal at the Schoolhouse: Management Ideas for Library Media Specialists and Administrators,* 21, 231
Cartledge, Gwendolyn
  Taking Part: Introducing Social Skills to Children, 199
  Teaching Social Skills to Children and Youth, 199–200
  Working Together: Building Children's Social Skills Through Folk Literature, 199

Cases in Literacy: An Agenda for Discussion, 56–57
Cassady, Marsh
  Creating Stories for Storytelling, 149
  Storytelling Step by Step, 149
Cazden, Courtney B., *Classroom Discourse: The Language of Teaching and Learning*, 63
CD-ROM for Librarians and Educators: A Resource Guide to Over 300 Instructional Programs, 28
Celebrate: Holidays, Puppets and Creative Drama, 147–48
Celebrating Diversity: Building Self Esteem in Today's Multicultural Classrooms, 225
Censorship and Selection: Issues and Answers for Schools, 27–28
Center for Civic Education, *National Standards for Civics and Government*, 112–13
Center for Research and Development in Law-Related Education (CRADLE), *We, the People of the World*, 116–17
Center for the Study of Reading, *Teaching Reading Strategies from Successful Classrooms*, 54
Challenge of Technology: Action Strategies for the School Library Media Specialist, The, 22–23
Challenge: Reaching and Teaching the Gifted Child, 214
Challenging the Gifted in the Regular Classroom, 214
Champagne, Audrey B., *This Year in School Science 1989: Scientific Literacy*, 85–86
Chapman, Gerald, *Teaching Young Playwrights*, 146–47
Chapman, Laura H.
  Adventures in Art, Teacher's Edition, 135
  Approaches to Art in Education, 130–31
Characteristics of Emotional and Behavioral Disorders of Children and Youth, 196
Charlesworth, Rosalind, *Math and Science for Young Children*, 177
Chatton, Barbara, *Using Poetry Across the Curriculum: A Whole Language Approach*, 74
Chavkin, Nancy Feyl, *Families and Schools in a Pluralistic Society*, 223
Child Development, 165
Child Goes Forth: A Curriculum Guide for Preschool Children, A, 172
Childhood Education, 180
Children and Painting, 134
Children and Their Art: Methods for the Elementary School, 131
Children, Clay and Sculpture, 134
Children Moving: A Reflective Approach to Teaching Physical Education, 154–55
Children with Disabilities: A Medical Primer, 195
Children with Special Needs: Family, Culture, and Society, 171–72
Children's Book Council, *Children's Books: Awards and Prizes*, 76
Children's Language and Learning, 64

Children's Literature and Social Studies: Selecting and Using Notable Books in the Classroom, 119
Children's Literature in the Elementary School, 79
Children's Machine: Rethinking School in the Age of the Computer, The, 231–32
Choosing Options and Accommodations for Children: A Guide to Planning Inclusive Education, 183–84
Chukovsky, Kornei, *From Two to Five*, 58
Clark, Barbara, *Growing up Gifted*, 205–6
Classroom Creature Culture: Algae to Anoles, 93–94
Classroom Discourse: The Language of Teaching and Learning, 63
Clay, Marie M.
  Becoming Literate: The Construction of Inner Control, 44
  What Did I Write? Beginning Writing Behavior, 61, 175
Cochran, Judith A., *Reading in the Content Area for Junior High and High School*, 46–47
Cohen, Herbert G., *Teaching Science as a Decision Making Process*, 91
Colangelo, Nicholas, *Handbook of Gifted Education*, 206
Colborn, Candace, *What Do Children Read Next? A Reader's Guide to Fiction for Children, Collaboration through Writing and Reading: Exploring Possibilities*, 74
Collection of Math Lessons: From Grades 1 Through 3, A; From Grades 3 Through 6; and From Grades 6 Through 8, 109
Collection Program in Schools: Concepts, Practices, and Information Sources, The, 29
Collier, Laurie, *Major Authors and Illustrators for Children and Young Adults*, 73
Coming to Know: Writing to Learn in the Intermediate Grades, 69
Common Bonds: Anti-Bias Teaching in a Diverse Society, 171
Compendium of Readings in Bilingual Education: Issues and Practices, 222
Comprehensive Curriculum for Gifted Learners, 205
Comprehensive Multicultural Education : Theory and Practice, 217
Computer Essentials in Education, 229
Computing Teacher, The, 238
Concannon, Tom, *Using Media for Creative Teaching*, 150
Conceptions of Giftedness, 207–8
Concepts and Experiences in Elementary School Science, 88
Consortium of National Arts Education Associations, *National Standards for Arts Education: What Every Young American Should Know and Be Able to Do in the Arts*, 122, 140
Content Area Reading, 47

Author and Title Index

Control Theory in the Classroom, 34
Control Theory Manager: Combining the Control Theory of William Glasser with the Wisdom of W. Edwards Deming to Explain Both What Quality Is and What Lead-Managers Do to Achieve It, The, 32
Cooper, J. David, *Literacy: Helping Children Construct Meaning,* 47
Cooper, Pamela J., *Look What Happened to Frog: Storytelling in Education,* 149–50
Cooper, Patsy, *When Stories Come to School: Telling, Writing, and Performing Stories in the Early Childhood Classroom,* 147
Cooperative Learning and the Academically Talented Student, 211–12
Cooperative Learning in the Social Studies Classroom: An Invitation to Social Study, 115
Copyright for School Libraries: A Practical Guide, 28
Copyright Primer for Educational and Industrial Media Producers, A, 230
Cornbleth, Catherine, *An Invitation to Research in Social Education,* 116
Cornia, Ivan, *Art Is Elementary,* 135
Cottrell, June
  Creative Drama in the Classroom, Grades 1–3, 142
  Creative Drama in the Classroom, Grades 4–6, 142
Council for Exceptional Children, 201
Council on Physical Education for Children (COPEC), *Developmentally Appropriate Physical Education Practices for Children,* 153–54
Counseling the Gifted and Talented, 208–9
Countryman, Joan, *Writing to Learn Mathematics: Strategies that Work, K–12,* 106
Covey, Stephen R., *The 7 Habits of Highly Effective People,* 37
Cox, June, *Educating Able Learners: Programs and Promising Practices,* 211
Crafton, Linda K., *Whole Language: Getting Started...Moving Forward,* 47–48
Cramer, Eugene H., *Fostering the Love of Reading: The Affective Domain in Reading Education,* 50–51
Cranston, Jerneral, *Transformations Through Drama: A Teacher's Guide to Educational Drama, Grades K–8,* 142–43
Craver, Kathleen, *School Library Media Center in the 21st Century: Changes and Challenges,* 21
Creating Classrooms for Authors: The Reading-Writing Connection, 65
Creating Stories for Storytelling, 149
Creative and Mental Growth, 131
Creative Drama Book: Three Approaches, The, 144
Creative Drama for the Classroom Teacher, 143
Creative Drama in the Classroom, 144
Creative Drama in the Classroom, Grades 1–3, 142
Creative Drama in the Intermediate Grades, 144
Creative Drama in the Primary Grades, 144

Creative Drama Resource Book for Grades K–3, 143
Creative Drama Resource Book for Grades 4–6, 143
Creative Expression and Play in the Early Childhood Curriculum, 169
Creative Problem Solver's Guidebook, The, 204
Creative Problem Solving: An Introduction, 204
Creative Puppetry in the Classroom, 147
Creative Sciencing: Ideas and Activities for Teachers and Children, 91
Creativity and Collaborative Learning: A Practical Guide to Empowering Students and Teachers, 189
Creativity in the Classroom: Schools of Curious Delight, 204
Creativity is Forever, 203–4
Critical Issues in Gifted Education: Defensible Programs for the Gifted, 209
Critical Issues in Special Education, 188
Criticizing Art: Understanding the Contemporary, 132
Cromer, Jim, *History, Theory and Practice of Art Criticism in Art Education,* 132
Cuffaro, Harriet K., *Experimenting with the World: John Dewey and Early Education,* 166
Cullinan, Bernice E., *Literature and the Child,* 79
Cunningham, Patricia M., *Phonics They Use: Words for Reading and Writing,* 53
Curriculum and Evaluation Standards for School Mathematics, 102
Curriculum and Evaluation Standards for School Mathematics, Addenda Series, Grades K–6, 109–10
Curriculum Compacting: The Complete Guide to Modifying the Regular Curriculum for High Ability Students, 213
Curriculum Considerations in Inclusive Classrooms: Facilitating Learning for All Students, 188–89
Curriculum Development for the Gifted, 205
Curriculum Initiative: An Agenda and Strategy for Library Media Programs, 16
Curriculum Standards for the Social Studies, 113–14
Curriculum-Based Evaluation: Teaching and Decision-Making, 184

Dailey, Sheila, *Tales as Tools: The Power of Story in the Classroom,* 175
Dame, Melvina Azar, *Serving Linguistically and Culturally Diverse Students: Strategies for the School Library Media Specialist,* 15–16
Daniels, Harvey, *Literature Circles: Voice and Choice in the Student-Centered Classroom,* 48
Danielson, Kathy Everts, *Integrating Reading and Writing Through Children's Literature,* 49–50
Danny Goodman's Computer Concepts: Using the Macintosh, 229
Dauer, Victor P., *Dynamic Physical Education for Elementary School Children,* 154
Dauntless Women in Childhood Education, 167

Davidman, Leonard, *Teaching With a Multicultural Perspective: A Practical Guide*, 114, 218
Davis, Gary A.
 Creativity is Forever, 203–4
 Education of the Gifted and Talented, 206
Day, Frances Ann, *Multicultural Voices in Contemporary Literature: A Resource for Teachers*, 76
De Vito, Alfred K., *Creative Sciencing: Ideas and Activities for Teachers and Children*, 91
DeBoer, George E., *A History of Ideas in Science Education: Implications for Practice*, 86
Deciding What to Teach and Test: Developing, Aligning and Auditing the Curriculum, 33–34
Delicate Balances: Collaborative Research in Language Education, 66
Derman-Sparks, Louise, *Anti-Bias Curriculum: Tools for Empowering Children*, 171
Dern, Daniel, *The Internet Guide for New Users*, 237
Deschooling Society, 36
Design Technology: Children's Engineering, 91–92
Designing and Renovating School Library Media Centers, 22
Designing Assessment in Art, 135
Developing a Quality Curriculum, 85
Developing and Implementing Individualized Education Programs, 184–85
Developing and Supporting Teachers for Elementary School Science Education, 82
Developmental Continuity Across Preschool and Primary Grades: Implications for Teachers, 167
Developmental Profiles: Prebirth through Eight, 164–65
Developmentally Appropriate First Grade: A Community of Learners (video), 179
Developmentally Appropriate Physical Education Practices for Children, 153–54
Developmentally Appropriate Practice: Birth Through Age 5 (video), 180
Developmentally Appropriate Practice in Early Childhood Programs Serving Children from Birth through Age Eight, 165
Developments in Elementary Mathematics Teaching, 103–4
Dewing, Martha, *Beyond TV: Activities for Using Video with Children*, 232–33
Dick, Walter, *Planning Effective Instruction*, 233
Dictionary of Reading and Related Terms, A, 42
Dimensions of Early Childhood, 180–81
Direct Instruction Mathematics, 194
Direct Instruction Reading, 193
Directory of Adaptive Technologies to Aid Library Patrons and Staff with Disabilities, A, 229
Directory of Video, Multimedia, and Audio-visual Products, 228
Disabilities, Children and Libraries: Mainstreaming Services in Public Libraries and School Library Media Centers, 17–18

Discipline: Appropriate Guidance for Young Children (video), 180
Discipline-Based Art Education: Origins, Meanings, and Development, 137
Distance Education: Strategies and Tools, 238
Dockterman, David, *Great Teaching in the One Computer Classroom*, 233
Doerksen, Donna, *Links to Literature: Literature-Based Units and Ideas for Teacher-Librarians and Teachers*, 19
Doing Our Homework: How Schools Can Engage Hispanic Communities, 222–23
Drama Themes: A Practical Guide for Teaching Drama, 146
Dramatizing Literature in Whole Language Classrooms, 146
Drum, Jan, *Global Winners: 74 Activities for Inside and Outside the Classroom*, 117
Dunn, Susan, *Design Technology: Children's Engineering*, 91–92
Dynamic Physical Education for Elementary School Children, 154
Dynamite in the Classroom: How-to Handbook for Teachers, 234
Dyson, Anne Haas
 Collaboration Through Writing and Reading: Exploring Possibilities, 67
 Multiple Worlds of Child Writers: Friends Learning to Write, 61
 The Need for Story: Cultural Diversity in Classroom and Community, 59
 Social Worlds of Children Learning to Write in an Urban Primary School, 63

Early Childhood Art, 136
Early Childhood Creative Arts, 122
Early Childhood Research Quarterly, 181
Eaton, Marcia, *Basic Issues in Aesthetics*, 131
Educating Able Learners: Programs and Promising Practices, 211
Educating Second Language Children: The Whole Child, the Whole Curriculum, and the Whole Community, 221
Educating Young Children in a Diverse Society, 223–24
Education of the Gifted and Talented, 206
Educational Consultant: Helping Professionals, Parents, and Mainstreamed Students, The, 185
Educational Imagination: On the Design and Education of School Programs, The, 33
Educational Leadership, 38
Educational Media and Technology Yearbook, 229
Educational Resources Information Center (ERIC). Clearinghouse on Information and Technology, 25–26
Educational Technology, 238–39
Educational Technology in the Classroom, 235

Author and Title Index

Educator's Guide to Macintosh Applications, 228
Edwards, Carolyn, *The Hundred Languages of Children: The Reggio Emilia Approach to Early Childhood Education,* 167–68
Effective Discipline, 186
Effective Programs for Students at Risk, 35
Eisenberg, Michael
  Curriculum Initiative: An Agenda and Strategy for Library Media Programs, 16
  Information Problem-Solving: The Big Six Skills Approach to Library and Information Skills Instruction, 18–19
Eisenhower National Clearinghouse for Mathematics and Science Education, 98
Eisner, Elliot W., *The Educational Imagination: On the Design and Education of School Programs,* 33
Electronic Learning, 239
Elementary School Library Collection: A Guide to Books and Other Media; Phases 1-2-3, The, 27
Elementary School Science for the '90s, 85
Elementary School Social Studies: Research as a Guide to Practice, 116
Elementary Social Studies: Challenges for Tomorrow's World, 118
Elkind, David
  The Hurried Child: Growing Up Too Fast Too Soon, 166
  Miseducation: Preschoolers at Risk, 166
Emergency Librarian, 29
Emerging Literacy: Young Children Learn To Read and Write, 45, 62
Emphasis Art: A Qualitative Art Program for Elementary and Middle Schools, 136
Encyclopedia of English Studies and Language Arts, 66–67
Engaging Children in Science, 94–95
Engaging Children's Minds: The Project Approach, 168
English, Fenwick W., *Deciding What to Teach and Test: Developing, Aligning and Auditing the Curriculum,* 33–34
Enrichment Triad Model: A Guide for Developing Defensible Programs for the Gifted and Talented, The, 205
Erickson, Fritz, *Computer Essentials in Education,* 229
Esler, William K., *Teaching Elementary Science,* 92
Essentials of Law Related Education: A Guide for Practitioners and Policy Makers, 114
Ethics of Multicultural and Bilingual Education, The, 223
Everybody Counts: A Report to The Nation on the Future of Mathematics Education, 102–3
Excellence, 34
Exceptional Children, 200–201
Exceptional Children: An Introduction to Special Education, 187

Exceptional Children/Exceptional Art: Teaching Art to Special Needs, 135–36
Exemplary Art Education Curricula: A Guide to Guides, 136
Experiencing Elementary Science, 96
Experimenting with the World: John Dewey and Early Education, 166
Eyeopeners II: Children's Books to Answer Children's Questions about the World, 78

Faltis, Christian J., *Joinfostering: Adapting Teaching Strategies for the Multicultural Classroom,* 220
Families and Schools in a Pluralistic Society, 223
Families, Professionals, and Exceptionality: A Special Partnership, 190
Farr, Roger, *Portfolio and Performance Assessment,* 43
Fishman, Joshua A., *Reversing Language Shift: Theoretical and Empirical Foundations of Assistance to Threatened Languages,* 220–21
Fiske, Edward B., *Smart Schools, Smart Kids: Why Do Some Schools Work?,* 32
Fitness Fun, 156
Fitzpatrick, Virginia L., *Art History: A Contextual Inquiry Course,* 133
Fleege, Pamela O., 163–64
Flexible Access to Library Media Programs, 14–15
Flood, James, *Handbook of Research on Teaching the English Language Arts,* 66
Focus on Research: A Guide to Developing Students' Research Skills, 18
For Reading Out Loud! A Guide to Sharing Books With Children, 19–20
Ford, Alison, *The Syracuse Community-Referenced Curriculum Guide for Students with Moderate and Severe Disabilities,* 196
Foster, Emily R., *Fitness Fun,* 156
Fostering the Love of Reading: The Affective Domain in Reading Education, 50–51
Foundations for Effective School Library Programs, 16
Foundations of Literacy, The, 62, 175
Frames of Mind: The Theory of Multiple Intelligences, 166
Free Appropriate Public Education: The Law and Children with Disabilities, 187
Freeman, Judy, *Books Kids Will Sit Still For: The Complete Read-Aloud Guide,* 76
Freericks, Mary, *Creative Puppetry in the Classroom,* 147
Freidl, Alfred E., *Teaching Science to Children—An Integrated Approach,* 92–93
Fresh Look at Writing, A, 69
From Library Skills to Information Literacy: A Handbook for the 21st Century, 15
From Page to Screen: Children's and Young Adult Books on Film and Video, 73
From Two to Five, 58

Fromberg, Doris, *The Full-Day Kindergarten*, 174
Frost, Joe, *Play and Playscapes*, 168–69
Fuel for Change: Cooperative Program Planning and Teaching (video), 14
Full-Day Kindergarten, The, 174

Gabel, Dorothy L.
  Handbook of Research on Science Teaching, 98
  Introductory Science Skills, 88
Gable, Robert A., *Assessing Students with Special Needs: A Sourcebook for Analyzing and Correcting Errors in Academics*, 191
Galda, Lee, *Language, Literacy and the Child*, 67
Gallagher, Arlene F., *Acting Together: Reader's Theatre Excerpts from Children's Literature on Themes from the Constitution*, 117
Gallagher, James J., *Teaching the Gifted Child*, 206
Garbage Pizza, Patchwork Quilts, and Math Magic: Stories about Teachers Who Love to Teach and Children Who Love to Learn, 103
Gardner, Howard
  Art Education and Human Development (Occasional Paper 3), 130
  Frames of Mind: The Theory of Multiple Intelligences, 166
Gardner, John W., *Excellence*, 34
Gay, Geneva, *At the Essence of Learning: Multicultural Education*, 117
Gega, Peter C.
  Concepts and Experiences in Elementary School Science, 88
  How To Teach Elementary School Science, 93
  Science in Elementary Education, 93
Genesee, Fred, *Educating Second Language Children: The Whole Child, the Whole Curriculum, and the Whole Community*, 221
Genshaft, Judy, *Serving Gifted and Talented Students: A Resource for School Personnel*, 208
Geography for Life: National Geography Standards 1994, 113
Gestwicki, Carol, *Home, School and Community Relations: A Guide to Working with Parents*, 173
Getting Reading Right from the Start: Effective Early Literacy Interventions, 51
Getty Center for Education in the Arts, *Beyond Creating: The Place for Art in America's School*, 136
Giangreco, Michael F., *Choosing Options and Accomodations for Children: A Guide to Planning Inclusive Education*, 183–84
Gifted Child Quarterly, 214
Gifted Child Today, 214
Gifted Children and Adults: Their Development and Education, 207
Gifted Program Handbook: Planning, Implementing, and Evaluating Gifted Programs with a Special Model for Small School Districts, The, 210

Gifted Students in Regular Classrooms, 213
Gillespie, John T., *Middleplots 4: A Book Talk Guide for Use with Readers Age 8–12*, 77
Gillet, Jean Wallace, *Understanding Reading Problems: Assessment and Instruction*, 51
Give Them Roots.... and Wings! A Guide to Drama in the Elementary Grades, 145
Glasser, William
  The Control Theory Manager: Combining the Control Theory of William Glasser with the Wisdom of W. Edwards Deming to Explain Both What Quality Is and What Lead-Managers Do to Achieve It, 32
  Control Theory in the Classroom, 34
  The Quality School, 32
Glatthorn, Allan A., *Developing a Quality Curriculum*, 85
Global Education from Thought to Action, 115
Global Paradox: The Bigger the World Economy, the More Powerful its Smallest Players, 37
Global Quest: The Internet in the Classroom (video), 238
Global Winners: 74 Activities for Inside and Outside the Classroom, 117
Glover, Donald R., *Team Building Through Physical Challenges*, 156
Glynn, Shawn M., *The Psychology of Learning Science*, 86
Gnys at Wrk: A Child Learns to Write and Read, 64
Going the Distance: Distance Learning Comes of Age, 235
Gollnick, Donna M., *Multicultural Education in a Pluralistic Society*, 34, 218
Gomez, Susan, 164
Good, Thomas L., *Looking in Classrooms*, 34
Goodlad, John I., *A Place Called School: Prospects for the Future*, 32–33
Goodman, Danny, *Danny Goodman's Computer Concepts: Using the Macintosh*, 229
Grace, Cathy, *The Portfolio and Its Use: Developmentally Appropriate Assessment of Young Children*, 170
Graham, George M., 153
  American Master Teacher Program Pedagogy Course Study Guide, and Self-Study Video, 158
  Children Moving: A Reflective Approach to Teaching Physical Education, 154–55
  Teaching Children Physical Education: Becoming a Master Teacher, 158–59
Graves, Donald H., *A Fresh Look at Writing*, 69
Great Explorations in Math and Science (GEMS) Teacher's Handbook, 88–89
Great Teaching in the One Computer Classroom (paper), 233
Great Teaching in the One Computer Classroom (video), 238
Grossi, Teresa A., 191

Author and Title Index

Grossman, Herbert, *Teaching in a Diverse Society*, 218
Growing Up Gifted, 205–6
Growing Up Literate: Learning from Inner City Families, 52, 60
Guidance of Young Children, 173–74
Guiding Young Children, 173
Gustafson, Kent L., 227

Hackett, Patricia, *The Melody Book: Three Hundred Selections from the World of Music for Autoharp, Guitar, Piano, Recorder, and Voice*, 124
Hall, Susan, *Using Picture Storybooks to Teach Literary Devices*, 74
Hamilton, Darlene, *Resources for Creative Teaching in Early Childhood Education*, 172
Hampton, Carol, *Classroom Creature Culture: Algae to Anoles*, 93–94
Handbook of Gifted Education, 206
Handbook of Reading Research, 41, 42
Handbook of Research on Science Teaching, 98
Handbook of Research on Teaching the English Language Arts, 66
Hansen, Jane
  Breaking Ground: Teachers Relate Reading and Writing in the Elementary School, 65
  When Writers Read, 65
Harris, Albert J., *How To Increase Reading Ability: A Guide to Developmental and Remedial Methods*, 42
Harris, Aurand, *Six Plays for Children by Aurand Harris*, 140–41
Harris, Judi B., *The Way of the Ferret: Finding Educational Resources on the Internet*, 235
Harris, Theodore L., *A Dictionary of Reading and Related Terms*, 42
Harste, Jerome C.
  Creating Classrooms for Authors: The Reading-Writing Connection, 65
  Language Stories and Literacy Lessons, 45, 61
Hassard, Jack, *Minds on Science—Middle and Secondary School Methods*, 94
Haycock, Ken, 12–13
  Foundations for Effective School Library Programs, 16
  Program Advocacy: Power, Publicity and the Teacher-Librarian, 23
  What Works: Research about Teaching and Learning through the School's Library Resource Center, 26
Hazen, Robert M., *Science Matters: Achieving Scientific Literacy*, 87
Health and Fitness Through Physical Education, 155
Heath, Shirley Brice, *Ways with Words: Language, Life and Work in Communities and Classrooms*, 59–60
Heilman, Arthur W., *Phonics in Proper Perspective*, 54

Heinich, Robert, *Instructional Media and the New Technologies of Instruction*, 233
Heinig, Ruth Beall
  Creative Drama for the Classroom Teacher, 143
  Creative Drama Resource Book for Grades K–3, 143
  Creative Drama Resource Book for Grades 4–6, 143
  Improvisation with Favorite Tales: Integrating Drama Into the Reading/Writing Classroom, 143–44
Helbig, Alethea K., *This Land Is Our Land: A Guide to Multicultural Literature for Children and Young Adults*, 77
Heller, Mary F., *Reading-Writing Connections: From Theory to Practice*, 50
Helmer, Dona, *Selecting Materials for School Library Media Centers*, 26–27
Helping Teachers Teach: A School Library Media Specialist's Role, 17, 246
Henley, David R., *Exceptional Children/Exceptional Art: Teaching Art to Special Needs*, 135–36
Herberholz, Barbara, *Early Childhood Art*, 136
Heron, Timothy E., *The Educational Consultant: Helping Professionals, Parents, and Mainstreamed Students*, 185
Heward, William L., 183
  Exceptional Children: An Introduction to Special Education, 187
Hiebert, Elfrieda H., *Getting Reading Right From the Start: Effective Early Literacy Interventions*, 51
Hildebrand, Verna, *Guiding Young Children*, 173
History of Ideas in Science Education: Implications for Practice, A, 86
History, Theory and Practice of Art Criticism in Art Education, 132
Hobbs, Jack, *The Visual Experience: Teacher's Edition*, 134
Hoffman, Andrea C., *Kits, Games and Manipulatives for the Elementary Classroom: A Source Book*, 236
Holdaway, Don, *The Foundations of Literacy*, 62, 175
Holt, Bess-Gene, *Science with Young Children*, 178
Home, School and Community Relations: A Guide to Working with Parents, 173
Hooked on Science: Ready to Use Discovery Activities for Grades 4–8, 89–90
Hopple, Christine J., *Teaching for Outcomes in Elementary Physical Education: A Guide for Curriculum and Assessment*, 155
Horgan, Dianne D., *Achieving Gender Equity Strategies for the Classroom*, 223
How to Increase Reading Ability: A Guide to Developmental and Remedial Methods, 42
How To Teach Elementary School Science, 93
Howe, Ann C., *Engaging Children in Science*, 94–95

278   Professional Collection for Elementary Educators

Howell, Kenneth W., *Curriculum-Based Evaluation: Teaching and Decision-Making*, 184
Huck, Charlotte S., *Children's Literature in the Elementary School*, 79
Hudelson, Sarah J., *Delicate Balances: Collaborative Research in Language Education*, 66
Human Characteristics and School Learning, 36
Hundred Languages of Children: The Reggio Emilia Approach to Early Childhood Education, The, 167–68
Hunt, Tamara
   Celebrate: Holidays, Puppets and Creative Drama, 147–48
   Puppetry and Early Childhood Education, 148
Hurried Child: Growing Up Too Fast Too Soon, The, 166
Hurwitz, Al, *Children and Their Art: Methods for the Elementary School*, 131
HyperCard: A Tool for Learning, 234–35

I Won't Learn From You: The Role of Assent in Learning, 224
Ideas and Insights: Language Arts in the Elementary School, 68
Illich, Ivan, *Deschooling Society*, 36
Illusion of Full Inclusion: A Comprehensive Critique of a Current Special Education Bandwagon, The, 187
Impact of School Library Media Centers on Academic Achievement, The, 14
Implementing Change: A Cooperative Approach, 25
Improving Reading: A Handbook of Strategies, 48
Improvisation With Favorite Tales: Integrating Drama Into the Reading/Writing Classroom, 143–44
In the Middle: Writing, Reading, and Learning with Adolescents, 46
Including Children with Special Needs in Early Childhood Programs, 172
Individuals with Profound Disabilities: Instructional and Assistive Strategies, 198
Information Power: Guidelines for School Library Media Programs, 13, 228, 245, 246
Information Problem-Solving: The Big Six Skills Approach to Library and Information Skills Instruction, 18–19
Instruction of Students with Severe Disabilities, 198
Instructional Classroom Management: A Proactive Approach to Managing Behavior, 186
Instructional Media and the New Technologies of Instruction, 233
Integrated Learning Activities for Young Children, 173
Integrating Reading and Writing Through Children's Literature, 49–50
Intelligent Eye: Learning to Think by Looking at Art, The, 130
Interactive Teaming: Consultation and Collaboration in Special Programs, 185

Interdisciplinary Inquiry in Teaching and Learning, 96
International Reading Association, 55
   Cases in Literacy: An Agenda for Discussion, 56–57
   More Kids' Favorite Books: A Children's Choices Compilation, 77
   Standards for the Assessment of Reading and Writing, 57
   Teachers' Favorite Books for Kids, 78
Internet for Dummies, The, 237
Internet Guide for New Users, The, 237
Internet Resource Directory for K–12 Teachers and Librarians, The, 26
Intersection of Cultures: Multicultural Education in the United States, The, 219–20
Intner, Sheila S., *Standard Cataloging for School and Public Libraries*, 24
Introductory Science Skills, 88
Invitation to Research in Social Education, An, 116
Invitations: Changing as Teachers and Learners K–12, 48–49, 68
Irwin, Judith Westphal, *Teaching Reading Comprehension Processes*, 45–46
Isenberg, Joan P., *Creative Expression and Play in Early Childhood Curriculum*, 169

Jacobson, Willard J., *Science for Children: A Book for Teachers*, 95
Jaggar, Angela, *Observing the Language Learner*, 63–64
Jane Asher's Costume Book, 150
Jennings, Coleman A.
   Plays Children Love, Vol.II, 141
   Theatre for Youth: Twelve Plays With Mature Themes, 141
Jensen, Julie M., 56
   Adventuring with Books: A Booklist for Pre-K–Grade 6, 75
   Stories to Grow On: Demonstrations of Language Learning in K–8 Classrooms, 67–68
Jensen, Robert, *Research Ideas for the Classroom: Early Childhood Education*, 104
Johns, Jerry L., *Improving Reading: A Handbook of Strategies*, 48
Johnson, Andra, 137
   Art Education: Elementary, 137
Johnson, Dale D., *Teaching Reading Vocabulary*, 53
Joinfostering: Adapting Teaching Strategies for the Multicultural Classroom, 220
Journal for the Education of the Gifted, 215
Journal of Educational Issues of Language Minority Students, The, 225
Journal of Educational Multimedia and Hypermedia, 239
Journal of Health Education, 160
Journal of Physical Education, Recreation and Dance, 161

Author and Title Index

Journal of Research in Childhood Education, 181
Journal of Research in Science Teaching, 99
Journal of School Health, 160
Journal of Science Teacher Education, 99

Kaleidoscope: New Visions for School Library Media Programs (video), 23
Kameenui, Edward J., *Instructional Classroom Management: A Proactive Approach to Managing Behavior,* 186
Kamii, Constance
 Achievement Testing in the Early Grades: The Games Grownups Play, 170
 Young Children Continue to Reinvent Arithmetic—Second Grade: Implications of Piaget's Theory, 104–5
Kase-Polisini, Judith, *The Creative Drama Book: Three Approaches,* 144
Kasten, Wendy C., *The Multi-Age Classroom: A Family of Learners,* 168
Katter, Eldon, 129
Katz, Lillian G., *Engaging Children's Minds: The Project Approach,* 168
Kaufman, James M.
 Characteristics of Emotional and Behavioral Disorders of Children and Youth, 196
 The Illusion of Full Inclusion: A Comprehensive Critique of a Current Special Education Bandwagon, 187
Kelley, Mary Lou, *School Home Notes: Promoting Children's Classroom Success,* 189–90
Kemp, Jerrold, *Planning, Producing and Using Learning Technologies,* 233–34
Kerr, Barbara A., 212
Kidvid: Fun-damentals of Video Instruction, 150
Kiefer, Barbara Z., *The Potential of Picturebooks: From Visual Literacy to Aesthetic Understanding,* 79
Kimmel, Margaret, *For Reading Out Loud! A Guide to Sharing Books with Children,* 19–20
King, Edith W., *Educating Young Children in a Diverse Society,* 223–24
Kirchner, Glenn, *Physical Education for Elementary School Children,* 156
Kits, Games and Manipulatives for the Elementary Classroom: A Source Book, 236
Klasing, Jane, *Designing and Renovating School Library Media Centers,* 22
Kobrin, Beverly, *Eyeopeners II: Children's Books to Answer Children's Questions about the World,* 78
Koegel, Robert L., *Teaching Children with Autism: Strategies for Initiating Positive Interactions and Improving Learning Opportunities,* 196
Kogon, Marilyn, *The Canadian Library Handbook: Orgainzing School, Public and Professional Libraries,* 24–25
Kohl, Herbert, *I Won't Learn From You: The Role of Assent in Learning,* 224

Kozol, Jonathan, *Savage Inequities: Children in America's Schools,* 33
Krashen, Stephen, *The Power of Reading: Insights From the Research,* 20
Krol, Ed, *The Whole Internet User's Guide and Catalog,* 236
Kuhlthau, Carol Collier, *School Media Library Annual,* 13–14
Kulik, James A., *An Analysis of the Research on Ability Grouping: Historical and Contemporary Perspectives,* 211
Kullesied, Eleanor, *Literature, Literacy, and Learning: Classroom Teachers, Library Media Specialists and the Literature-Based Curriculum,* 20
Kulm, Gerald, *Science Assessment in the Service of Reform,* 83
Kunesh, Linda, *Developmentally Appropriate First Grade: A Community of Learners* (video), 179

Lance, Keith Curry, *The Impact of School Library Media Centers on Academic Achievement,* 14
Language and Deafness, 197
Language and Learning: The Importance of Speech in Children's Development, 57–58
Language Arts, 54–55, 70
Language in Mathematics, 106
Language Learning Strategies: What Every Teacher Should Know, 221
Language, Literacy and the Child, 67
Language Stories and Literacy Lessons, 45, 61
Language-Experience Approach to Reading: A Handbook for Teachers of Reading, The, 48
Lankford, E. Louis, *Aesthetics:Issues and Inquiry,* 131–32
Laughlin, Mildred Knight
 Literature-Based Reading: Children's Books and Activities to Enrich the K–5 Curriculum, 20–21
 Public Relations for School Library Media Centers, 23–24
Lawrence Hall of Science, *Great Explorations in Math and Science (GEMS) Teacher's Handbook,* 88–89
Lawrenz, Frances, *Research Matters . . . To the Science Teacher,* 98
Leap Into Learning! Teaching Curriculum through Creative Dramatics and Dance, 142
Learning in Two Worlds: An Integrated Spanish/English Biliteracy Approach, 221–22
Learning through Feedback: A Systematic Approach for Improving Academic Performance, 186–87
Lee, Lauren, *The Elementary School Library Collection: A Guide to Books and Other Media; Phases 1-2-3,* 27
Leiva, Miriam A., *Curriculum and Evaluation Standards for School Mathematics, Addenda Series, Grades K–6,* 109–10
Lerner, Janet W., *Attention Deficit Disorders: Assessment and Teaching,* 196–97

Levenson, Elaine, *Teaching Children About Science: Ideas and Activities Teachers and Parents Can Use*, 89
Levi, Albert W., *Art Education: A Critical Necessity*, 137
Levine, John, *The Internet for Dummies*, 237
Lewis, Rena B.
  Special Education Technology: Practical Applications, 194
  Teaching Special Students in the Mainstream, 188
Library Media Skills: Strategies for Instructing Primary Students, 234
Library Talk, 29–30
Lima, Carolyn W., *A to Zoo: Subject Access to Children's Picture Books*, 25, 75
Lindfors, Judith Wells, *Children's Language and Learning*, 64
Linking Reading Assessment to Instruction: An Application Worktext for Elementary Classroom Teachers, 44
Links to Literature: Literature-Based Units and Ideas for Teacher-Librarians and Teachers, 19
Lipson, Eden Ross, *The New York Times Parent's Guide to the Best Books for Children*, 75
Literacy Development in the Early Years: Helping Children Read & Write, 175–76
Literacy Instruction in Multicultural Settings, 52, 59, 170–71
Literacy: Helping Children Construct Meaning, 47
Literacy's Beginnings: Supporting Young Readers and Writers, 45
Literature and the Child, 79
Literature as Exploration, 72–73
Literature Circles: Voice and Choice in the Student-Centered Classroom, 48
Literature, Literacy, and Learning: Classroom Teachers, Library Media Specialists and the Literature-Based Curriculum, 20
Literature-Based Reading: Children's Books and Activities to Enrich the K–5 Curriculum, 20–21
Living Between the Lines, 64–65
LM_Net, 22
Loertscher, David, *Taxonomies of the School Library Media Program*, 16–17
London, Peter, *Exemplary Art Education Curricula: A Guide to Guides*, 136
Lonner, Walter J., *Readings in Psychology and Culture*, 224
Look, Listen and Trust: A Framework for Learning Through Drama, 151
Look What Happened to Frog: Storytelling in Education, 149–50
Looking in Classrooms, 34
Loucks-Horsley, Susan
  Developing and Supporting Teachers for Elementary School Science Education, 82
  Elementary School Science for the '90s, 85

Lovitt, Thomas C., *Tactics for Teaching*, 191–92
Lowenfeld, Viktor, *Creative and Mental Growth*, 131

Machovec, George, *Telecommunications, Networking and Internet Glossary*, 237
Magazines for Kids and Teens, 28–29
Mager, Robert F., 35
Major Authors and Illustrators for Children and Young Adults, 73
Maker, C. June
  Critical Issues in Gifted Education: Defensible Programs for the Gifted, 209
  Curriculum Development for the Gifted, 205
  Teaching Models in Education of the Gifted, 210–11
Making Choices for Multicultural Education: Five Approaches to Race, Class, and Gender, 219
Making Meaning: Integrated Language Arts Series (videos), 54
Mallow, Jeffry V., *Science Anxiety—Fear of Science and How to Overcome It*, 87
Managing the Social and Emotional Needs of the Gifted: A Teacher's Survival Guide, 208
Marantz, Kenneth, *The Picturebook: Source and Resource for Art Education*, 134
Marion, Marian, *Guidance of Young Children*, 173–74
Martin, Ralph E., *Teaching Science for All Children*, 95
Martinello, Marian L., *Interdisciplinary Inquiry in Teaching and Learning*, 96
Master Curriculum Guides in Economics Teaching Strategies: K–2, 3–4, 117–18
Math and Literature (K–3), 109
Math and Science For Young Children, 177
Mathematical Power: Lessons from a Classroom, 103
Mathematics Assessment: Myths, Models, Good Questions, and Practical Suggestions, 107
Mathematics for the Young Child, 106–7
Mathematics: Teaching for Understanding (video), 110
Mathematics Teaching in the Middle School, 111
Mathematics Their Way, 177
Mathematics with Reason: The Emergent Approach to Primary Maths, 105–6
McCaslin, Nellie
  Creative Drama in the Classroom, 144
  Creative Drama in the Intermediate Grades, 144
  Creative Drama in the Primary Grades, 144
McGee, Lea M., *Literacy's Beginnings: Supporting Young Readers and Writers*, 45
McLoughlin, James A., *Assessing Special Students: Strategies and Procedures*, 184
McNeil, John D., *Reading Comprehension: New Directions for Classroom Practice*, 46
Meaning Makers: Children Learning Language and Using Language to Learn, The, 62–63

Author and Title Index

Meaningful Movement: A Developmental Theme Approach to Physical Education for Children, 169
Means, Barbara, *Using Technology to Support Education Reform*, 231
Measuring Up: Prototypes for Mathematics Assessment, 106
Media & Methods, 239
Megatrends: Ten New Directions Transforming Our Lives, 37–38
Megatrends 2000: Ten New Directions for the 1990's, 38
Melody Book: Three Hundred Selections from the World of Music for Autoharp, Guitar, Piano, Recorder, and Voice, The, 124
Mental Retardation, 195
Mercer, Cecil D.
   Students with Learning Disabilities, 197
   Teaching Students with Learning Problems, 192
Middleplots 4: Book Talk Guide for Use with Readers Ages 8–12, 77
Miller, Elizabeth, *The Internet Resource Directory for K–12 Teachers and Librarians*, 26
Miller, James Hull, *Self-Supporting Scenery for Children's Theatre . . . and Grownups', Too*, 150
Miller-Lachmann, Lyn, *Our Family, Our Friends, Our World: An Annotated Guide to Significant Multicultural Books for Children and Teenagers*, 224–25
Mime and Masks, 148
Minds on Science—Middle and Secondary Scool Methods, 94
Minority Education: From Shame to Struggle, 219
Miseducation: Preschoolers at Risk, 166
Model Drama/Theatre Curriculum: Philosophy, Goals and Objectives, A, 140
Moffett, James
   Student-Centered Language Arts, K–12, 68
   Teaching the Universe of Discourse, 58
Mohnsen, Bonnie, *Using Technology in Physical Education*, 155
Moore, Ronald, *Aesthetics for Young People*, 132
More Exciting, Funny, Scary, Short, Different, and Sad Books Kids Like About Animals, Science, Sports, Families, Songs, and Other Things, 76
More Kids' Favorite Books: A Children's Choices Compilation, 77
More Than Graham Crackers: Nutritional Education and Food Preparation with Young Children, 178–79
More than Stories: The Range of Children's Writing, 69–70
More than the ABCs: The Early Stages of Reading and Writing, 176–77
Morris, Betty, *Administering the School Library Media Center*, 22
Morrow, Lesley Mandel, *Literacy Development in the Early Years: Helping Children Read and Write*, 175–76

Moss, Joyce, *From Page to Screen: Children's and Young Adult Books on Film and Video*, 73
Moving and Learning: The Elementary School Physical Education Experience, 157
Mudpies to Magnets: A Preschool Science Curriculum, 178
Multi-Age Classroom: A Family of Learners, The, 168
Multicultural Classroom: Readings for Content-Area Teachers, The, 218–19
Multicultural Education, 225–26
Multicultural Education in a Pluralistic Society, 34, 218
Multicultural Education: Inclusion for All, 97
Multicultural Education: Issues and Perspectives, 217
Multicultural Perspectives in Music Education, 123
Multicultural Teaching: A Handbook of Activities, Information, and Resources, 118, 220
Multicultural Voices in Contemporary Literature: A Resource for Teachers, 76
Multiethnic Education: Theory and Practice, 216–17
Multiple Worlds of Child Writers: Friends Learning to Write, 61
Music Connection: Teacher's Edition, The, 125
Music Educators National Conference, 127–28
   Bring Multicultural Music to Children (video), 126
   Sing! Move! Listen! Music and Young Children (video), 126
   Teaching Music of African Americans (video), 126
   Teaching Music of Asian Americans (video), 126–27
   Teaching Music of Hispanic Americans, 127
   Teaching Music of the American Indian, 127
Music in Childhood: From Preschool through the Elementary Grades, 123–24
Music in Prekindergarten Planning and Teaching, 124
Musical Games, Fingerplays, and Rhythmic Activities for Early Childhood, 125

Nagy, William E., *Teaching Vocabulary to Improve Reading Comprehension*, 53
Naisbitt, John
   Global Paradox: The Bigger the World Economy, the More Powerful Its Smallest Players, 37
   Megatrends: Ten New Directions Transforming Our Lives, 37–38
   Megatrends 2000: Ten New Directions for the 1990's, 38
National Art Education Association (NAEA), 138
   NAEA Task Force, *Purposes, Principles, and Standards for School Arts Programs*, 130
National Association for Gifted Children, 215
National Association for Multicultural Education, 226

National Association for Sports and Physical Education Committee, *Outcomes of Quality Physical Education Programs*, 154
National Association for the Education of Young Children, 182
  Developmentally Appropriate Practice: Birth Through Age 5 (video), 180
  Discipline: Appropriate Guidance for Young Children (video), 180
National Association of Elementary School Principals, 39
National Center for History in the Schools, *Standards for United States History and World History*, 113
National Council for Geographic Education, *Geography for Life: National Geography Standards 1994*, 113
National Council for the Social Studies, 119–20
  Curriculum Standards for the Social Studies, 113–14
  Social Studies Curriculum Planning Resources, 115
National Council of Teachers of English, *Standards for the English Language Arts*, 57
National Council of Teachers of English, 71
National Council of Teachers of Mathematics, 111
  Assessment Standards for School Mathematics, 101–2
  Curriculum and Evaluation Standards for School Mathematics, 102
  Professional Standards for Teaching Mathematics, 102
National Council on Economic Education, *Master Curriculum Guides in Economics Teaching Strategies: K–2, 3–4*, 117–18
National Excellence: A Case for Developing America's Talent, 203
National Research Council
  Everybody Counts: A Report to the Nation on the Future of Mathematics Education, 102–3
  Measuring Up: Prototypes for Mathematics Assessment, 106
  National Science Education Standards, 83
National Science Resources Center, *Science for Children: Resources for Teachers*, 99
National Science Teachers Association, 100
  NSTA Science Education Suppliers, 99
National Standards for Arts Education: What Every Young American Should Know and Be Able to Do in the Arts, 122, 140
National Standards for Civics and Government, 112–13
National Visual Arts Standards, The, 130
Natural Learning and Mathematics, 107
Need for Story: Cultural Diversity in Classroom and Community, The, 59

Neelands, Jonothan, *Structuring Drama Work: A Handbook of Available Forms in Theatre and Drama*, 145
Nessel, Denise D., *The Language-Experience Approach to Reading: A Handbook for Teachers of Reading*, 48
Neuman, Donald B., *Experiencing Elementary Science*, 96
New Directions for Elementary School Mathematics, 108
New Handbook for Storytellers: With Stories, Poems, Magic, and More, 174–75
New Read-Aloud Handbook, The, 78
New Technologies for Education: A Beginner's Guide, 230
New York Times Parent's Guide to the Best Books for Children, The,
Newkirk, Thomas
  More Than Stories: The Range of Children's Writing, 69–70
  Understanding Writing: Ways of Observing, Learning, and Teaching K–8, 70
Nichols, Beverly, *Moving and Learning: The Elementary School Physical Education Experience*, 157
Nobleman, Roberta, *Mime and Masks*, 148
Norlin, Dennis, *A Directory of Adaptive Technologies to Aid Library Patrons and Staff with Disabilities*, 229
Norton, Donna E., *Through the Eyes of a Child*, 80
NSTA Reports, 100

Observing Development of the Young Child, 170
Observing the Language Learner, 63–64
Ohanian, Susan, *Garbage Pizza, Patchwork Quilts, and Math Magic: Stories about Teachers Who Love to Teach and Children Who Love to Learn*, 103
Organization of School Health Programs, 156
Ostlund, Karen L., *Science Process Skills—Assessing Hands-On Student Performance*, 83–84
Our Family, Our Friends, Our World: An Annotated Guide to Significant Multicultural Books for Children and Teenagers, 224–25
Outcomes of Quality Physical Education Programs, 154
Overby, Lynette, *Early Childhood Creative Arts*, 122
Owens, Douglas T., *Research Ideas for the Classroom: Middle School Mathematics*, 105
Oxford, Rebecca, *Language Learning Strategies: What Every Teacher Should Know*, 221

Paley, Vivian, *Wally's Stories: Conversations in the Kindergarten*, 62
Palmer, Mary, *Music in Prekindergarten Planning and Teaching*, 124

Author and Title Index

Papert, Seymour, *The Children's Machine: Rethinking School in the Age of the Computer*, 231–32
Parents Speak Out: Then and Now, 190
Parke, Beverly N., *Gifted Students in Regular Classrooms*, 213
Parker, Ruth E., *Mathematical Power: Lessons from a Classroom*, 103
Parker, Walter, *Renewing the Social Studies Curriculum*, 115–16
Parsons, Michael, *Aesthetics and Education*, 132
Partnerships: Developing an Integrated School Library, 18
Passion for Excellence, A, 38
Pate, Russell, *Health and Fitness Through Physical Education*, 155
Pathways to Investigative Skills: Instructional Lessons for Guiding Students from Problem Finding to Final Product, Grades 3–9, 212–13
Patterns of Influence on Gifted Learners: The Home, the Self, and the School, 209
Paul, James L., *Children with Special Needs: Family, Culture, and Society*, 171–72
Paul, Peter V., *Language and Deafness*, 197
Payne, Joseph N., *Mathematics for the Young Child*, 106–7
Pearson, P. David, *Handbook of Reading Research*, 42
Perez, Bertha, *Learning in Two Worlds: An Integrated Spanish/English Biliteracy Approach*, 221–22
Perkins, David N., *The Intelligent Eye: Learning to Think by Looking at Art* (Occasional Paper 4), 130
Peters, Tom, *A Passion for Excellence*, 38
Peterson, Carolyn Sue, *Reference Books for Children*, 27
Phelps-Teraski, Diana, *Teaching Competence in Written Language: A Systematic Program for Developing Writing Skills*, 194
Phi Delta Kappa, 39
Phi Delta Kappan, 38
Phonics in Proper Perspective, 54
Phonics They Use: Words for Reading and Writing, 53
Physical Education for Children: Concepts Into Practice, 157
Physical Education for Children: Daily Lesson Plans, 157
Physical Education for Children: Instructor's Manual, 157
Physical Education for Elementary School Children, 156
Picturebook: Source and Resource for Art Education, The, 134
Piirto, Jane, *Gifted Children and Adults: Their Development and Education*, 207
Place Called School: Prospects for the Future, A, 32–33

Planning Effective Instruction, 233
Planning, Producing and Using Learning Technologies, 233–34
Play and Playscapes, 168–69
Playing the Game, 151
Playmaking: Children Writing and Performing Their Own Plays, 147
Plays Children Love, Vol.II, 141
Polloway, Edward A., *Strategies for Teaching Learners with Special Needs*, 192
Poppe, Carol A., *Science Learning Centers for the Primary Grades*, 89
Portfolio and Its Use: Developmentally Appropriate Assessment of Young Children, The, 170
Portfolio and Performance Assessment, 43
Postman, Neil, *Teaching as a Subversive Activity*, 36
The Potential of Picturebooks: From Visual Literacy to Aesthetic Understanding, 79
Poulter, Christine, *Playing the Game*, 151
Power of Reading: Insights From the Research, The, 20
Power Teaching: A Primary Role of the School Library Media Specialist, 17
Presenting Reader's Theater: Plays and Poems to Read Aloud, 73–74
Preventing Early School Failure: Research, Policy, and Practice, 35
Primary Voices K–6, 71
Primaryplots 2: A Book Talk Guide for Use with Readers Ages 4–8, 78
Principal, 38–39
Professional Standards for Teaching Mathematics, 102
Program Advocacy: Power, Publicity and the Teacher-Librarian, 23
Promoting Health and Safety: Skills for Independent Living, 192–93
Psychology of Learning Science, The, 86
Public Relations for School Library Media Centers, 23–24
Puppetry and Early Childhood Education, 148
Purcell, Theresa M., *Teaching Children Dance: Becoming a Master Teacher*, 159
Purposes, Principles, and Standards for School Arts Programs, 130
Purves, Alan C., *Encyclopedia of English Studies and Language Arts*, 66–67

Quality School, The, 32

Raines, Shirley C., 163
   Stories: Children's Literature in Early Education, 176
   Story S-t-r-e-t-c-h-e-r-s: Activities to Expand Children's Favorite Books, 176
   The Whole Language Kindergarten, 174
Raizen, Senta A., *Assessment in Elementary School Science Education*, 84

Ratliffe, Thomas, *Teaching Children Fitness: Becoming a Master Teacher*, 159
Rawlins, George, *Look, Listen and Trust: A Framework for Learning Through Drama*, 151
Reaching Potentials: Appropriate Curriculum and Assessment for Young Children, vol. 1, 165–66
Read Any Good Math Lately? Children's Books for Mathematical Learning, K–6, 108–9
Reading and Writing Together: New Perspectives for the Classroom, 50
Reading Comprehension: New Directions for Classroom Practice, 46
Reading in the Content Area for Junior High and High School, 46–47
Reading Strategies and Practices: A Compendium, 49
Reading Teacher, The, 55
Reading-Writing Connections: From Theory to Practice, 50
Readings in Psychology and Culture, 224
Ready-To-Use Music Activities Kit, 122–23
Recommended Practices in Gifted Education: A Critical Analysis, 207
Reconstructing Mathematics Education: Stories of Teachers Meeting the Challenge of Reform, 104
Redican, Kerry, *Organization of School Health Programs*, 156
Reference Books for Children, 27
Reflective Practice in Social Studies, 114
Reichman, Henry F., *Censorship and Selection: Issues and Answers for Schools*, 27–28
Reigeluth, Charles, *Systemic Change in Education*, 232
Reis, Sally M., *Curriculum Compacting: The Complete Guide to Modifying the Regular Curriculum for High Ability Students*, 213
Relationship of Grouping Practices to the Education of the Gifted and Talented Learner, The, 212
Renewal at the Schoolhouse: Management Ideas for Library Media Specialists and Administrators, 21, 231
Renewing the Social Studies Curriculum, 115–16
Renzulli, Joseph S.
  The Enrichment Triad Model: A Guide for Developing Defensible Programs for the Gifted and Talented, 205
  The Revolving Door Identification Model, 210
  Schools for Talent Development: A Practical Plan for Total School Improvement, 209
  The Schoolwide Enrichment Model: A Comprehensive Plan for Educational Excellence, 210
  Systems and Models for Developing Programs for the Gifted and Talented, 207
Research Ideas for the Classroom: Early Childhood Education, 104
Research Ideas for the Classroom: Middle School Mathematics, 105

Research Matters . . . To the Science Teacher, 98
Resources for Creative Teaching in Early Childhood Education, 172
Restructuring America's Schools: A Blueprint for Action, 236
Rethinking Elementary School Mathematics: Insights and Issues, 105
Reversing Language Shift: Theoretical and Empirical Foundations of Assistance to Threatened Languages, 220–21
Revolving Door Identification Model, The, 210
Rhodes, Lynn K., *Windows Into Literacy: Assessing Learners K–8*, 43
Richard-Amato, Patricia, *The Multicultural Classroom: Readings for Content-Area Teachers*, 218–19
Rigg, Pat, *When They Don't All Speak English*, 60
Risk Makers, Risk Takers, Risk Breakers: Reducing the Risks for Young Literacy Learners, 52, 60–61
Robinson, Ann, *Cooperative Learning and the Academically Talented Student*, 211–12
Rodriguez, Rodolfo, *Compendium of Readings in Bilingual Education: Issues and Practices*, 222
Rogers, Karen, *The Relationship of Grouping Practices to the Education of the Gifted and Talented Learner*, 212
Role Drama: A Teacher's Handbook, 146
Role of Imagery in Learning (Occasional Paper 1), The, 129–30
Rollins, Jean, *National Visual Arts Standards, The*, 130
Rosenblatt, Louise M., *Literature as Exploration*, 72–73
Ross, E. Wayne, *Reflective Practice in Social Studies*, 114
Routman, Regie, *Invitations: Changing as Teachers and Learners K–12*, 48–49, 68
Ruddell, Robert B., *Theoretical Models and Processes of Reading*, 42–43

Saber-Tooth Curriculum, The, 36
Salisbury-Wills, Barbara,
  Theatre Arts in the Elementary Classroom, Volume One: Kindergarten Through Grade Three, 145
  Theatre Arts in the Elementary Classroom, Volume Two: Fourth Grade Through Sixth Grade, 145
Sargent, Laurence R., *Social Skills for School and Community: Systematic Instruction for Children and Youth with Cognitive Delays*, 200
Savage Inequities: Children in America's Schools, 33
Sawyer, Ann, *Developments in Elementary Mathematics Teaching*, 103–4
Scarcella, Robin, *Teaching Language Minority Students in the Multicultural Classroom*, 222
Schickendanz, Judith A., *More than the ABCs: The Early Stages of Reading and Writing*, 176–77

Author and Title Index

Schifter, Deborah, *Reconstructing Mathematics Education: Stories of Teachers Meeting the Challenge of Reform*, 104
Schiller, Pam, *Where Is Thumbkin?: Five Hundred Activities to Use with Songs You Already Know*, 169
Schmitz, Connie C., *Managing the Social and Emotional Needs of the Gifted: A Teacher's Survival Guide*, 208
School Arts, 138
School Home Notes: Promoting Children's Classroom Success, 189–90
School Library Journal, 30, 239–40
School Library Management Notebook, 21
School Library Media Center in the 21st Century: Changes and Challenges, 21
School Library Program: Teacher-Librarian Resource Manual, The, 15
School Media Library Annual, 13–14
School Science and Mathematics, 100
Schools for Talent Development: A Practical Plan for Total School Improvement, 209
Schoolwide Enrichment Model: A Comprehensive Plan for Educational Excellence, The, 210
Schuman, Jo Miles, *Art From Many Hands: Multicultural Art Projects*, 133–34
Schurr, Sandra L., *Dynamite in the Classroom: How-to Handbook for Teachers*, 234
Schwartz, Dorothy, *Give Them Roots . . . and Wings! A Guide to Drama in the Elementary Grades*, 145
Science & Children, 100
Science Anxiety—Fear of Science and How to Overcome It, 87
Science Assessment in the Service of Reform, 83
Science Curriculum Activities Library, 90
Science Education, 100
Science for All Americans, 82
Science for Children: A Book for Teachers, 95
Science for Children: Resources for Teachers, 99
Science in Elementary Education, 93
Science in the Multicultural Classroom: A Guide to Teaching and Learning, 97
Science Is: A Source Book of Fascinating Facts, Projects and Activities, 87
Science Learning Centers for the Primary Grades, 89
Science Matters: Achieving Scientific Literacy, 87
Science Process Skills—Assessing Hands-on Student Performance, 83–84
Science with Young Children, 178
Seaver, Alice, *Library Media Skills: Strategies for Instructing Primary Students*, 234
Seefeldt, Carol, *Social Studies for the Preschool-Primary Child*, 118, 178
Selecting Materials for School Library Media Centers, 26–27
Self-Supporting Scenery for Children's Theatre . . . and Grownups', Too, 150
Selwyn, Douglas, *Arts and Humanities in the Social Studies*, 118
Serving Gifted and Talented Students: A Resource for School Personnel, 208
Serving Linguistically and Culturally Diverse Students: Strategies for the School Library Media Specialist, 15–16
7 Habits of Highly Effective People, The, 37
Sewall, Susan B., *Hooked on Science: Ready to Use Discovery Activities for Grades 4–8*, 89–90
Shanahan, Timothy, 40
  Reading and Writing Together: New Perspectives for the Classroom, 50
Shearer, Arleen P., *Linking Reading Assessment to Instruction: An Application Worktext for Elementary Classroom Teachers*, 44
Shore, Bruce, *Recommended Practices in Gifted Education: A Critical Analysis*, 207
Siccone, Frank, *Celebrating Diversity: Building Self Esteem in Today's Multicultural Classrooms*, 225
Silbert, Jerry, *Direct Instruction Mathematics*, 194
Silverman, Linda Kreger, *Counseling the Gifted and Talented*, 208–9
Simpson, Carol Mann, *Copyright for School Libraries: A Practical Guide*, 28
Simpson, Richard L., *Autism: Information and Resources for Parents, Families, and Professionals*, 197–98
Sing! Move! Listen! Music and Young Children (video), 126
Sinofsky, Esther R., *A Copyright Primer for Educational and Industrial Media Producers*, 230
Six Plays for Children by Aurand Harris, 140–41
Skeel, Dorothy J., 112
  Elementary Social Studies: Challenges for Tomorrow's World, 118
  Small Size Economics: Lessons for the Primary Grades, 118
Sklar, Daniel Judah, *Playmaking: Children Writing and Performing Their Own Plays*, 147
Skutnabb-Kangas, Tove, *Minority Education: From Shame to Struggle*, 219
Slaughter, Judith Pollard, *Beyond Storybooks: Young Children and the Shared Book Experience*, 49
Slavin, Robert E.
  Effective Programs for Students at Risk, 35
  Preventing Early School Failure: Research, Policy, and Practice, 35
Sleeter, Christine E., *Making Choices for Multicultural Education: Five Approaches to Race, Class, and Gender*, 219
Small Size Economics: Lessons for the Primary Grades, 118

Smart Girls, Gifted Women, 212
Smart Schools, Smart Kids: Why Do Some Schools Work?, 32
Smith, Deborah Deutsch, *Effective Discipline,* 186
Smith, Frank
 Understanding Reading: A Psycholinguistic Analysis of Reading and Learning to Read, 43
 Writing and the Writer, 70
Smith, Ralph A., *Discipline-Based Art Education: Origins, Meanings, and Development,* 137
Snell, Martha E., *Instruction of Students with Severe Disabilties,* 198
Snyder, Agnes, *Dauntless Women in Childhood Education,* 167
Social Education, 119
Social Skills for School and Community: Systematic Instruction for Children and Youth with Cognitive Delays, 200
Social Studies and the Young Learner, 119
Social Studies Curriculum Planning Resources, 115
Social Studies for the Preschool-Primary Child, 118, 178
Social Worlds of Children Learning to Write in an Urban Primary School, 63
Sorenson, Juanita, *The Gifted Program Handbook: Planning, Implementing, and Evaluating Gifted Programs with a Special Model for Small School Districts,* 210
Sorrow, Barbara Head, *CD-ROM for Librarians and Educators: A Resource Guide to Over 300 Instructional Programs,* 28
Southern, Thomas W., *The Academic Acceleration of Gifted Children,* 203
Special Committee on Youth Education for Citizenship, *Essentials of Law Related Education: A Guide for Practioners and Policy Makers,* 114
Special Education Technology: Practical Applications, 194
Spolin, Viola, *Theater Games for the Classroom: A Teacher's Handbook,* 151
Spring, Joel, *The Intersection of Cultures: Multicultural Education in the United States,* 219–20
Stage of the Art, 151
Stahl, Robert J., *Cooperative Learning in the Social Studies Classroom: An Invitation to Social Study,* 115
Stainback, Susan, *Curriculum Considerations in Inclusive Classrooms: Facilitating Learning for All Students,* 188–89
Standard Cataloging for School and Public Libraries, 24
Standards for the English Language Arts, 57
Standards for United States History and World History, 113
Starko, Alane, *Creativity in the Classroom: Schools of Curious Delight,* 204

Stenmark, Jean Kerr, *Mathematics Assessment: Myths, Models, Good Questions, and Practical Suggestions,* 107
Stepans, Joseph, *Targeting Students' Science Misconceptions: Physical Science Activities Using the Conceptual Change Model,* 96–97
Sternberg, Les, *Individuals with Profound Disabilities: Instructional and Assistive Strategies,* 198
Sternberg, Robert J., *Conceptions of Giftedness,* 207–8
Stevens, Gregory, *Videos for Understanding Diversity: A Core Selection and Evaluation Guide,* 236
Stewig, John Warren, *Dramatizing Literature in Whole Language Classrooms,* 146
Stires, Susan, *With Promise: Redefining Reading and Writing for "Special Students,"* 51–52
Stoessiger, Rex, *Natural Learning and Mathematics,* 107
Stoll, Donald, *Magazines for Kids and Teens,* 28–29
Stories: Children's Literature in Early Education, 176
Stories in the Classroom: Storytelling, Reading Aloud and Roleplaying With Children, 149
Stories to Grow On: Demonstrations of Language Learning in K–8 Classrooms, 67–68
Story S-t-r-e-t-c-h-e-r-s: Activities to Expand Children's Favorite Books, 176
Storytelling Made Easy with Puppets, 148
Storytelling Step by Step, 149
Strategies, 161
Strategies for Teaching Learners with Special Needs, 192
Strickland, Bonnie B., *Developing and Implementing Individualized Education Programs,* 184–85
Strickland, Dorothy S., *Emerging Literacy: Young Children Learn to Read and Write,* 45, 62
Stripling, Barbara, *Brainstorms and Blueprints: Teaching Library Research as a Thinking Process,* 19
Structuring Drama Work: A Handbook of Available Forms in Theatre and Drama, 145
Student-Centered Language Arts, K–12, 68
Students with Learning Disabilities, 197
Swartz, Larry, *Drama Themes: A Practical Guide for Teaching Drama,* 146
Synthesizers in the Elementary Classroom: An Integrated Approach, 124–25
Syracuse Community-Referenced Curriculum Guide for Students with Moderate and Severe Disabilities, The, 196
Systemic Change in Education, 232
Systems and Models for Developing Programs for the Gifted and Talented, 207

Tactics for Teaching, 191–92
Taking Part: Introducing Social Skills to Children, 199
Tales as Tools: The Power of Story in the Classroom, 175

Author and Title Index

Targeting Students' Science Misconceptions: Physical Science Activities Using the Conceptual Change Model, 96–97
Tarlington, Carole, *Role Drama: A Teacher's Handbook*, 146
Taxonomies of the School Library Media Program, 16–17
Taylor, Barbara J., *A Child Goes Forth: A Curriculum Guide for Preschool Children*, 172
Taylor, Denny, *Growing Up Literate: Learning from Inner City Families*, 52, 60
Teacher's Guide to Including Students with Disabilities in Regular Physical Education, A, 193
Teachers' Favorite Books for Kids, 78
Teaching as a Subversive Activity, 36
Teaching Children About Science: Ideas and Activities Teachers and Parents Can Use, 89
Teaching Children Dance: Becoming a Master Teacher, 159
Teaching Children Fitness: Becoming a Master Teacher, 159
Teaching Children Games: Becoming a Master Teacher (paper & video), 158
Teaching Children Gymnastics: Becoming a Master Teacher, 159–60
Teaching Children Mathematics, 111
Teaching Children Movement Concepts and Skills: Becoming a Master Teacher (book & video), 158
Teaching Children Physical Education: Becoming a Master Teacher, 158–59
Teaching Children Science, 90
Teaching Children with Autism: Strategies for Initiating Positive Interactions and Improving Learning Opportunities, 196
Teaching Competence in Written Language: A Systematic Program for Developing Writing Skills, 194
Teaching Elementary Physical Education, 161
Teaching Elementary Science, 92
Teaching Exceptional Children, 201
Teaching for Outcomes in Elementary Physical Education: A Guide for Curriculum and Assessment, 155
Teaching Gifted Kids in the Regular Classroom, 213
Teaching in a Diverse Society, 218
Teaching Individuals with Physical and Multiple Disabilities, 195
Teaching Language Minority Students in the Multicultural Classroom, 222
Teaching Models in Education of the Gifted, 210–11
Teaching Music of African Americans (video), 126
Teaching Music of Asian Americans (video), 126–27
Teaching Music of Hispanic Americans, 127
Teaching Music of the American Indian, 127
Teaching Music with a Multicultural Approach, 123
Teaching Reading Comprehension Processes, 45–46
Teaching Reading Strategies from Successful Classrooms (videos), 54
Teaching Reading Vocabulary, 53
Teaching Science as a Decision Making Process, 91
Teaching Science for All Children, 95
Teaching Science Through Discovery, 90–91
Teaching Science to Children—An Integrated Approach, 92–93
Teaching Social Skills to Children and Youth, 199–200
Teaching Special Students in the Mainstream, 188
Teaching Strategies for Ethnic Studies, 217
Teaching Students with Learning Problems, 192
Teaching Students with Moderate to Severe Disabilities: Use of Response Prompting Strategies, 198–99
Teaching the Gifted Child, 206
Teaching the Universe of Discourse, 58
Teaching Vocabulary to Improve Reading Comprehension, 53
Teaching With a Multicultural Perspective: A Practical Guide, 114, 218
Teaching Young Playwrights, 146–47
Teague, Fred, *Technology and Media: Instructional Applications*, 234
Team Building Through Physical Challenges, 156
Technology & Learning, 240
Technology and Media: Instructional Applications, 234
TechTrends, 240
Telecommunications, Networking and Internet Glossary, 237
TESOL Matters, 226
TESOL Quarterly, 226
T.H.E. Journal, 240
Theater Games for the Classroom: A Teacher's Handbook, 151
Theatre Arts in the Elementary Classroom, Volume One: Kindergarten Through Grade Three, 145
Theatre Arts in the Elementary Classroom, Volume Two: Fourth Grade Through Sixth Grade, 145
Theatre for Youth: Twelve Plays With Mature Themes, 141
Theissen, Diane, *The Wonderful World of Mathematics: A Critically Annotated List of Children's Books in Mathematics*, 107
Theoretical Models and Processes of Reading, 42–43
This Land Is Our Land: A Guide to Multicultural Literature for Children and Young Adults, 77
This Way to Books, 74
This Year in School Science 1989: Scientific Literacy, 85–86
Thomas, Carol Chase, *Interactive Teaming: Consultation and Collaboration in Special Programs*, 185

Thomas, Jerry R.
  Physical Education for Children: Concepts Into Practice, 157
  Physical Education for Children: Daily Lesson Plans, 157
  Physical Education for Children: Instructor's Manual, 157
Thomas, Rebecca L., *Primaryplots 2: A Book Talk Guide for Use with Readers Ages 4–8*, 78
Thornton, Carol A., *Windows of Opportunity: Mathematics for Students with Special Needs*, 108
Thought and Language, 58–59
Thoughts on Art Education (Occasional Paper 2), 129
Thousand, Jacqueline S., *Creativity and Collaborative Learning: A Practical Guide to Empowering Students and Teachers*, 189
Through the Eyes of a Child, 80
Tiedt, Pamela, *Multicultural Teaching: A Handbook of Activities, Information, and Resources*, 118, 220
Tierney, Robert J., *Reading Strategies and Practices: A Compendium*, 49
Tolman, Marvin N., *Science Curriculum Activities Library*, 90
Tomlinson, Carol Ann, *Challenging the Gifted in the Regular Classroom*, 214
Topal, Cathy Weisman
  Children and Painting, 134
  Children, Clay and Sculpture, 134
Trafton, Paul, 101
  New Directions for Elementary School Mathematics, 108
Transformations through Drama: A Teacher's Guide to Educational Drama, Grades K–8, 142–43
Treffinger, Donald J.
  The Creative Problem Solver's Guidebook, 204
  Creative Problem Solving: An Introduction, 204
Trelease, Jim, *The Read-Aloud Handbook*, 78
Trostle, Susan L., *Integrated Learning Activities for Young Children*, 173
Turnbull, Ann P., *Families, Professionals, and Exceptionality: A Special Partnership*, 190
Turnbull, H. Rutherford
  Free Appropriate Public Education: The Law and Children with Disabilities, 187
  Parents Speak Out: Then and Now, 190
Turner, Philip, *Helping Teachers Teach: A School Library Media Specialist's Role*, 17, 246
Turner, Sandra, *HyperCard: A Tool for Learning*, 234–35
Tye, Kenneth A., *Global Education from Thought to Action*, 115
Tyler, Ralph W., *Basic Principles of Curriculum and Instruction*, 37

Understanding Reading: A Psycholinguistic Analysis of Reading and Learning to Read, 43
Understanding Reading Problems: Assessment and Instruction, 51
Understanding Writing: Ways of Observing, Learning, and Teaching K–8, 70
University of California at Berkeley Wellness Letter, 160–61
Using Media for Creative Teaching, 150
Using Picture Storybooks to Teach Literary Devices, 74
Using Poetry Across the Curriculum: A Whole Language Approach, 74
Using Technology in Physical Education, 155
Using Technology to Support Education Reform, 231

Vacca, Richard T., *Content Area Reading*, 47
Valencia, Sheila W., *Authentic Reading Assessment: Practices and Possibilities*, 44
Van Houten, Ron, *Learning Through Feedback: A Systematic Approach for Improving Academic Performance*, 186–87
Van Orden, Phyllis, *The Collection Program in Schools: Concepts, Practices, and Information Sources*, 29
Van Tassel-Baska, Joyce L.
  Comprehensive Curriculum for Gifted Learners, 205
  Patterns of Influence on Gifted Learners: The Home, The Self, and the School, 209
Vandergrift, Kay, *Power Teaching: A Primary Role of the School Library Media Specialist*, 17
VanSchuyver, Jan, *Storytelling Made Easy With Puppets*, 148
Videos for Understanding Diversity: A Core Selection and Evaluation Guide, 236
Visual Experience: Teacher's Edition, The, 134
Visual Handicaps and Learning, 194
Vygotsky, L.S., *Thought and Language*, 58–59

Wachowiak, Frank, *Emphasis Art: A Qualitative Art Program for Elementary and Middle Schools*, 136
Walker, Hill M.
  Antisocial Behavior in School: Strategies and Best Practices, 198
  The Walker Social Skills Curriculum: The ACCEPTS Program, 200
Walling, Linda Lucas, *Disabilities, Children and Libraries: Mainstreaming Services in Public Libraries and School Library Media Centers*, 17–18
Wally's Stories: Conversations in the Kindergarten, 62
Wanamaker, Nancy, *More Than Graham Crackers: Nutritional Education and Food Preparation with Young Children*, 178–79
Warner, Allen R., 31–32
Watson, Dorothy J., *Ideas and Insights: Language Arts in the Elementary School*, 68

Author and Title Index

Way of the Ferret: Finding Educational Resources on the Internet, The, 235
Ways with Words: Language, Life and Work in Communities and Classrooms, 59–60
We, the People of the World, 116–17
Webb, Norman, *Assessment in the Mathematics Classroom: 1993 Yearbook*, 108
Wells, Gordon, *The Meaning Makers: Children Learning Language and Using Language to Learn*, 62–63
Werner, Peter H., *Teaching Children Gymnastics: Becoming a Master Teacher*, 159–60
Westberg, Karen L., 202
What Are You Teaching My Child? (video), 110
What Did I Write? Beginning Writing Behavior, 61, 175
What Do Children Read Next? A Reader's Guide to Fiction for Children, Collaboration through Writing and Reading: Exploring Possibilities, 74
What Works: Research about Teaching and Learning Through the School's Library Resource Center, 26
Wheetley, Kim A., 139
When Stories Come to School: Telling, Writing, and Performing Stories in the Early Childhood Classroom, 147
When They Don't all Speak English, 60
When Writers Read, 65
Where Is Thumbkin?: Five Hundred Activities to Use with Songs You Already Know, 169
White, Melvin, *White's Readers Theatre Anthology: 28 All-Occasion Readings for Storytellers*, 141
Whiteley, Sandy, *American Library Association Guide to Information Access: A Complete Research Handbook and Directory*, 230
Whitin, David, *Read Any Good Math Lately? Children's Books for Mathematical Learning, K–6*, 108–9
Whole Internet User's Guide and Catalog, The, 236
Whole Language: Getting Started . . . Moving Forward, 47–48
Whole Language Kindergarten, The, 174
Wiggins, Jackie, *Synthesizers in the Elementary Music Classroom: An Integrated Approach*, 124–25
Wilde, Sandra, *You Kan Red This!: Spelling and Punctuation for Whole Language Classrooms, K–6*, 66
Williams, Robert A., *Mudpies to Magnets: A Preschool Science Curriculum*, 178
Willis, Barry, *Distance Education: Strategies and Tools*, 238
Windows Into Literacy: Assessing Learners K–8, 43
Windows of Opportunity: Mathematics for Students with Special Needs, 108
Winebrenner, Susan, *Teaching Gifted Kids in the Regular Classroom*, 213
Wings to Fly: Bringing Theatre Arts to Students with Special Needs, 148–49

Wirth, Marian, *Musical Games, Fingerplays, and Rhythmic Activities for Early Childhood*, 125
Wish in One Hand, Spit in the Other: A Collection of Plays by Suzan Zeder, 142
Wishnietsky, Dan, *Assessing the Role of Technology in Education*, 232
With Promise: Redefining Reading and Writing for "Special Students," 51–52
Wolery, Mark
  Including Children with Special Needs in Early Childhood Programs, 172
  Teaching Students with Moderate to Severe Disabilities: Use of Response Prompting Strategies, 198–99
Wonderful World of Mathematics: A Critically Annotated List of Children's Books in Mathematics, The, 107
Wood, Judy W., *Adapting Instruction for Mainstreamed and At-Risk Students*, 189
Wood, Terry, *Rethinking Elementary School Mathematics: Insights and Issues*, 105
Working Together: Building Children's Social Skills Through Folk Literature, 199
Workjobs: Activity Centered Learning for Early Childhood, 177
Wright, June L., *Young Children: Active Learners in a Technological Age*, 179
Wright, Keith, *The Challenge of Technology: Action Strategies for the School Library Media Specialist*, 22–23
Writing and the Writer, 70
Writing to Learn Mathematics: Strategies that Work, K–12, 106

Yarbrough, Cornelia, 121–22
You Kan Red This!: Spelling and Punctuation for Whole Language Classrooms, K–6, 66
Young Children, 181
Young Children: Active Learners in a Technological Age, 179
Young Children Continue to Reinvent Arithmetic—Second Grade: Implications of Piaget's Theory, 104–5
Young, Jane F., *Meaningful Movement: A Developmental Theme Approach to Physical Education for Children*, 169
Young, Wendy, *Partnerships: Developing an Integrated School Library*, 18
Youth Theatre Journal, 152
Ysseldyke, James E., *Critical Issues in Special Education*, 188

Zarnowski, Myra, *Children's Literature and Social Studies: Selecting and Using Notable Books in the Classroom*, 119
Zeder, Suzan, *Wish in One Hand, Spit in the Other: A Collection of Plays by Suzan Zeder*, 142

Subject Index

Advertising, the professional collection, 250–51, 253
Aesthetics, 131–32
Anthologies, theatre, 140–42
Art criticism, 132
Art education. *See* Visual arts
Art history, 133
Art studio, 133–34
Attention deficit disorders, 196–97
Authors & illustrators, information about, 73
Autism, 196, 197–98

Behavior management, special education, 185–87
Bilingual education, 220–22, 223
Book fairs, organizing, 254
Book reviews, keeping up with, 247–48
Booktalks, to promote the professional collection, 253

CD-ROMs, health & physical education, 160
Children's literature, 72–80
    author information & media adaptations, 73
    early childhood education, 176
    instruction & activities, 73–74
    journal, 80
    keystone works, 72–73
    selection aids:
        general, 74
        specific, 76
    textbooks, 79
Civics. *See* Social studies
Classic works. *See* Keystone works
Community resources
    for developing professional collection, 254–55
    file for teachers, 256
Computer center, development, 257
Computers. *See* Instructional technology
Copyright, 28, 230
Creative drama, 142–46

Cultural & linguistic diversity. *See also* Multicultural education; Multicultural resources
    language arts, 59–60
    reading, 52
Curriculum & instruction. *See also* Instructional methods; Instructional technology
    children's literature, 73–74
    early childhood education, 172–73
    general education, 33–35
    gifted & talented, 205
    science, 84–85, 87–97
    social studies, 115–16
    special education, 191–94
    visual arts, 135–36
Curriculum guides & documents, 255

Dance, 159, 161
Deafness, special education, 197
Directories, yearbooks & manuals, instructional technology, 228–30
Disabilities. *See* Special education
Distance education, 235, 238

Early childhood education, 163–82
    approaches, 167–68
    art, music, and play, 168–69
    assessment, 170
    cultural diversity & special needs, 170–72
    curriculum, 172–73
    guidance & parenting, 173–74
    journals, 180–81
    keystone works, 164–67
    kindergarten, 174
    language & literacy, 174–77
    mathematics, science, and social studies, 177–78
    memberships, 181–82
    nonprint materials, 179–80
    nutrition, 178–79
    technology, 179

Educational technology. *See* Instructional technology
Exceptional children. *See* Gifted & talented; Special education

Games
 health & physical education, 158
 instructional technology, 236
 theatre, 151
General education, 31–39
 changing schools, 32–33
 classics, 36–37
 curriculum & instruction, 33–35
 journals, 38–39
 memberships, 39
Gifted & talented, 202–15
 acceleration, 203
 creativity, 203–4
 documents/guidelines/standards, 203
 general background works, 205–8
 girls, 212
 guidance, 208–9
 journals, 214–15
 memberships, 215
 nonprint material, 214
 program development, 209–11
 program models, 210–11
 research, 211–12
 teaching strategies, 212–13
Guidance
 early childhood education, 173–74, 180
 gifted & talented, 208–9
Guidelines & standards
 gifted & talented, 203
 health & physical education, 153–54
 instructional technology, 228
 language arts, 56–57
 math, 101–3
 music, 122
 reading, 40–41
 school library media programs, 13
 science, 82–83
 social studies, 112–14
 theatre, 140
 visual arts, 129–31
Gymnastics, 159–60

Health & physical education, 153–62
 documents/guidelines/standards, 153–54
 early childhood education, 169
 general works, 154–56
 journals, 160–61
 memberships, 161–62
 nonprint materials, 160
 special education, 193
 teaching, 156–57

 text, manual, lesson plan package, 157
 textbook & accompanying video, 158–60
History. *See also* Social studies
 of art, 133

Individualized Education Programs (IEPs), 183–85
Information problem-solving, 18–19
Instruction, integrated, reading, 49–50
Instructional materials, collecting, for use with students, 255
Instructional methods. *See also* Curriculum & instruction
 reading, 47–49
Instructional technology, 227–41. *See also* School library media programs; Videos
 directories, yearbooks, & manuals, 228–30
 documents/guidelines/standards, 228
 improving schools, 230–32
 instructional applications, 232–35
 journals, 238–40
 memberships, 240–41
 nonprint materials, 238
 resource guides, 235–36
 telecommunications, distance learning, and the Internet, 237–38
Integrated instruction, reading, 49–50
Internet, 235, 237–38
 resource-sharing and, 257

Journal collections, 4
Journals
 access to, and collection development, 247–48
 children's literature, 72
 early childhood education, 180–81
 general education, 38–39
 gifted & talented, 214–15
 health & physical education, 160–61
 instructional technology, 238–40
 language arts, 70–71
 math, 111
 most frequently used by teachers, 10–11
 multicultural education, 225–26
 reading, 54
 school library media programs, 29–30
 science, 99–100
 social studies, 119
 special education, 200–201
 theatre, 151–52
 visual arts, 137–38

Keystone works
 children's literature, 72–73
 early childhood education, 164–67
 language arts, 57–59

Subject Index

reading, 41–43
school library media programs, 13–14
visual arts, 130–31
Kindergarten, 174

Language arts, 56–71. *See also* Reading & writing
  cultural & linguistic diversity, 59–60
  documents/guidelines/standards, 56–57
  emergent literacy, 60–63
  journals, 70–71
  keystone works, 57–59
  language, 63–64
  memberships, 71
  reading and writing, 64–66
  research/reference works, 66–67
  teaching, 67–69
  writing, 69–70
Language resources, multicultural education, 220–22
Leadership. *See* Professionalism & leadership
Learning disabilities. *See* Special education
Library media specialists. *See* School library media specialists
Literacy. *See also* Language arts; Reading & writing
  early childhood education, 174–77
Literature-Based programs, 19–21

Mainstreaming, 188–89
Management, school library media centers, 21–23
Master teacher programs, health & physical education, 158–60
Math, 101–11. *See also* Science
  documents/guidelines/standards, 101–3
  early childhood education, 177–78
  experiences & issues in implementing change, 103–4
  journals, 111
  memberships, 111
  nonprint materials, 110
  research, 104–5
  special education, 194
  teacher resources & references, 105–9
  teaching & assessment activities, 109–10
Media. *See* Instructional technology; School library media programs
Memberships
  early childhood education, 181–82
  general education, 39
  gifted & talented, 215
  health & physical education, 161–62
  instructional technology, 240–41
  language arts, 71
  math, 111
  multicultural education, 226
  music, 127–28

reading, 55
school library media programs, 30
science, 100
social studies, 119–20
special education, 201
theatre, 152
visual arts, 138
Minorities. *See* Multicultural education
Multicultural education, 216–26
  general resources, 216–20
  journals, 225–26
  memberships, 226
  special resources:
    language, 220–22
    other, 222–25
Multicultural resources
  early childhood education, 170–72
  language arts, 59–60
  music, 123, 125–27
  reading, 52
  science, 97
  visual arts, 133–34
Music, 121–28
  books, 122–25
  documents/guidelines/standards, 122
  early childhood education, 169
  memberships, 127–28
  multimedia package, 125
  nonprint materials, 126–27

National survey, xvii-xviii, 1–11
  data in table form, 261–67 (appendix)
Networking, 257
Nutrition, early childhood education, 178–79

Parents
  collection of books & pamphlets for, 256
  working with, special education, 189–90
Phonics, 53–54
Physical education. *See* Health & physical education
Play, early childhood education, 168–69
Plays. *See* Theatre
Playwriting, 146–47
Professional collections
  contents, xvi-xvii
  designating space & staff for, 244
  development of, 246–48
  district-level, 5, 265–67
  easy access, 248–50
  importance and identity, xv
  library checkouts & hours, 249–50
  location, xvi, 263
  national survey, xvii-xviii, 1–11, 261–67
    most popular titles, 5–11
  organization, 248–49

promoting development & use, 242–46, 250–55
selection criteria, xviii-xx
size, 3, 263
uses, xvi, 264–65
Professional organizations, memberships. *See* Memberships
Professionalism & leadership, school library media programs, 25–26
Program advocacy, school library media programs, 23–24
Program marketing, school library media programs, 23–24
Program planning. *See also* Curriculum and instruction
gifted & talented, 209–11
school library media programs, 14–21
information problem-solving, 18–19
literature-based, 19–21
Public relations. *See* Program advocacy
Puppetry & masks, 147–48

Reading & writing, 40–55. *See also* Language arts
assessment, 43–44
beginning, and emergent literacy, 44–45
comprehension, 45–46
content area & upper grades, 46–47
documents/guidelines/standards, 40–41
early childhood education, 175–77
instructional methods, 47–49
integrated instruction, 49–50
journals, 54
keystone works, 41–43
language arts, 64–66, 69–70
literature-based programs, 19–21
memberships, 55
motivation, 50–51
nonprint materials, 54
problems, 51–52
special education, 194
special populations, 52
vocabulary, 53
word recognition, 53–54
Reference works
for teachers, 256
language arts, 66–67
Research
gifted & talented, 211–12
language arts, 66–67
math, 104–5
science, 98
social studies, 116
Research skills, 18–19
Resource sharing, 256–57

School districts, role in development of professional collection, 243–46

School librarians. *See also* School library media specialists
most frequently used books, 6–7
School library media programs, 12–30. *See also* Instructional technology
cooperative program planning & teaching, 14–21
information problem-solving, 18–19
literature-based, 19–21
documents/guidelines/standards, 13
journals, 29–30
keystone works, 13–14
management, 21–23
marketing and advocacy, 23–24
memberships, 30
organization of resources, 24–25
professionalism and leadership, 25–26
selection of resources, 26–29
School library media specialists. *See also* National survey
funding the professional collection and, 243–44
most frequently used books, 7–8
other professional services, 255–58
role in development of professional collection, 243–46, 250–55
School library selection aids, introducing teachers to, 252
School reform, general education, 32–33
Science, 81–100. *See also* Math
assessment, 83–84
curriculum, 84–85
documents/guidelines/standards, 82–83
early childhood education, 177–78
general resources, 85–87
instruction/activities, 87–90
instruction/methods, 90–97
journals, 99–100
memberships, 100
multicultural classroom, 97
research, 98
selection aids, 98–99
Social skills, special education, 199–200
Social studies, 112–20
documents/guidelines/standards, 112–14
early childhood education, 177–78
experience & issues in implementing change, 114–15
foundations for reform, 115–16
journals, 119
memberships, 119–20
research, 116
teacher resources & references, 116–19
Special education:
Part 1—cross-categorical issues and methods, 183–90
assessing student needs & developing IEPs, 183–85

Subject Index

    collaborating and teaming with colleagues, 185
    effective instruction, classroom organization, and behavior management, 185–87
    foundations, contemporary issues and perspectives, 187–88
    mainstreaming and inclusion, 188–89
    working with parents & families, 189–90
    Part II—curriculum content and disability areas, 191–201
    academic content area, 191–92
    curriculum content, 192–94
    disabilities, 194–99
    journals, 200–201
    memberships, 201
    social skills, 199–200
Speech. *See* Language arts
Standards. *See* Guidelines & standards
Storytelling, 149–50

Teachers
    fulfilling interests & needs of, 246–47
    most frequently used books, 8–10
    most frequently used journals, 10–11
    reference collection for, 256
Teachers as Readers program, 252
Technology. *See also* Instructional technology
    adaptive, 229
Theatre, 139–52
    anthologies, 140–42
    creative drama, 142–46
    documents/guidelines/standards, 140
    games, 151
    journals, 151–52
    memberships, 152
    playwriting, 146–47
    puppetry & masks, 147–48
    special populations, 148–49
    storytelling, 149–50
    technical, 150

Videos
    books on, 73
    early childhood education, 179–80
    gifted & talented, 214
    health & physical education, 158–60
    instructional technology, 238
    marketing and advocacy, 23
    math, 110
    music, 126–27
    program planning, 14
    reading, 54
Visual arts, 129–38
    aesthetics, 131–32
    art criticism, 132
    art history, 133
    art studio, 133–34
    content reference, 134
    curriculum, 135–36
    documents/guidelines/standards, 129–31
    journals, 137–38
    keystone works, 130—31
    memberships, 138
    policy, 136–37
    theory, 137
Vocabulary, reading, 53

Whole language approach, 47–48, 74, 146, 174, 248
Writing. *See* Reading & Writing

SMYTHE GAMBRELL LIBRARY
WESTMINSTER SCHOOLS
1424 WEST PACES FERRY RD NW
ATLANTA GEORGIA 30327

WITHDRAWN